Traders of the New Era:

Interviews with a Select Group of Day and Swing Traders Who Are Still Beating the Markets in the Era of High Frequency Trading and Flash Crashes

Fernando Oliveira

Expanded Edition

ISBN 13: 1547020482

Cover design by Leandro Oliveira based on a Nanex chart.

To Nathaniel Branden (1913-2014).

Table of Contents

Foreword	By Joel Elconin	1
Introduction		3
Chapter 1	The Fundamentals of High Frequency Trading	7
Chapter 2	Gregg Siabicca: The Home Run Swing Trader	13
Chapter 3	Adam Whiting: The Futures Scalper	61
Chapter 4	Jim Cash: The Futures and Options Veteran	83
Chapter 5	Flemming Kozok: The Big Bet Sniper	107
Chapter 6	Dennis Dick: The Base Hit Trader	129
Chapter 7	Jeffrey Goldman: Market Maker Turned Prop Firm Trader and Manager	163
Chapter 8	Eric Scott Hunsader: The Market Structure Expert	183
Chapter 9	Mitch Semon: The Veteran Stock Operator	211
Chapter 10	Wayne Kulcheski: The Trend Fighter	231
Chapter 11	Anonymous: The Former Winner	265
Chapter 12	Anonymous: The Secrecy of the Bot Destroyer	279
Chapter 13	atticus: The Options Expert	287
Chapter 14	The Trader ToolBox	305
Chapter 15	Additional Advice, Resources and Tips	327
	The Boost Your Discipline Mini-Course	332
Chapter 16	The Core Principles of Good Short-Term Trading	343
Epilogue		353

Foreword

By Joel Elconin - Trader, Radio show host

My name is Joel Elconin and I have been active in the financial markets since 1985 as an investor and trader. My first exposure to the markets was as a clerk, then as a trader in the S&P 500 index futures pit at the Chicago Mercantile Exchange. At that venue, I learned a lot about the psychology of the markets and still incorporate the lessons learned into my current trading strategies.

I have been a proprietary trader/market-maker for a Wall Street firm, ran my own office for Bright Trading, one of the largest day trading firms in the US, and have continued on as an independent trader. I now host Benzinga's Premarket Prep radio show (along with Dennis Dick, who is featured in this book). Along the way, I have been witness to fortunes made and lost and can tell you firsthand, the key to long-term success is to be able to adapt to your trading environment.

The markets have evolved considerably over the past decade, and automation has become the industry norm. Many traders have had difficulty adjusting to this new automated trading world. The author of this book, Fernando Oliveira, was one of these traders. But where many other traders refused to learn and adapt to the new market environment, Fernando went a different route. Instead of falling prey to the HFT crowd, he took it upon himself to find traders who had adjusted to this new environment and researched their tactics in order to compete.

Keep in mind that Fernando is of Portuguese descent, with Portuguese being his native language. Imagine the difficulty of interviewing, transcribing, and writing in something other than your native tongue. The endless hours of interviews, considering his language barrier, makes this book an even more impressive achievement.

When reading the collection of interviews in this book, take note of mistakes made by these traders and try to relate them to your own experiences. Concentrate on the traders that most closely fit your own mentality and trading style. Be what you are, not what you want to be. Take special note of the lessons learned from the traders interviewed at the end of each chapter. In fact, you will notice that many of the same lessons are reiterated in one way or another by multiple traders, no matter how or what they trade.

A common theme is that it is important to define your time horizon and be cognizant that much of the real short-term trading and or scalping in all markets is controlled by high-frequency traders. Simply stated, it is extremely difficult to compete with them on speed and short-term scalping strategies. But by expanding your time horizon from seconds to minutes (or hours or even days), you eliminate the pressure of precise executions, and slippage becomes less of an issue. This creates risk/reward ratios (strategies) that can be productive even in an environment where the short-term odds are stacked against you.

Finally, one common thread among many of the traders interviewed in this book is the ability to keep an open mind. By that, I do not mean hopping from chat room to chat room searching for the next superstar, what I mean is being willing to share your success and failures with others.

A great example of this is the interview with Adam Whiting backed by Futex. Despite having great success in the markets, Adam could have easily left the firm and traded his own funds. However, he placed significant value on the services offered by the firm and credits some of his success to surrounding himself with other great traders. Whether it is learning from their mistakes or adding a new twist to create his own strategy, Adam is glad to share some of his profits in order to receive the benefit from being around other traders.

I hope you enjoy reading this book as much as I have, and do not hesitate to break out the highlighter and revisit many of the important tips offered in this book. With hard work, a lot of discipline, and a little luck, Fernando just may be contacting you when he composes his next edition of "Traders of the New Era."

May the trade be with you,
Joel Elconin

Introduction

It was April 15, 2011. I was in my desk checking out some news and threads in a poker forum when all of a sudden a rumor broke out: the FBI had seized a number of major online poker websites. A few minutes later, I realized it wasn't a rumor at all when I tried going to these sites and found a message on each explaining that the domain names had been seized by the FBI pursuant to an arrest warrant obtained by the US Attorney's Office for the Southern District of New York.

I immediately logged on to my poker platform in a panic and tried to withdraw my funds. My logic was that the news might create a run on the bank on these sites and that they might not have all the money they needed to pay their players. I figured I could withdraw all my funds and then wait until things were settled before depositing again. But I soon realized my effort was futile. Posters on the forums were talking about how these sites' bank accounts had been frozen. Supposedly these poker websites had been breaking all kinds of financial regulations, and there was no way they could process the withdrawals.

I was outraged. I thought, "I'm not American. Why am I being dragged into this?" It was questionable whether poker was even gambling anyway. Why were US taxpayers' dollars being used to stop people from playing a skill game they played voluntarily? But it was a waste of time to complain. I had no idea if I was ever going to see any of the money I'd deposited with those sites, and Americans had been effectively banned from playing online poker.

Eventually I was able to get access to my funds, but the poker games were never the same. Instead of playing against mostly recreational American players, now I had to go up against tougher and harder-working Europeans and Asian players. My playing was still profitable, but my income had gone down. To make matters worse, in early 2012 the poker site I used made a major change to its bonus system, which cut my income even more. At that point, I decided that poker had had its run in my life. It had been a good job over the years due to all the freedoms it gave me, but now I had to move on to bigger and better things.

I didn't want a nine-to-five job, so I thought, "I'd better get into day trading." Trading was a natural transition for me because I'd been a "position" trader since 2007. I would make trades based on macroeconomic trends, buy and hold or short stocks I felt were incorrectly priced, etc. I had made some good profits off my macro account over the years, sometimes even more than in poker, so diving deeper into markets and trading felt completely appropriate to me. The issue was that in 2008, during my first try at day trading, I struggled with profitability. I would make some and give it back. Commissions would add up. Overall, I posted a small loss after a month or two. When I came back to day trading in late 2011, I wanted a solid strategy that I could rely upon so I wouldn't struggle like I had in 2008. I decided to go with a popular NYSE opening imbalance strategy.[1] Essentially, you would provide liquidity against opening imbalances and take the other side, along with the specialist. You would get in long or short on a stock that was away from its theoretical "fair value," and you would profit as the stock approached its fair value.

I started to use this strategy every day; however, I began to notice a number of strange things in the stocks that I traded. For instance, I would short a stock in the opening print, and if I put in a limit order to buy a stock at, for example, $20.15, sometimes the stock would trade down to right above my price, say $20.17 or $20.16, and it would stop there. If I did get hit, it would then drop another 10 cents very quickly, which means I left money on the table. There was also a situation in which I sent a market sell order for 600 shares, got filled at the exact low of the day, and then the stock proceeded to rally a lot. Before I sent the order, I saw in the Level 2 that the bid wasn't that low. The quotes moved as soon as my order was sent.

After months of trading with this strategy, I had almost no profits. I'd made about $2,000 and then gave all of it back. At that point, I realized that I had to improve my trading by learning from other traders that were already doing it well. I wanted to understand these markets so that I could develop sounder strategies. I wanted to make a living off this business and was willing to do whatever it took to get there.

I decided to pay for subscription services, day trading chat rooms, and interview and learn from as many traders as I could. I wanted to talk to the best guys I could possibly find and try to learn how they were able to extract profits when it seemed impossible for me. I'd always been a big fan of trading books that featured interviews with the best traders and really dove deep into what they thought it took to become a winning and consistent trader. I really liked the diversity of views, strategies, and styles in those books. I wanted to write a book like that, but up to date for the modern markets and with a focus on short-term trading. I wanted to find good short-term traders and essentially pick their brains.

The result of all of that was this book. By interviewing successful traders and learning from them, I discovered all kinds of traps that I was falling into due to the rise of High Frequency Trading and the new era of electronic markets. I discovered that I had to dramatically change the strategies I used. If I wanted to succeed, I had to focus more on the basic fundamentals of good day trading, key risk management rules, and technical changes. I implemented several changes, and a few months after I started these interviews and thought about the advice I received, I achieved profitability—finally, consistent profitability. I actually struggled to write this book, because once I'd done the interviews I already knew what changes I had to make and could refresh my memory by listening to the audio files any time. So why even

---

[1] This strategy is explained in more detail in Chapter 6.

put in the time and effort to produce a book? I knew it wasn't likely to be a good source of income (especially compared to the significant number of hours I had to put into it). But ultimately I decided to write it because I just wanted to do something nice and give back to other people.

For most of my life, I was not a charitable guy. I was always too busy with my own projects and goals. This time, I thought, why not do something nice and help struggling or new traders who might be making the same mistakes I or my profiled traders had made? Supposedly, you're only truly happy when you help other people. Giving is said to be one of the major ways people can be happy. I wanted to find out if this was true.

This book is the result of my blood, sweat, and tears, as well as of these traders. I hope you find the information contained in it as helpful as I have found it.

Best,
Fernando Oliveira
April, 2016

Chapter 1

The Fundamentals of High Frequency Trading

High frequency trading (HFT) is a term that is used these days to describe many different styles and strategies. It can mean anything from basic stock market trading using an algorithm (algo) to the use of news algos that parse news and buy or sell futures, stocks, or bonds. In this chapter, I'm going to go through some of the main characteristics of HFTs and why it's important to understand them if you want to be successful at day trading these days.

According to the *Financial Times*:

"High-frequency trading (HFT) is high-volume trading used by proprietary traders and a new breed of electronic trading outfits (typically privately held). It relies on synthesizing information faster than other traders using sophisticated trading algorithms and powerful computers, often co-located near the electronic matching systems within securities exchanges. By co-locating their trading systems close to the exchanges' matching 'engines', these firms can speed up their orders to the exchanges ever so slightly (the time savings are in the milliseconds) and thus provide a competitive advantage over other traders whose systems are not as fast.

HFT firms' orders are designed to be not only faster but also potentially more nimble by strategically and swiftly placing buy and sell orders (and, in many cases, quickly canceling them). In this way, HFT firms can detect or anticipate changes in the depth and direction of order flow from institutional and retail investors.

For example, the HFT traders can position themselves to profit from momentary order imbalances and fleeting intra-day price trends by placing aggressive buy and sell orders (thus putting them first in line to gain by either first buying low and selling slightly higher in less than second or by first selling high and then buying moments later at a slightly lower price)."

According to the NASDAQ:

"[HFT] refers to computerized trading using proprietary algorithms. There are two types high frequency trading. Execution trading is when an order (often a large order) is executed via a computerized algorithm. The program is designed to get the best possible price. It may split the order into smaller pieces and execute at different times. The second type of high frequency trading is not executing a set order but looking for small trading opportunities in the market. It is estimated that

50 percent of stock trading volume in the US is currently being driven by computer-backed high frequency trading. Also known as algo or algorithmic trading."

In addition to high frequency trading (the above definitions), HFT is commonly used to mean high frequency trades and high frequency traders. Back in the old days ('90s and early 2000s), the HFTs were the day traders. They would try to manually make markets in stocks with sufficiently large spreads (buy at the bid and sell at the offer). They would read the news then try to reprice a stock. They would also try to read the supply and demand by looking at things like the Level 2 (L2) window, arbitrage securities, and profit from mispricings. Many of these activities have been taken over by HFTs these days simply because computers are more efficient at this job than any human could ever be. They can make all the calculations and predictions, create/submit/cancel orders, before a human can even finish looking at the screen.

Some of the main strategies by HFT firms are statistical arbitrage (exploiting deviations from statistical relationships between different securities), market making, news trading (trading after using an algorithm to "read" the news and make a quick assumption of how much an asset should change its value based on that news), and latency arbitrage (arbitraging differences between the faster direct data feed that they pay for and the slower SIP feed that everyone else gets).

HFT firms frequently "collocate" their computers by placing them inside the exchanges. This guarantees them a fill before everybody else given that their latency will be the smallest among all the market participants in a specific financial instrument. This compounds their speed advantage over other participants even further.

In addition to colocation, HFT firms also get special benefits from exchanges and ECNs. According to the book *Dark Pools*[2] and the *Wall Street Journal*, firms with special connections get special order types that are not available to regular market participants.

This enables them to get an advantage that they would otherwise not have, especially in terms of avoiding adverse selection.[3] *Adverse selection* is an important concept to learn in order to understand these modern markets, but instead of using sophisticated language to explain the term, I'll give you an example.

Let's say you want to buy a stock that's currently trading at $15 with a spread of 6 cents (meaning a bid at $14.97 and the ask at $15.03). You send a limit buy for $14.98. Frequently (as in virtually every time), the HFT who's making markets in that stock will immediately join you at $14.98 or "penny jump" your order at $14.99. You might think, "This is fine. Maybe we'll both get filled, and I'll save some money

---

[2] Scott Patterson 2012.

[3] For Superfast Stock Traders, a Way to Jump Ahead in Line - WSJ - Scott Patterson and Jenny Stratsburg - September 19, 2012.

by not having to hit the ask." You then proceed to see a lot of trades going off at $14.9901 – so called **subpenny trades** – which, according to rule 612 from Reg NMS, are fully legal when they happen **off**-exchange. These are liquidity taking orders that are intercepted by some HFT firms and they don't interact with your limit order because they paid for the order flow privilege. You might think, "This is strange. How come I'm not getting these fills?" A few minutes later, you start to get frustrated, then all of a sudden you get filled, but the problem is that the stock is now down to trading at $14.90 with a bid of $14.85 and $14.92 offered. Yes, you got your fill and a rebate, but the cost was that you got filled because the stock was going down so much (as supply and demand shift) that the HFTs stopped playing their games and your order was filled.

In this case, your order was suffering from adverse selection, meaning it was likely to get filled only when you were wrong (in the short-term), and it was unlikely to get filled when you were right (in the short-term). This creates a huge problem for you because you get stuck with 100 percent of the losers of your trading strategy, but you miss out on some winners because you never get filled.

What are some of the games that HFTs might play against your order? First, there's payment for order flow. HFT firms pay for retail brokerage houses' order flow and trade against them. That's where most of the subpenny trades come from. The retail traders and investors are usually the most uninformed participants in the markets, meaning that they're the least likely to be right about the short-term direction of a security. When they take that order flow all to themselves (and provide a negligible "price improvement" in return), your order gets exposed to order flows that are more toxic. They're more likely to know more about short-term price direction than you. The flow could be other market-making HFTs (that can tell that the supply and demand has shifted before you can), news algos (that can read and trade on the news way before any human can even understand what's going on), professional traders, institutions reacting to news, etc. The result of trying to save a few cents by not hitting the spread is something that might cost you way more than that in a particular trade.

An order to take liquidity might have been improved by a subpenny, but a resting and displayed order had its fill taken away by somebody else with a special advantage. The truth is that markets are rigged against players who are not engaged in the business of trying to get special advantages.

In addition to payment for order flow, there are also many different special orders that firms can get these days. The *Wall Street Journal* exposed the hide-not-slide order in 2012.[4]

---

[4] How 'Hide Not Slide' Orders Work - WSJ - Scott Patterson and Jenny Strasburg September 2012.

That special order type gave an HFT firm order priority over a regular order and enabled them to be executed first. The nonprivileged order was only filled later, which means its way more exposed to adverse selection than the order that's on top of the others. In market making, avoiding adverse selection is the name of the game, and being at the top of the queue is the best way to achieve that.

This might be only the tip of the iceberg however. It's Wall Street, after all. If the stuff that's being openly talked about looks unfair, imagine what's being done behind the scenes by people with questionable ethical standards.

Eric Hunsader, founder of Nanex Research, uncovered a scheme in which some HFT firms were being given the news before everybody else. (He's profiled in this book and explains more about it in his chapter.) When I say they got the news before everybody else, I mean a matter of milliseconds before. But in today's electronic markets, that timeframe can amount to millions of dollars in profits during a big event.

It's said that HFT market making is good for markets because it tightens up spreads. But that's only part of the story. While spreads have decreased from the early 2000s to today (mostly due to electronic trading), the actual displayed size of the bids and asks has also decreased. In the old days, you would see much thicker bids and offers, but these days a lot of stocks are 100 shares each side. When there are more than 100 shares, if you try to hit an entire level for all the liquidity available, frequently HFTs will cancel their orders, and you will get a partial fill. (Even worse, your size will be displayed in the Level 2 window because your buy/sell order will become the ask/bid after you clean up that particular level. You just showed your hand to the HFTs, who now know your intention to buy/sell.) This problem was immortalized in the book *Flash Boys* by Michael Lewis.

If you want to get in and out of size these days, it's harder than ever. There are all kinds of algos and computers programmed to try to detect big orders that are being worked in a specific security. As soon as a "whale" is detected, they'll immediately try to make that big buyer or seller pay or lose more than would otherwise be the case.

This chapter is not meant to be a complete guide to HFTs and how they affect the markets. Such topics are beyond the scope of this book. If you want to know more about it, I would encourage you to read the books *Dark Pools* by Scott Patterson, *Broken Markets* by Sal Arnuk and Joe Salluzi, and *Flash Boys* by Michael Lewis. You can also find more materials about it on the website and Twitter feed of Nanex Research (nanex.net and @nanexllc). This book is more about the necessary adjustments you have to make if you want to succeed at day trading in an HFT world. In the following interviews, I asked traders how to do that and what they think are the keys to making a living off day and swing trading.

The traders I selected had to meet a certain criteria to make sure I was sourcing advice from folks who knew what they were doing rather than trying to sell something. They had to up $150,000 per year *minimum* in the period leading up to the interview and they had to be experienced. This means they were around for many years and had seen the markets change. There are two interviews that are exceptions for the income criteria (The Former Winner and The Market Structure Expert). The reason why they were included will become clear once you read their chapters.

Keep in mind that during these interviews I had to be careful as to not make the trader become defensive by specifically asking about their main money-making strategies right away. As a result, I had to have a more indirect/patient interview style (with longer interviews) and try to learn from their little snippets of info, or pick up on when the trader volunteered strategic information. At the end of each chapter, I list the lessons I learned from each trader. Now, the interviews.

Chapter 2

Gregg "lx21" Sciabica - The Homerun Swing Trader

Gregg Sciabica, popularly known by his nickname "lx21" (Twitter @lx21), is the number one ranked trader on Profit.ly, a website that verifies trades and lets users search their trade database. He has uploaded trades that add up to more than $10 million in gains.

It's a large amount but it understates his results given that he has not updated his full 2014 and 2015 trades. 2014 in particular was a phenomenal year for him given the extreme volatility in small cap stocks, his bread and butter niche, brought by the bull market in US stocks. He profited over $5 million in that year alone.

He is quite well known for being a short seller of high flying low float small cap momentum stocks that often can make unbelievable moves. MDBX is an example of such a stock.

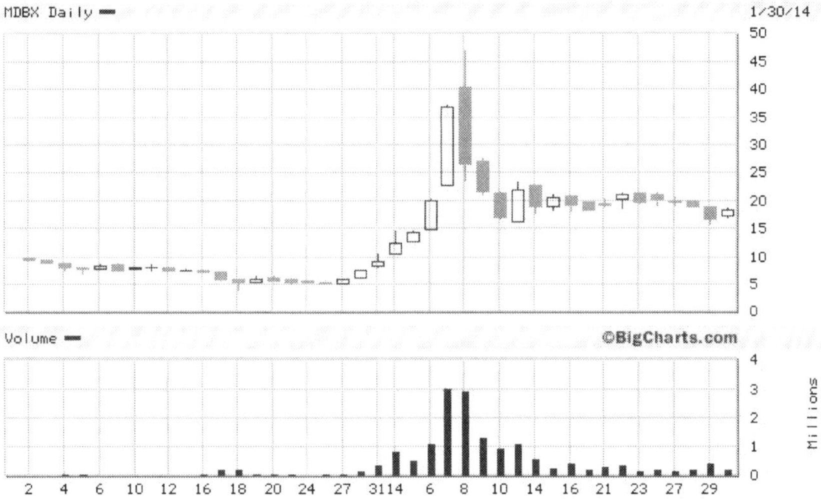

Source: Bigcharts

I know quite a few traders who specialize in that approach, but Gregg is the type who will bet bigger and hold for longer than most traders. Some of his greatest trades involve taking significant short positions in parabolic charts and then scaling out of the position on the way down. Sometimes he will hold at least part of these short positions for weeks. A lot of traders can`t stomach such an approach given that it's hard to turn down a significant profit, but Gregg is the type of trader who will try to think in terms maximizing profits rather than doing the comfortable thing, which is to take profits and move on.

His strategy is not just for anyone. Getting involved in these stocks requires a significant amount of knowledge, experience and respect for what he calls "the tremendous amount of damage the market can do to you."

A lot of traders get carried away by shorting these large moves because they did their fundamental research and concluded that the stock has no way of ever sustaining their valuation. This is true, and in the long-term they will be right, but the problem is that the world is somewhat biased against short selling. Things such as buyins (when a short position is closed by your broker against your will due lack of shares to borrow), asymmetric risk exposures (the most you can lose in a long is 100% but in a short you can lose an infinite amount), short squeezes, lack of locates of shares to short, etc. can make these moves last far longer than expected. They can also deliver gigantic financial and mental losses before they finally reverse.

Gregg is the type of trader who will come up with the story that explains what is going on by combining the fundamental data, the technical understanding of what the stock is doing, along with the catalysts/news that are moving it. Once he does that, he can actually come up with an actionable trade idea, with the focus on proper timing. As he puts it, while talking about a stock that went from $7 to $30s (before eventually coming back to earth at $8), "Whether the trader was bullish or bearish, you could have screwed this trade big time or you could have made a lot of money. It's not a matter of whether you are bullish or bearish in the company, it's all about timing."

This interview was conducted in October 2014 and updated in February 2016

Back when you started, how were you approaching trading? How did you come up with the ideas of how to trade?

Before I even placed my first trade, I spent a lot of time researching stocks. I would pore over data and charts looking for a repeatable pattern that I could trade. I suppose you could say I was looking for a mechanical system even before I knew what system trading was. I spent a couple of months reading, researching and digging – it was almost a full time job. One night I discovered something that had a lot of promise. Shortly thereafter I opened a SureTrade[5] account and implemented it. I placed my first trade in January 1999.

How have these ideas of how to trade improved? Did you backtest things, or was it just trial and error with observations when you noticed patterns and situations that repeated? Did books or chat rooms influence you in that regard?

I did a ton of backtesting. In the beginning I was a bit naïve and I believed that if I researched enough I would figure out the Holy Grail of the market - a system that I could trade consistently and profitably without much effort. I found a few patterns that worked, and I even designed one system that I ran successfully for a few years. I designed and tested tons of technical indicators, but ultimately I made far more money integrating discretionary trading with patterns.

I spent years searching for a good book or service that could help me learn how to trade. It took me a long time until I could find a good book or service. In retrospect I'm glad that I didn't find a chat room or service to learn from. I believe that I never would have been successful if I wasn't forced to test ideas and learn what worked the best on my own.

What were some of the interesting market discoveries you made early on through your backtesting?

Markets and stocks can stay overbought or oversold for a long time and they usually become more overbought or oversold before they eventually reverse.

Most stocks that are undervalued are undervalued for a reason. Often if a stock is undervalued the price doesn't catch up to the fundamentals, but the fundamentals catch up to the price.

Most technical indicators have little predictive value. I think too many traders assume something should work because they read about it online or in a book. When I backtested trading ideas, I discovered that many widely held beliefs hold no water.

You mentioned you made more money when you integrated your backtested patterns with your discretion. Would you say that this is the key to your success these days?

I would say it's a part of it. It's not that I am advocating a new approach or some advanced hybrid strategy of "backtested patterns with discretion." It is really just a reflection of the path I took when I learned how to trade. I was in search of

---

[5] No relation to SureTrader. SureTrade is no longer in business.

mechanical trading systems. When I started trading, it gave me an enormous advantage to be thinking in terms of systems. I was trying to trade the odds. I was sticking to things that had a positive expectancy. I was looking for clear, definable set ups. I would argue that these are all good approaches to trading - and I was doing them right from the beginning.

Backtesting is a reflection of how I got started. It was a big part of how I learned to trade. It had a lot of influence on learning what works and what doesn't. It had even more of an impact on me in learning what doesn't work. There are a lot of widely held beliefs about technical analysis or price action patterns, indicators, setups that a lot of people think work but when you test them they don't work. If you were to get into the debate of technical analysis, you have two extremes. Some people swear by it, and that's all they use. They will insist that by looking at the chart and the indicators you get a reflection that is everything that is known in the market. Therefore you wouldn't need to get to know the news events, catalysts and fundamentals.

Then you have the other extreme, where people think that technical analysis is like superstition or astrology. When you look at both of those arguments, there is some truth to both of them but there are also some big assumptions made by both camps. I believe the truth lies in the middle. And the reason for that is because it's true that a lot of it doesn't work and is a bunch of garbage but that's not necessarily true of everything. You can't throw it all out. It's kind of like some medications. They have proven to be very valuable. That doesn't mean, though, that all drugs are good. A lot of people believe in alternative medicine, or homeopathic medicine. Herbs and some of the stuff might work but, like in technical analysis, a lot of that stuff might be false too. Sometimes there are outrageous claims and nothing to back it up. Going back to your questions about backtesting, when I first learned to trade I focused a lot on technical analysis. Many of my discoveries through backtesting steered me clear of using various ideas that I read about because there was just no value there.

Do you still do a lot of backtesting these days?

No. I still enjoy doing some research on systems but the truth is that I got myself to the point where discretionary trading is so much more profitable. There comes a point in your own experience and skill that you become better than any system can be. I think that is because the human mind is so much more adept at taking into account practically an infinite number of variables in the decision making process. A computer is only as good as the programmer. There comes a point where a lot of the decisions that people make aren't simple black and white, black box setups. You have to take into account a multitude of factors. It would be next to impossible to truly test and program them all into a trading system. You graduate into a new level and move past it. This is not to say that systems are no good or that there is no value there, but I've never seen a system that can make the kind of money that a good trader can make in terms of percentages.

Did you also cut back on backtesting because you accumulated so many setups and strategies that you no longer needed more of them? You maybe already maxed out the productivity of your trading time?

I wouldn't say that is true. To this day I still try to research for new ideas, new setups. On the one hand, when you are making good money as a trader you have a finite amount of time to work with. If your time as a trader is very productive and you have one more hour to work with, you need to decide if you are going to spend that hour looking for a trade/researching a stock you are watching or developing a new system. What's the most productive use of your time? If that answer is consistently to research stocks that are currently on your radar, then slowly you start to spend less and less time coming up with new systems and setups. That's because where the value is, it's been worth it for me to spend more time on trading and less on new systems. In an ideal world I would love to spend plenty of time on research, but I have a family. I have a life to live. I already spend enough hours trading.

I don't mean to imply that I no longer spend time looking for it because I don't need setups. In the last year or two I still found some new setups. Obviously, after a number of years you find some at first and over time you start to find these more nuanced, little patterns. You can still add these to your library. I wouldn't say I'm not looking for it. I'm just spending less time backtesting things. At this point I have enough experience and knowledge to determine the value of something even without a full statistical analysis of a particular pattern or setup.

Because you have been trading for so long, how much have you noticed that the structure of the market has changed?

The biggest changes from when I started to now were the decimalization of the quotes and the move from a market maker/specialist-based system to something that is now ECNs and dark pools based. These differences are very large. A casual observer probably wouldn't even care. But, for a trader, the difference is big.

When these changes started to occur, did you have some difficulties adapting? Did you have to alter your trading a bit?

The first change, which was to move to ECN trading, was certainly a welcomed change for a trader. It enabled our orders to be placed and executed much more rapidly. The move to decimalization certainly helped my style of trading because it decreased my slippage. Unless you were scalping the bid and ask, it was beneficial to have that. Over the last few years, we have seen the rise of the HFTs and what that led to was a narrowing of the bids and ask, which was welcomed. Over time we started to see that our ability to get filled at the bid and ask gradually become more and more difficult. If you are trading 100 share lots, you are fine. If you are trading 5,000 shares, your ability to get filled on offer or the bid is certainly more difficult these days in all but the most liquid stocks.

Do you add liquidity a lot of the time or do you take?

Again, it really depends on the circumstance. More often I'm probably adding liquidity but it really depends. Sometimes it's all taking, sometimes it's all adding, a lot of the time it's mixed.

Usually do you add when you are fighting the trend a bit, and take when you are going with it?

It really depends on the circumstance. There are a lot of different setups that I trade. There are a lot of different ways that I will add or take liquidity. Unfortunately I don't have a simplified answer for this. It's hard to generalize my trading.

I think my best trades are when I'm adding liquidity. Most times that I'm taking liquidity, it's usually because something is not going right and I'm trying to exit a position that is already moving against me, or I'm caught up in the moment. I think my most profitable trades were the ones in which I was adding liquidity.

Do you think a trader needs a skill to choose the right level to put the orders in to add liquidity?

I believe that can be beneficial. I don't think that's required though. It helps if you improve your average by just a few cents because if you tend to have a good read of where the support and resistance level are, you will certainly increase your profits. It won't necessarily make or break your ability to make the trade though.

Would you say you have that skill?

Yes. I spent a lot of time analyzing charts in that kind of manner.

By reading your comments on Twitter it seems that you use quite a bit of fundamentals to judge stocks. Do you use that to gauge how much downside a stock has so if it's really bad you can stay short for longer, and if it's not it becomes more of a scalp? Would this be accurate?

Yes, there are different types of trades that I make. If I'm looking to short a company, especially for a longer-term hold, it certainly helps to know where a company stands fundamentally.

What's the typical timeframe of your trades? Are you more of a swing trader or day trader?

Some of my biggest profits are from swing trading but the majority of my trades are day trades. This is simply because there are more setups there, yet there is more money to be made in the swing trades. I would do more swing trades if the proper setups could be found, the good setups that I like. If I'm finding one or two of those but five or ten day trades, obviously I will end up doing more day trading. Yet swing trading might still be profitable in the end, even though it's a smaller portion of my activity.

Some of these swing trades are big shorts in parabolic stocks that you made. How do you judge the right moment when you put the big position in? If you do it too early, a lot of the time you can go broke. It seems to me that the risk control part is really crucial in this strategy. I believe you dodged some losses on LAKE before it went into the $30s. Are you always really careful when they are still in an uptrend, allowing yourself to put the big short in when they start to turn? Or it's a case by case basis?

It's a case by case basis. I feel that whenever I talk to traders it seems that so many answers I give sound evasive, but the reason I give answers like that is because it's true. Each circumstance is different, so it's hard to generalize hundreds of trades with one explanation. If you were to look at what I think of as my best swing shorts, those as a group are actually very few. When I find really good ones, generally they are very profitable per trade but in terms of the quantity of trades I make, they are actually very few. It's a rare setup when I got really big on a swing short. Those types of trades may get a lot of attention when I share them, but if you were to look at my Profit.ly or on Twitter I'm not actually making that type of trade all the time.

When it comes to these best ones, I'm looking at the market as an observer. I'm observing the crowd. When the market gets to a point where things have reached a level of complete disbelief, when the stupidity reaches a crescendo, there comes a point where I know that it can't last. Of course, it's always dangerous and risky. We all know that with short-selling the loss can be theoretically unlimited, but there is also a point where a stock reaches such a ridiculous level that I know it will work. Timing will always be important even in those types of stocks because if I time it better I will have either a larger profit or a smaller loss if it doesn't work. There is something that differentiates this type of trade from almost all my other trades. Most of the time I don't have a lot of confidence, yet there is a point where everything just kind of clicks and I just know that what the market is doing is absolutely ridiculous. It's a completely different feeling. When I observe this madness, I know that whatever the market is doing can't be sustained much longer, so it becomes just a matter of timing.

When you are observing the crowd, do you use Twitter and social media to get a feel?

Rarely will I be watching a stock for the first time when they are ready to be traded in the way that I'm explaining. By the time it reaches that level, I would have already followed the commentary in chat rooms, Twitter, the various press releases from the company, the Seeking Alpha articles. I'm trying to get a pulse of the entire trading community. As much as everything adds some color to the picture that you are trying to paint, the biggest piece is still the chart. The chart contains the actual trading from people with real money, while everything else is just opinion.

In these types of big short trades, do you think there is a bit of a misunderstanding by people who see your profits? They see the big profit, but they might not know what your net worth is. If you had a loss in that trade, it might not have been that huge as a percentage of your net worth. But people might be thinking you were risking a huge amount because for them it's so much money. Do you think there is some of that going on?

I think, as with any kind of social media, there are going to be a lot of different misunderstandings. Even though I use Twitter, I still don't recommend anybody to use it for anything other than entertainment when it comes to following traders, and that includes myself. If you follow me on Twitter for a trading idea, you don't know my risk tolerance, you don't know my time frame. There is so much that you don't know. Why take a trade based on what I'm doing, or someone else? I think there is a lot of that going on, especially in chat rooms. People blindly following a so called "guru." I've never been able to do that, so I don't see how someone else would be able to do that following me.

In these better setups, the big shorts, is there a percentage that you would be comfortable losing? What is that number? When I look at these sort of trades I'm usually thinking, "Well, what if the stock went Volkswagen?" I'm always afraid I'm going to be short on that and exposed to a huge loss. I usually will bet a bit less so I'm not exposed to that.

When I establish a large short position, I like to look at a worst-case scenario because of exactly of what you are saying. "What if it's a Volkswagen? Or an LOTE, the BB stock that went to an obscene level?" There are various nightmare scenarios and you need to be able to survive those. You either are going to survive by taking a loss at some point, or by weathering the storm and stomaching that loss all the way to the top. In either case, you need to plan it out for sure. Trading is risky without a doubt, and it's not easy either. I have a tremendous amount of respect for the amount of damage the market can do. Whenever I let my guard down, I'm usually about to take a big loss. I always have to be thinking in these terms: "How far can a stock go?" "What would happen if it gets there?" "Are you going to survive?" "Will I add to the position?" "Will I get out at the worst moment possible?" These are all real possibilities which have to be taken into consideration.

Riding losses all the way up. Is that something that happens frequently in your trading?

I'm not a big fan of using stops, at the least hard stops. As a long as the original thesis still holds up, I want to stay in that trade. When the thesis of the trade starts to disintegrate, I want to get out. It's similar to a stop but it's not based on price. It's based on whether the original reason of why I got in is still there. Another way to look at this is: if I pull a stock chart and if it was the first time I looked at it, with all the information that I know about it, would I be buying, shorting or doing nothing?

If I was already short and I am carrying a loss but the answer to the question is "I would short here," then the question becomes "Why am I getting out with a stop?" Using the mentality of a stop, sometimes I would be getting out when in an alternative universe I would be entering your first short. It's a contradiction. Other times, the answer will be that you would be buying the stock or doing nothing, so the question then is "Why am I still short?" despite the fact that I have to take a loss. That doesn't change the odds of success.

So instead of a price stop, your risk is controlled by determining how big you want to be at any given point?

Yes. The key to me as a trader is that you have to be very honest with yourself. Once you have a position, you will start to think of the stock and the chart differently. As soon as you are long, everything that you read will seem positive for the company. And vice-versa for shorts. It's confirmation bias. Every time the bar moves down a bit, you think, "Here's the big break." Every time there is a press release, you think, "This must be BS." There is a very strong tendency to do that. It's a bias. Stubbornness. These are all strong factors that influence us heavily as traders. Especially when you have a big position, you become even more vulnerable to these things. When you see message boards or Twitter, you see the same things playing out, where longs and shorts get into this battle. It's as if the ego is more important than the profits. They just dig in deeper and deeper into their rationale and their beliefs. Our job is not to be political talking heads, always defending the same position, creating new arguments to defend that position. Our job is to make money and we need to read the current situation correctly. The current situation has nothing to do with whether or not you are already in the stock. Where the stock is going has nothing to do with whether you are already in. These things are irrelevant to the market. It doesn't care what your position is. We tend to be influenced by the knowledge that we already have a position. We all do it. We sit there and look at where our breakeven level is, our profit objective, our risk tolerance based on how much money we can lose. These are arbitrary things. The market doesn't care if you are about to lose $1,000 or $10,000 in a stock. It only cares about where it is going.

To have an objective ability to analyze a situation, you have to remove the fact that you are already involved in that situation. This forces you to be brutally honest with yourself when you are being subject to these biases. I try to answer the question, "What is the best decision to do now, based on all the available information?"

Would you say that this style is not really recommended to traders without a lot of experience? If they make some position sizing and timing decisions incorrectly, they are exposed to a total wipe out. Would you agree with that?

I agree, but on the other hand I don't know if any trading strategy is appropriate for inexperienced people. All trading is risky. The failure rate for new traders is very high. I'm not aware of a strategy that can magically guarantee success. The failure rate is high in all approaches. Even though on paper my approach is very risky, I'm not sure it's actually so much worse than any other method.

Really? Because I feel that it's so asymmetric. If you do it wrong, the loss is so huge compared to the gain. For instance, if you short LAKE at $12 and cover in the $30s because you can't take it anymore you can lose nearly everything. If you are long biased, you always have the zero bound price to protect you.

That's true, but that's not because they are using my strategy. That's because they are doing a very poor job as a trader. Any strategy that you screw up that badly will make you go broke very quickly. Maybe not all at once, but it will be quick no matter what. You have to understand your strategy, your setups. You have to respect the market. There is also another element. If I were to short LAKE at $12 and ride it to the $30s, even if I could survive that, it's very important not to get myself into that kind of situation. There is more to it than whether your account can survive. The mental stress of taking such a large loss will certainly affect your performance beyond that particular trade.

Yeah, absolutely. I talked about it in the first edition of this book. Mental capital, you drain it and then you lose in other trades. It's one of the reasons why taking low-profit and lower quality trades can sometimes be detrimental.

True. Yes, it's hard to understand it until you are in that position. I've seen this in other traders and I have experienced it many times myself. One large loss leads to another large loss because mentally you are not in the right place.

What do you do to deal with these tough periods? Do you just stop trading? Take vacations?

The answer will be different for everybody. There is no recommended approach that I can recommend to all traders. You have to know yourself. In my case, I feel that it's important to double down on discipline, rules and re-establish the things that made me successful in the first place. Sometimes the reason why I got myself into a bad trade in the first place is because I misread a situation, got in early, or went too big on something. A lot of the time it's a reflection of the market environment. It's often the case that there are different good opportunities because of that. Rarely does the loss happen in a vacuum. Usually it's a reflection that something in the market is reaching an extreme. If, and this is a big if, I can be extremely careful, very cautious and disciplined, then I can sometimes stay active in the market environment and capitalize on the next opportunity. There is some self-awareness that a big loss leads to. The shift in the market environment that I was slow to adapt to the first time around, but a week later there might be an even better opportunity. By remaining focused, alert and disciplined, I can profit on the next opportunity, which sometimes can be bigger than the loss.

Let's go back to the worst case planning. On ICPT, which was a great trade for you, what was your worst case there?

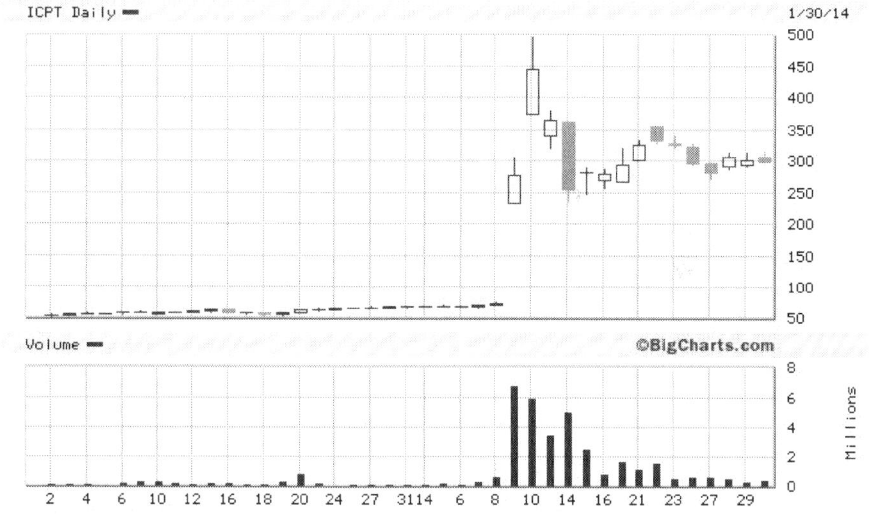

Source: Bigcharts

That stock ran up to a high of $497. It had gapped up almost $100 from the previous day's close. A lot of that was a short squeeze and margin calls. Essentially we were looking at an extreme move, both in percentage and in dollar terms. Things were just reaching an absurd level. If I recall, several analysts were coming out with price targets and we were already overshooting some of these targets. It just seemed to be a continuation of what was an insane amount of momentum from the previous day. It wasn't exactly a valuation call. I wasn't trying to predict where the stock was going to go even a week later. It was a trade based on a capitulation move.

We had a big gap and immediately after the open it started to rocket higher. It just moved to such absurd levels that not only did I short some at the open, but I also added to the short on the way up. I spaced out my orders too, every $10 or $20 up. By the time it peaked at $497, I was short most of the position and, if I recall, I added a bit after it peaked out. My average was a reflection of many entries.

You asked me about the worst case scenario. I did think about it. I remember that at some point, as it was moving up, I was already in a drawdown and was adding to the position with 500 share orders. I had two more to go to get to a 10,000 share short. If the stock went above $500, I would be holding a $5 million position. I thought to myself, "What is the craziest move that this can possibly make?" and, "Am I willing to stomach it?" I thought, "Hey, anything is possible, but if it moves another $100 and went to $600, it would be a reflection of absolute madness and it probably won't go any higher than that." I did the math, and, if it went there, I would have been carrying a drawdown of $1.5 million. Of course that was a very disturbing thought, yet on a risk-reward basis I saw that it was acceptable. Even though I was willing to do it, it doesn't mean it's easy or not scary. Of course it was very scary.

I wanted to make sure that I would not be capitulating. You want to short into capitulation and not give another short seller a great entry, should it make another massive squeeze.

Fortunately, it didn't go above $500. The stock pulled back pretty early in the morning.

You asked the question of whether picking your levels is important. Here is an example: had I picked better levels, I could have made more money and had a much less stressful day. It was stressful watching the stock moving such a dramatic amount after I established the short position.

Had the stock breached $500 and kept going higher, it would be a discretionary decision to exit or stomach the loss right?

Yes.

So the plan for the exit wasn't set beforehand?

Well, this was such a quick event. Most setups are not so quick. The stock, even in the pre-market, didn't give a hint that it was about to do what it did. This was a decision that had to be made on the fly. Most of the big trades that I do aren't made so quickly without contemplation. In this case there was no choice. I either enter or I miss the opportunity.

Your thought process in these trades is, "There is a 90% chance this will implode and a 10% chance that I will have a problem."

Right, but in this case I think there was even a less than 10% chance but I had to acknowledge the fact that there was a chance. In the trading world, you occasionally see people make comments like, "There is no way this stock will go higher," or, "It's impossible for this to happen." There are no such things. Anything is possible. Anything can happen. Those chances may be tiny and very remote, but you still have to acknowledge the possibility.

What ICPT did was already a very rare type of move. If I could accumulate a database of chart setups with a big gap and a humongous run like that, ICPT was already in the 10% probability distribution. It was a fairly unique situation to have such a huge move.

Were you comfortable analyzing the actual biotech company? Understanding the drug trial tests and everything?

That's one area where I would love to improve a lot. I really regret having very little knowledge in analyzing the biotech data, understanding FDA results, etc. I know very little about it and for that reason I have historically avoided FDA news stocks. It's only in the last few years that I actually ventured into that, and I do it very cautiously for that reason.

In this particular stock, the first day was the day of the news. This is where you have to understand the actual data. With each day, the news gets older and the technicals start to matter more. As the catalyst becomes more stale, price action becomes more important. On the first day, I did make one trade but it was relatively small compared to the one in the second day.

So when you are analyzing a situation like this, you look at all the variables, like number of up days, size of the move, catalyst, float, short interest, likelihood of an equity offering, etc. You put it all together and come up with a bias?

You want to piece together an entire story. You want to put together all the pieces and make a story out of it so you can explain each step of the move. As the move proceeds, you can start to interpret what you are looking at with more precision. (If consistently wrong, does that give you pause?)

When it comes to big morning moves, do you think on average they are a losing proposition to the buyer?

Usually, but there are many different circumstances, so not always.

Would you say that you'd rather be short a big morning move rather than a big mid-day move?

It really depends on why the stock is moving. You can have two identical charts on two different stocks. With two different catalysts for each, you can interpret the same exact charts in different ways. I really believe you cannot trade in a vacuum. You have to understand the catalyst, the environment you are in and all the surrounding information. I think the best way to answer your question is, "It depends."

I guess the point that I'm trying to make is that a lot of the time there are overextensions in the morning and it seems a key of your trading to capitalize on that is in the entry part of your shorts in a good setup rather than a random situation.

Yes.

For instance, there is a company that you think has terrible fundamentals. It then has a big gap up and a morning run Wouldn't you start to get interested in that?

Sure. But now you are adding information to that setup. If you just took that chart in a vacuum and didn't tell me what that company was, why it is up, or any other information, I would be very reluctant to trade. In the past I have traded charts purely on technicals, and I still do occasionally.

Sometimes I have found setups that are so good that I have traded them without any knowledge of what the company does, why is it up and other variables. But, honestly, that is very rare. The more I trade the rarer that occurrence is. I just feel that there is too many exceptions to these things. I have to look into them, make sure you know what is going on.

Did you look at EGLE the other morning?

Yes.

On October 15 it closed at 68 cents. In the next morning pre-market it started ticking higher. In no time it doubled. By 8:15 it was at $3. It more than quadrupled. 99 times out of 100, if I saw this type of absurd move I would short it. It's a great setup on the chart. By 8:36 it was higher than $5. Not much later it was up tenfold from the previous close. This is, by all measures, a parabolic move. By any form of technical analysis, this is a great short. It kept going higher and higher until it halted right before the open. By that time it had peaked it hit a high of $15.33, and this is all just pre-market! A 68 cent stock went to $15.33. Anyone who trades solely on the chart could easily have shorted this at $5, at $6.80, at $10. Yet every one of these entries ended up being a loss. 99% of the time, these types of entries would make money. Here is an example in which you would have lost, depending on your entry, 50% to 200% of your initial trade capital.

This is perfect example of what I'm trying to say when I say you can't trade in a vacuum. Why I avoid speaking in black and white, why you have to know the circumstances, the variables, etc. That's why I give evasive answers sometimes. I don't want to say, "Yes, you can short a stock that is up 100-200% pre-market," because there are exceptions. This is a classic exception. Even if I was following this company even a little bit, and I thought, "This is a junk company," I would still get hurt. The reason the stock made such a huge move was because the previous shareholders were diluted massively and they issued new shares. It started trading the next day and this wasn't the same stock anymore, but almost nobody knew that.

The stock was all over Twitter and the chat rooms and no one picked up on the reason for the move right away. People thought this little shipping company was making this huge move when in fact this was a new stock being revalued.

Don't they usually add some letter to the end of the ticker or choose an entirely new ticker?

That's a good point because that's what they should have done and they usually do. I believe that was a blunder by the company and the exchange. That cost some shorts a lot of money. They should have halted it even before the first trade that morning and put out some kind of press release to clarify it, but for whatever reason they didn't, and it was very strange.

Does this happen on the NYSE too? This was on the NASDAQ.

I'm not sure if it is a function of the exchange or the fact that small companies don't usually trade on the NYSE. I will try to notice it in the future and see if there is a pattern there.

How much of your profits come from the big swing trades and how much of it comes from the day trades that you said is most of your trading activity?

Just to clarify, the big swing trades aren't my only swing trades. I have plenty of other swing trades. Not every setup is a stock that is making an extreme move. There are plenty of setups. Some of them don't merit a big position, and for some of them the profit objective is nothing spectacular. There is a lot of different stuff.

The balance between day trading and swing trading tends to cycle a bit depending on what kind of market we are in. What kind of setups there are. In terms of my activity, I would say that it's ¾ day trading and ¼ swing trading. The big swing trades are probably 1% of it but in a really good market it's going to be more than that, maybe as much as a 5%. This is as a percentage of trades, not capital, shares or profits.

In terms of profits, let me check my trade records here…

Is that something you keep? All of your trading records in an Excel file or something?

Yes, I have the ability to sort through my trades in Excel. I do some programming so I built some macros to auto-import my trades from my brokers.

At least 80% of the profits come from 20% of the trades. This doesn't mean it's all in the big short swing trade. There are some big day trades mixed in there. The point is that we all make a lot of trades. A lot of the time they are the best trades that are available at the moment but the really good stuff is what makes most of our P&L. Those opportunities aren't always there every day. We have a lot of activity as traders but sometimes without a lot of results. This doesn't mean we are not having a good day. It just means that there is not a lot of opportunity that day. I think sometimes as much as 90% of the profits are made by 10% of the trades. That could be pushing it but it's somewhere in that range.

I wish it was easy to sit there as a trader and say to myself, "I'm only going to focus on the best trades," but the only way to find those good trades is by being active and participating. Being involved in some of the more mediocre trades is not necessarily because I'm bored and have nothing better to do, but it's part of the process in which I discover the good ones. The good ones don't pop up out of nowhere and become a great trade. They start off as a mediocre setup which evolves into a better and better trade.

Now that you have more experience, are you focusing more on those great trades than in the past?

Actually no, because I can justify my time as a trader even when I don't have the great setups. It's hard to sit idle. The way I see it is that you have to be in tune with the market. You have to be in sync with what's happening. You can't do that just by firing up the computer in the morning and checking things, finding out that there is nothing great and walking away. You need to be participating, scanning, etc. Just by placing a few trades you tend to get a feel for stocks, how it behaves.

Sometimes those really good trades start off as a typical trade, and as you become more familiar with the situation you can become more aggressive. It's just not as simple as you looking at the stock and saying, "Oh, this is a great one." You have to put together all the information, and being involved when the setup is still not that great can assist in that process. It's what we were discussing previously. You have to put together the whole puzzle. It's not something you can do in 5 minutes. By being there every day, trading, and watching these stocks you can get a sense of what makes it move so that the next time it makes a big move you are right there with it. You can anticipate and react to the move.

One thing that I think is related to this is that sometimes the best thing that can happen for a trader is for him to have a loss because he will tend to wake up and be more alert. Sometimes when I start the day I don't feel like taking trading risks, but after a loss, it's like I wake up and I'm ready to go. This is a particular problem for me on Mondays because I'm still on weekend mode. After a loss though, it tends to go away.

I agree with you. I believe what you are saying is very similar to something I was trying to describe earlier. It's in a different time frame. Sometimes you take a big loss and it can lead to a turnaround in the next week or two and become a new equity high. It's the same principle in play. I don't think this is something that applies to all traders. Everybody is going to react to a loss differently.

Sometimes a really good day can start with a small loss because it snaps you back into the right mode of thinking and that can be such a positive thing. As a trader, you have to be thinking right and be mentally in the right place, not being subject to your emotional ups and downs. A small loss can snap you back there. Now, of course I'm sure that there are a lot of people that start into a downward spiral with that small initial loss.

I tell myself that sometimes my biggest gains come after my biggest losses. It's a way to give myself a positive spin. Of course, I have to be careful to not go into denial and just double down on my next bet. The key here is to not double down on my bet but to double down on my discipline and on the main aspects of my trading that make me successful. I need to refocus on these things so that a small loss can be something that snaps me back to doing things the right way.

I think I noticed that a lot of good traders of your style usually have that pattern: big loss followed by big gains. Some of that I believe has to do with the mean reversion of these stocks but some has to do with the loss putting you into a more risk taking mode. This can be a bad thing in the wrong hands, but in good hands it can lead to boldness level the person wouldn't normally have. The trader would then put a big position and hold it in a situation where there is a large edge.

I fully agree with that. A big loss in the wrong hands will just get worse and worse until you are broke. I hope no one takes this the wrong way. I'm not trying to say taking that loss is a good thing or it's easy. It can be very painful. It's very important to not let yourself slide into the dangerous mode of thinking of, "I want to make my money back," or increasing the size of your next bet regardless of the setup's merits. Going from a precise calculating trader to a gambler can be expensive. No one is immune to these urges. The difference is if you can catch yourself before it happens you can stop it. I have these same thoughts too and occasionally I go in the wrong direction, but it's the self-awareness that is the key. One of the most important traits for a person to be a trader is the ability to self-observe and have self-awareness. All these different psychological weaknesses aren't things that everybody is immune to. The real difference is how we handle them. No one person is immune to the various forms of greed, fear, impatience, etc. The list is endless. How we respond to them, how we handle them, is the main difference between great traders and the rest. You need to be aware of those issues and not become a victim to them. If I catch myself trading in the "I got to make my money back" mentality, I try to catch myself and say, "Well, I'm doing that thing and this is probably not going to end well. I better be very careful here and not give in to it."

What is the trade that you are most proud of that you made this year?

Off the top of my head, I would say the MDBX short. There is also BLDP which was a very profitable one, but it doesn't stick out in my mind as a great trade. At the same time as MDBX there was GRNH. It peaked out in the same day as MDBX. That was also a big trade for me. But if I had to choose, I would go with MDBX.

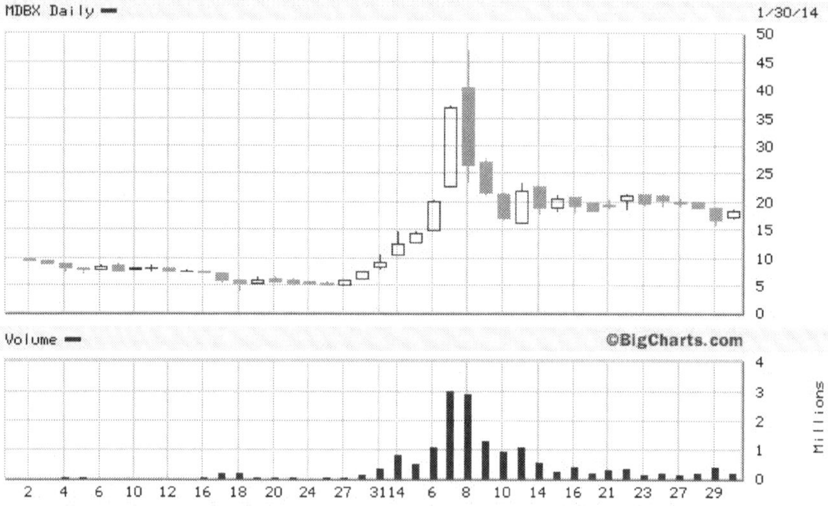

Source: Bigcharts

What's the particular reason you like this one?

It was a very tempting short for the first few days. I was quite pleased with myself because I didn't short too early. Those types of moves can draw me in because of how much they are running up. I felt that I did a good job of letting it set up all the way. My position sizing was pretty well done. At one point that day, my largest position was 15,000 shares. It wasn't a very liquid stock, but I balanced the need to push for a big enough size to maximize the profit from the setup and the need to respect the lack of liquidity of the stock. It's a OTCBB stock so it was harder to get executions.

The chart was a great setup. It was a textbook parabolic setup. I shorted some the day before the big run and collapse. I believe I shorted 3,000 shares and then I added about 12,000 on the big day. I was a little bit early on some of the shares, but I saved plenty of ammo for that big move up. My average entry was $43, which in this type of stock is a great entry. It's hard to get killer entries in these bulletin board stocks. It's hard to get fills with these market makers at precise levels, especially when compared to an NYSE or NASDAQ stock.

The fact that it collapsed from the high to the low about $23 in one day is what made this trade so exciting. It's rare that you have such a big profit in such a short period of time. I didn't have to wait several days or weeks to get that.

Did you take the profits on those lows because you saw that? You knew it was such a rare move down that you just had to take it?

Well, there is a point in the stock when it collapses a lot where I might feel that there is a good chance that it's going lower, but as it drops you can run into two different problems. One is that if you don't cover at least part of your position, you lose your ability to re-short higher when it bounces. Even if I feel that it is going lower, it can be a good idea to lock it in because I might get such a great reentry on a re-short that day or the next day that I would be a fool to be so stubborn with it. And two, once it drops so much sometimes it might not go lower at all. It might just recover and you will be sitting there cursing yourself for the rest of your life thinking "Why didn't I take profits?" It's always a trade-off. Nobody knows for sure what a stock is going to do and that applies to me as well.

This goes back to our conversation about backtesting. In situations like this, I start to revert back to my earlier days of trading and I start to think in terms of odds. When a stock drops like this to such an extreme level, the odds of it going lower or higher becomes like a 50/50 proposition. Why should I continue to hold? I don't have much edge in holding it. Now, if I cover there then I have the opportunity to re-short if it bounces a lot. In these pink sheets and BB stocks, I have seen some violent bounces. There is the infamous FNMA day where it collapsed. If I recall, it bounced almost 100% from the low. These bounces can be just as violent as the initial drop. It's just a risk-reward thing that leads me to these decisions. There is no magical crystal ball that tells me what to do. It's just a matter of assessing the risk and the odds.

Do you play these bounces at all? You go long in them?

Yes. They are very tough. Most of the time I will watch them. Only occasionally will I play them. Sometimes I do it successfully, and sometimes I find myself being a bag holder.

What was your worst trade this year?

I had one bad trade in LAKE that was very costly. On October 09 the stock started to breakout, gapped up to $12.30, previous close was $11.62. It was a decent sized gap. Then it started to run pretty high. I still got mixed feelings about this trade because by some measures a short there was not a horrendous trade.

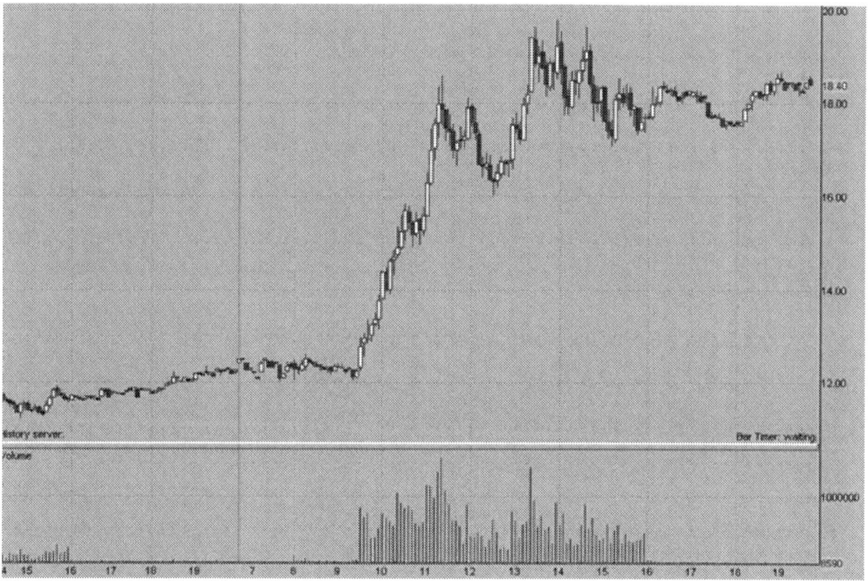

Source: MBT Desktop pro

I think what happened was that I managed it poorly. My initial entries in terms of the overall setup weren't a mistake even in hindsight. Even a great setup has a chance of failure, and this happened to be one of those. I shorted a relatively large amount of shares, but the setup was for a short-term day trade. I wasn't getting married to the short. My intent was to play the early morning setup. It's a pattern that I had played before many times. This particular stock on that day for some reason had an enormous amount of volume and momentum. The volume that day was the biggest volume that stock had ever had in all its history, even with all the big days it has had since. It traded 40M shares that day. I should have recognized how much momentum was plowing into that stock in the morning by looking at the price action and volume. Instead, I traded the setup without fully accounting for that. What should have been a decent setup with a confined amount of risk just got worse and worse. When I entered it, and even when I added to it a couple of times, I didn't feel that it was a bad trade yet.

The stock had a few moments when it pulled back. It then did something that is a sign that the trade will not work: it came really close to several of my orders to exit the position, but then it went higher without any fills. This kind of thing happens too often to not be true. It's almost like the market knows you are trying to get out and it's going to tease you like that. I say *almost* because the market is not really thinking like that. What is happening is that too many people are in the same boat you are in. They got short too early and are looking for break even, or at least a little bit of a pullback to cover into. As soon as the stock pulls back a little bit, a ton of short sellers are trampling over each other to buy that pullback. As a result, the pullback becomes very quick. It's one thing for the stock to miss your exit and a few minutes later you can adjust your price and get out, but in this case the momentum would just resume every time.

It's such a painful loss to take when you almost get out several times. The first time you would have a small profit, the second maybe you would break even, etc. Over and over the stock just keeps taunting you. By the time I actually got out, my frustration level was through the roof. It just snowballed into a much bigger loss. I looked back and thought, "Damn, I was almost out at one point with a small profit." It's one of those days where you are slightly too early getting in, being aggressive and greedy. These little problems just accumulate until they became big problems.

By the time I actually got out, I had lost over $230,000. Unlike the other trades we discussed, I didn't start the morning thinking "I'm willing to risk a large amount on this one." This was supposed to be "enter at point A, exit at point B and if the trade is not working, just exit after a certain amount of time," but when the momentum is so out of control when you go take your loss, it's at a point where you just never expected it. There are a lot of things that in hindsight I should have noticed. I don't remember where my first entry was, but I felt that I was being patient waiting for a big move up. I wasn't being too early. But, looking back, I was *WAY* too early.

You covered it all and carried none of that overnight?

Yes. I got out completely. At least I stuck with that part of the plan. I ended up covering much higher than I hoped and much later in the day than I intended to. I know that in the past I would get myself in situations like this and I would get stubborn and carry overnight. A small trade idea would turn into a horrible disaster. This one qualifies as a disaster, but at least I didn't let it get worse and I covered.

What was the particular reason you were so averse to holding this one as a swing trade? I remember looking at the balance sheet and they needed money fast. A lot of shorts got bent all the way into the $30s because of that.

I find it to be a very difficult trade to short a stock because a company needs to raise money. I don't know if there is any truth to this, but sometimes it seems that the fact that they need to raise money is bullish for the stock. Almost as if whoever wants to do the capital raise tries to get the stock inflated just for that reason. Of course, an impending dilution can be very bearish for a company. But just like we were talking about earlier, just because a company is a great short doesn't mean that timing is not important. Timing is everything.

In the case of LAKE, the stock went from $7 all the way to $29 on the daily chart. In the after-hours it actually went all the way to $35. Whether the trader is bullish or bearish, he could have screwed up this trade big time or he could have made a lot of money. It's not a matter of whether you are bullish or bearish on the company. It's all about timing.

So you don't get overly excited about capital raise needs because it tends to get crowded and sometimes it gets manipulated up?

I'm reluctant to believe in any of these conspiracy theories, but the truth is that it seems sometimes that companies have some kind of promotion of the stock in order to get the price up for the capital raise. You see it all the time when the company gets a delisting notice from the exchange because their market cap is too low. Then they get their stock promoted, push it up and stay on the exchange. There are a lot of clean companies out there but there are plenty of dirty ones too. It really seems that there is someone pulling the strings, manipulating the price in a lot of these companies that need cash.

Long-term, yes, it's very bearish to have an impending capital raise. But short-term I don't think it's a very good reason to short. I tried to trade that way in the past and lost money, even though I was right in the long-term.

As an example, look at NETE in September. That stock made a massive run. They did the capital raise. Yes, the price eventually came down, but in the meantime it went up an enormous amount. If you had shorted that first day up, eventually you would make money but you would have to endure a huge amount of pain. It ended up going higher by 60-70% from the first big move. I have no idea if it's true or not but it did feel like someone was pushing the stock up for that capital raise.

Sometimes you see this stuff happen far too frequently to be random. Do you agree with that as a trader? You see this stuff too.

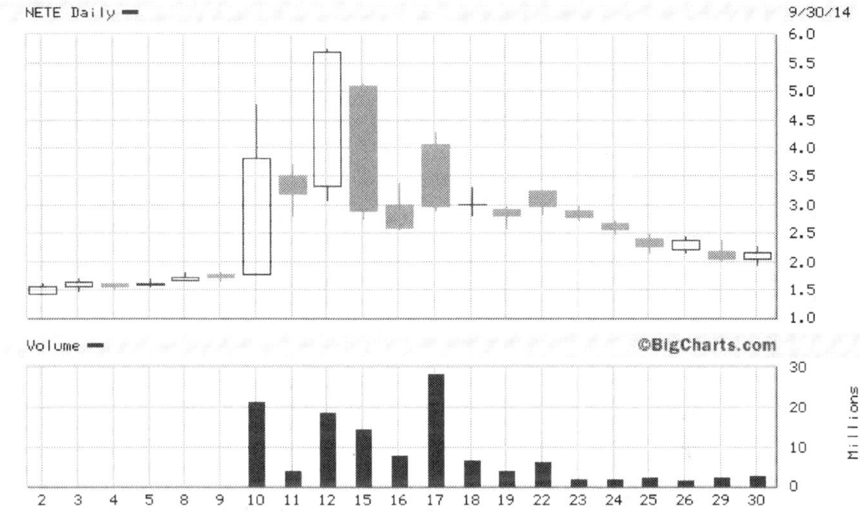

Source: Bigcharts

I wouldn't even say it's a conspiracy. I would say it's a reality. I'm confident that there is something shady going on. Not for every ticker, maybe not even for those mentioned here, but a lot of these companies have no idea how long their stock will stay up. Any competent CFO would quickly try to raise money and shore up the balance sheet the next night. The fact that they keep waiting and waiting tells me that they know it's going higher. Sometimes they help the move with more press releases too. It appears too orchestrated to be random.

Yes. Further proof that sometimes there is manipulation is what you see in a lot of these offshore companies. For instance, Israeli or Chinese companies. When the companies are offshore, listed in the US but operated and managed outside, they seem to do this kind of stuff a bit more often than the US ones. This is another hint that there is something going on behind the scenes. It really makes you wonder, "Who is doing this?" There are laws against this, but somehow they keep it under the radar and don't get caught.

Would you say offshore companies are a little more risky because of that? If they get caught they won't go to jail so they can be more aggressive with the manipulation, press releases, etc.?

When you follow companies long enough, you can get a feel for how shady a company is. You can have a scale of shadiness. Some companies come across as shadier than others. When they are offshore, that is certainly one variable, but there are plenty of offshore companies that are clean, too. The fact that they are offshore certainly adds another element to the puzzle. It's harder to track the actions of the insiders and the people behind the stock. These types of things can come across as allegations which makes me reluctant to say anything publicly, but there is a surprising amount of shadiness in the market. Fraud is not even the right word, because a lot of times they are very careful to not break the law, but that doesn't mean what they are doing is ethical or right. You can be deceptive, manipulative and shady, but it doesn't mean what you are doing is illegal.

A perfect example are some of the debt offerings that companies participate in. They sell these convertible bonds to offshore hedge funds, and these deals just stink of shadiness. The terms are very obscure and are extremely favorable to the hedge funds. It makes you wonder, "Why would they do that? Are they that desperate to raise capital? Or are there some backroom deals going on?" It's hard to know for sure, but there are so many question marks when you try to decipher the terms that it just doesn't make sense.

So that is another variable that you look at when considering an eventual short, the degree to which the company is breaching its fiduciary duty to shareholders?

Yes, you can put it that way. It goes back to what I was saying earlier. You have to put together the whole story to figure out why the stock is going up. What are the elements that are making the stock trade where it is at? The shadiness factor is certainly a part of it. That will influence my decision whether to short the stock.

The thing is, even a perfectly legit company can be a good short. It's all about timing and the price. The shadiest company in the world is not a good short just because the stock is almost worthless. You always need the stock to be up, overvalued by some extreme measure. Even legit companies can be shorted if they fit the bill. They can't just be overvalued. It has to match some technical criteria that tells me that it will be pulling back soon. Keep in mind that there are a lot of players involved here too. It's not just a matter of a company being valued too much or too little. There are also the hedge funds manipulating it, analysts getting involved, etc. There are plenty of other people involved and profiting by manipulation or getting involved in the stock. There are plenty of times that the company has nothing to do at all with the shady activities going on. It could be just somebody that owns a lot of the stock and they are paying to promote it.

Sometimes you can have a clean company but there are plenty of analysts that are being ridiculously bullish, essentially pumping the stock. Then people short it too early and the whole thing turns into a short squeeze. These are all factors that are external to the company. These are the types of factors that create the trade.

Sometimes the company itself is irrelevant to the trade. More often than not though, it's a combination of factors that compose the story that leads to the trade.

What would you say is your main weakness as a trader?

The biggest weakness that I have identified is my urge to make trades. I can't stand the feeling of missing out on something. If a lot of people are making a lot of money in a particular stock and I'm missing out, or if a stock makes a big move and I didn't participate, I want to get involved. Sometimes it's too unbearable to resist. When I get myself into a trade that I don't belong in, it's usually not a good thing. So many of my biggest losses have come from that exact problem.

Sometimes it's just not a good setup. It's not a stock I necessarily understand. It's just not a good trade, but either I feel unproductive because it's a slow day, or I see others talking in chat rooms or social media about how a stock is going to move. Sometimes I just succumb to that urge of "I need to be involved in this." This can be extended to other things as well. If I'm watching a chart closely and it looks like the stock is about to breakout, the inability to resist the urge can hurt me. As I jump in these breakouts, it seems to fail every time. So many losses I had I can trace back to my inability to resist the urge to trade. I can assess how good a trading session went just by looking at which setups I traded, and this has nothing to do with whether I made money or not.

Is tape reading a key part of your style?

I read charts very closely, pay attention to key parts of the charts, but I don't think that's what most people mean by tape reading, so I would say no. I do some of that, but it's not a big part of my trading. Occasionally I might pick up something that might have an influence on what I'm doing. When I pull up a stock I will look at the chart, the L2 and the times and sales. Usually the chart will have the biggest influence on me.

I guess the difficulty, at least for me, with tape reading is that there is so much noise in it. Especially if you are looking at stocks like Facebook, etc. They move back and forth so much it's hard to know what is going on.

Tape reading in big cap stocks like Facebook is useless to me. Perhaps some people have the skill to do it, but I have no idea how. I agree with you, it's a lot of noise. In the less liquid stocks, sometimes you can decipher something from tape reading. Sometimes you can pick up on a very large buyer or seller and figure out at what levels he is at. There is some value there.

You are having a very great year while a lot of traders are struggling due to low volatility and HFT activity. What do you think is the reason you are succeeding and they are not?

Because of the types of stocks that I trade. There has been a lot of opportunity in the universe of stocks that I follow. From my conversations with other traders that use a similar style, they are also having a very good year.

Would you say that HFTs have had a harmful impact on your trading?

Yes.

Any particular practice that may have caused that?

One example of something that has harmed me is when I see multiple participants on the offer at $10. Maybe there are 500, 300 and 200 shares showing on Level 2. Then I go to buy 1,000 shares. I get filled on 200 and the price jumps up 15 cents. That kind of scenario plays out a lot. And this is not even the worst case scenario. Stocks in the $40 to $60 range are usually the worst in this kind of situation, like if I try to buy 2,500 at $45 and the offer lifts and then they run the stock because they sniffed out a large order looking for liquidity. And 2,500 is not really that much, Mid-day when liquidity is dry, it's almost as if there are no real participants there. Then the 100 share bids start to show up and they start to go in front of each other over and over again. You try to hit at $45, get filled on 200 shares, maybe 1,000 if you are lucky. The offer goes instantly. It jumps 15-20 cents and then you see the bids start stepping up, first at 10 cents, then 12, 15, etc. 10 minutes later, this thing is 70 or 80 cents higher. Until you realize what is going on, you might not get the rest of your order until 70 or 80 cents later. If you do know what is going on, you can actually short into that artificial false move.

This is one way to combat HFTs. This might not be a great strategy on its own because you have to risk getting the 2,500 in order to get that pop. But if you are trying to get out you can short those moves, because they essentially moved the price on nothing. These are the types of games that I've experienced personally

When that first started to happen, I was slow to adjust to it. But these days I've wised up. It's still frustrating to trade with these games going on, though.

It's possible that a few years ago that same stock would have had a huge bid-ask spread, so maybe all this complaining is for nothing. These days it feels like the liquidity is there, but it's really the same as the old days when the spread was large and the market makers played their games.

When routing orders, do you use stuff like stacking iceberg[6] orders at levels that you are interested in?

It really depends on the stock, liquidity, and situation. If I'm trading Facebook, there is no need for that, but if I'm trading a thinner small cap, I certainly need to have multiple orders or I never get filled.

There are just too many scenarios to give a general answer.

Do you use hidden orders? I find them useful in higher priced, big spread stocks. In low priced stocks with tight spreads I often just go ahead and hit that spread.

I use hidden orders in low priced stocks too. It all depends on how quick I need to get in and out, and how aggressive I am. If I am scalping for a few pennies, my P&L will be very sensitive to the spread. If I am playing for a big move and I am afraid I am going to miss it, I will just take liquidity. If I am in a stock that has very large bids and offers already displayed, by joining them I wouldn't expect the stock to react much. If everybody is showing 100 shares and I show up with 10,000, everybody will step back. There are many different scenarios, situations, setups, etc. I try to use the order type and route that I believe is the most appropriate for any given situation.

What percentage of longs compared to shorts do you have in your trading? Are you a always a short seller?

I'm far more short biased, however, I'd like to emphasize that I'm a contrarian trader. In a bull market I will be shorting far more and in a bear market I will be buying stocks more often. In the depths of the 2008 crisis, I was buying far more than I was shorting. As a contrarian, I was buying the deeply oversold plays. We are in a 5 year bull market, so as a contrarian I end up shorting more than going long.

It's interesting that you mentioned 2008. There was a point there that seems similar to the parabolic shorts that you like to trade. In October 2008, prices reached a point of total disbelief, but to the downside. Did you make a lot playing the long side there?

Yes. I played all kinds of bounces and some overnight holds. Mostly day trades. I didn't hold stuff for very long.

---

[6] Iceberg orders are orders where you only show part of the size that you intend to get done. For example, you might be trying to sell 30,000 shares but only display 100. You are only showing the tip of the iceberg to other participants.

Why not play like some of your shorts? There was a point where buying stocks in general and holding for like a month or so seemed like an excellent trade.

I wish I had. I have a reluctance to buy and hold anything. When it comes to the market, I'm very skeptical as a whole. I tend to be cynical about stocks. That probably saved me from a lot of losses, because I started trading in 1999 during the NASDAQ bubble. Back then, buying and holding could have made you filthy rich. But then you also could have lost all the gains and then some. It's a mixed blessing.

I watched your presentation in the penny stock conference on YouTube where you talk about hard work.[7] Can you share your thoughts to the readers on this?

There are a lot of people, especially those who subscribe to newsletters and trading alerts, who view trading as a get rich quick scheme. A lot of people don't really appreciate that those who have had success had to work really hard to get there. I believe this is true in all endeavors. I don't think there is anyone who reached a high level of success without working hard. In trading, people tend to run into this misperception quite often. They think trading is easy. They think that anyone can come along and retire as a millionaire by picking the right stocks. Usually, they quickly learn the lesson that it doesn't work that way.

So you try to gain an edge in all parts of trading from order execution, learning routes, new setups, programming your own software, etc. in order to stay ahead of the competition?

Yes. I don't think trading is easy. Therefore, I feel that I have to try much harder to be good at it.

What is your advice for beginning, struggling and intermediate traders?

Everybody has to find the approach to trading that fits their personality. You can't become good at something that's not a natural fit for you. If my approach doesn't fit your risk level or your understanding of the markets or people, it's not going to work for you. The method that will work for you is the one that is natural for you. People ask, "What is better? Breakout trading or momentum trading, short selling or scalping?" My answer is "What is best is what works for you." I've seen some people criticize some types of trading and that is misguided in my view.

Even for traders who have a similar style to me, I've seen some big differences. It doesn't mean I'm right and they are wrong. We just found different things that work for ourselves. That is an important part of success. I can give you some examples: I

---

[7] https://www.youtube.com/watch?v=PKHFWuhrCEk

have not had great success trading ETFs. My historical track record has been terrible. I have not been good at trading breakouts. I have not been able to profit off alerts in chat rooms or newsletters. I'm sure there are people that can do all of these things. But that is not because I'm not a good trader. It's because I know what I'm good at and I focus on that. If it's not working for you, the first thing you probably should check is whether it suits your personality.

What do you do with your trading gains? Do you buy real estate, stocks, keep in cash in order to avoid distractions?

Usually half of it goes right to the government. The other half, I like to compound it. One of the modern marvels of the world is compounding. That's one of the reasons why I became successful. From the very beginning I wasn't looking to make a small amount or a certain amount of money. I was looking to grow my accounts as much as I could. To maximize opportunities. There is no better way to do that than to compound your gains.

That said, I've reached a point where it has become difficult to compound because a lot of these opportunities have a limited capacity for how much capital they can absorb. I'm at the point where I have to actively search for trades that have more capacity. I'm also looking for other investments as well. I've started other projects, such as launching a fund of funds to invest and manage. I'm working with other traders to set up hedge funds for them so I can invest in them and help them grow. These are in the early stages though.

I believe it is important to give back. I am very fortunate that I have the ability to support charities and try to make a difference in the world.

A lot of people reach some kind of success but then they reach a point where they are just not comfortable anymore and they reach a plateau. You seem to keep reaching new highs. Was that something that you always had as a child or you did you have to develop that?

When I got started in trading, there were a lot of people who made a lot of money. There was one guy I knew who said he was making $10,000 a day trading, and all kinds of figures were being thrown around. What that did for me was set the bar very high. That was my early impression of what traders make.

Then I read the *Market Wizards* book series by Jack Schwager. A lot of those traders were making tens if not hundreds of millions. Don't get me wrong: $100,000 a year is a lot of money for anybody. $1 million a year is an extraordinary amount in any profession, but in relation to what other successful traders are making it's not a lot. I have been comparing myself, perhaps naively, to traders who make a lot of money. From the very beginning I wasn't getting a sense that I was succeeding to a point where I was going above and beyond what other traders were making. Even to this day I don't feel that way. Sure, for a day trader I do well, but you still can't compare me to a hedge fund trader or a market wizard. If you do, you can still argue that I don't actually make that much. A lot of this is relative, depending on who you compare yourself to. I never had a mental ceiling. If I made $1 million a year trading, I still might not feel that I was on top of my game. With the Profit.ly website, you can compare amounts of different retail traders. I had no idea that some of my gains would be at the top. For many years I was still naively comparing myself to traders that I knew from early on.

A lot of this is mental: if you don't think a certain amount is a lot, then you aren't going to be limited by it.

So your role models are so much higher than you that you never felt that you accomplished anything amazing, which could limit your future gains?

Yes. And this is still true to this day. If you look at the investment legends, I'm nothing compared to them. Maybe I will never reach their level, but that is ok because I have a great lifestyle and I'm happy with my success. 100 years from now, people will talk about George Soros and Carl Icahn, but my name won't come up. In day trading circles yes, I have been successful, but I can't even hold a candle to those guys.

What change do you think they should make to the market structure?

If you put in an order, they should force you to honor it. There should be a one second cancellation policy. No one should be allowed to send orders if they don't plan to honor it, even for just one second. This probably would lead to a big difference in our ability to get fills. They won't be able to play games, get in front of our orders, etc. I don't know if this would solve all problems, but it would be a simple step to take to minimize the unfair advantage of HFTs.

The thing is, there have been games in the stock market ever since there was a stock market. I don't think they will ever end. If they fix one problem, another one probably shows up. A lot of the HFT stuff seems to be the law of unintended consequences. The exchanges were being unfair, then electronic trading started to rise, leading to the irrelevance of the specialists and market makers.

It certainly seems that someone has the regulators in their pocket because the solutions aren't difficult or complex. There are probably a dozen solutions that they could try out to fix the problem.

In the end, we all pay a small amount to HFTs. Depending on the stock, it can average one tenth of a penny or 5 cents per share. It's almost as if a private institution places a tax on trading. That tax might not be much, but can you imagine if on your statement if it said there was a 2 cent per trade tax? We would all be outraged. That's essentially what is happening here. They skim a tiny piece out of every order and we tolerate them as if it's ok. They use the excuse of adding liquidity, but I don't think any real trader would agree with that. Only people who don't know what they are doing would think that is a legit argument.

Since you short a lot and your universe of stocks tends to be small cap, hard-to-borrow stocks, what are your thoughts on the Reg Sho list? Does a stock added there tend to be higher risk? How can investors adjust to that?

First, I would say that I do keep track of the Reg Sho stocks. I believe the answer is that it doesn't matter all the time, but occasionally it matters. Just like my other answers, it depends on the circumstances.

A lot of people believe that when a stock is added to the Reg Sho list, A) they are going to get bought in their shorts and/or B) It's impossible to short. Both are false. Is there a higher chance of buyins? Yes. Is it harder to borrow? Yes, absolutely. A lot harder. But in neither case is it definitely true. Usually it's harder to borrow and often there are buyins, but it depends on the broker too. It goes back to what I was saying before about putting together the story of a stock. Reg Sho to me is another piece. It's not usually a big piece, but it can be. You have to take it on a case by case basis.

To me, it seems that it used to be a bigger deal. The SEC loosened up a little bit on the rules for the brokers. It seems to be less consequential these days than it used to be. Do you agree with me on this?

Well, the thing is, I've heard some short sellers say that a few years back it was easier to get borrows and there weren't many buyin problems. These days this happens more.

I would say emphatically that the Reg Sho rules, not the list, have made it harder for short sellers. When they made the regulatory shift, it impacted how these stocks setup and our ability to short them. It goes beyond on whether or not a stock is in the list.

I think in my first five years of my trading career, I had about two buyins. On the stocks I trade, I would get buyins 90% of the time if I wasn't careful. That did not used to be the case. If I shorted something in the old days, I had it, and I didn't get bought in. When the Reg Sho rules were implemented that changed.

But, to be honest, the Reg Sho list used to be a bigger deal. These days the Short Sale Restriction[8] (SSR) has far more impact.

With regards to the SSR, is the way you adapt to that to short into strength more often than you are used to?

Yes, but I don't want to overplay how much the SSR impacts a stock. If it's trading normally, it's going to zig-zag and you are going to get filled. For my style of trading, it's more difficult to get a fill, but it's not that bad. What is different is the way the stock trades. It really seems that after reaching the SSR, longs are more confident and shorts are more scared, or something like that. It seems that stocks tend to have a more positive bias when the SSR is on. It's harder to take it down. It does make the timing of a short more difficult.

It does seem like you need to wait for the SSR to be off for you to get your pay day. Not always, but more often than usual.

I read a guy on Twitter talking about how a NASDAQ stock with the SSR is similar to a pink sheet or OTCBB stock. When the upside momentum turns, everybody is trying to get short but it's too late because no one is getting any fills. The stock will drop 10-20 cents and then the fills appear, but by then it's too late and the stock pops.

Oh yes, it's quite similar. Sometimes, as traders, we are so stubborn that we just can't let the idea of the trade go. We just keep chasing it down and create these types of moves. What you just described is a long setup to play the bounce, but as traders we can be so stubborn that we just won't let go.

It's similar to the HFT example I gave earlier, where they run the stock on air by 70 cents. A bad trader will just complain about it. A good trader will just short it because it has run on nothing.

What are your thoughts on mid-day trading? Sometimes I feel like the most profitable thing is to walk away. You can watch it for 4 hours, drain yourself of energy and have small losses, and 80% of the time the move will only happen in the last hour anyway. All the energy spent there hurts you for that last hour as you lose confidence and you don't bet big when the move finally happens.

I tend to agree with that. The thing is, you have to strike the right balance. Some people leave it completely and don't trade it at all. I feel that's too extreme. On the other hand, I agree with you. If you watch it too closely, you can drain yourself.

---

[8] Stocks with the SSR can only be shorted on a uptick. Short selling on the bid is restricted.

Personally, I feel that there is more to be done with research, catching up with things from earlier in the day. I don't agree with walking away completely, but pushing too many buttons can be a problem too. You got to strike a balance.

Occasionally, there are mid-day setups, but if you are too bored you will be prone to entering them too early and get yourself in trouble. If you are careful, though, it's quite possible to make money mid-day. You must be selective. If a catalyst comes out mid-day, a rumor or news, those stocks can be good trades.

80% of your returns come from 20% of your trades, but what about trades that get initiated and closed mid-day? How much as a percentage of your returns are they?

It can be difficult to answer these types of questions with accuracy. For one thing, the answer will change depending on the market environment. Another issue is that just one or two very good or very bad trades can alter the percentages a surprising amount. Lastly, the answer will also vary depending on how far back I look. The numbers will vary depending on whether I look at the last 6 months or the last 2 years. All that being said, I can give you approximations that are decent representations of what I feel is typical for me (regardless if it's accurate in the current market environment).

Most trades initiated and closed mid-day have a very poor relative performance. Many traders, including myself, feel the need to keep busy and will take trades simply because a very small profit is better than no profit at all. The danger is if I begin to move the threshold of what qualifies for a set up too much. I will start losing money on those trades. It is important to be extra patient and selective mid-day. It is possible to make money on mid-day trading, but likewise it is too easy to get sloppy and lose money on mid-day trading as well.

Do you believe that they are maybe 3% or less of your profitability? I'm backing out trades initiated mid-day and closed in the last hour or the next day because those trades can be frequently initiated later and the mid-day period served just as a grind and didn't add much value. I guess the point I'm trying to make is, since the hourly dollar return of mid-day trades is so much lower, isn't it worth it for you to use that time to do other things at this point in your career, since you've already accumulated a large library of situations and setups in your head?

I am not a "once in, once out" trader. Therefore, even the mid-day trades are often adds or exits to pre-existing positions. This makes it next to impossible to say it is not worth it to make these trades. These trades are just part of a continual watching, monitoring and adjusting of current positions. That being said, it is rarely worth my time to day trade the mid-day setups (enter and exit fully in mid-day). Although it is uncommon, there are some very good mid-day opportunities. As I said, the key is to be very selective. If I am already watching and monitoring the market, then finding these opportunities is certainly worth it, as long as I don't allow myself to get sucked into trading the "boredom" trades.

2016 Update

I remember last year there was one day where GENE was at $10 and it went down to $8.50. For the rest of the day it just kept grinding up, all the way to $10. Then, at the end of the day, it put a squeeze to $10. And then shortly after that, the stock just went straight down for days. I remember you said that you were short before that end of the day squeeze. You added during it and added more after it. How did you know that wasn't going to be another round of buying that could take the stock much higher? There was a lot of volume in the buy side there.

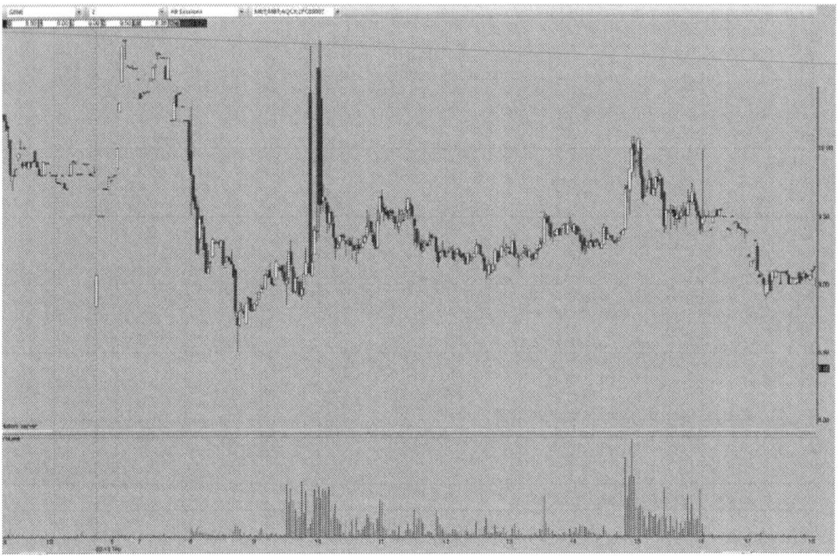

Source: MB Trading Desktop Pro

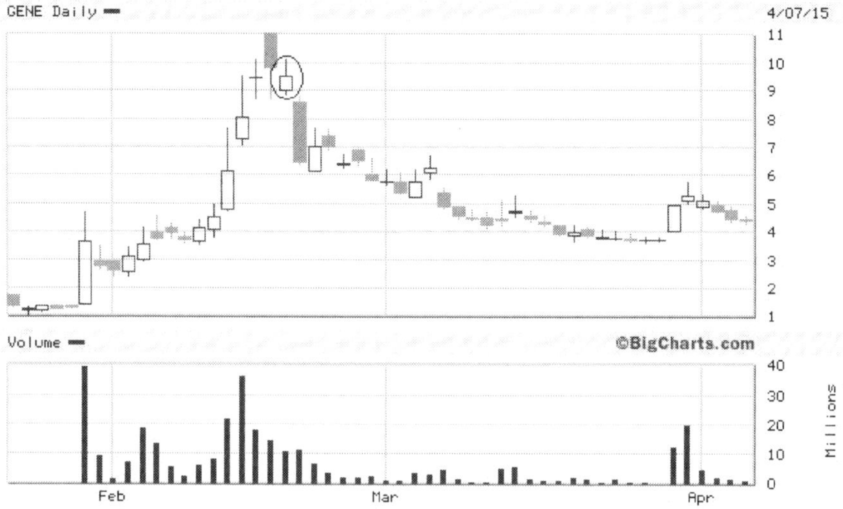

Source: Bigcharts

I wouldn't necessary say I knew; it was not a certainty. A better way to put it is, "what made me think the stock was done?" I'm sure there were a lot of reasons when I put together my trade thesis. I'm always trying to look at it from all the different angles and perspectives. In this particular case, it had to do with how much it had already run up, the type of volume, the fact that the day before the stock had a huge gap up that got sold really hard. Combine that with the stock's catalyst. The last step was to understand the other side of the trade. If you look at it before the big move happened, when it was trading in the $3.50 to $4 range, - there were a lot of shorts accumulating positions, so when it broke above $4.50 it surged all the way to $7.50. A lot of that was due to a short squeeze. Put all of this together up to the day that you are referencing, and most of the squeeze was over. The shorts who were swinging it were either out, or they weren't going to get out, no matter what. I remember that I was a little nervous. It could have gone higher, but the price action made it look like it was the last hurrah. The longs had been making easy, quick profits and they were boldly chasing it at $10 thinking, "this was going to be another easy move." The shorts who were getting hurt day after day were all capitulating. All of these elements were in play, and yet it couldn't get above $10. The same thing happened during the previous three days; the pumpers and chasers were pilling in and the shorts were being squeezed, and yet this time it couldn't move higher.

I always try to put together lots of pieces of information. I think of it as "creating a story." Every situation is different and I try to put together a story of how and why the stock got there. I try to understand all the different angles.

The stock had quite a run from the low ones to the 10 dollar area. It was exhausted. One last piece of that story: I recall that I sensed someone was behind the move, trying to get it up to sell shares into the move.

Do you think they made a decision to sell there because if they let another round of rallies happen it would be too costly for them to let all the momentum chasers profit off the move?

No, not really. I think they got the price they wanted. Earlier in the run it seemed that someone was manipulating it. They were buying the stock. On paper they had to be making a lot of money. Once they got it up to the price that they wanted, they had to transition out of a huge long position and dump the stock. They couldn't just dump their shares on the market as soon as it was up, because that would crush the price very quickly. I don't think that the rally at the $10 area was manipulated... and it was the perfect opportunity for them to start selling.

Of course so much of what I'm saying is speculation. I don't have any proof that the company or anyone else was doing something illegal.

VLTC was another big runner that was tough for shorts for a while and then it made that final move up. On the day before the top there was a big rapid squeeze from $16 to $19. Did you play that?

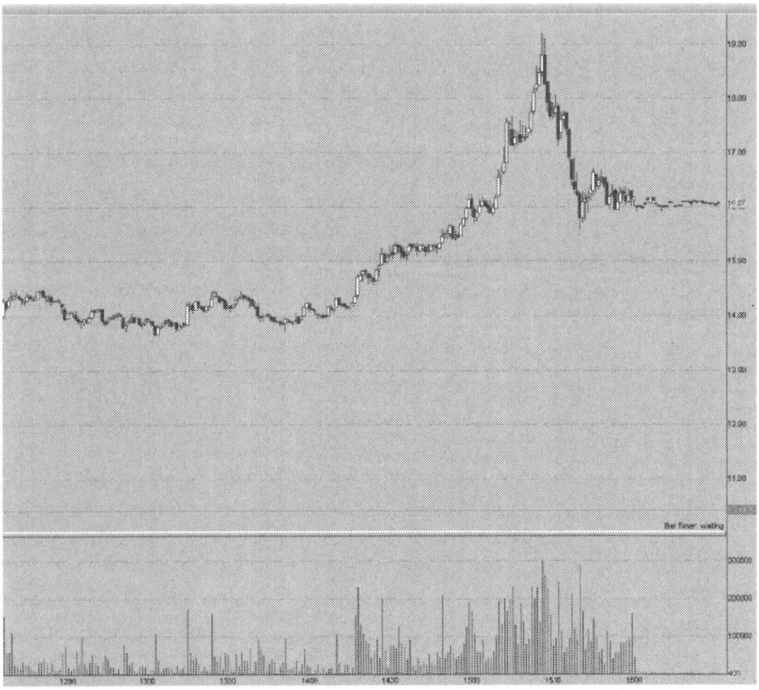

Source: MB Trading Desktop Pro

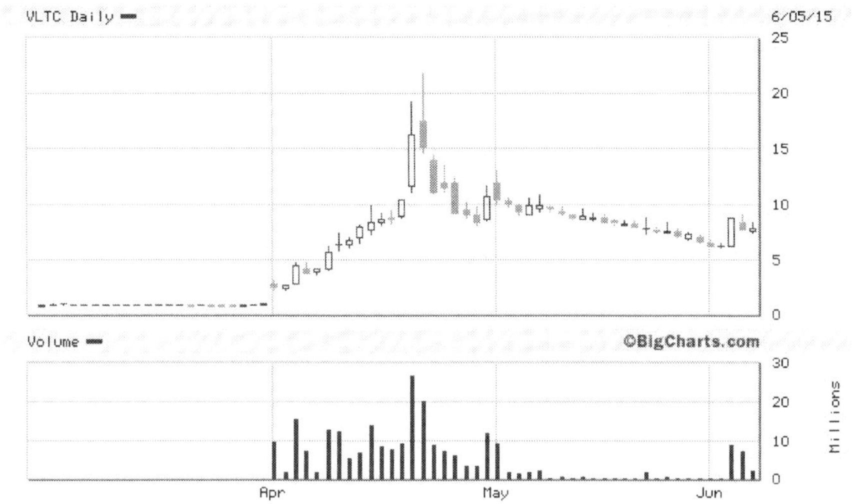

Source: Bigcharts

I had three fairly large trades that day. There comes a point where the stock is so volatile and getting so out of control that I have to just pick a spot and go with it. Even if I had very good timing, I wouldn't be able to build a large position right at the top. As the stock is making a big move like that, there are multiple points where the stock is making a potential top. If you're trading a small position, it's no big deal. You can take a stab at it and if you are proven wrong you can get out, sometimes even for a small profit, or at worst a small loss. If you have a big position, forget about it. You are not going to be able to do that. Not only it will be hard to get the position in right at the top, but you'll also have a hard time getting out without serious damage if you're wrong.

Even though I still try to time it, I also accept that I will not top tick it with a big position, and that is not my goal. My goal is to get a good average entry price, and potentially add later. With that in mind, I tried to short VLTC three times that day. The first two times were premature. I took a stab at it, and got out a couple of times. The third time was when I built up pretty good size. At that point there was no more getting out; I got a good enough price, and I was sticking with it no matter what happened.

It was tough when the stock collapsed into the close. At that point I had to make the decision between whether to chase it lower and add, or to wait for the next day to try to get a better price. I had built a decent sized position. It wasn't huge, but I was pretty well positioned in case the stock collapsed the next day, and it didn't.

With regards to AQXP and KBIO, what were some of the lessons you drew out of those moves? They went far higher than either longs or shorts ever expected. I assume these were the toughest trades for you last year.

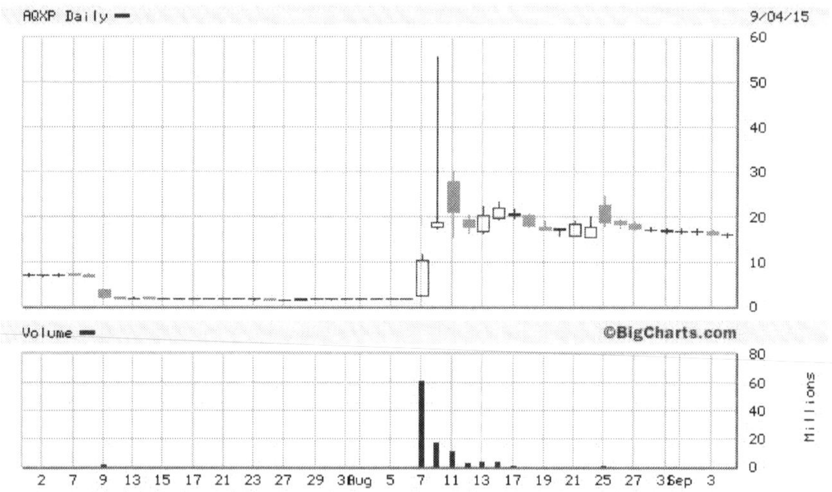

Source: Bigcharts

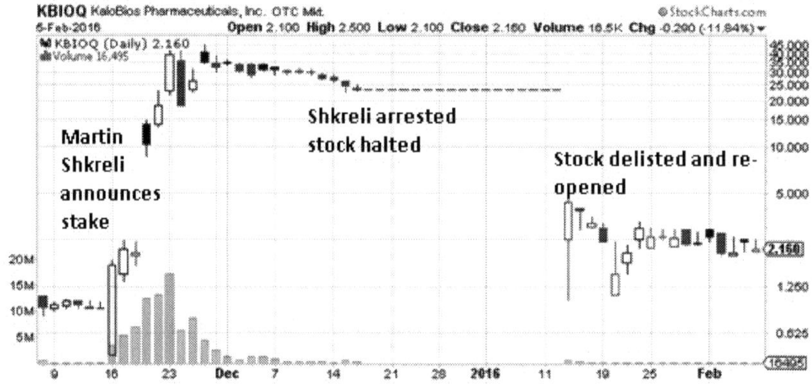

Chart courtesy of StockCharts.com

KBIO is such a good example of an outlier. You can look at hundreds of thousands of stock charts in all different scenarios, and no matter how long you study, there are going to be some occasions when something happens that is not only rare, but completely unique. What happened with KBIO had never happened before. The circumstances and how it played out were so outside the realm of what can ever possibly be reasonably anticipated, that it stands out as a complete outlier event.

A giant squeeze was created because of the way that the stock was purchased for the shell. There were so many other ways they could have acquired the stock without causing the squeeze.

The real lesson is: you will not always be able to anticipate what is possible. The realm of possibilities is enormous. Sometimes things will happen that you can neither predict nor prepare for in your risk management models.

The biggest problem was the way they announced their stake through SEC filings ***after-hours***, when there was no liquidity. You could have the best risk control measures possible, but if you held a stock like this overnight, no risk control model could have protected you from what happened. Either you were lucky, and you were sitting in front of the computer when that news hit, or you were going to take a huge loss. There is literally nothing you can do when it's after-hours and you have a significant short position. Even if you start covering immediately on the news, you are still risking a massive loss.

This is an example of how things can happen in the market that are outside of anyone's expectations. It will humble you if you think you are managing risk properly. You cannot apply any type of risk management to those situations other than sticking to tiny positions.

AQXP had some parallels, but they were nowhere near as The big move on day 2 was similar in the sense that something quite unexpected happened, but at least in this case there was liquidity. You could actually exit it if you were short. When KBIO spiked you would have been stuck if you were short because there was no liquidity. These scenarios can really test your imagination of what is possible.

Despite all this, I don't believe I should make any excuses for my bad trades. Traders need to be accountable because anything can happen.

Are you going to have smaller overnight short positions to protect against that in the future?

The only adjustment I will make as a result of that is to make sure my overnight shorts are smaller in relation to the float. I won't have smaller overnight positions in general. The reason why KBIO did what it did was because there was no liquidity. The company already had a tiny float, and then Shkreli and his friends bought roughly 70% of the float. Of course it's going to squeeze on that, but how could I have known that? If someone told me at $2.50 that, "70% of the float is cornered by a group of investors," of course I would have avoided shorting the stock.

Quite frankly, I'm disappointed at the regulators. They could have stepped in so many times when it seemed that something fishy was going on. When the SEC fillings came out after the close the exchange could have halted the stock. I'm sure it would still have gapped up a lot in the next day but it would have been much more orderly. Major news came out when the stock was very illiquid and they let it continue to trade. They halt large cap stocks a lot of times for news dissemination.

How did you ended up managing this trade? I believe you were short at $2. Did you get out at $10 or $15? On AQXP, also, if you short at $30 and it goes to $55, what do you do?

It was really tough. On KBIO, I did get squeezed and it was pretty nasty. I held a good portion of it overnight, because I didn't want to be covering all of it during the illiquid after-hours session. I covered the next day at a lot of different prices. I even covered a good chunk as low as $10. It was extraordinarily stressful to do that. Although I lost a lot of money on it, at least it created a lot of excitement in the small cap world, which led to a lot of other good trading opportunities the following week. Fortunately, I was able to make back a lot of that loss. I even eventually made some back trading KBIO, but nowhere near as much as I lost. A lot of other stocks caught fire because of KBIO, and it became a highly profitable time period.

On AQXP, how did you manage the trade?

Although I traded AQXP, it was over the summer when I'm usually a lot less active in my trading. I don't remember all the details, but I did short on the way up. Similar to KBIO, it surpassed my projections of how high it could go. I ended up with a poor average entry. I was able to add some when it was near its highs. With KBIO, I couldn't really add because the position had grown so large. If I have a short position worth $200,000 and the price goes up 10 fold, then I'm suddenly short $2 million worth of stock. That's an ugly situation. AQXP wasn't nearly as bad in that sense. I was able to manage it better by scaling in. It wasn't quite as dramatic as KBIO.

Is that something that you do a lot? Take the summer off for life-work balance reasons?

Yes. I have been doing that for the last five or six years. I need to force myself to take a break. I usually have a lot of overlapping positions, and that makes it hard to take even a little time off. If I take just one week off I would need to unwind a lot of positions first. When I'm trading, I usually I end up working every day. I know that if I start watching the market when I'm supposed to be off I tend to get sucked back in. I eventually need to take a break and the best way for me to do that is to completely remove myself from all trading by taking summers off. I usually take at least two full months without any trading at all.

Is there anything special about the summer?

My daughter is off from school so I can spend some time with her. Also, historically, the market is slower.

Would it be accurate to describe your style as catalyst analysis trading?

Yes, that's a good way to put it. I mix it with technicals. I analyze the catalysts along with the events surrounding the situation.

People often simplify trading to 2 types, based on either technical or fundamental analysis. Traditionally, these are considered the two ends of the spectrum. I feel that those descriptions miss the mark. There is a lot more to it than just looking at a chart or just looking at the fundamentals of a company. I am not a purely technical trader, and I'm definitely not a fundamental trader.

When a stock is making a move, I want to understand the context of that situation, which means understanding the catalysts. Why is the stock moving? You wouldn't want to short KBIO after it went from $2 to $4 after-hours simply because "it's up 100%." You have to understand why it is up, and adjust accordingly. Creating a bias, understanding why a stock is moving, and understanding the perspective of the other traders are some of the key elements. Combine those with technical data to help determine support and resistance levels, potential reversal spots, et cetera... This all goes hand in hand. Technical analysis alone misses some of the elements that are required to be successful. Trading solely on technicals, to me, is incomplete.

So you want to understand the likely impact of news, catalysts, market positioning and technical levels to develop a bias and position yourself accordingly?

Yes. For example, if a biotech came out with good news, you could look at the news and say, "Yes, that's very positive, and the stock price should rise." But it's the market's reaction to the "good" news that could make the stock either a good long or a good short. Overreactions and under-reactions happen all the time. I look at the price in context of the catalyst. The technical aspects need to be overlapped with an understanding of the catalyst. I like to have an idea of what the move should be worth.

The context includes more than just the news from the company; it includes the sentiment of the market as well. What have the day traders been doing recently with these stocks? When you have certain types of stocks making big moves, the expectations of big moves is much higher. My trade entries shift to higher levels to account for that. I need to give them more room to run, and vice-versa. In a quiet market, a stock with a certain type of catalyst could be overbought following a 20-

30% move. In another type of market, that same catalyst and stock could run 100% on the same news! You really have to piece together a lot of different variables.

A lot of guys avoid shorting these momentum stocks during the uptrend and try to get in short when they show some kind of reversal. Guys like you seem to be more comfortable starting in when the stock is still showing strength. Does that mean you don't make this distinction of uptrend and downtrend as far as your positioning is concerned?

A lot of that depends on the situation. In some cases I would completely avoid the uptrend just like those guys. I agree that I tend to get in against the uptrend more often than some guys, but it really depends on what I'm looking at.

There are so many different setups that it's hard to boil it down to a simple answer. When I have a high conviction trade, I am not going to be scared out as easily. I won't be concerned about losing money as much, because I know it's just a matter of time until I make it back.

Right now, we are in a type of market where there aren't as many opportunities. The high flyers that we had a few months ago are gone. In this market I'm not holding shorts as much. The moves are quicker. I will take what the market offers, and right now it's not offering big moves. This is not an environment where conviction is high. The moves are quicker now. For example, take INO, one of the Zika virus stocks. It made a decent move from $5.25 to $7.20, but in a more speculative environment the stock would have moved a lot more than that. It was still a good move and there was an opportunity to short, but I am not going to trade it the same way as I would VLTC. It's very different. The opportunity was smaller and quicker.

What is the best advice you can give to people who want to learn how to trade small cap stocks?

For someone who is just starting, my advice would be to thoroughly research your strategies and setups. You have to understand how stocks trade. Also, you have to understand how extreme outliers can be, like KBIO and AQXP have shown. You could trade 100 times in a row and make money with a great success rate, but it only takes one outlier to blow you up. You have to familiarize yourself with all the different possibilities. There can be false feedback when traders have success. They might not realize how big the underlying risk is. There's only a small chance of facing an outlier, but it is high enough to blow you up or cause you to lose a lot of money.

It's important to understand this and not make too many assumptions, especially when it comes to managing your risk.

So, be careful about risk management.

Yes, the thing is that people think risk management is all about stops. They think, "I will risk 20 cents on this stock and I'll stop out when it gets there." But if you are holding something overnight, I would argue that your risk management has much more to do with position sizing than with where your stop is. Position sizing on an overnight short is the only true risk management that you have. With KBIO, it wouldn't have mattered where your stop was.

In the first edition of this book, I wrote a rule for risk control, which is to assume that a short would gap 300% against you as a form of a stress test that you could survive a short squeeze. A loss of 30% or more in the stress meant you were too big. Do you think that can work as a protective method?

I think that's smart. One hundred per cent of the money in a trade is at risk. You can't pretend that you are risking 1% of your account. If you lose 500%, that's five times of your investment that was at risk. Sometimes it's even more than that - as in KBIO.

If you are in a trade, obviously you will have to take these risks. The trades that pay off more are usually the riskier ones. Often the stocks that move a couple of percent per day aren't the ones that make a lot of money.

Do you ever worry that one day you will see a 5000% gap? The mother of all short squeezes?

No. I guess it's possible. I could worry so much about getting hit by a car that I would never leave my house. It's always possible to get hit by a car, but we live our lives with a certain amount of acknowledged risk. We need to live with it otherwise we would be paralyzed with fear. If I had worried about risks like that then I wouldn't be where I'm at now. Something that extreme? Yes, it's possible. But it's probably more likely I will get hit by a car tonight than I will see a gap that big. Both would be terrible, but in either case you can't just stop what you are doing.

Do you feel like the HFT industry has peaked now because of the regulatory scrutiny, the criticism, Congress, etc.? Do you feel they will struggle going forward?

Quite possibly. The growth of HFTs may have peaked because they all squeezed each other's profit margins. The easy money is gone. In the early days, it was so easy to make money that a lot of firms flocked to it. Now there's enough competition that, while there is still money to be made, it's not as automatic as just setting up a shop.

I remember you saying that you never made much money trading ETFs. Do you know why that is?

With ETFs I don't usually see the same overreactions and underreactions that are in stocks. They also don't have the same types of catalysts. They have broad economic news, but even then sometimes they barely move.

We have as many as 10,000 stocks to choose from. Out of those, you only have to choose a few of the best to make a good living. The ones that are defined as the best can rotate depending on the situation of that day. In ETFs, it's a different story. How many good opportunities in ETFs do we have? While there are a few hundred ETFs out there, only a small number actually have sufficient liquid. Even out of those few hundred, many are just variations of each other. There is a VIX ETF, an Inverse VIX, and a leveraged VIX, sometimes many of the same type. All of them are highly correlated with SPY, which also has an inverse and leverage ETF and so on. Even though there are a lot of ETFs, they are so correlated that it's only really a few ETFs. Out of 10,000 stocks to choose from, there are a lot of opportunities compared to just a handful of ETFs.

This is not to say that ETFs can't have good opportunities. It's just that out of a basket of 10,000, mathematically, you are going to have vastly more opportunities.

So you don't get involved much when the SPY and VIX are going crazy?

If the SPY is going crazy I'm usually going to find a better opportunity in an individual stock that is making a more extreme move.

A few times a year there are opportunities, times when the markets are making big moves, and everything becomes highly correlated. Everybody is dumping stocks, regardless of the name. We had that a few weeks ago when the indexes were getting hammered in the beginning of January. All the big name stocks, and even the small cap stocks, were dropping. It didn't matter what you were holding. In times like that, there are some opportunities on SPY, yet I still feel like there will be better opportunities with a stock that (even though it's correlated to SPY) is capitulating to more of an extreme. My ability to time the reversal seems a bit easier in that situation.

One of the issues that I have with shorting small caps is that when the moves are not extreme, it's hard to get involved. I see guys shorting these 1 day or 2 day runners, and I don't understand how they are comfortable getting in so early in these plays. Whether these stocks die early, or whether they die after a huge run, they look very similar early on. How do you think a trader can get more comfortable with that?

I can relate to that. I see some guys shorting some of these symbols and I don't see why. That goes back to what I said. We have 10,000 stocks to choose from, so just pick from the ones that you *do* understand. You don't have to trade the ones you that you don't understand.

There are plenty of times where I'm trading something, and the other guys don't understand my setup and what I see on it. And that's fine. We all see something different. That is probably a good thing. We don't want to all trade the same way.

Lessons from Chapter 2

1. The importance of precision. The thing that struck me about Gregg's style and personality is that he really cares about having a precise view of what is going on, and his view on things. Frequently, he would avoid making any kind of blanket statement or generalization. He said many times "it depends" over the course of the interview. I suspect this is due to him being a contrarian trader who deals with asymmetric scenarios constantly. The price of a mistake in a high flying stock can be large. In order not to be wrong, Gregg tries to analyze all the variables at play for the stock, to come up with a view on the stock (or what he calls a "story"). The long list includes: the chart, volume, the catalysts, how hard it is to borrow the stock, how profitable (or not) the company is, the shadiness level of the company's management, presence in the Reg SHO list, the company's need to raise cash, what the insiders are doing, the press releases, short interest, the analysts' comments, and many others.

Being too quick to trade something or missing key pieces of fundamental information can turn a quick attempt at a profit into losses that are several times the profit target.

The way a trader should apply this principle is to do a lot of research on the stocks or instruments that he trades. Once you feel you have a precise idea of why the price did what it did, then you can actually go ahead and take a significant risk in either direction.

2. The point of complete disbelief. Gregg talks about how he knows the top is close when things get to a point of total disbelief. When these stocks are up so much, and shorts are hurting so badly, that it all "clicks," and he just "knows" the trade will work. Prices have reached a point that are not just fundamentally unsustainable, but more importantly, technically unsustainable. I have been involved in the stocks mentioned in this interview (MDBX, LAKE) and recall the days when they peaked. The feeling is different from other days when those stocks were up. The acceleration in the price action, the ridiculous price targets being thrown around on Twitter and chat rooms, the amount of people blowing up shorting it, etcetera, distinguish those days. For any contrarian trader, it just feels like a top. Longs are up so much and are ready to take profits. Shorts are losing so

much, getting margin calls, bought in, etc. When they stop, there are no more buyers, and an avalanche of sellers comes in.

This is not to say that it can't go any higher. Even when things are at a point of complete disbelief, you can see one last wave of buying, driven by short covering or any number of possibilities. The price that the stock can finally go to can amaze anyone, because buy-ins have to be executed, no matter what. The brokers face a regulatory liability if they don't. We live in a world with a lot of black swans and you have to be prepared to face some of them in your lifetime. Risk management is still important, and hence the next lesson.

3. Plan for the worst case scenario. Gregg talks about how he shorted ICPT on its monster run to $500, but he had planned that, in a worst case scenario, the stock might actually keep going to $600. He would be down $1.5 million at that point. While he did not disclose his net worth to me, I feel comfortable saying that the loss figure is not over 20% of all his assets. A loss like that in an extremely unlikely scenario is consistent with proper position sizing (for more information on position sizing, check the Lessons section in Chapter 11). This is especially true when you consider that in his estimation, there was over a 90% chance that the stock would come in, and his gain would be as big, if not bigger, than the loss.

As he puts it, "I wanted to make sure that I would not be capitulating. You want to short into capitulation and not give another short seller a great entry, should it make another massive squeeze."

4. Be "cautiously aggressive." I once read about a term from a poker player that I believe applies to this interview perfectly. The player was talking about how in No Limit Texas Hold'em you have to be cautiously aggressive. You are aggressive by raising pre-flop, attacking other players' blinds, making stabs at pots, small bluffs, etc. But at the same time you are cautious so as not to make a big mistake with a lot of your chips. You only really go "all-in" when you know you have a big advantage. The "all-in" term in poker can be a bit of a misnomer, given that most good players only have a fraction of their bankroll at the table. The point is: you make an aggressive big bet when you are certain, and aggressive small bets when you are not. Gregg talks about how most of the time he is in trades without a lot of confidence. These are not high percentage trades, but they are profitable. When they turn against him, he is quick to get out, though. The LAKE trade is an example of a trade that he perhaps could have cut sooner, but he did exit the trade. Had he not, he would have faced a gigantic loss, given the stock's massive run.

Gregg will only really go for the huge gain when the setup shows him that the odds are massively in his favor. In that case, he will be quite aggressive with significant position sizes, yet he still has that worst case plan, as mentioned in the previous lesson. Through the combination of exiting lower confidence trades and planning for the worst case in high confidence trades, he remains cautious, despite the fact that he is being an aggressive short seller going against huge trends.

5. Improve all aspects of your trading. Another thing that struck me about Gregg is that he knows a lot about order execution, routes that are best for each scenario, best brokers for each style, etc. I know quite a few good traders that are completely oblivious to any aspect of trading that doesn't involve knowing when to buy and sell. They make good money, but they could make even more if they improved other areas of trading. That additional profit compounded over a decade adds up to huge sums of money. I've had conversations with Gregg about order execution, and ended up learning a great deal. This principle applies not just to market structure and order execution knowledge, but also to psychology, setups, fundamental analysis, and more. In his YouTube video, Gregg talks about how he still to this day reads trading books, goes to conferences and tries to improve his trading. The philosophy of constant improvement is probably a key element in his success. Although possible, it's hard to be a winning trader without it, and it's even more unlikely that you will be among the top of winning traders without it.

6. Be careful with buy-ins. Due to regulatory changes put forward by the SEC, buy-ins have become more common these days. When you are short a stock, if your broker is unable to keep the shares that they borrowed, they will cover your position. It doesn`t matter what the price is—even if it's ridiculous to be a buyer at that level, they will close you out. The way Gregg adapts to this is to monitor how easy it is to borrow the stocks, whether they are on the Reg Sho list, whether buy-ins have happened recently, etc. If he concludes that the chance of a buy-in is high, he will focus on quicker profits, and won`t ride losses for very long. It becomes more like day trading. Holding overnight (especially if in a loss) becomes extremely dangerous. If the chance is low, or he expects a massive move in a short period (like at the point of total disbelief), he will hold the short longer and try to capture bigger moves.

7. Be careful betting against stocks that need to raise equity. These stocks frequently will end up going far higher than you think. Gregg suspects this has to do with manipulation happening behind the scenes, so more can be raised in the equity offering. I've seen a lot of shorts get crushed with a simplistic thesis such as "the company needs to raise money, it has to go down." Whether the company needs to raise cash is just one input to take into account when putting together the story of what is going on in a stock.

8. Be careful with offshore stocks. A similar principle applies here. Offshore stocks involve management that is from a different country than where the stock trades. This enables them to be bolder with manipulation, create aggressive press releases, etc., due to less fear of suffering law enforcement action. This does not mean that these stocks run for longer or go higher than domestic stocks. It simply means that you should expect the unexpected more in these stocks. It`s another variable to take into account when putting together the story of the stock and deciding how to trade it.

9. When considering whether to take profits, consider re-shorting opportunities. If you have a short position with a large gain, one variable to take into account is what you think the chance is that it will give you a nice re-shorting opportunity. Even if you think the stock ultimately is going lower, it might be a good idea to take profits, just so you have a chance to re-short it higher and profit even more.

10. Pick role models who are much more profitable than you are. A key element that enabled Gregg to keep growing as a trader and reach new levels of profitability was the fact that he never thought he was doing anything amazing. By choosing the Market Wizards as his role models, his profits looked tiny by comparison. He experienced less anxiety and difficulty. He bet bigger, making bigger amounts, and became one of the top US retail traders as a result.

11. Size your overnight shorts by taking into account the size of the float. KBIO shows how dangerous it is to have a significant short position in a stock with a small float. Stocks of this kind warrant a small (or no) position for an overnight short.

12. When judging whether to enter in a stock, take into account what day traders did in similar stocks recently. Gregg talks about how in some periods stocks can put in big runs or small runs based on similar catalysts. Market sentiment is a key component of timing your entries. When markets are hot, you have to be more patient and careful with short selling. When they are not, you can be more aggressive, and play for the mean reversion earlier.

13. Risk management has more to do with position sizing than it has to do with stops. Due to such things as gaps, halts, breaking news, etc., you have to consider that you might not be able to exit your position at your desired price, and therefore size your position more carefully when you are exposed to those risks.

14. You have 10,000 stocks to choose from. US stock markets have a significant amount of diversity of setups, plays, news, sectors, etc. that enables you to find a trading style that you are comfortable with.

Chapter 3

Adam Whiting - The Futures Scalper

Adam Whiting (Twitter @apwtrader) is a self-described futures trader and HFT hater. He is a member of the futures prop firm Futex. I came across him on Twitter while trying to find a profitable futures trader that was HFT aware and could guide me on how to reach success trading index futures.

Futures trading has always appealed to me. The liquidity, the amount of different markets you can trade and the huge leverage you can deploy in that market. It's the type of market where, as trading skills develop, your income can grow with almost no limit, sometimes exponentially.

The transition from being a stock trader to a futures trader is something that has interested me so I decided to get in touch Adam in order to understand how the mind of a futures trader works.

Adam is a London-based trader who is a big advocate of screen time. He is an active scalper who rarely holds things for many hours, nevermind overnight. He is most active in the European stock index futures markets. This was yet another reason I wanted to interview him. A lot of traders report that the US crisis of 2008 was great for their profitability. Europe seems to be going through a crisis almost every year with a lot of volatility in their equity indexes. Trading their markets made sense to me. Instead of hoping volatility would come back, why not go after volatility globally by choosing which stock markets to trade based on that? If the trader can adapt to the different work hours, it looks like a good solution to me.

At the start of his career, Adam was backed by Futex. The firm provided him the capital, hardware and basic instructions so he could begin. To this day he has stayed in the firm.

This interview was conducted in June 2015

When did you start trading and how was that?

I started trading pretty much as soon as I left university, which was back in 2006. I joined a firm for a couple of weeks where my dad knew the chairman. I was there for a couple of weeks and I saw all the guys that were there making money and doing well. Then I asked if I could stay a little bit longer and they said no problem. Since then it just has been growing and growing and I have been trading ever since.

That was a UK prop firm?

Yes, it is called Futex. I work in their London office. They are even in Poland now.

Did you start in futures right away or you were trading something else?

They were solely futures, basically. Some of the guys there would trade some options every now and then, but it has always been pretty mainly focused on futures. I have been a futures trader since day 1 really.

In the US, futures prop firms are rare because it is so easy to get leverage in the contracts with a retail firm. Why do they exist in the UK?

These firms exist because obviously there is a lot of money in there. There is not a huge amount of prop firms in the UK. We certainly are not one of the biggest. Some of the biggest traders of the firm do about 2,000-5,000 roundtrips per day, the real big guys. The firms will take a few pence per contract and then a percentage of the profits. When you start, you tend to be in some kind of 60/40 split, or 70/30 or 80/20. They take a cut of the profits but also make a small amount out of every trade. There is a lot of money for them. The traders can still make a lot for themselves though.

What is in it for the traders? Why not just open a regular retail brokerage account and keep 100% of the profits?

The main reason really is the support you get. You are based in an office, you get IT support there. If something goes down they can ring up a broker and close pending orders for you. They provide everything, so you have all the computers, screens, etc. If something breaks they will just replace it for you. In addition, you are in an office with like-minded people. People that are trading, often the same markets as you. This helps everyone to learn from each other. While everyone is competing in the same market, you are still a very small portion of the market so everybody can help each other. If you go to a retail brokerage, these days they are starting to offer price ladders[9], but in the UK a lot of them are more like spread betting. You pay a spread, say in Eurodollar, and you would have to pay up like 5 cents to get in or

[9] The price ladder is referred to as Depth Of Market (DOM) in the US. It's like a vertical L2 window.

out. However, when you are trading on futures using price ladders, you can be in the best market price.

How were those first few months and years for you?

It was tough for two years. Most people that come through the door take a while to learn. There are a couple of guys that made it in like 18 months. But the majority of the people that are making money in the firm have been there for a long time. Usually it takes a good two years before they were solidly profitable. You have profitable months, a good couple of weeks. But to make money weekly and monthly consistently, it usually takes a couple of years to learn that skillset. For me it was no different. It took a good two years to make money that one could actually consider a good wage. I was quite lucky that I was young and was just out of university. My mom was letting me live at home rent free, and my dad gave me some cash to supply the basics. After two years it all kind of clicked and I started to build it up from there.

What was the best advice that you got from the guys in the firm?

I have been asked that quite a few times, but I don't really know how to answer that. You always pick up little snippets. The best pieces of advice are always things that help here and there but nothing like a big quote or anything that stands out to me. A lot of the guys in the firm were always very supportive. They said you just have to be patient. In this business you are forever learning. The market is always changing every day, month and year. I'm lucky enough to have traded through the end of the bull market in 2006/2007, through the massive financial crisis in 2008/2009 and since 2009, one of the biggest bull runs in history. I also traded through the European debt crisis in 2011. I traded a lot of different markets. You are always learning, and you always have to discover new things. You can't ever stand still. You have to be adapting the way you trade.

What are the main contracts that you trade?

I trade the German DAX, the FTSE 100, the German Bund which is the 10 year government bond, and the S&P500 emini. Sometimes I trade the Russell or the NASDAQ, but not very often these days. Also, the Eurostoxx is the more liquid European stock index, while the DAX is very thin. I trade oil as well. Occasionally I dabble in currency, but not too much.

Have you tended to gravitate towards the European contracts more because of the crisis there and the extra volatility it has brought?

Most of the guys in the firm tend to do well in markets that are more volatile. By volatile, I mean intraday swings, a market that is not stuck in a range. The DAX is one of the most illiquid and volatile markets out there. In the last 2-3 years, it has been my bread and butter. Having said that, recently it has gotten to the point where it's almost too illiquid. The slippage to get in and out is almost like half the trade. I'm more of a scalper. I'm in and out for a few ticks rather than being in the big trades. What I tend to do is to trade the European markets until 2:30 UK time, which is when the S&P500 futures open. Then from 2:30 to 4:30 I will generally trade the ES.

What is the main difference between the DAX and the ES contract?

They are vastly different. The S&P500 is the most liquid stock market in the world. Even right now, which is the thinnest that I have seen in a long time, you still have bids and offers of 200-300 contracts, albeit it can rip through them in no time. The DAX at the moment is trading with anywhere from 1 to 5 contracts in the bid and offer.

Wow.

It is unbelievably different. If you hit a market order in the DAX and it is a big enough order, you will get filled through 3-4 prices. In the ES you will tend to just get one price.

Do you believe that the DAX, because of this thinness, is more inefficient, so there are more edges to exploit?

Sometimes, yeah. Generally, if it is going in a massive run up, you certainly get some extremes where it goes even further than you think because of the illiquidity and the stops. You certainly can take advantage of that. It has massive ranges. Even recently we had days with 400-500 tick ranges. It is priced at half a tick so it is actually 1000 prices. So it certainly offers advantages because of the way it moves. A DAX swing might be 100 ticks whereas an ES swing could be 5 to 10 handles, which would be about 40 ticks. You certainly get inefficiencies working in your favor that way when you are in extremes in markets. However, it can also become inefficient in the way it trades. As I mentioned, the slippage could be quite an issue. Getting in and out sometimes might entail a spread of 3 or 4 prices. Just to get in or out you would have to pay up 4 prices. So it can work both ways.

You describe your trading style as a scalper. Always quick trades, in and out?

I would say that for 80% of my trades I am in and out certainly in less than 10 minutes. I will get in for a 20-30 tick winner and that's it. If I'm trading the ES or the Eurostoxx, it might be a little longer. Maybe 30 minutes. I might be looking for a new low while we are in the middle of the range. Predominately, I scalp. I am in and out quite quickly. Everything is pretty much intraday. 95% of my trades are intraday as well. Very rarely I will hold something overnight. Occasionally I do it if I really believe in a trade and I manage to get a good price getting in. If the trade is in the profit and I have some breathing space on it, I might hold it overnight. Most of the time I'm intraday and a high percentage of those trades I'm out quite quickly.

Do you have a long or short bias?

No. I have never had a bias of long or short. I like to come in completely fresh, working what the markets are doing and go from there. Through the day, I will obviously develop some kind of bias based on what I'm seeing. I might say, "Hey, this market is feeling bullish here," and then generally focus on long trades. But I certainly don't prefer one or the other for most of my trades. I just go with what the market is doing that day. I might even have a long bias, but have my first few trades that day be shorts, just because that's what the better setup is at the given time.

Most of the traders I interviewed are stock traders and they complain about things like HFT cancellations and sub-penny trades, among other things. In the futures markets, what do you like and dislike about HFT activity?

The big problems with HFT tends to be in stocks where the bids or offers get cancelled, but what I see in futures are predatory algos. They have to be algos because it is too quick to be a human doing it. You will go to the market with a bid, and as soon as your bid goes in, let's say in the middle of a 5 price bid offer spread, you would expect to be hit because you are paying up. But as soon as your bid hits the market, a bid goes in front of you and the next two offers also get pulled. You know it is not a human that is doing that. I believe it is quite obvious sometimes how the market trades around your bids and offers. It is not just me in the office that sees this. Everyone I work with sees this every day. We see the market churn 2,000 lots at one price, at the bid/offer several times in the Eurostoxx or the ES. Because you don't know what is going on, you then decide to get out, and instantly it stops churning and orders go in front of you. For some mysterious reason it just churned 2,000 lots but it can't do another 5. I don't really think there are too many advantages of having HFT, certainly for us. The only advantages is when we see all these stories about the spoofing and layering, you can actually scalp and take advantage of that, because you know essentially what the spoofer is trying to do. He is trying to get other algos to buy or sell in front of him. Then he can pull orders and move the market the other way. If you see what the algo is doing, you can take advantage of that. You just have to go against what the algos are doing. That's the only real advantage that I can see. Sometimes you can see what they are doing and trade with that information in mind. You are such a small player compared to the size that they are dealing with that you use that in your favor.

With regards to the spoofing, I believe you traded with Navinder Sarao, the guy who was accused of causing the flash crash way back in 2010. What were your impressions about the guy?

I sat next to him for 6 to 9 months. This was quite a while ago, back in 2007 I think. He was one of the best traders I ever saw trade. He was awesome at trading pretty much any contract really. He just kind of knew what was going on and traded huge size. I will say this about the charges against him: I'm pretty much convinced that they are just making him a scapegoat. If someone is trying to accuse a person of causing the flash crash, then they are just stupid. There is just no way can one person cause a flash crash in the US stock market of 10%. It is just impossible.

Do you still see a lot of spoofing going on?

Yes. It is funny actually. After the story broke that he was arrested and charged, for the next two weeks we saw spoofing like we never had before. It was just uncanny. It was happening all the time. It almost started the day the story broke. You saw it in the ES, the DAX, Eurostoxx, everywhere.

Do you believe that the case against him gave other people the idea of how to make money and they started to do it as well?

I don't think so. I believe it just happened to be a coincidence, but it was funny how those things happened at the same time. It certainly has cooled down lately. It still happens but not as much as in that two week period. I don't think it had to do with the announcement of the arrest or anything like that.

Is it accurate to say that you learned how to trade futures markets by just watching the price action and over time you developed a sense of how things are likely to move?

Yes. I follow a lot of guys on Twitter who talk about having a plan, trading your plan, having your stops, targets, etc. I believe that certainly helps, especially in big events like Fed or ECB announcements. If you think ahead about the different possibilities, it clears things up in your head. Then you know how to react when the markets are moving very quickly. But most of the guys in our office are discretionary traders. We essentially make decisions on impulse. Obviously, we have charts in front of us. We see setups that exist and trade them accordingly, but it is not something that is set in stone. We see things that we have seen before and we think, "Buying should come around here and I will go long because of that." The stop and exit are based on how the market moves once you are in. Watching the ladder is probably one of the most beneficial things a trader can do. You study that ladder for one or two years, every day, and you are bound to learn how it moves. You will see things that can help you get better entries and better exits. This is something that is constantly evolving. You are constantly learning.

Anyone can look at a chart, see a flag or head and shoulders and know what they "should" do. But the ladder actually tells you how to trade according to how the market is moving. I am not so rigid as "Once the market breaks this trend line I'm going to do XYZ."

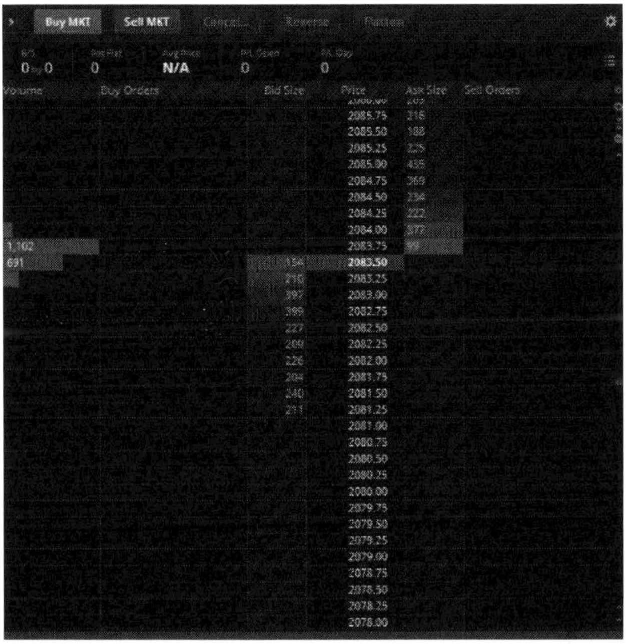

"Ladder" S&P500 e-mini futures. Source: ThinkorSwim platform

With regards to these discretionary instinctive styles of trading, do you think that the computers haven't closed those edges because of the limited position size that these strategies support, or is it because it is almost incomputable given the number of discretionary variables?

The second reason. One thing I will say: the computers can see things that people see. They can see a flag form in a chart, and then they will take the price through the flag. That's the point where a lot of people will get in. Then they will take it the other way and get all of those people out. They might even do it a few times until eventually it does a real run off the flag pattern. They program chart patterns in these computers so they know where to expect people to get long or short. When they see enough people get in one side, they slam it the other way and get them out. That's the beauty of the ladder. You can often see these things. You can see them holding a price but you know it eventually is going to go upwards or drop. If you just look at a chart, you don't get a feel for what the market is actually doing. In a candlestick chart, you might see a long candle with a 20 tick range, but you can't see what happened in that 20 tick range. You know the highs and lows but you can't know what happened inside it. And that's where you get the edge as a discretionary trader. Just watching what is going on you get a feel. You might get it half way through the candlestick that it is going lower. You wouldn't get that opportunity just looking at a chart.

A discretionary trader might be able to see a situation that is technically different from another though still pretty similar so he can play it the same way, but a computer might not realize that. Do you think that's part of how you can get an edge?

I believe so. Day to day the markets are always going to move because the biggest players want the market to move. The computers and algos can sense where people are getting long and short because they usually have a lot of their orders on the bids and offers. They can tell when a lot of people bought or sold. They know when people are trapped as well. They know where people had been buying so they know where they can squeeze people out. By looking at a ladder, you can trade those movements. I don't think you can compete against this kind of knowledge, the knowledge of what is actually going on in the market. If you see what is going on, you know what is eventually going to happen.

Had you traded other styles before you became a scalper?

Not really. I have always been a scalper. But as I said, occasionally I will do a long-term trade. In the couple of blogs that I write for the company, I make basically daily recommendations, show daily setups or longer-term setups. That sometimes gives me my bias. I can look at the daily and think, "Ok, this is long-term where the market is going." The thing is it might take two weeks or two months to get there, and you don't know what is happening in between. So I trade predominantly in the scalping style because I believe it is one of the easiest ways to trade. For some people it is best to come in and take two trades a day, but for me and everyone in the office we like to be very involved with the market.

The iceberg orders that the computers and sometimes the buy/sell programs use, do they hurt you or do you like them?

I think they can be more of a help than a hindrance really. The only time they are a hindrance is when you are long and the icebergs are on the offer, essentially stopping the market from going up. But as a whole it helps you read the market. If there is an iceberg on the offer, this is obviously one order. It is one guy trying to get out. If everyone else is constantly hitting him, you can tell that the rest of the market wants to go the other way. It might not get through the first time, but you can see if the iceberg adds another 100 or another 10. Does the market come off straight away? Because if it does, it might indicate that there wasn't much buying going on. If someone is in the DAX and he is iceberging for 100, lots and people keep buying it almost instantly. You kind of know that the market is strong there and eventually he is going to get taken out. In a way, icebergs help you see how strong/weak the market is, but that's it really. They are not that important.

Do you believe that a key component of trading futures is choosing which days you want to be more active and bet more and which days you want to be less active and maybe not even get involved at all?

Yes. You can usually get a feel during the opening hour or the first two hours. You can get a sense that "Ok, this is going to be a range day and I shouldn't be trading much, and if I do it will be around the edges of the channel. Buying the lows and selling the highs." Also when it is very busy, you can usually see that there is a lot of volume and that can shape the way you trade. The more volatile it is the more involved you should be because there is that much more opportunity. I definitely think it helps to identify the day type. Also, you know that holidays tend to be very quiet days, at least most of the time. Most of the Mondays after the non-farm payrolls are usually very quiet. Heading towards a long weekend with the holiday on Monday, the Friday before tends to be quiet. The morning before an ECB meeting also tends to be quiet, because everyone is waiting for the announcement. Those are the days you have to remember to not expect too much. So I definitely think it helps to know what kind of day you are dealing with.

And after the ECB or Fed announcements, is there an increase in your profitability as a result of the volatility?

Yes, usually after the market becomes much more volatile and there are more opportunities. A lot of people wait for the announcements just in case there is a surprise. Once they start to get involved, the volatility will pick up.

What would you say are the key elements of your success?

I definitely think that perseverance and hard work are important. It is a bit of a cliché, but the harder you work the luckier you get. You can see that the people who come through and do well are generally the ones that work very hard. They are at it from before the market opens all the way until after the market closes. I am in a stage now that I do not necessarily need to do that. If I want to take a morning off, I can do it. I don't have to be there all day to be learning. I have already acquired all the basic skills. When I started, though, I worked really hard, read a lot of books and shaped my view of how markets move and things like that. That is by far my biggest strength. I see people come through the door and when they don't put in the effort, 10 times out of 10 they won't make it as a trader. You have to be quite humble when you come in. As I said, it takes a couple of years to get profitable in futures markets generally.

One of the great advantages of trading futures markets is the liquidity. Do you force yourself to play bigger and bigger so you can reach new levels of profitability?

Certainly. I'm a big advocate of the principle that if you are trading well you should up your size as often as possible, because at the end of the day all that will do is add marginal gains to your account. If you are already trading a 5 lot, if you add another lot to that, you will only be adding 20% to your profit or loss. Then if you get comfortable trading a 6 lot, if you add another lot to that it will be less than 20% to your profit or loss. Each lot you add becomes less of a strain mentally. That's why people say that the hardest change is to go from a 1 lot to a 2 lot. That's the only time you double your size. After that, the percentage will only go down.

If I'm in a good run, I will generally add a few lots depending on what I'm trading. At the end of the day, it is just going to make you more money.

Do you do any backtesting at all?

Not really. There are a couple of guys in the office that do but I don't. I do bring up charts to study things that happened on a certain day or in a certain situation, or how the market reacted to certain events. But backtesting is not something that I do.

And when you are trading, do you focus solely on the ladder?

No, I have charts as well. I use Market Delta or IQ feed. I've got 4 screens of charts. They allow me to form an opinion of where the market should go or where I think it is going, but my execution is based on the ladder. I might notice an area on the chart, a level where if the market is falling I might be looking to get long. I get that information from the chart. When the market gets to that level, that's when I use the ladder to get my entry. If you have a 5-6 tick range of where you think the market is going to find support, it might find support on the first tick. It might find support in the sixth tick. It's down to you as a skilled trader to use the ladder to get in at the price that is the most optimal. Sometimes it will bounce at the top of the tick range and you have to buy higher, and sometimes it will go through it and you can wait and buy after at a lower price. The ladder essentially allows you to fine tune your execution almost to the tick, really.

The chart tells you what the market did already, and the ladder can tell you what the market might do in the future. The chart can't tell you anything about what is going to happen in the future, but it can tell you what you might expect. But the ladder can help you see things in absolutely real-time down to the millisecond what is going on. You get a taste over time of the price action, like how a market looks when it gets to lows. Let us say it made a low, had a quick bounce and went back down again by one tick. Then it couldn't find any sellers. You might think, "I see this all the time, it's a great situation to buy." You can buy it, stop near the low and you can just ride it.

Again, you can use the chart to see potential areas of interest to get long or short, and then you can see areas where you can potentially scale out. But using the ladder, sometimes you can take the trade for a little bit longer because even though you might expect support or resistance in a certain area, your reading of the ladder tells you the price it is going to get through.

Do you look at the times and sales as well?

I use that quite a lot actually. In the S&P500, it is always good to know how the market reacts when a big trade goes through. If somebody buys 350 contracts and the market barely budges, it tells you that the guy might be screwed. He just bought a lot at the high or near the high and the market did not even flinch. That would give you a clue to maybe go short. Likewise, if he does buy it and immediately it starts to get bid up or maybe another big buy order comes in, it tells you that the money is going long here.

So in that kind of situation you would be able to buy on the offer and flip it higher, taking advantage of the fact that these big guys can't do that because they have too many contracts to buy?

Essentially, they can do that. There is nothing stopping a guy from buying 350 lots and then selling 350 lots. But when you are trading that kind of size, in theory it should move the market. It's the same in the DAX, but in that case a 30 lot would have the potential to move the market, because people will try to front run that since the market is so thin. In US stocks, it would have to be 1,000 lots to move the market. As a scalper, sometimes before you get a trade right you might buy and sell a trade three or four times before you get the buy that keeps going. You might buy it and it doesn't really move so you get out for a small loser or a scratch. Do the same thing 2-3 times so you get a feel for it before you eventually get one that really shows a profit. You will rack up commission costs when you do that, but they are very minor compared to the profits you are making.

Do you try to minimize those costs? How?

Some of the guys in the firm do a huge amount of round trips, but I don't do that many. If you do 5,000 round trips a month, you get a certain amount back as a form of rebate. If you do 10,000 you get an even bigger rebate. You can negotiate a slightly cheaper commission per trade if you do a lot of volume.

Do you still give a certain percentage of the profit to the firm?

Yes, they do take a percentage of my profits. Many of the people when they come in are in on 50/50 splits. As you make money you can switch to 60/40, 70/30, 80/20, etc. Eventually it tops out at 90/10 or 92.5/7.5. There are some people that come in and put all of their money from the start and they will keep 100%, but generally the people that come to the firm, because they are backed by the firm, will give up a certain part of their profits.

At this point in your career, isn't it worthwhile to move to a retail brokerage and keep 100%?

It can be but at the same time being a member of a prop firm can be very beneficial to me. I have the support I need, and I have brokers to get in and out of trades. I have the IT guys there. People will disseminate the news too so I know exactly why the market is reacting at a certain time.

What are some of the trading rules that you follow?

The biggest one is that you have to have a daily stop. If you lose X amount of money, you stop for the day. I know that if I go through that and continue to trade, 9 times out of 10 it will keep getting worse. If I am not reading the markets right, I know from experience that it is better for me to go home, come back the next day and start fresh. Sometimes I will give myself a few more hundred pounds after I reach it but you have to have a stop in place.

Another one is to keep looking for is ways to up your position size, because at the end of the day it is going to increase your profitability.

If I have two or three bad trades in a row, I always try to take a break, go outside for a walk or just leave my desk. It is not a hard rule though. Sometimes it is good to take a break if you have many good trades in a row. To keep your focus, and make sure you keep those profits. The same way I have a daily loss stop, I have a daily profit stop. But it is different for profits: if I reach a certain amount, I will only be willing to give back X amount. If I lose that, I am done for the day. There is nothing worse than losing money that you made.

Regarding the issue of 9 times out of 10 a trader not being able to get out of a hole, do you think that is due to the fact that our judgment gets impaired and we misread situations?

It certainly can be that. When you have a few bad trades in a row, you tend to get frustrated and let emotions take over a little bit. That stops you from having 100% focus. This usually leads to putting another trade right after, which is simply stupid and just costs more money. Another problem is that when you hit your stop loss for the day but you give yourself another few hundred to play with, that stifles your ability to manage that trade. That trade might need a few hundred more than the amount you set as your new stop loss and, as a result, you might be forced out for reasons unrelated to the trade itself.

In the stock world, many traders report that the noise levels have increased due to HFT activity. Is that something that you noticed in futures over the years since 2006?

I believe it depends on the times, really. At the moment in Europe, we have very volatile markets. The German Bund just came out of this huge bull run that we had and it absolutely collapsed from the highs. Now it is really thin and volatile. Before we only had a 20 to 30 tick range on the day and the noise might be 5 to 10 ticks, whereas now the market is going down and you know it is going to continue to go down. Yet, it can go to the lows and then bounce 15 ticks in 20 seconds. That is the noise you have to deal with. You know that the trend is down but, because it is so thin, the bounces are much more exaggerated. You get squeezed more. You are put under pressure. If someone wants to get out of significant size, they must move the market. So there is certainly noise in that sense.

I do not know if there is more noise in general but it does happen when you have markets that are more volatile.

In this German Bund situation, how did you play? Did you short the rallies and cover sell-offs?

In the first couple of days of the collapse, everyone was trying to buy it because it was coming off a large run. If you look at the daily chart, it is incredible how far it ran and how quickly it dropped compared to how long it took to get there.

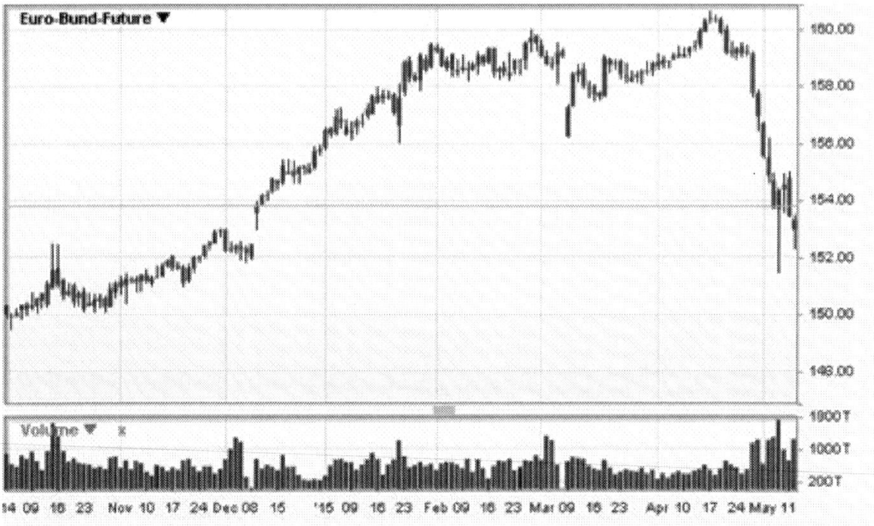

Source: Frankfurt Boerse

I'm generally a contrarian trader: sometimes I will buy near the high because I think it's going higher, but most of the time if the market is dropping I will be looking for a place to buy. I will look for a small bounce because I believe there will be some support at a level. Then I will get my 10 to 15 ticks and that is good enough for me.

That is how I played the Bund sell-off. I would buy it in where I thought were good support areas, looking for quick bounces. But sometimes I would also go short those bounces because it looked like it was going to keep dropping. But it was all very quick in and out style trading, looking for quick trades.

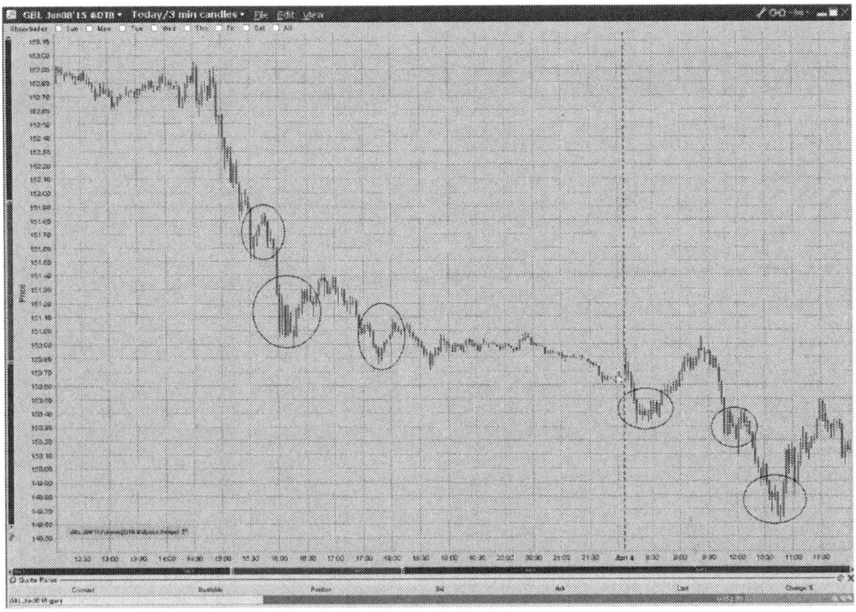

Bund 3 min chart. Source: Interactive Brokers TWS

These bounce plays, do you try to find some kind of buying interest in the ladder and times and sales in sell-offs that are getting overextended, and then get in and out?

When it gets volatile, you can see things like the contract move 40 ticks in three minutes. And nothing really happened. It is not like it's news-related or anything like that. So it starts to look a bit overdone. Then you look at the 2-3 support points below there. When it gets there, that is when the ladder, time, and sales can sometimes help you to make the decision. I try to find areas where the market might turn and then wait to see how the market trades around that level. If the market goes straight through, then I do not want to be getting long. Or if I do get long, I want to have a very tight stop. But if I see the market struggling to get through the level, then I will think it is safe to get long and play it for a quick bounce.

Do you look at cross correlations between different markets and trade off that?

Sometimes. Correlations really come and go between different markets all the time. At the moment, the European stock market is very correlated with the EUR. If you see a weak EUR, you will see the DAX being very strong. Generally, I look at the other markets to shape my bias. If bonds are selling off, I try to figure out what that means for stocks, or if the currency is doing this or that, how that will impact equities, etc. However, I will not put a trade on in another market just because a market had done this or that.

Is there a trade you made this year that you are proud of?

This year has been very quiet. It has picked up recently in recent weeks. I believe March has been my best month of the year so far. There was a period of a couple of weeks where I was very in tune with what was going on. I was making money every day. I do not think there was one day or trade that I was especially proud about. As soon as a day is over, I try not to think too much about it. I like to start a new day completely fresh. Whether I made or lost money, I don't want to dwell on that.

What are some of the tough losses that you had in your career?

The tough losses a lot of the time are not really about money. You have losing trades and lose money all the time in trading futures. That is just the nature of the game. The problem arises when you have a trade on that you like but the market keeps going against you to a point where you hit market out. As soon as you do that, the market completely turns and goes in the direction you were positioned for. Those are the ones I get the most angry about. You were right but you got out at the low or the high. You can see how it was manipulated against you and when you eventually paid up to get out, it went the other way.

Were some of your best periods during the financial crisis?

Not really because I was still new. I was trading for a couple of years but I had just started to be profitable. I was still trying to find my main market during that time. I was profitable but I was doing relatively small size. By money made, it certainly was not my most profitable period. My most profitable period was in 2011 when the European market was moving a lot every day on news about the sovereign debt crisis. In that year, people really thought that shit was going to hit the fan. My best month ever was probably August of 2011 because of the volatility that it brought to the markets.

Would you say during that time you could play the same ideas that you had about setups but you would make more with the same risk?

I would say that there was more risk because it was so volatile. In a quiet market, you can sort of know that you are wrong when it goes 3 or 4 ticks against you. In a volatile market, it can go 5 or 10 ticks against you and you are not wrong yet. It has only done that because there are a lot of people pushing that way, but you know that it's eventually going to turn around. So there is more risk but the reward also increases a lot. In situations where you would look for 10-15 ticks, now you would look for 20-30 ticks. If you managed to buy one of the lows on the Bund a couple of days ago, it bounced about 1%. You basically caught 50 ticks in less than 10 minutes. That is a huge range. Even if you only played 10 lots, that is €5,000.

During these volatile periods, does your win rate go higher, are there more plays available or are the risk-adjusted gains larger?

I would say it is a combination of these. When it is volatile, I would say it is certainly easier to read the market because there is less noise. What I call noise in the market is when there is a lot of churn. Algos trading with each other, stopping the market from moving up or down. When it is volatile, you get a lot less of that kind of noise. When the price bounces, it goes straight up and gives you a good winner. I definitely think when your win rate goes up a little bit it is easier to read. However, you also get bigger gains because you can run things for a lot more.

If you divide the monetary value of the wins by the losses, will the ratio be higher than the periods where the markets are slow?

Yes.

When you enter a position, do you immediately set a stop?

Sometimes, but not always. It depends on why I got in the trade. If I got in a trade in the middle of the range and I am looking for new highs or something, I will give some room, try to feel when I think I am wrong, and that is when I will get out. If the DAX is falling off a cliff and I am picking a low, as soon as I am long I will put a stop. If it hits a level and bounces a little bit, I might buy it thinking it is a possible low. In that situation, I will immediately put a stop below the low. If it goes below that, I know my idea was wrong. I do not want to risk many stops getting hit and the slippage that it would cause to my fills. So it depends on what kind of trade I am in. If I am picking highs or lows, I put a stop right away. If I am doing discretionary trading in the middle of a range, I will try to feel out when I am wrong and get out.

Do you think the algos try to purposefully hit stops?

Absolutely. The algos know where the stops are. They know where everyone is long and short. They definitely try to push in areas where they would be hit. You have to be careful against that.

How do you prevent being gamed by that?

There is really nothing you can do. If you want to be out at a certain price, you have to put a stop in. Sometimes what you can do is to have your long stop hit, notice that market is not going any lower, then you can get back in at the same price or a bit higher. But at the end of the day you need a stop and you cannot prevent the market from going to where it is going so there is not much you can do.

Could you try to get in right after the stops are hit, when the price is being distorted by the market orders?

Yeah, but you do not know where the stops are. Certainly if I see many stops go off, I am likely to be fading that move. If the Bund goes through the lows and takes out 20 ticks in one second, I will definitely be looking to buy that. Maybe not looking for a reversal to where the stops started, but half way there or something like that. In the DAX, you get many stops in the highs and lows and that is where you can try to fade them. You do not tend to get that in the ES as much, because it is such a liquid market. You need to have many stops in place to what I call blip. Blip up or blip down. It is not really a trading strategy. It is more about being alert and reacting to the market.

Do you have the confidence that you can continue to beat the futures markets in the coming years?

You never know what is going to happen. I guess that is the real risk with this job. There is no guarantee. There is no certainty. As I said, 2011 was probably my most profitable year even in terms of money made even though now I am more experienced and I am trading far bigger sizes. That is the risk of this job, and you never know how much you are going to be making. You never know. There could come a time where the style that you have is not working anymore. I have seen some people who made money for 3 or 4 years and still ended up leaving because what they were doing stopped making money. There are no guarantees. But so far I have adapted to everything the market has required me to. I am certainly confident that whatever happens in the coming years cannot be so different that I would not be able to adapt.

I read on your Twitter that you believe HFT provides liquidity to the markets when it is not necessary, but none when it is actually needed. Can you expand on that?

It is obvious that when the market is on a tight range, trading normally without a lot of volatility, the bids and offers are very thick. That is because there are a lot of computers and market makers in there. But when fear really comes in the market, these market makers just pull their orders. They disappear. This makes the market even more volatile because there is not enough liquidity in there to trade. There are humans doing that as well. When you see things getting out of hand, you tend to cancel orders. It's human nature to do that. HFT basically claims that they provide liquidity, but they only do that when it is not volatile. When things get volatile and you need market makers to get the market functioning in a normal manner, they disappear.

In the stock market, there are certain HFT firms that get special advantages. Do you think this happens in futures?

Yes. I do not know it but I am convinced that some people pay the exchanges to have knowledge of other people's orders, whether someone has been partially filled or not, etc. It definitely happens. You cannot know, but just the way the market trades around your bids and offers, you can tell that something is up. It cannot be a coincidence.

You mean the icebergs? They know how much people have behind it?

Not necessarily the icebergs. Sometimes you see the market churn. It trades on the bid and offers 500 lots, 1000 lots, constantly trading on the bid and offer. As soon as you decide, "Ok, I am going to buy it here," you join the bid. It immediately stops churning and it goes bid up, bid up. How can it trade 2,000 lots in the last 3 minutes and as soon as my orders goes in, it totally stops doing that?

So they know when it is a lot of small orders and they know when it's just one guy trying to buy those 300 lots?

Yeah. They definitely know when people have been partially filled. They know when people drag orders around. I have seen it myself. There was an option in a charting platform that a guy showed me a couple of years ago that enabled you see when people were dragging their orders, when they would move it up or down the entire order. Sometimes you see stops being triggered with 1 lots. The big players definitely know many things and they take advantage of that.

What advice would you give to traders that are trying to learn how to trade the futures markets?

They have to have a lot of patience and perseverance. They have to stick to it. It is a forever-learning process. It will take you one or two years at least. Sit in front of the ladder for as a long as possible with the charts around you. It is going to feel like it is not going anywhere but will eventually click. I am convinced that 9 out of 10 people could become a good trader if they had the time, but most people do not have the time. I am convinced that if you trained someone for 2 years and paid them for 2 years, they could become a successful trader. It just takes time. Also, find out your market. Certain personalities are better for certain markets. I am much better in thin volatile markets. The ES is the only thick market that I trade, and even that is not very thick these days. Some people might like short-term interest rate products because they move a lot slower. Find out your best market and study it as much as you can.

The ES contract, when you trade it, do you stick with just the open and that is it? It tends to be more volatile and thinner around that time.

No. I will trade it for 2 hours day, from when it opens to when Europe closes. If it is going to be a busy day or if it is the last day of the month, I will trade till the close. Days of Fed meetings, I will trade until the close as well. However, most of the time I am done by the European close.

Because it is the most profitable period?

I tend to find that after the European close, things usually quiet down a lot. Another thing is, I am in the office at 7:30 every day. By the time of the Europe close at 4:30, it has been a long day for me. It is mentally challenging. You cannot trade every day all the way to the US close because otherwise you would be doing 15-16 hour days. If for whatever reason I was not making much money in the European market but was on ES, I would just change my hours. I would come in at 2:00 and trade all the way to the American close. I trade it when it opens, because it is the more dominant market and Europe equities tend to follow it around anyway.

What would you say is the breakdown of your activity in terms of open/mid-day/close?

I would say that the European open, the first 90 minutes, is probably when I am the most active. After that, my most active period would be the US open all the way to the European close two hours later. However, if it is a busy day I will be trading all day.

What do you do when the market is not that active? Do you leave the desk? Do something else while at the computer?

Sometimes I will watch something online, maybe the soccer highlights. If it is quiet, I might watch something on Netflix. Even if it is busy, I might take a break sometimes, go for a walk or get my lunch or something. However, yeah, if it is quiet, I will take breaks. Chat with other traders, etc.

Do you hold trades through news announcements at all?

No. Unless I really thought something was going to happen I wouldn't be in during news announcements.

Lessons from Chapter 3

1. The importance of the price ladder (DOM). Adam emphasized several times in the interview how much the ladder is a key component of his success. The idea is to accumulate enough screen time watching the action of the ladder to the point where your unconscious mind will give you clues about what is likely to happen next. You might end up getting little indications of supply and demand imbalances or shifts that can make your entry or exit decision more precise. Before this interview I never realized that it was even possible to obtain an edge in this manner. I had developed the limiting belief that the computers had somehow closed all the edges of mechanisms like that. Having spoken to him and observed the index markets with more of an open mind, I have now reversed that belief. It won't happen all the time, but certain times you can tell where something is likely to happen by the action of the bids, asks and executed trades.

This is not to say that you can jump in and out over and over again solely based on the ladder. This instrument is only one key of his approach. There are more, hence the next lessons.

2. Look for key support and resistance levels in the chart, particularly in overextended markets. One of his trading setups is to look for counter-trend moves in overextended charts at key support or resistance levels. A great example of that were the Bund trades. He would wait for the market to start a significant sell-off, reach some kind of support point in the chart, and then watch the ladder to detect a shift from selling to buying. At that point he would jump in and scalp on the long-side.

3. The importance of market positioning. Adam uses his experience to understand how traders are positioned in any given futures market. If he senses a certain trade got crowded due a certain technical chart formation or indicator, he will take that into account when making his decisions. In this HFT-driven world, according to Adam, a lot of the time the HFTs will try to exploit a crowded trade by taking prices in the other direction.

4. Surround yourself with great traders. This is a key component of Adam's success, so much so that he is still willing to give up a certain percentage of his profits in order to stay in contact with other good traders. Through this book you will see that this is a common trait of good traders. Good traders have other good traders around, with whom they share ideas, experience, tips, mistakes, trades, etc.

5. As you get profitable, don't be afraid to increase your size. The key advantage of futures markets is the incredible liquidity that they offer versus other financial assets such as stocks. As you accumulate experience and prove to yourself

that you can be consistently profitable, don't be afraid to push yourself to increase your position size. As Adam says: "At the end of the day, it's just going to make you more money."

6. Respect your daily loss limit. Adam believes it's very important to have a maximum loss amount for any given day and stick with it. In his experience, when he gets over that, 9 times out of 10 he will just lose more. Whether we like it or not, our decision making tends to be worse when we are losing. Avoiding trading decisions when our judgment is inferior is a way to win by not losing.

7. Screen time is king. As Adam emphasized through the interview, it's very important to observe markets for a long time. He believes it takes a couple of years for a trader to be able to notice predictable patterns and setups in real-time.

Chapter 4

Jim Cash - The Futures and Options Veteran

Jim Cash (@TraderJim64) is a former floor trader at CME. He made the switch to screen trading before the internet was widely used. He also worked as a Commodity Trading Advisor (CTA) and a Commodity Pool Operator (CPO). He has managed a hedge fund and traded for a number of high net worth individuals. Jim was also a radio host on Power Trader Radio and has published a trading newsletter for active traders. As you can tell, he is a very experienced trader who has been active in the world of futures for a long time. I was excited about interviewing him for that reason.

Currently, he is an independent trader working with a Family Office with a good capital base.

We did our interview during one of the most volatile periods for the stock index futures markets in years. This provided an interesting opportunity to understand how this veteran trader thinks and manages risk in volatile times.

When did you start trading?

I started trading in 1986. I was on the pits in the Chicago Mercantile Exchange. A couple of years before that I was working for a broker as a runner. Then I moved up real fast to phone clerk, then arb clerk. Eventually I took over a currency arbitrage operation. From there I moved to the pits as an independent trader. That is when I started.

Trading your own capital?

Yes.

How was that?

It was ok. I did not realize at that time how many other people were backed by either brokerages or other order fillers. It took some time for me to understand the political aspect of trading in the pit. You have to know who is connected to who and whether or not you can get order flow from certain people. Once you figure that out and develop your own style of trading, then it becomes easy to make money.

Because your strategy was mainly to just make markets?

I was an independent liquidity provider. I was on the other side of order flow. If the order flow came in and they were all sellers, we would be buyers. Or, vice-versa.

Could you be filled at discounted prices and get some expected profit on those trades?

Yeah. In the early days, there was still a good amount of movement. I remember trading in the Eurodollar interest rate market and there was still some good movement in there. The problem was that I saw that computerized trading was going to take over this job. Even as far back as 1991, I could tell that computers were going to be the future. Several of the brokerage firms that had desks on the floor, they were using laptops connected to the data providers. They were getting real-time charts at their desks that we were not getting. I was just standing in the pit. There was no room for me to have a computer there. They were able to see things before we did. The edge of being on the pit started to disappear much more quickly as computers started to become more popular in the trading business.

All your data came from those big boards on the exchange?

Yes. They also had some monitors with stuff like news and even some charts. However, these charts were very antiquated. It was a daily chart, not even intraday.

At what point did you decide to leave the pits because you could not see a future in being a human market maker?

It's not that I thought there wasn't a future in it. I just wanted to be on the cutting edge. It was around late '92 when I left the floor. Then I spent the next two years getting computers, software, learning how to use all of that so I could trade. Now mind you that, at that time, there was no widespread use of the internet. I was using satellite feeds, which had their own delay. Then you had to phone your order. I knew how that process worked, so I knew of the problems that could happen. If a runner did not make it fast to the pit, you could really be delayed. The market could move away from you and you would never be filled. In one regard, it was much better when the internet came around and the electronic trading platforms really developed because I was able to get the same fills as my counterparts on the pit were getting.

When you moved away from the floor, did you immediately start to do more directional trading as opposed to making markets?

Yes, definitely. Back then, in a typical day on the pit, the Eurodollar market would move 3 to 5 ticks. In that range, I would never get the high or the low, so I would only get the inside of that tight range. What that means is that you really had to scale up your size in order to make money. That was helpful to eliminate fear because I got used to trading bigger. Moving off the floor, I was able to capture bigger moves because I did not have to trade just the Eurodollar. I was trading the equity indexes, foreign exchange and 30-year bonds. I was able to have a bigger picture by expanding my period. I was able to make more profit with less at risk.

In this process of playing for bigger moves, were you profitable right away?

I would say I was profitable about 80% of the time. However, I was trading very small and I did not take many trades. They had to be great setups. Let me put it this way: imagine the market is like a train and that train is in the station. I was never the locomotive, but I was never the last car either. I wanted to see that train leaving the station, and then I would jump on a couple of cars behind the locomotive. Then I would ride that train until it looked like it was about to stop and get out. I would never get the best fill on the high side of the day if I were shorting or the lowest side of the day if I was buying. I do not try to do that. I just try to get a good chunk of that move and then look for the next opportunity.

The fact that you made money right off the bat, what do you attribute that to? Your experience on the floor?

No. Being off the floor was so tremendously different from being on the floor. On the floor, you always had someone to lean on. You knew that there was order flow, like a big broker nearby that was bidding. If I was long and I needed to get out, I pretty much knew I could exit my position on that broker that was bidding. When you are off the floor, you do not see that. You do not feel it, you do not hear it. There were services like Ben Lichtenstein and some others that would call out the activity on the S&P500 futures. What they were calling out is nothing compared to actually being on the pits. When you are looking at the order flow, looking at people's expressions, the date from the boards on the walls, etc., you really feel like you are on it. What I mean by that is it's kind of like being a spider in the middle of a web. When you are off the floor, you do not feel that wind in that web, the little vibrations, etc. You do not feel the traders getting anxious at the bid or offer.

Off the floor, I really had to hone my skills of chart reading. Some people spent a lot of time solely with Level 2. You really cannot be a one-faced specialist. You really have to focus on a few things that will help you make instantaneous decisions and jump on a market movement.

So you developed your skills as you went along.

I studied chart reading for a long time. This even goes back to when I was on the floor. BarCharts used to put out a book that I bought every week. This book had charts of all the commodities in it. I would literally update the charts, every single es they would have intraday charts for the most active commodities. y would have 30-minute charts and time frames like that. We would make photocopies of them, take them with us to the pits and update them every 30 minutes. I would trade with the charts in my pockets. That would give us a better view of what was going on. This enabled me to get familiar with chart reading. When I moved off the floor, the computers really allowed me to expand on that and develop my ability to read the charts.

When did you notice that the computers really started to affect the futures trading business with all the new platforms, quotes and things like that?

I would say in the late '90s, when Globex came out. The attention wasn't taken off many people until that. When it finally did, you had many hardware, software and data companies throwing a lot of money into research and development in order to provide traders with better tools. When Globex came about and you were able to enter the orders on your screen, that is when the whole world of trading changed. The edge that people thought they had by being on the floor started to disappear much faster in favor of the people that were reading charts and entering orders electronically. In addition, some algorithms were created to do that execution for them because they were much faster at reading the charts and sending orders.

When that happened, did your methodology change?

At that point, I was pretty much down the road of playing for longer periods. I was no longer scalping for ticks. I tell this to the traders that I mentor sometimes. There are a couple of styles for futures trading. If you are a person that scalps for ticks, you have to do a lot of work. You've got to be 100% focused in whatever market you are trading because you've got to be in and out so many times through the day, you really better be focused. However, as an intraday trader, you can enter a position, have your profit target, stop loss, and let that work. I try not to focus on how much I can make but how much I can lose so I prevent the losses. Once it starts going in your favor, you can add fuel to the position. What I mean by that is adding contracts, adding to the winner. It is very different from scalping. They would be in and out five times by the time I had a full position on. The benefit of the intraday style is that you do a lot less work. I can even take a phone call or talk to someone in the middle of a trade.

You were holding the position for like an hour or two?

It is difficult to say because it depends on the volatility of the market. I could have positions that I held anywhere from five to 15 minutes but I was building a long position because I believed the market was going to turn then I had to be much more patient. I might have had to hold from 15 minutes to several hours because you needed to have that market position to develop. I would throw out some "loss leaders." What I mean by this is that if the market had been down all day and I felt that it had reached a bottom and was going to start to turn up, I would throw out a few contracts long just to get me in the game. I knew that they were likely to go against me but it was not going to hurt me because it was just one or two contracts. If it did go against me, I could continue to add a little bit because I was developing that position. If the market continued to steam roll in that direction and I knew that I was wrong, I would just exit and wait for setup. Remember what I said about the train? That is a situation where I tried to be the locomotive. I would start to throw those small leaders to see if I could be on the leading edge of a market turn. Those positions would take longer.

My average hold for the first two hours of the day was probably from three to 10 minutes.

You said that you could feel that the market was turning. A lot of your trading is based on a feeling that you get from looking at the chart.

When I say feeling, what I mean is that I have seen patterns so many times that I have a pretty good read for what patterns are profitable for a counter-trend trade. For instance: if I see that we are way oversold, that is when I would start to throw out those leaders. It is an intuition sort of thing. You have seen this pattern so many times that you are willing to step in just a little bit early and risk taking a small loss if you are wrong.

When did you notice that the HFT activity on the futures markets started to increase a lot?

Probably around 2005. I saw that mostly in the S&P500. In 2005, 2006, and 2007 I noticed an increase in price action moves that were not there before. You have to understand that these computers got charting programmed into them too. Some programmers put the same things that we see into these algorithms. Whatever the myriad of indicators that are out there, the bots know them too. These bots will often suck people into a move, and then they will come in and squash the move in the other direction. Then when we had the financial crisis in 2008, I really saw the bots come to life in a major way.

What do you like and dislike like about HFT?

Trading against HFTs is like playing chess against a computer. As a human, I have one significant advantage that they do not: I can read emotions. Computers have no ability to read the emotions of the trading community. I can be watching CNBC or Bloomberg, and I can see that the more the media is touting that the market is down

X amount of points, the more anxiety they are creating for retail traders. These days everybody has a smartphone and they can look at their positions at any time. As the media covers the drop, it can actually make the drop every worse. The computers cannot read the psychology of the marketplace like that. All they can read is the indicators, momentum, price action, and volume, but they cannot read why is something happening. It is interesting to play against them sometimes. Sometimes you can force the bots to do things that you would not.

For example, I can see that the anxiety is all over the market. I can step out and not trade. Whereas the bots, when they are on, they are on. Sometimes they will go too far in one direction, then they have to get out of trades, and then they move in the other direction. I saw that happen right after the flash crash in 2010. It was interesting because I was trading in the after-hours session. Some firm, or firms, left their HFT trading in the crude oil market. We were trading in 75-cent ranges where we could force the bots to stop themselves out, causing them to push up the market. Then we would sell into their buying. They would stop themselves out and it would roll back down. That afternoon was extremely profitable to play against these bots. We were messaging other trader friends and saying, "Hey you got to jump in on this because someone walked away from their bot and it's just going crazy right now." So it is challenging sometimes, but if you understand what drives the HFTs then you can work against them or work with them. You just have to figure them out as another participant.

In that particular situation, you could tell it was an HFT because of the quick and mechanical way it was reacting.

Yes, absolutely. One of the things that bots do is to step in front of order flow. What I saw happening was, let us say crude was trading an x.60. If I were to put an order at x.61, the bot would step ahead of me and bid x.62. I would go x.63, it would go x.64. Every time I would put an order in, the bot would just keep stepping in front of me. That's not human. That computer is trying to stay on top as the leading bid. Then when the bids underneath it evaporate, all of a sudden they start forcing it down. Offers start collapsing and they push it the other way. I was able to take advantage of knowing that the bots do that, and that allowed me to force them to keep bidding up. Then I would keep my sell orders out there, and they would bid right into my sell orders. I would stack my bids much lower, then they would drop their offers because now the bot is long near the high of the move. They do not want risk so they will always lean on the bid, so if the bids disappear they will keep offering lower and lower until they can find a bid. You have to remember one thing: they cannot trade against themselves. I believe that is an exchange rule and an industry rule. You cannot trade against yourself in order to create false volume. An

HFT that keeps stepping in front of a bid has to hit an ask from someone else. It cannot hit its own ask. They can only manipulate to a certain degree.

These days, which contracts do you trade?

All the equity index futures, the 30-year US Treasury bond, the Euro and Canadian currency contracts and crude oil, of course.

What would you say are the key elements of your success?

Patience, patience, patience. As a screen trader, you do not have to be there for every single trade. You have to be prepared and you have to know how you are going to take advantage of movements. However, you have to be patient and wait for the perfect setups so you do not force yourself into a trade that inevitably becomes a loser. Forced trades are typically losers.

When I say perfect setups, that can happen every two minutes or five minutes. Therefore, it is not like I am waiting for hours and hours. However, it is like when I was trading in the stock market. If the stock that you are trading is not moving, you would go just look for another stock. There is always something moving. If I am trading ES and it is not moving, I would look for a different index, or a currency or crude. Look for another contract, but more importantly do not force a trade in any of them. You really have to be patient and wait for a setup.

I imagine you traded a lot last Friday when the market was falling hard.

Yeah, Friday was a very interesting day.

Is it accurate to say that you would be long on the bounces along the way to those panic sell-offs?

I definitely traded the bounces. The thing that I was looking at the most was the failure of support. It seemed that every time we would come into a support area, we would fail that area.

Source: ThinkorSwim platform

The more the media was exploiting that type of market activity, the more we exacerbated the move. I believe we were heavily oversold on Friday because of the media giving so much attention to these so-called critical levels. From Monday to Friday, what changed? What valuations changed? What economic fundamentals changed? Was there a war that broke out? Was there a drastic interest rate change? Nothing really changed, so when we look at a big move that occurred, if you are not a scalper, you have to be looking for opportunities to get in on the buy side. Therefore, to answer your question, yes there were many times I bought for the bounces. After those sell-offs on the open, there was a shift from selling to buying and I caught 16 points on the Russell. Which, on that contract, is huge.

When the market is failing at every support level, would you short those or would you rather short the rallies?

Well, you have to look at what the trend is for the day. If the trend is down, then you look to short rallies, unless you have a real bottom put in and one of the keys of those bottoms is volume. Sufficient volume coming into the bottom, trading at the bottom and coming out of that bottom. If you do not see that kind of action, then you have to be shorting the bounces because they happen due to the price arriving at technical areas. The sellers are gone and the buyers come in.

I believe in the last hour there was a bottom like that, some good volume. It failed but a scalper could have perhaps made some money there.

Yes. Unfortunately, it came very late in the day. Not all of the people who were long had to get out. They could hold those positions overnight. There were some people who were playing the idea of, "Well, the shorts are trapped now so they will have to cover. It's a weekend coming and all the headline risk from China and the Middle East." That is what the longs were thinking. The shorts were thinking the exact opposite: "Well, they had their little bounce, can it hold it? If it can't, when will they start to sell?"

Therefore, the markets were pushing up pretty well, then the market turned and most indexes closed on their lows.

The markets had a quick pop after-hours, so it seems that it was as you are saying. People wanted to get out before the weekend.

It was bizarre because of the longs and shorts. You had to be long at the event risk during the weekend. The Chinese could lower interest rates. Central banks could decide to provide liquidity. You really have to look at things at a macro level and determine, "Do I want to take that risk?" The longs who were riding it up that last rally of the day really had to think about, "Do I want to take that risk?" The HFT bots did not care about any of that. Once they saw that the bids started pulling and the sellers starting coming in, the bots started hitting the market hard. Selling begets more selling which begets more selling.

When you are looking at this type of action, do you look at L2, the DOM or just charts?

I would say it's mostly charting but I would pay attention to L2. In the futures industry, there is not much information on L2 though. In the equity industry, you can see which ECNs are bidding and offering. You used to be able to see which brokerages were making the markets and you could get an idea if it was institutional trading, retail, etc. These days with mostly ECNs, it is not about who is on the L2 but what they are doing there to determine if the HFTs are on the bid or the offer.

In the futures world, you do not get that kind of information. We cannot know who is doing what. We do not know where the order flow is coming from. All we see is how many contracts are bid and offered. This is why charting is the main tool to watch.

Couldn't one use the L2 to time an entry off a good chart setup?

I do not think so, for me anyway. I will keep the L2 on the corner of my eye just to see if the bids are vanishing, or if they are absorbing it. I will get a feel for how much volume is actually trading there. If I see that the bids are evaporating, it will appear to me that there are many scared buyers out there. When that happens, in my view, the bots read that. They will push the market in the direction of the weakness. When you start seeing blips, what I would consider market orders, 30 or 50 contract orders hitting the markets, that's when you've got to figure out what is happening. Look at the news and see if there is anything out there. However, more importantly, you have to look at the chart and see if we are at a technical level in some period that is causing people to want to use market orders to get out. The futures markets are the most fluid of any market, more so than equity. That is because it will typically trade every single tick up and down as the move develops. It is very rare for the price to jump ticks. When that happens, generally there is going to be due news.

You want to keep an eye on the L2, but for me most of the work is done by looking at the charts.

Therefore, you pay a lot of attention to support and resistance levels and come into the day knowing the key levels.

I do that to some degree. However, because the market is very fluid, it does not pay to stick to your guns in the static support and resistance levels.You cannot just look at a daily chart and say, "Ok, these are my support and resistance levels,' because the HFTs might be looking at the one minute timeframe support and resistance. Maybe the 5, 10, or 25 minute. Whoever wrote the HFT algo, they have different periods that they are analyzing. Your support and resistance on the daily chart might be invalid against an HFT. A screen trader such as myself, I look at multiple periods simultaneously. I am always looking at support and resistance on all periods. That helps me stay out of trouble in those areas.

When you use those areas, do you try to give some space to the trade to avoid those stop hunting ticks that happen?

I love when the HFTs go after the stops. You have to know which levels are the most probable for that to happen. Round numbers are always an area where they are going to have stops. You would think that after so many years people would realize that you should not put your stops at whole numbers. Give yourself some room or stop out earlier. These days, the computers all know that is where the stops are.

How do you set stops?

I never put hard stops. I use mental stops, because I am never in a situation where I am all in. For example, if I am going to be trading 40 or 50 contracts, I do not do all 50 contracts at once. I will scale in, which gives me the flexibility of adding if the position is going against me. If I had stops in and used that approach, I would have to buy into my own positions being stopped out, which would make no sense. I look at the bigger picture. Now, if I were long and the market were about to collapse, I would just do a marketable order to get out. However, the last time that happened was in 2010.

What is the period of the charts that you are looking at?

The lowest period that I look at is the one minute. I only look at them if I am really trying to hone in a specific buy or sell. Typically, I am looking at intermediate trends intraday through the 15 or the 30-minute. Typically, this is what I tell the traders that I mentor: whatever timeframe that you are going to be trading off, you have to anticipate holding that position 4x that timeframe. If you trade off a five-minute chart, you really have to be looking at the next four bars. If you are in it for one minute, you are really a scalper so paying attention to a higher period is kind of fistula. For me, I look for bigger moves, so I am looking at the 15/30 minute charts then I will execute off a five-minute or one minute depending on which contract it is.

Therefore, you would be willing to hold your position for one hour or maybe two hours.

If I were in a 30-minute chart, I could easily be on a hold for one hour or maybe two, and sometimes even three hours.

Days like last Friday are great because of all the volatility and the predictability of some of the moves, but what about on the slow days? How do you trade them?

For me, I look at volatility with my profit expectations. If the market is not moving a whole lot, then I have to reduce my profit expectations. If I am generally looking at two to four points of a move and the market is quiet, I might take profits at one or two points. If it is busy like it was on Friday, I could be going for four to 10 points.

How do you manage your total risk exposure? Do you have a percentage of your total capital that you are willing to risk or something else along those lines?

No, I manage my risk through anticipated volatility. What is the average trading range for that contract? Then I will adjust my size accordingly. If you are trading in the Russell and you have a very small account, if you use multiple contracts on a day like Friday, you are just asking for trouble. You are taking on so much risk. A typical move in a day like that can put six, eight or even 10 points in the red very fast. If you do not manage your risk depending on the volatility of the day, you might have a very short lifespan in this market.

One thing I do not understand is how SPY affects ES and vice-versa. SPY has a smaller spread than ES so it trades more cents per tick of ES. Do the bots look at

SPY to gauge demand or supply and predict which level of ES will be taken next? Do you have any thoughts on that?

You have to look at SPY as the little brother of ES. The SPX is what you really should be focusing on. The SPX and ES are directly fungible. The SPY is 10% of the SPX. If you look at SPY at 197.63, the SPX would be 1970.89. Retail traders trade SPY. Some institutions trade that too, but predominately that is a liquidity instrument. With the SPX, you cannot really trade it because it is an index. You can only trade it through options. However, you can trade the ES as a fungible contract for the SPX. The thing is, the SPY can flicker around a lot without really influencing ES because it is that much smaller.

Do you use fundamental data on your trades? News and people's reactions to new data coming in? Things like that.

Typically not. Number one, when I look at the news media, they are sensationalist in nature. They are out there really exploiting whatever news event is happening and making it bigger than it really is. Their job is to report the news. Do they do that unbaled? Probably not, because they are emotional. They get in there and embellish on what is happening. If that is what they are doing, they create anxiety amongst the retail traders. I would have to say that most of the professional traders that I know do not pay attention to the news until there is a big move in the markets and they need to find out what is causing it to determine whether they want to be a participant.

I just want to know what the catalyst to the move is. If there was a surprise interest rate hike, I know that it would mainly affect interest rate instruments, secondly currency, and thirdly it would affect equity indexes. However, you just have to know how each one would be affected individually.

Was last week one of the most profitable weeks for you?

No. I do not think so. It was probably an above average week but not the most profitable.

What were some of the good trades you had this year?

Off the top of my head, I am not sure. Back in May I think we had some good volatility in crude oil. The whole move has been good. During the entire collapse, as you see crude going down, you see this affects many industries and equities. The shipping industry gets affected too. Therefore, this has created many interesting anomalies. The more volatile we get, the more activity I am going to have, but not by a lot. I am a very stable trader.

Would you describe your style as a counter-trend or contrarian?

Yes. I definitely I look at this from a contrarian point of view. Because I do not necessarily want to be in the herd. Typically, the herd is wrong. However, that can be a very dangerous thing, especially for a new trader. You really have to be good at reading the charts and understanding risk.

In 2008, when markets just kept plunging, how did you deal with that style then?

Back in that period, I actually played with the trend. I saw those issues coming way ahead of time. I was working for a different firm at the time. We were able to take swing positions and do pretty much anything that we wanted to do. I was shorting oil and the euro at their peaks and riding them all the way down. Then I started to see brokerages beginning to get into trouble. The whole mortgage collapse was going in full swing, so we were short many of the brokers. We looked at who had risk exposures. I traded a lot with the herd in that period.

You only swing traded during that period?

We did both day trading and swing trading. It was probably 50/50.

These days, do you swing trade much?

Not very much. My situation has changed. I am not with that firm anymore. I am not deploying anywhere near as much capital so I do not have the need to swing trade. If you are trading with $200K, you can be very profitable as a day trader. If you are trading with hundreds of millions of dollars, it is very difficult to get good returns with two-to-three-day traders. You really have to expand your periods.

These days, you are strictly a retail trader?

I do both trading for my own account and trading for a firm account.

What is the advantage of trading for the firm?

Capital. It is all about capital. I have a specific dollar amount that is allocated to me. They have been pushing me to take more capital. I do not want to take more capital. I am comfortable taking my percentage every day, being profitable and consistent. You are also trading in an environment where there is a strict set of rules. With a prop firm, you have somebody else who will cut you off if you are not disciplined enough to do it yourself.

By capital, you mean that they put up 100% of the money?

In my situation, yes.

You keep a percentage of the profits and that is it?

Correct.

How does a new futures trader go about developing this library of setups that you have?

The first thing they have to do is to determine what kind of trader they want to be. Do they get very anxious if a position goes against them? Alternatively, are they ok with putting their targets out there, letting things develop, etc.? It depends on their personality. Of all the people that I mentored over the years, the very first thing that I do is put them on a simulator. I put a trade on and tell them to manage. I do not tell them if it is going to be long or short. I just tell them, "You take it from here." I try to learn, based on their actions, what kind of trader they are. Whether they are risk averse or too risky. Whether they are quick to take profits, or whether they will hold their losses more than they need to.

After that, you just need the screen time to be able to identify the setups?

Screen time is so important. I have a person that I have been mentoring for about one year. He and I are vastly different. He likes my trade setups but he does not have the capital necessary to trade my style. As a result, he had to alter my style to make it work for him, which is very acceptable. You can watch a professional trader, you can watch someone who has been doing it for years, but until you start doing it yourself with real money you will not learn what kind of trader you are. You will not learn how much emotion you have and how anxious you get when you have a live trade on.

You seem to use quite a few indicators in your trading.

Yes. I use a variety of indicators.

Do they help you find some key levels? Like in a self-fulfilling prophecy kind of way? Alternatively, do you really think they add something more than that?

They indicators that I use, I do it to find out where the herd is at. This past week you saw people on the media talking about the "death cross," which is when the 50 day MA moves below the 200 MA. You have to be aware of what those levels are, and that is why they are on my charts. I need to know why markets are moving in a particular way at certain levels.

However, I do not play them hard and fast. I will not put my buy/sell orders at those levels and expect my trade to work out. To me it is fun when the market breaks through those levels, whether it is to the upside or to the downside.

So the indicators can help you read the psychology of everybody and it can help you build a bias?

Correct.

I understand that you do quite a bit of options trading as well. What is your overall approach on options?

Options to me is all about the direction of the underlying. I use options as an advantage. I would have to say that almost all of my options trading these days are swing plays. I do not use intraday trade options anymore, but I used to though. The HFT algos have taken over that business too, so it is nowhere near as profitable as it used to be.

The algos understand when momentum will push the underlying and then take advantage of the options before a human can react?

Yes, and the computers can read the volatility. They can streamline the calculations for the delta and the gamma. They can read those and the changes so much faster than a human can. They are making markets based on their read of the underlying and of the Greeks. It is very difficult for a human to compete with that.

When you play multiday strategies in options, which strategies do you use?

I will typically be directional. So I will be long premium with calls if I am bullish, but if not I am very sure about it I will do a long call spread. Sometimes I will do credit spreads as well. If you like to think like a contrarian, do the credit spreads. If you are bullish, you have to be thinking like a contrarian to be shorting puts and take in premium. The issue with taking premium is that you have to cap your risk. Because, if you are wrong, you can have a premium expansion that forces you out. Always know your risk when it comes to options.

When you short those puts and perhaps on the call side as well, do you buy the wings to cap the risk?

Always. I buy the protection put way out of the money and short the more near money put, what I call "profit put." You need a profit and a protection when playing these. The most you will make is the difference in the profit and the protection puts. If you trade outright long premium, your potential profit is almost unlimited.

However, as I said, the HFTs have really exploited the options markets. You get premium expansion around events, whether it be earnings or Fed announcements, etc. Therefore, you get that premium expansion and then you get the collapse in volatility. You get the move you were expecting in the underlying but the option does not move and that is because volatility shrinks. That is a mistake that many retail traders make: not understanding what is causing your option to not move. They overextend their stay because they think, "It's going to keep going up so I will hold into my calls," and the option never moves. They keep losing moves during time decay.

I noticed that in some of the pharma stocks, when they are up a lot, it seems almost impossible to make money being long options. The premiums are so high.

Yes, and that was the point I was making a moment ago. Computerized trading has taken over that sector. They know when to expand the implied volatility and when to collapse it. For the retail trader, it is just not worth it to be in those stocks unless you are willing to short the options. That is the only thing that you can do, short the premium.

Therefore, you prefer to be on that side.

If I am trading options, I will be looking to be short expanded volatility.

You are looking for an overreaction in the IV?

Yeah. There was a pharma company about a week or two ago that went from $2 to $50. First day was from $2 to $10. The next day was from $10 to $27 and the following day was from $27 to $50. The last time I looked was at $17 I think. You can see it was a very limited life span on that move. However, the important thing is to know what the potential trade there was. As this thing was trading from $2 to $50, you want to be thinking, "If this thing retraces, I want to be riding that." As they are killing the premium on the puts, what I would do would be to ladder myself in the puts. If it were trading at $55, I would buy the 40s, 35s, and 30s. I would use the same dollar amount of them to increase my size at every level going down.

What are some good trades you have made in options recently?

I would say it was a directional trade. I believe it was on GALE. I laddered a bunch of call options anticipating a move back over $100. I believe that was my biggest play this year. My primary focus is on futures.

That was one of those one-day big spikes that you predicted was going to keep going?

No, it was actually a contrarian play. I was looking at the chart and thinking it was crazy that it had been sold out so much. I thought that if it started to get back momentum to the upside, it would spike a lot. I believed that the pharma industry was going to get a lot more attention. That was a good blue chip name in that industry.

So essentially it was a dip buy in a good pharma name during a pharma/biotech bull market?

Yes, it was a reversal play.

What about good options plays that you did on the short premium side?

A few years back, FAS and FAZ were very active. Everybody was trading them. These were the three bank sector ETFs. If I remember correctly, FAZ was trading at the $200 area and the premium on the calls were so high it was just incredible. I believe Bank of America was trading at a low price, something like $3. All the bank stocks were down to the garbage level. You just knew that this would not keep going. Bank of America was not going out of business. JP Morgan and Wells Fargo were not either. However, they did have an extreme move to the downside, so, if you could afford the risk, you could sell premium on FAZ. As the market started to create bounces, FAZ would fall huge and so would the premiums. I was selling the ATM calls premium on FAZ. FAZ is the inverse of the financials: as they go down, FAZ rises and vice-versa. I was anticipating that the market was going to start to bounce. Over time, that was pretty much what happened. It was a steady methodical plan of always selling premium and having some protection in case there was an extremely adverse move.

Those ETFs are structured in a way that they always go to $0, are they not?

They are. If you do not understand them, your account is going to $0 too.

Do the options pricing consider those?

I am sure that it does but I am not really an expert on options pricing. I trade more the action in the underlying. I use options to try to exploit those moves.

How much of your gains come from futures and how much come from options?

For the last three or four years, it has been 70-80% futures and the rest in options.

Is your options approach is similar to the futures? You are very selective, and you wait for the good setups?

Yes. Options to me is all about the leverage. They give me the leverage without tying up a lot of capital.

How does your trading setup look?

I got a couple of laptops with a couple of external monitors attached to them. This is far different from what I used to have.

You used to have many monitors?

I used to have three computers with eight monitors.

You had more monitors than futures contracts you were trading.

Yes, exactly. Things have changed a lot because the monitors have more resolution these days. In addition, the software is better these days. You can expand and shrink things, etc.

Do you look at cross correlations between different futures?

This is definitely part of my analysis. As of late we have seen many correlations break down. NASDAQ has been hit hard lately. It was down 174.5 points Friday and the S&P500 was only down 57. One of the things that I watch is the risk-spread, which is how the NASDAQ is doing against the S&P500. If you see something like the Dow being down a lot versus the S&P500, you take that as being more retail trading. Meaning, the retail public is reacting more to the Dow Jones Index on TV.

Going into Monday, what is your plan for trading?

My plan developed on Friday, late afternoon. I got long going into the sell-off on the close in anticipation of a bounce Sunday night and into Monday.

If you get that pop, are you a seller right away or are you going to ride this one?

It depends how much of a pop and whether or not there seems to be volume pushing that momentum. If the market pops by, say, 200 points on YM at the open, then I would sell my position. You never look at a gift horse in the mouth. If the market hands you a gift, you take it and say "thank you very much."

If you get a gap down, are you bailing right away?

My position is relatively small, so even a gap down would not prevent me from staying with my position. If it was a 200-point gap down, yes, that could create some anxiety for me. I would look at a gap down as a potential buying opportunity unless there is something else going on.

And through the day you will try to get a read on whether the market wants to bounce or continue to go further down and then position yourself for that?

Yeah. One of the sayings I have on the top of my monitor is "trade what you see, not what you think." I try not to come into the market every day with a particular bias. I really want to see what develops and trade that. For Monday, I am coming in with a bit of a bias for the long side because I already have long positions. I have to be very careful that I do not turn that into too much of a bias.

I noticed that issue with overnight trades. On top of that, when you have a loss you tend to get upset and the decisions that you make after that tend to be hurt by that loss.

I tell this to new traders: if you take a swing trade and immediately it opens up against you and you stop yourself out, the best thing you can do is get up and walk away. Take a walk. Go get some coffee. Clear your mind so you can come back and look for the next opportunity.

What would you say has been your worst mistake you ever made?

Fighting the trend. Trying to stop the locomotive if you will. However, in terms of a particular trade, it was back in 2010 during the flash crash. I was trading some stocks that were being thrown out to ridiculous levels. Trading down to the pennies. Anderson Consulting was one of them. I saw this thing go from $40 to less than $1. I thought, "This is insane. This company still has value." I went in and started buying some of that stuff. However, I did not hold it for a long time. It was just a trade. If I were up $7-$8 on it, I would sell it. It was a good gain. What started out as a good trade turned into a bad one. Later we found out that the exchanges were going to bust trades. I do not know who caused them do to this. They cancelled a bunch of trades down there. Problem was that they cancelled my buys but not all my sells. As a result, I had a short position and went from a gain to a loss.

Therefore, your 7-8 point gain turns into a 20-point loss.

I do not remember exactly but the loss was something like 2.5 times the amount I thought I had gained. It took them quite a while to even notify traders that they were busting all those trades.

In futures would you say your worst mistake has been fighting the trend?

In futures, if you get stupid and step in front of the freight train you are going to be run over.

What was the best trade you ever made?

It was being long on options and interest rate futures in '87. It was more luck than anything else to be honest. I just thought interest rates were not going up anytime soon. Then the crash started to occur. I was calling my broker in Singapore and asking what was happening. He was saying the market was going crazy. He was giving me quotes but I did not know what he was talking about. It seemed to be only up 12-15 ticks higher from the close. I called him again two to three more times and I finally asked him, "What handle are we trading in?" He said we were 200 basis points higher than where we were on Friday's close. That was a huge move for me.

In recent years, are there any trades that you are particularly proud of?

Right now, I am more looking for consistency than I am about big moves. These days, if I have a $100,000 day, that is good. I am happy about that.

Therefore, you are more of a base hitting than a home run style trader these days?

Absolutely. I will push five, six, seven base hits and then I will get lucky, be on the right side, and catch a bigger move. However, even with that I will not catch the whole move. I will be scaling out to lock in my profits. Those are the $100,000 days.

The mentorship that you mentioned, is that something that you do as part of your deal with the prop firm?

Unfortunately, sometimes I have to mentor new traders at the prop firm. Usually though, if someone wants to get into the business, I do this on the outside when I have time.

In addition to finding the right style in terms of being a scalper or intraday trader, what are some of the top things that you tell them?

Preserve capital. The most important thing is to make sure you have enough capital to come back and play tomorrow.

In terms of watching the markets, how long do you think a trader needs to watch before he can consistently anticipate moves?

It is different for different people. I have seen people pick it up real quick, within two to three months. The most important thing when you are trying to develop your reactionary skills is respective activity. The longer you spend in a realistic simulated mode, the better. What I mean by realistic simulated mode is if your account is going to be $20,000 or $30,000, do not be trading 10 contracts. That is unrealistic. Trade one or two. What you are trying to do is to create repetitive activity. The more times you do something, the better you are going to get at it. Whether you are a quarterback or a pitcher, what these people do all the time is to practice their skills. They are constantly doing the same thing repeatedly. That is what simulated trading does for you. It causes you to create a repetitive activity. Then when you start to deploy real money, you have to continue that repetitive activity and not think about the money. As long as you can press the button at the right times, you should be successful.

What would you say is your greatest weakness as a trader?

I would say it is getting too subjective. Violating my primary rule of trading what you see not what you think. I start to think, "This is what the market should do," and I step in front of the freight train.

That happened to me on SPY Friday. I would think that the market had to bounce, and it would bounce, but then the rally would fade and the profits would evaporate. Do you think that happens because we build a theory and then we fall in love with that theory?

You hit the nail on the head there. You thought like everybody in the market thought: "We sold off far enough, we should rebound." Some people would say, "We hit a 50% retrace," or, "We hit this support level." You had a massive herd that started to get in there but you had no follow through with mass volume. Without the continuation, the move started to dissipate and then it failed. That is what happened to me, to you and to a whole bunch of other traders. Fortunately, many traders saw that happening sooner than others did so they sold their positions out. They can still believe in the idea but they can wait for better opportunities. I got out of the way of the sell-off by waiting.

Were you able to sell the longs before they totally turned, or did you sell at the break of the lows of the day?

For me, I was able to see it turning in the smaller periods. If the bounces did not have the continuous upward momentum then the downside momentum from the major trend of the day was going to kick in. So I got out of the trades quickly.

You mentioned that you had an important rule on your monitor. What are some other rules that you have?

Another one is, "If you hit your maximum loss for the day, that doesn't mean that you are a failure. It just means that you were wrong. Stop. Why add more losing trades to a losing day?" Sometimes I will see that early on in a day where I am making bad decisions. I will not even hit my max loss for the day. I will just stop, walk away, and clear my head. When I come back, I will try to look at it from a different perspective. Look at multiple periods and try to figure out what am I missing. Another rule is if you have losing trades, go back and look at the charts to try to figure out why you traded at those times. Did you have a valid reason? Were you trading what the chart was telling you or were you trading what you thought should happen? I will tell you that 9 out of 10 times when I trader does that, he will find out that he was trying what he thought should happen instead of what the chart was telling him should happen.

So even in a highly liquid market that is supposedly more efficient, you are still going to see some reliable chart patterns and things like that?

Let me put to you this way: the markets relate to the charts much like the heart of a human relates to the heart rate. As a long as there are markets and the heart is beating, you are going to have an edge.

What do you do with the money that you make from trading? Do you invest in real estate, stocks and things like that?

Back when things were good, leading up to 2008, I was diversifying a bit. About 50% of what I was making I was taking out and putting into real estate. Unfortunately, that proved to be a bad decision. I was overinvested in real estate and we were killed in the collapse. These days, if I am not keeping it safe in the bank, then it is in the trading account.

Do you push for more size as the trading accounts grow larger?

Not very much. I aim for consistency. I have a model that depends on how much I have in the trading account and that will determine how much size I can trade. It is not an incremental thing like going from 10 contracts with $50,000 to 11 contracts with $55,000. I am looking to take $50,000 to $100,000 and then trade 20 contracts. However, I scale a lot, so it will not be 20 all at once. Instead of starting with two lots, I might start with three or four lots.

What would you say is the easiest contract for someone to start out trading futures?

That probably would be the Dow futures, YM. You get nice movement but relatively low risk. Its only $5 a tick. There is plenty of liquidity. With the ES, I find that people that start tend to get frustrated. Even though it looks like there is tremendous liquidity there, they do not always get to take advantage of it. There is so much liquidity there that you are not likely to be filled without paying the spread.

At YM, I can be hit at almost every level that I want to be hit.

Post interview update

The Monday after the interview (August 24 2015) markets crashed (with a mini flash crash at the open). Here is what Jim had to say about his trading:

So on Sunday night I saw the market was selling off and I stopped out of the long positions. Monday morning the market continued to sell off. I worked a little on the short side to recover some of the losses from the longs. When I saw the Russell was bottoming in crazy action down around 1075, I started chasing some by orders and got filled in the mid-80s. I continued to aggressively buy on the shallow dips and sold in the 1139-1140 area. Huge turnaround day for the big account. Unfortunately, the little accounts did not fare so well. Took some stock losses and was unable to trade those accounts because I was too busy on the big account. Crazy far for sure. Expect to see more volatility over the next several days. Must be very careful not to hold overnight positions with so much turmoil in the market.

Lessons from Chapter 4

1. Don't fight trends. One of the most significant mistakes Jim has made has been fighting the "locomotive" as he puts it. Trends driven by momentum can be powerful and traders who don't respect that usually don't last very long.

2. Chart reading. Chart reading is one of the key components of Jim's success. He has seen and accumulated a long history of charts and patterns and that enables him to act during the heat of the battle without hesitation. For traders looking to get good at that, screen time is the first step in order to develop this ability. The more you observe futures charts, the more you are going to get familiar with how it moves. Saving charts of important situations or lessons is also another step. This will enable you to review and "relearn" lessons you have derived from the charts.

3. Patience, patience, patience. Jim looks to only trade high quality setups. This does not mean waiting for hours for a trade but, rather, it means you will be looking for other futures contracts until you find something that your experience tells you is a good trade, the same way a stock trader can move on into other stocks if he doesn't find action in the first one.

4. When you are struggling with a market, look at a longer time frame. This might show that you are missing something that you are not seeing by just looking at the intraday chart.

5. Stops placement. When deciding where to put your stops, be careful about setting them in obvious spots. Algos will frequently take prices in a direction and trigger them to enhance their profitability. As Jim says, "Give yourself some room or stop out earlier." If you are worried about a position, you might be better off exiting it right away rather than having the stop at a round number level or a few

ticks below/above a support/resistance point. Either exit the position or set the stop with extra room to the obvious level.

6. Find out what kind of trader you are: scalper or intraday trader. Depending on the level of your patience and ability to be logical during a loss and discipline, you might be better off being a scalper or an intraday trader. If you are the type of person who gets nervous easily when losing, playing for small moves as a scalper is probably a better option. If you have no problem being disciplined, can scale in positions with no emotions and like to play for bigger moves, being an intraday trader would be a superior style.

7. Consistency. Jim's main focus these days is to be consistent. He no longer tries to go for home runs on every trade. He is looking for "base hits" and daily profitability. Home runs are a bonus that happen every once in a while. Mentally, this is an easier approach to take. Its low stress trading and, for some traders, pretty much the only way to trade due to mistakes that arise when that trader is in a drawdown.

Chapter 5

Flemming Kozok - The Big Bet Sniper

I came across the following trader (Twitter @flemmingkozok) while in a trading chat room. Everybody was talking about FNMA and FMCC, two Over the Counter (OTC) stocks that had been hot lately and had just had a large crash and rebound. People were pleased that they made a few thousand dollars in the stock. Some even made $10,000. Flemming, on the other hand, said he made more than $100,000. Even though it sounded like a lot, it was very doable given that the stocks were extremely liquid and put in some huge moves.

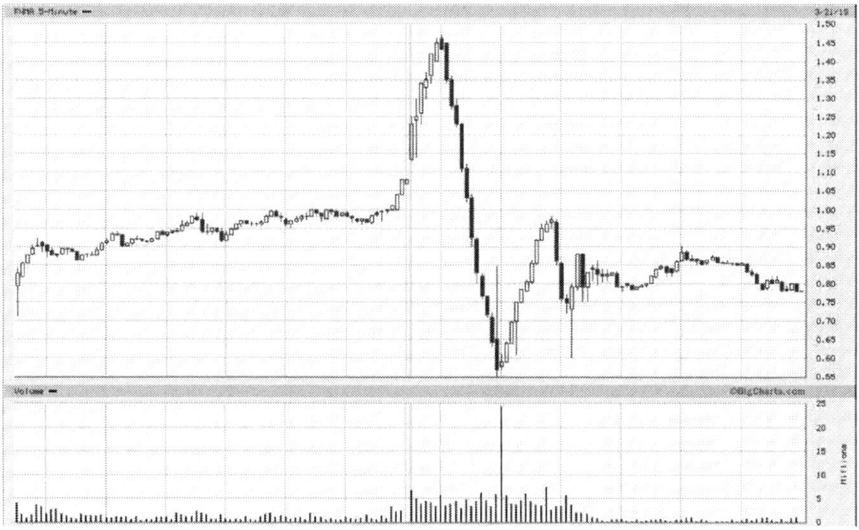

FNMA 5min chart. Source: BigCharts.com

After that day, I realized I had to push my comfort zone more if I wanted to make big money in the markets. I decided that when the right setups came along, I would go for it more aggressively. What was amazing was that those two stocks came back and made an even more impressive run, going from $0.50 in March all the way up to $5 in May.

It was the same sort of setup, a parabolic mini-bubble, fueled by retail traders and "investors." It was doomed to failure. Such a greater-fool speculation is self-reinforcing on the way up and down. It's only a matter of whether you can stand the losses that happen when you short the move too early. You can also play the bounce that inevitably comes when the stocks overshoot on their way down as well.

Chart courtesy of StockCharts.com

I decided to play the move in May with a bigger position than normal, and I ended up making about $7,000, mostly on the short side but some on the rebound as well. That was my best day ever at that time and I was quite pleased. Flemming then posted screenshots of his platform, and the results were staggering. He had just made almost $800,000 in a single day! It sounds huge but these stocks were so liquid, and the moves so gigantic, that he even said he left a lot of money on the table. After that, I decided that I wanted to learn as much as I could from him, and I contacted him for an interview.

I'm glad I did as he has a very interesting perspective on what it takes to get good at trading. Contrary to what some people might think, he's not a big-swinging-dick-style trader who makes huge bets every day and has large swings. He has a patient style and only bets big when the right setups come along. "I'm more patient than ever," he says. He's similar to a sniper who takes his time, waits for the right opportunity—the perfect headshot—and then pulls the trigger.

He's based in Copenhagen, Denmark, is thirty-five years old, and started day trading with $4,100 in 2000. He has executed more than 350,000 trades, and has made nearly $4.5 million after trading costs and fees.

This interview was conducted in August of 2013

When did you become a trader, and why did you want to?

Being from Copenhagen, I started trading Danish stocks many years ago. I immediately felt that it was an interesting line of work, and I also felt a natural ability to assess how certain stocks would behave in the market. From the very beginning, I felt that it was only going to be a matter of time before I made a lot of money, even if I made nearly nothing in the beginning. I started in 1997 but only started to day trade US stocks in 2000. I became attracted to the US market because of the large number and high variety of stocks. I have always been drawn to stocks with the highest possible volatility, as those stocks are the ones that can deliver the fast money. But, of course, they're the most risky as well. So basically my job is to manage risk while I seek risk.

Did you start out well, or did it take some time to make money?

When I switched to day trading US stocks, I was very profitable right away. Prior to making the jump, I spent many months analyzing how to approach day trading. My strategies actually worked from the very beginning. The fantastic thing for me is that to this day the main principles of the approaches I used in 2000 are the same. As such, I have never needed to alter them fundamentally. My main line of thought is the same but, of course, I have refined them due to changes in the marketplace. But yes, I was profitable right away.

Starting in 1997, how did you do?

I made money but gave it back. That was not day trading, however. At the age of fifteen and sixteen, I was just finding out what this trading thing was all about, so it went slower. I started with $1,100 and probably made around $130,000 in a period of three or four years, and then I lost everything. That's when I realized that I needed to take what I had left, which was around $4,100, and move into day trading with a different strategy. So overall, I didn't make money. It was slower and harder than day trading.

Do you think it was important to have lost everything?

Yes, absolutely. I lost everything and I was indebted. You learn in a very intensive way when you lose everything, but you don't have to do that in order to learn. In 2000, I almost did it again. I didn't lose it all but it felt that way. I made $800,000 in the first four months of day trading, and then I lost more than half of that in five weeks. It really felt like I was losing everything once more. Those two losing periods are important to me to this day, as they added some substantial fundamental knowledge of how to do things and how *not* to do things.

Those two times that you lost a lot, was it that you just bet too big in a single trade?

The first time around, it was a trading combination that I don't really remember the specifics of. I do know I was using lots of margin leverage. Now, in general, I seek not to use margin and recommend others not to use it. The second time was a mistake of breaking the rules of the strategy. I tried to convert into swing trading, but I'm not a swing trader. I wanted to try to do it because I could see some big opportunities in it. I also used margin, so I lost most of what I'd made.

Do you have an educational background? A college degree?

I have a master's degree from college, but it's never helped me in stock trading. Stock trading to me is a game of psychology, it's not a game of who can crunch numbers. I let other people, like analysts, crunch numbers. For trading purposes, I have no interest in reading reports and that kind of thing. The result of the number crunching is what you see in the ticker tape—price action. The price action is the key, not reading reports.

What are some of the great trades that you had early on in your career?

I must admit that I remember the bad trades better. They were short sales where I mistimed entries. I was convinced that things were going to break down. So the combination of mistiming and holding stubbornly to positions resulted in large losses, and eventually I got margin called. Having executed so many trades in my life, I must admit I don't really remember the specifics of many of the good ones. I do remember having done some short sales as well as great bottom plays on the long side. Being primarily a short seller, I'm very happy about catching a good long, especially if I let my profit run more than I'm used to. I have never been really good about letting my profits run.

There are many categories of good trades. An amusing category of a good trade is the ones that you enter and flip three, five, seven seconds later. You make $500, $1,000—it's not a lot of money, but when you consider that the operation only took a few seconds, it's actually a very good trade. I remember not so long ago I traded 100,000 shares and made $7,000 in eleven seconds. Flipping a position that was this big so fast is uncommon, but I managed to do it in a matter of seconds, getting hit on the bid and the ask. That was a very good trade because of the beauty of the trade, the way it was executed.

In the early 2000s a lot of traders were using the strategy of buying the bid and selling the ask, scalping-style market making. Was that a big part of your approach?

I have many different approaches. One of them is market making. I have done lots of that. It has become harder to do that over the years because of the market changes and higher costs related to trading. I have had to shift my focus to other strategies.

So over the years your market making has become less important and the other strategies more important?

Absolutely. I have always sought to have multiple strategies and approaches to different types of stocks. I have always been afraid that some areas would stop working, so I would have the other areas to rely on. I have about twelve different types of trading that I do, different kinds of setups and other strategies.

A lot of traders say that the US markets are difficult because of the computers and lack of volatility. You live in Europe. Why don't you trade the European markets, which seem to be moving more?

I'm not all that fond of the European stocks. You don't have any market in the world where you have such a huge volume of stocks and different markets as in the United States. Also you have extreme volatility in many different stocks in different exchanges. Stocks also trade in a technically different manner on different exchanges, which is both fun and interesting. You also find different ways to approach them. I don't see that happening in Europe. I also like the consolidated tape in the United States. If you look at the Danish market, you don't see a lot of games being played in the way they are in the United States. You have people trying to manipulate stocks in the United States because of the different kinds of routes you can use. You don't see much of that happen in a less fragmented market like in Denmark. Those are the kinds of games that I like to observe.

I first came across your results in March of 2013 when FNMA and FMCC had a big day. You made more than $100,000 that day. Then in May, you made $800,000 in an even bigger volume day. How do you go from making small trades to all of a sudden making a huge bet like that?

It's a good question. In March, I was actually feeling more insecure, even though I felt it was the right thing to do. The thing was, I had seen those kinds of setups in those stocks in 2009, but just not that extreme. I'd also seen those kinds of setups in other OTC stocks multiple times in the past. I felt very safe in doing what I did. I even felt safer in May with the bigger bets than in March with the smaller ones. It was all the result of having observed similar setups many times before. There were many traps along the way in those plays, but I didn't have any significant unrealized loss on them, so I was able to think straight when I had to. When the time came, I knew that this was it and it could be a big trade. I wasn't questioning that there was going to be a big move at all.

These other stocks that you saw similar patterns in, do you have an archive of charts saved somewhere, or is it all in your head?

The archive is in my head only.

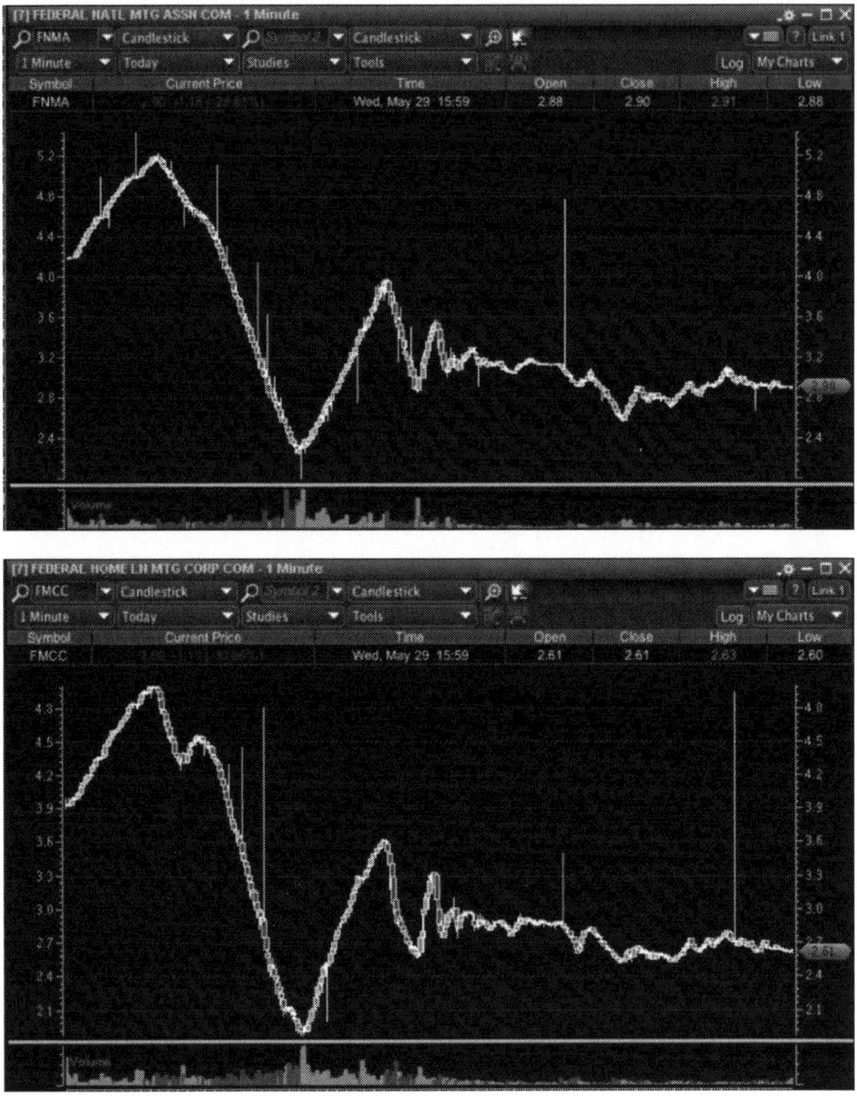

FNMA FMCC 1 min chart. Source: E-Trade Pro

You made more money on the way down or on the way up from the rebound?

I think it was fifty/fifty. I was short pretty heavily in FMCC because it was hard to get borrows on FNMA. Both FNMA and FMCC couldn't bounce after the first attempt, so I thought, "This is going to flush down strongly." I held it for quite a while. I didn't really care about how much I was making, as I was focused on covering and catching the bounce on the long side. I ended up catching the very bottom, focusing only on FMCC due to a slight laggard delay relative to FNMA. I did well that day because I was mentally strong and able to think straight when I had to. Problem is, you can look at a great setup, but if you time it wrong one, two, three times, and you're down $10,000 to $20,000, you have a bad beginning in a nice setup, and then you always get weaker the more you try. That day I was strong because I had a good start. I made something like $150,000 on the first drop, so I thought, "This is the point you have to get in the long side." I bought something like 400,000 shares averaged slightly below $2.

You mentioned catching the bottom in those stocks. I was trading those stocks that day...

You traded them?

Yes, I made some money but not $800,000, not even close. I noticed that ARCA and NITE would flip sides and then the stock would change directions from downtrend to uptrend or vice versa. Did you get in before the flip or after?

Did you look at the bounce in FNMA/FMCC in March?

Yes.

Which one did you trade?

I believe I traded FMCC.

FMCC had trades at $1.88 and $1.89. That was the bottom. I had an average of $1.92 on 400,000 shares. The thing was FMCC trailed FNMA.

I remember that.

That's what I used to guide me. When FNMA confirmed the bottom, there were still huge ask orders in FMCC that needed to be taken off. I always get in gradually, never all at once, so I started buying 25,000 to 50,000 shares at a time. Opening the position, I wasn't nervous at all, but I managed to get a bit nervous as FMCC was still heavy on ask, having problems getting released from its low. But at that point, FNMA confirmed the move once more as it started getting released. That's when it was OK to add to the position, even if I was already loaded. I knew that everyone else thought that when ARCA switched sides it would be the time to buy. It would confirm the bottom. At this point in time, I was loaded and wanted the stock to move, so then I bought more using ARCA so it would switch, knowing more people would start to jump in the trade. I bought all the way up to $2 using ARCA. I hope you understand what I'm saying here.

Yes. You took the displayed liquidity from ARCA, and when it crossed, everybody started to jump in because it was a sign of rebound.

Yes, because, for whatever reason, ARCA wasn't being used by other traders, so I was the one who made the decision to use it aggressively. Even if I didn't really need to add to the position, it was important to send that signal to get others to pull the trigger.

You said you have problems letting winners run. That day you just knew it was going to move, so you just held for the whole thing?

I didn't hold for the whole move. It went all the way to $3.5. I started selling at $2.8, scaling out because it had some bumps along the way. I probably sold my last shares at $3.10 or $3.2, but I don't really remember. I held them percentage-wise much further than what I would typically do. It's always been my problem that I have to do lots of trades, because I don't let my winners run. If you can let them run, you need fewer good trades. I let these run much more than I normally do, but in hindsight I could have let them run much more, I left a very significant amount of money on the table.

I noticed that in those stocks, that day was great, and the next day was good, but then it started to get choppy and the range got smaller. Did you still make money in them for a while?

I continued as a long as there was liquidity. I only focused on those for a while. I made nearly $100,000 the next day, then nearly $50,000 on the third day. Then it decreased to $40,000, $20,000, $10,000, etc. I was active in them for a while, but level of activity will always correlate with level of liquidity.

What is the feeling of making almost $800,000 in a day?

Most people think that I was screaming to the sky, being really happy and all, but the thing is, I never really react that way to the money I make. I have always had an extremely humble attitude toward the market, and I'm very fearful about it. When I make money, and it doesn't matter how much money, I only really feel one thing, and that is *relief*. I never feel too much happiness about making money. I'm much more grateful than happy. When I made $795,000 in three and a half hours, I felt a huge relief. When I lose money, even smaller amounts, I suffer a lot. There's a very significant mental imbalance there. The negative emotion related to losing is much more profound than the positive emotion related to making money. I've always been aware that I felt that way, so I try to handle that mental imbalance.

If you don't handle it, you will suffer so much in trading that you will go crazy at some point.

So you don't over celebrate, because otherwise you get attached too much, and that is going to hurt down the line?

That's not the way to put it actually. I never celebrate, but not for that reason. You don't celebrate for things that are just necessary. Making money is something that is necessary. You have to do it. It's not like I over-accomplished in any way. For me, it's a necessary step toward the overall objective. The other thing is that I'm very fearful about the market. I'm humble, so I don't dare to be too happy. I know that the market is a black hole that can take everything away from you, and you don't even get an "I'm sorry" or anything. Just stay humble no matter how much you make.

Take money out of your trading systems and only leave what is needed to execute your strategies. Always take some off the table.

Did you trade AAMRQ two weeks back?

It was a very classic setup for me, and I would have traded it, but I was on vacation. When I got back I looked at, and I was like, "Damn, I would have definitely traded it."

How important is tape reading for your style?

It's very important. I'm very much focused on that and price action, getting a very good sense of what is happening with the stock. There are no two stocks that are equal, which is fascinating. I always viewed stocks like a living organism, which has a heart and rhythm. You need to be able to feel that heartbeat. What is the state of this organism? That's why L2, tape reading, and all of that are the most important tools to get you close to that heartbeat, the state of it. You can look at a chart, but it doesn't get as close as tape reading.

Is that just for OTC stocks, or is it for NASDAQ and NYSE too?

It's for everything.

Do you trade mostly on the OTC or a lot of NASDAQ and NYSE as well?

Sometimes, for some reason, you have some crazy times in the OTCs. You have liquidity flowing into many different kinds of stocks. When there is significant volatility in the OTCs I choose to trade it. I like the price action, the way the pendulum swings. They're dangerous. You have to be right, but to me it's always been fairly easy to pick the bottoms and tops because of the way the Level 2 acts. But when there is no liquidity, I tend to avoid OTCs.

Would you say that you got good by watching markets a lot and remembering situations?

Yes, absolutely. When you trade so many years, and you've seen so many setups, it's like having a small library in your head. The good thing is that when you sit down and look at action in a stock, you don't necessarily feel as if you analyze it. Everything is very mechanical. That's when you've reached the next level of learning. Everything becomes automated, and you don't feel like you're struggling with analysis. Your analysis is very relaxed. It's all the result of having the library and so many experiences, observations, etc. The library increases the ability to identify the ideal setups: the low risk, high probability setups. Those that are golden.

Did you have a mentor, or did you learn everything by yourself?

I never had a mentor. I never read books about it. I always thought that I could do this by myself. When I found a system in the Danish stocks, I went with that system. Then I had theories on how I could I improve, various ideas. The same goes for the way I day trade US markets.

I didn't want to mess with my pretty clear picture of the markets by taking on indicators and analysis from others. I still want to continue to refine what I feel is *my* truth about the markets. How *I* can make money. I've always been afraid of taking on many indicators. At some point, when you respect the indicators too much, you have too much contradictory information. Then you'll be paralyzed by your analysis and you won't be able to act. I've only read books like *Reminiscences of a Stock Operator* and Jack Schwager's interviews with top traders.

A lot of traders say the markets are difficult now, but in 2013 you had your best year ever. What do you attribute that to?

To a great extent this is due to the success in those two particular stocks. If you take those two stocks out and just look at all other stocks combined, I made about $400,000. In total around $1.5 million, so yeah, this year has been good, and I say that there are two elements to it. For one I'm very relaxed. I'm more relaxed than ever. I'm more patient than ever. This year I've made fewer mistakes than ever before. At the same time, I'm not as trigger-happy. I'm sitting on my hands in a way that I've never done before. For instance, if I see a stock that just keeps rising, and I know that I want to short it, I'm better than ever now at just waiting for the right moment. If I miss out on the really big spike, I don't really care. I'll wait, and I'll hit it in the sideways action instead of hitting it in the high-risk parabolic move. That's when you have those days where you can lose a lot. If you time the parabolic wrong, you can get forced out at really bad prices.

I'm more patient than ever, and that means I don't take many losses. When you don't take many losses, you will be surprised at your results. It doesn't really feel like you have to have that many good trades before you make a lot of money. I've always taken lots of losses, and then I had to make up for those losses. At the end of the year you can look back and say, "Hey, I made a lot this year." But then you look at how much you've lost along the way. If you could cut just half of what you lost, then you could make extreme amounts of money. That's my focus right now. Be more patient, take fewer losses.

Would you say that your approach right now is to do fewer but bigger trades when the right setups come along?

Yeah, I think you're right about that. It needs to feel safe to increase size. I'm trying to cut down on the number of trades, to be better at timing things. More patient. Then hit it with large size.

What are your thoughts on HFTs. Do they hurt you?

They definitely have cut some areas of activity. I only trade stocks that have thick layers and thin spreads, like 1-cent spreads. You see that in low priced stocks, like $3 to $7 a share typically. In a higher priced stock, you would see that in Gold ETFs, but I like trading $5 stocks in which there's huge liquidity, thick bids and offers. The thing with these HFTs is that they're faster than you. Let's say you need to make 1 cent to cover your costs of entry and exit. You'll probably lose at least 1 more cent from the HFTs, as they're faster than you. You used to have to make 2 cents to profit. Now you have to make at least 3 cents. You have to be even more secure. When you enter the trade, you need to have the right timing, because you need to make 1 or 2 cents more per trade. That's why I've cut lots of that scalping activity. The risk/reward is not good anymore.

In those thick (lots of liquidity), low-priced stocks, do you wait for the right daily chart setup and news, and then you jump in?

Actually, I don't care about news. I would like to know what is moving a stock so I can know the context, but the interpretation of the news I don't care about, because the whole market is the result of accumulated interpretations. No matter what my opinion is, I just need to look at what the market feels about the news. When I look at these stocks, I look at the correlation to the Dow Jones, S&P500, or gold. Then I look at the L2. If that looks good, I'll trade combined with a short-term bias of the S&P500 or gold. When it aligns, then you have a good setup. I also never show my real size when sending orders.

Do you use stuff like hidden orders or icebergs?

I don't do hidden. I use iceberg. When I sell a stock, I will never, ever show my real size.

Are some ECNs better than others?

I usually do ARCA. The fees aren't cheap, but relative to others it's fair enough. You get a rebate if you're hit. ARCA seems to be working very well for me. I use Interactive Brokers (IB) along with some other brokers. At IB I also use their SMART router for some orders.

You mentioned that you have many different strategies. Do you have one for trend following, one for reversals, etc.? Do you have many different sorts of biases in these strategies?

Trend following is actually one that I do very seldom. Generally, I'm a pessimist. If a stock has a nice trend upward, I can't put my money on a bet that it will continue higher. The same applies to something that has been beaten down. I would wait for a contrarian move rather than try to participate in the trend. I don't do trend following, even though I feel it's potentially very profitable. I do shakes and bounces, mainly in momentum stocks.

Sometimes I play some momentum stocks that are in an intermediate top intraday. They form a base, and because they're like this living organism, they can't simply stay in the same level for the rest of the day. They give a cue that they'll go up or down, and you have to follow that cue. Sometimes I play breakouts. If I feel that the support is there and buy orders are imminent, I just remove everything in the book, assuming there's not too much out there and there will be some follow-through. I can easily be the one guy who takes the step and removes everything, and then others can follow. You need to be able to time it well, because if you buy everything and there's no follow-through, you'll have a problem.

In general, I like overextended stocks in both ways. I like sideways action too. If there's a fairly tight range for a number of days, I try to get a feeling on the stock, because I know that at some point it has to make a directional move. You need patience with that. Sometimes it takes weeks or even months. I'm often the one who starts removing either support or resistance in a stock that has traded sideways for a while. At that point, I can be quite aggressive. I like playing lagging stocks too. You just need to be familiar with a lot of stocks and be able to sniff out what is going on.

I also do "magnet play" to round numbers as well as breakouts through such levels. It's a very basic psychological human thing. People love round numbers. I love that they love them, because if you have the right timing, you can play the breaks and typically get some follow-through, and you can dump everything at 10, 20, or 40 cents higher or whatever.

These breakouts to round numbers, do you have a software that alerts you it's about to happen, or is it just in the stocks you follow?

Just in the stocks I follow.

How many stocks do you follow?

Typically, in my system it will be two hundred at a time, and that changes on a daily basis. The stocks that are no longer interesting are removed. Early on it was four hundred, but I changed to two hundred. In addition to that, I do some scanning for volatility and momentum. If you find a stock that has momentum, there are some reliable setups that you can trade there. When that momentum disappears, it's not necessarily thrown out. It can be sideways for weeks, and there are some setups on sideways action as well. That's why I like to have many different ways to profit. Many traders would say they're momentum traders, and they just stick with that. I used to do that but no longer. I also like blue sky breakouts.

What do you mean by blue sky?

Blue sky is like when a stock reaches its highest level ever, or a level it hasn't seen in a long, long while. This means that everybody is watching closely, especially the shorts. If you have a stock that's close to the blue sky breakout, then you have some real potential. If it's rejected because of the resistance of the former high, then you can play it short instead.

I also like red to green, green to red moves. If a momentum stock has been red all day but has been slowly rising and going toward the green, you can buy and ride them a bit. You also have that reverse setup on the short side with green to red moves. A stock turning red is a cue for many people to sell it, and if you call such a move early, it may make for a good short. Again, this is for stocks with momentum, otherwise you don't have as many eyes following these signals.

I also have the preplay approach. Sometimes you look at stocks and you feel that something is brewing there, especially in the smaller stocks. It's not a scanner. I have always been good at sniffing out when there's something about to happen. You need to look for slow accumulation in some stocks, and you have to be part of that accumulation just before it makes a good move.

The preplay stuff, is that for subpenny or one-penny stocks that start to go to two, three, and four?

Yeah, some are 2 to 3 cent stocks. Some are 10 cents, but I'm not so interested in them anymore.

Usually OTC stocks?

Mostly, but sometimes AMEX, NYSE, and NASDAQ too.

How important is the daily chart for your approach?

The daily is something that I use for context. When I get a stock I think is interesting, I take a look at the daily, then I get the overall feel for where the stock is.

Do you avoid stocks like AAPL, AMZN because of the spread?

Yeah, I don't like to trade those. Ever since I started, in '97, it was natural to me to avoid the largest stocks. It wasn't really all that interesting to me. I always focused on small and medium size stocks.

Would you say that your approach is about finding key points and predicting human psychology there?

Human psychology is deeply embedded in everything that happens, so yeah, it's a major part of activity.

It's not everything that you do? It's just one part of the puzzle?

Yes, the beauty surrounding chart reading is that history has a nice way of repeating itself. This is due to human psychology, but there's also the L2, the manipulation there. You can't look at the chart and say, "It's overextended, oversold, so it should bounce." It's more complicated than that. It's the game of manipulation, with many factors that all come together, but to a large extent it has to do with what people believe right now. So you're trying to predict how that will change in seconds, minutes, hours, etc.

In terms of discipline, were you always disciplined from the start, or did you have to build that up?

I was almost always very disciplined. When I was not, that's when I lost the most, and I knew that was the reason. One thing I always have been extremely disciplined in is taking my losses. I'm blessed with having no problems taking a loss. Most people have a hard time with that. For some reason I always knew that if I was to survive in trading, I needed to take my losses. I could also see that I was mentally able to do it as well. It's absolutely necessary. I view that as the single most important thing. My rule has always been: seek protection before you seek profit.

A recent example of protecting against losses is a fat finger error I did, selling short 650,000 FNMA shares at $2.48. For some reason I mistakenly hit the "submit order" button instead of the "cancel order" button. The order was absorbed right away, meaning that the stock had underlying strength. Even if it hurt, within just fifteen seconds I was covering the whole position, taking all the shares I could get, resulting in a $6,000 loss. Five minutes later, the stock was 8 cents higher than my cover, which would have meant an additional $11,600 loss had I not covered right away. Most people would hesitate to take an immediate loss of $6,000 based on a fat finger mistake, but my conclusion was clear, and when the conclusion is clear, you don't have an argument for hesitation.

Which software do you use for your trading?

I use three different brokers, but I only use one information system.

So you have one just for the charts and other data and the others for entering orders?

Yeah, the one with the charts and data can also take orders, but the others are only for orders and trading.

Which one is it?

It's integrated in one of the trading platforms offered by a small New York broker called Track Data Securities. Not many are acquainted with them. I like their system and their AIQ charts. They have lots of indicators, but I never use them. I have my own way of doing chart reading, without the use of indicators.

You mentioned that you went on vacation after your big win. How important for you is to take breaks, vacations, and things like that?

Actually, I have never been good at vacationing and taking breaks. Because of my discipline, I always felt I should never allow myself too much freedom, because of some goals that I want to achieve. About six years ago, I started to allow myself to travel more. I usually travel two to three months every year. Sometimes I trade and travel as well. Now I'm thirty-five and have made nearly $4.5 million. As I've gotten older and felt privileged to have made quite a bit of money, I've allowed myself the privilege of traveling more.

When you travel and trade with a laptop, what kinds of adjustments do you make?

The screen real estate shrinks a fair amount, so I set up the software in a different way, but the main problem is being in sketchy places without a backup Internet connection. If the connection is lost, you don't want to get caught in a big position.

In these situations, I'm cautious about size, and I take trades that I don't have to hold the whole day or for the next day. I prefer to do trades that I hold for seconds, maybe minutes. I will take positions that I have to hold for hours if they're potentially very profitable, but I prefer not to.

When you're trading in your house, what kind of computer do you have?

In recent years, the computer chips have become so super powerful that even a laptop will have sufficient processing power. I like the freedom of a laptop. I also have two external monitors.

I don't have a huge setup. My strategy doesn't demand six or eight screens. I have always tried to keep things as simple as I can without compromising the efficiency of my strategy. I just have one high resolution laptop and two large external screens. Typically, I don't need more than that. In that setup I can see what I need, which is eight L2 windows and four order books, like ARCA, NSDQ, and so forth, to see the extra depth of those books. I don't need ten or twenty charts.

So even though you're following two hundred stocks, you only have a handful that you're paying attention to on a given day?

The thing is, I can see the L1, volume, price change, etc. Just by switching pages I can see forty stocks at a time. I don't look at the two hundred all the time, just the ones that qualify. The most important thing is for them to qualify to be in the 8 L2 windows. The four most important ones I'll put in the windows with the extra-depth books.

When you're flipping pages and looking at forty stocks at a time, you're looking to see big moves, big volumes, that kind of thing?

The main thing is the price change and the volume. I usually can sense when the volume is higher than what it usually is. I also build in some scans in all the two hundred stocks I follow, so I know if there's something unusual going on. I also do some market-wide scans.

The money you take out from trading, do you just keep it in the bank, or do you buy stocks, bonds, etc.?

I don't run risk with what I take out. I always viewed the market as a dangerous place to be. So with my trading capital in a dangerous place, I need to know that the rest is at zero to little risk. I don't own one single stock, not even bonds. I only have cash and a couple of real estate properties. I need the feeling that this is secure in order to be able to fully focus on trading in the risk zone.

When you're going to make a trade, how do you decide how much to bet? Do you use a mathematical algorithm, or is it just a feeling?

It's just a feeling. It depends on liquidity. You need to know when you're pushing the limit with regard to your exit. Sometimes you can easily buy a lot of stock, but it's not the right thing to do. The stock has to be liquid enough to absorb your exit. It's always a matter of liquidity.

When FNMA and FMCC were trading hot, you could easily buy 200,000. I bought about 600,000 shares in March and sold it way too early. The stock easily would absorb that. Buying 600,000 right now would be suicidal.

What kind of advice do you give to traders that are starting out or are trying to get better right now?

First, focus on protecting yourself before seeking profit. It's a typical mistake not to do that. People come to the market wanting to make money fast, so they focus on the opportunities, and then they get killed because they are wrong and don't know how to exit. They need defined exits and clear stop-loss strategies. They need to learn that opportunities will always come. They need to focus on living to fight another day.

Also, a new trader needs to focus on developing a tight relationship with the market in the particular stocks that they want to trade. You want to feel the heartbeat of the stock so you're much more likely to be able to assess what's going on. You need to dive into the tape, L2, understand the mechanics behind it. It's a process, a journey.

They need to watch the markets to develop an instinct, a feeling of how things will move?

Yes.

Do you do any backtesting at all?

Everything I do is inherently a backtest in the sense that I always evaluate what I do. When I tweak, modify something or do something new, I move slowly. I try to feel how it works on a smaller scale. It's not simulated trading. It's with real money. I never had a system that I only tested on a theoretical basis. Everything was trial and error with real money. You will always get a better feel with real money, because that's when it hurts. You get a sense of what you're doing because you know it hurts. It's practice, not theory.

It's backtested, but it's in your head?

Everything is in my head.

Would you say that your secret is your observational skill combined with your discipline to take losses?

Absolutely. It's all about instincts, charts, and a history of observations. Between chart reading and instinct, I would say 60 to 70 percent is instinct. It has always been like that. The beautiful thing is that technology gives us great tools. For instance, the order book is a tool, the chart is a tool, and so forth, and the tools can help confirm the hypothesis that your instinct provides. It's a very nice combination.

Does it concern you that HFTs are becoming more present in the markets and some opportunities are being closed by these computers?

Yes and no. It's always a concern if your profits get squeezed in some areas of activity, but in many stocks you don't have that many HFTs, or they don't affect you that much. Lots of traders got hurt because they got squeezed out of the particular stock group they traded. I always traded a wide variety of stocks and strategies.

I also trade stocks that are slightly illiquid, not too illiquid, usually above $10. You can swing plays in them and hold for a few days. You'll capture the order flow movement that the HFTs can't control.

What kind of Internet speed do you have in your country?

I think it goes as high as 50 to 100MB. I have 20MB, but it seems to have a similar response delay as that of 5MB.

Now that you're trading less, doing bigger positions, and having more patience, do you think the tendency for you is to become a swing trader at some point?

I have been thinking about it. After thirteen years, I'm considering setups in which I can extend my time horizon. I tried to do that in 2000 and I failed, losing more than ever before. Now I'm considering it again, but I'm moving slowly with it because of my past experience. In an ideal world, I would convert to swing trading at this point in time.

Lessons from Chapter 5

1. Experience is king. Flemming was able to make huge bets in FNMA and FMCC because he had seen those patterns before. He had stored in his head the way those moves play out when he watched them in other stocks. If you're starting out, realize how important it is to accumulate information about charts, situations, patterns, etc. Don't try to go for a big trade if you're not feeling confident about it.

In Chapter 15, in the section titled "How to Best Accumulate Market Knowledge become a Student of Price Action and Market Situations," I describe my favorite way to speed up the information accumulation process and develop a mental library of market situations.

2. Have the courage to bet big. If you've seen the situation before and you know what the course of action is, don't be too afraid of making a big bet. The thing to keep in mind is that in an HFT world there are fewer opportunities to make consistent money every day, but there are still plenty of opportunities to make big money every once in a while, when the right setup comes along. Days like the flash crash, Knight Capital, some Fed announcements, FNMA, and FMCC are days on which, if you have courage, you can make your entire year.

3. In ideal setups, **it's very important to be mentally strong**. Flemming says he was more secure in May making bigger bets than in March with smaller bets while trading FMCC. It's very important not to ruin a good setup by weakening yourself psychologically by accumulating losses immediately prior to the big play. You have to be patient, even risk being a little late. If the setup is good and the move will be big, there's plenty of time to get in. What you can't afford is to be upset by losses then play a fraction of your normal size when the move finally occurs.

4. Don't be afraid of being the one who takes the first action. Flemming mentions being the one who took the ARCA displayed liquidity on FMCC. That made the L2 look bullish to everybody watching the stock and sent the signal to other people that the stock would bounce. He also talks about playing round-number breakouts in listed stocks and being the one who makes the first move and takes out the ask, as well as often being the first to remove support or resistance orders after periods of sideways action. If you trust the situation, don't be afraid of being the one who makes the first move.

5. Seek protection before profit. He says his ability to take losses is his most important trait. While it's great to have the courage to go for it and take chances, you always have to keep in mind that even the best setups may fail. If you have problems taking losses, realize that you have to work on it. Your survival and profitability as a trader will depend on it.

6. Addition by the lack of subtraction. Decrease the amount of losses you have. Flemming talks about how your year-end results can be improved significantly by simply focusing on cutting down the amount of losses you have. This will also improve your mental clarity, given that losses can be debilitating. How exactly can you decrease the amount of losses you have if you don't know if a trade will work out or not? That's when lesson seven comes in.

7. Focus on the best setups—ideally, what Flemming calls "low risk, high probability" setups. By only taking what you would consider the best setups, you can be sure that your ratio of dollar return to time invested in trading will be very high. If you're new and don't have a lot of trading experience, it can be detrimental to only take great setups, because then you don't accumulate market knowledge and learn from different situations. If that's your case, you're probably better off only **playing with very small size in many different situations**. Save the bigger bets for situations in which you're familiar and have seen the results before. If you're already experienced, consider improving your results by playing less frequently but playing bigger when you do. The good news is that this style leaves you with more free time to travel and enjoy the money you make.

8. Develop a tight relationship with the market. Get to the heart and rhythm of the stock. Flemming talks about stocks being like living organisms that have heartbeats. Your job is to use tools, like the chart, L2, order books, tape, etc., to get a read on those heartbeats so you can make a tradable call. You can develop this relationship by watching stocks very closely. They have to be stocks that are "alive," meaning they're momentum stocks, stocks with news, etc. If you watch some illiquid HFT-driven stocks, you're just seeing the result of random action, and you won't learn much.

9. Avoid HFT games by playing lower-priced stocks with thick layers (lots of volume on the bid and ask). Numerous NASDAQ and NYSE low-priced stocks have a lot of volume with plenty of liquidity on both sides of the L2. From time to time, they're also in play with news and catalysts, so they can make some nice moves. The spread is less of a factor in these stocks so the "HFT tax" is smaller as a percentage of the move that you are trying to capture.

10. Watch out for limiting beliefs. If you think markets are terrible and there are no opportunities, you might end up missing some huge days that become available every once in a while. It's true that HFTs have decreased the consistency of day trading, but if you're always on the watch out for those special days—and don't worry, they'll come—you can capitalize on them big time. Flemming had his best year ever by May, being up more than $1 million at that point, even though markets were supposed to be bad.

11. Your instincts drive a hypothesis that you can confirm using trading tools. When you accumulate a lot of price action knowledge, you'll develop a feeling when things are about to happen. You can't merely trust the feelings blindly, but you can construct a hypothesis that you seek to confirm via tools such as the L2, chart, order book, ticker tape, etc.

12. The power of ARCA. In listed stocks, ARCA balances out with good execution, rebates, and liquidity. ARCA also allows you to place iceberg orders, which are important when using limit orders. Never show your hand if you have significant size.

13. Order books as an additional tool for developing a read in a stock. Most people have the L2 in their platforms, but not all have depth of the book from sources like ARCA or NSDQ, because they come with a cost, and many believe that L2 is sufficient. In the L2 you only see the best price from any given ECN or exchange. By diving deeper into the depth of the book, you can get a sense of the overall supply and demand of that exchange or ECN. This can provide you with additional information that might tell you if a stock has true support, or if a stock will break out or fail to break out. Because there are fewer people looking at that data, there is potential for an edge there.

14. The power of focusing on one stock only. When FNMA/FMCC are in play, Flemming doesn't trade anything else. He focuses 100 percent on those stocks. That's what enables him not to miss critical turns and to make huge bets. If you try to watch other stocks, you might make an additional $500 to $1,000 in them but miss a $10,000 profit in the stock in play.

15. Price action is more important than crunching numbers and reading reports. The market price already expresses the collective opinion of people that are processing the fundamental data. If you pay attention to price action, you don't necessarily have to know the data behind it.

16. "It needs to feel safe to increase size." When pushing yourself to bet bigger, remember that it needs to be a solid setup with plenty of liquidity, otherwise you might find yourself caught with a big position and not know how to get out.

The decision to go bigger should be based on technical and logical factors, not on gambling urges or the fact that your results have been hot lately.

Chapter 6

Dennis Dick—The Base Hit Trader

I first heard about Dennis Dick (Twitter @TripleDTrader) when I contacted Don Bright (one of the founders of Bright Trading, LLC, a professional stock trading firm) to ask him for an interview with one of his top traders. He sent me Dennis' e-mail address, along with his SEC testimony for the Commission's Concept Release on Equity Market Structure, which I immediately read.[10]

What struck me about that testimony is how well he explained issues like informed order flow, internalization, and how subpenny trades lead to situations where limit orders sitting on the order books tend to be filled when they're wrong (in the short-term) and not filled when they're right. This was exactly the experience I had while doing day trading on my own, but I was simply not aware of what was going on. That testimony opened my eyes and made me realize that things were not as simple as the older trading books could lead one to think. (Most of the older books say people who blame the markets for losses are just making excuses. It might be true in a lot of situations, but in an HFT world it's less true than you would expect.)

What also caught my attention about him was that he's the exact opposite of the big-ego Wall Street trader. I found him quite friendly and humble about trading and his experiences. Of course, everybody has a little bit of an ego, but Dennis is the type of guy you would want to have a beer with after a long trading day.

He exemplifies a principle that I heard a long time ago, with which I agree wholeheartedly: "If you can't explain something to a ten-year-old, then you don't understand it." He's not the type of guy who will get all fancy with indicators or algorithms. He tries to make trading as simple as possible, probably because it leads to lower stress and it fits his easygoing nature. (This might be true for his hedging tactics that you will read about in the interview.)

He's the type of trader who rarely goes for big gains. This limits his losses dramatically and makes his results "shockingly consistent" on a week-to-week basis, as he says. For those who are familiar with the book *Moneyball* by Michael Lewis, Dennis would be like the hitter Jason Giambi, a player that is very consistent

[10] http://tinyurl.com/o652gh6

at getting singles and is known for his plate discipline and high on-base percentage. Sure, he might not get big scores all the time, but he'll grind out his profit in a low-stress fashion.

He also hosts a free Benzinga Internet radio show called "Premarket Prep" along with his friend Joel Elconin. Every morning before the market opens, they go through the major news pieces of the day, stocks that are moving, key support and resistance levels, market structure lessons, trading tips, etc.

This interview was conducted in August of 2012 and updated in November of 2013

What initially made you want to become a trader?

I started trading back in university. My dad and uncle had some money invested in some stocks, and I was helping to manage their money a little bit. This was from 1996 to 1998, in the bull market. I think by pure luck I did well, because everything went up back then, but looking back now, I see that I probably didn't know what I was doing. In those markets, everything seemed to be rising no matter what you bought. I can remember buying Amazon at $100 and selling at $130 a week later. It was just a crazy tech bubble back then. I was pretty much hooked on trading at that point. I graduated in 1999 and knew that I wanted to trade. I had a friend that was trading with Bright Trading in Detroit. I went over there and checked it out, met the trading supervisor, Joel Elconin, and opened my account the next week. The first few months, I struggled, but that was part of the learning curve. After a while, I started to become consistent.

What do you think was the difference that enabled you to get better?

I think it was just learning the basics. Learning what works and what doesn't work. I started in May of 1999, and in the first few months I was kind of all over the place. I actually remember that in my first week I got lucky and made money. But in the second week I got killed. I had seventeen or eighteen losing trades in a row, and I was thinking, man, I suck at this. But I was trading small. I was only trading 100 share lots, so when I lost on that many trades in a row, I was only losing $150 or $200. I wasn't really getting slaughtered and that's what Bright had taught me: start with 100 shares, learn how to trade, and slowly bring in size when you start to become consistent. The key factor that made me turn the corner was discipline. Learning to cut your losers and hold onto your winners a little bit longer.

But was your overall edge something they provided you or something you learned on your own?

A lot of stuff came from myself. We did a lot of filter trading back then, where we would have filters searching through the market for certain criteria. I started doing a lot of market making too, basically trading to scalp the spread. We traded in 1/16 fractions back then. I remember trading Lucent Technologies. I would be sitting on the bid and sitting on the offer trying to make the spread. As opposed to making market calls, we were just making markets, trying to capture the bid-ask spread. Obviously, that game doesn't work well anymore, but back then it worked for a number of years. I can remember trading Lucent almost exclusively in the year 2000. The stock was bouncing around, and I was just capturing the spread.

You didn't have much of a directional bias?

We listened to Ben Lichtenstein on Traders Audio and we would get a feel for the market. You would see the S&P500 start to take off, and back then we were pretty quick. If the market started to take off, we would start grabbing stocks in the S&P500. So you would grab GE, Lucent, IBM, and they would start to take off too. There was a lag of a few seconds back then between the equities and the futures, and it was just enough time to profit. It wasn't instant execution on the NYSE. You had to send your order to the specialist on the floor and the order execution time was as much as eight seconds. If you went to Instinet or another ECN you could get an instant execution, but at that time even the market makers had around fifteen seconds to respond to your order.

You have a CFA charter, right?

Yes, I do. I got it in 2002.

Did it help?

With overall market structure understanding, yes, I would say so. But do you need a CFA charter to be successful in trading? I don't think so. It doesn't hurt. I think it gives me a good understanding of the overall picture, like who's on the other side of my trades. A CFA charterholder can paint the big picture of how everything works. Institutions with a longer-term horizon seeking liquidity, with short-term traders providing that liquidity. I think it's an asset, but I don't think it's a necessity.

So you were trading that market making strategy for a number of years. When did you notice that things started to change and some inefficiencies started to go away?

I can take you back to the root of when everything started to change, which would be in 2001 with decimalization. That's what changed everything, because with fractions market makers would make $1/16^{th}$ of a point. Then, all of a sudden the spreads tightened up, which put a lot of human market makers out of business, and that's what led to the rise of the machines. There were some HFTs before that, however, that was when the pendulum swung, so to speak, where the machines started to dominate the humans. It didn't start immediately, but if you wanted to pinpoint where it started, it was with decimalization.

So the market maker's edge started to dry up after that?

Yes, because a computer is much more efficient at market making, as they can adjust quotes faster and get to the top of the order queue. Before Reg NMS you would have computers that would step in front of your order not by a penny but sometimes by a subpenny. Eventually the SEC, under Reg NMS, enacted rule 612, which banned subpenny trading on the exchanges, but these days we still see subpenny trades away from the exchanges. Once the spreads tightened up, the computers were probably more efficient at doing it, but we still did well. We would still make markets. The market makers on the floor probably suffered more once we got to decimals, because of this battle to be at the top of the order queue, and computers can be very efficient at doing this.

Did you use the opening trading strategy that Bright is known for?

Yes, and I still do some of that. In 2000, 2001, and 2002 it worked very well. The basic strategy is just to provide liquidity into an opening imbalance of a NYSE stock during the opening print. You would be trading on the same side as the specialist. Now they're called designated market makers, DMMs. You would basically provide liquidity to a stock that was opening below fair value. A simple way to calculate that would be if the market was going to open down 1 percent[11], a stock that has a beta of 1 would typically open down 1 percent, all other things being equal, meaning there's no news on that stock. If the stock were to open down 1.5 percent, we would possibly buy it, and vice versa. If the stock was opening down only 0.25 percent, we would short it. It worked quite well for a number of years, but I think over the last few years the strategy has got crowded. There are too many participants playing that strategy, and all of a sudden, when they need to hit the exits, the liquidity isn't there for them.

I noticed that sometimes with this strategy when you get filled, you don't want that fill, as the stock just keeps going in the wrong direction.

It's a crowded issue, for sure. I think Bright was one of the first firms to focus on this strategy, but now it's being done by a number of firms. HFTs do this strategy as well. When you get everybody on one side of the trade like that, it can lead to

---

[11] This can be inferred by looking at the S&P500 futures.

shakeouts. I did a video on IBM yesterday, and it's on YouTube[12]. It talked about the shakeout that IBM had yesterday at the open. When you get too many short-term traders on the same side of the trade, they start to look for liquidity and bids. If the bids aren't there, then they start to hit whatever bids they can find, and that can start a shakeout. This gets a lot of traders scared. Eventually, they sell their stock and the stock just continues to go down.

You never really want to be on the same side as all the short-term traders if you can avoid it, because it usually goes the other way. That's probably what a lot of my trading is based on: identifying which side what I call "the trading herd" is on, and trying to go the opposite way.

Is the opening strategy still profitable?

I would say it cycles. I've been saying this for a number of years. It will be good for a while, then everybody catches on and thinks it's working again. Then everybody goes back to trying it, and the strategy gets crowded and stops working. As it stops working, and people stop doing the strategy, then it gets less crowded and starts working again. It keeps going from working to not working. In the last couple months, it hasn't been working well. If you look over the last number of years, it has cycled a lot. Because of this tendency to cycle, I never stop doing the strategy, but when it's not working I decrease my size so I don't lose very much. That's a way of monitoring it. If I were to do well with it again, then I would increase my size. Instead of stopping the strategy, I would rather change my size.

It seems that Don Bright doesn't use stop losses in the opening strategy but just profit-taking exits. Is that something you do?

Don automates in and automates out. I automate in on this strategy because it would be cumbersome or impossible to send hundreds of OPG orders manually. I know a lot of people (like Don) automate out too. I don't. I manually trade out of my opening positions. These days we have so much more information than we used to. We have the continuous book price that tells us where the stock is about to open, so we can tell which stocks we're going to get filled on. If I'm going to get filled in all the longs, I would quickly hedge it with SPY or something. I do a lot of hedging tactics off the open to eliminate market risk. The whole point to the strategy is to capture the trading anomaly of a stock opening too high or too low relative to its fair value. If I get filled on a bunch of longs, and the market starts to tank, I'm going to lose on all of those positions. But if I hedge out the market risk, I can still make

---

[12] "IBM Shake-out" by premarketinfo. http://tinyurl.com/p39bbop

money on those positions, even if the market tanks. This allows me to stay in the trade longer.

Right off the bat, there's often a shakeout, because the trade is crowded. If you can hold through the initial shakeout, the stocks will often come back to their fair value. That's where hedging helps me. It can keep me in the trade. You would probably be better if you walked away from your computer for thirty minutes once you're hedged, and then you wouldn't have to have the stress of holding through the opening shakeout. I never do that, but I wish I could. It's also loser management. When you get filled on twenty or thirty stocks off the open, there are going to be winners and losers. The key is to work out of those losers as best you can and try to let the winners run.

Cutting down size a little bit?

Yes, maybe selling half or maybe hedge with something. That's kind of what this job is, to minimize damage as much as possible. If you have a bunch of bad trades it can ruin your week or your month. That's what I've been good at, minimizing damage so I don't have the losers that can destroy my week or my month.

Is that how you deal with your other strategies as well?

Yes. In thirteen years of trading, I've probably been through hundreds of strategies. It's funny, a strategy that hasn't worked in years can all of a sudden start working again. So I try to monitor them. But it's all feel for me too. I watch the technical aspect very closely and would consider myself to be a technical trader, but there are intangibles as well. On my online radio show, "Premarket Prep," I talk about technical issues all the time. However, I do trade a lot on feel. I can feel whether the market's been really holding up well or it's starting to turn, and that's a hard thing to teach. You need a lot of screen time. Sitting there and being able to feel the market, feel the turns, and being able to feel that the trading herd is short is a huge asset. For example, a few days ago when we had a vicious short squeeze in the market, we had a gap up the next day. I could feel that the trading herd was really caught short. It was predictable that it was probably going to continue to rally, at least until we had some macro or fundamental news knock the market back down.

Do you think intuition can be an edge because it sometimes can involve inputs that can't be computerized and backtested so easily, so it's not as easily exploited?

I would say that backtesting is good to find an idea that has worked in the past. I don't do a lot of backtesting with my overall strategies. I just play around. I'm always researching and developing new strategies. I always have a strategy that seems to work, and that's where I make my money, but I'm always playing around and doing things differently. I'll try some new strategies with small size to see if they work. If I find something that clicks, I start to increase my size. I'm not a big fan of backtesting, but I'm a big fan of research and development. I think you have to always be researching new strategies, especially in these markets, because there's always new stuff that seems to start to work.

The key to being successful in an HFT world is to stay ahead of the bots. The machines are just doing what they're programmed to do. When there's some type of new strategy, it takes some time for them to find out. Then they have to give it out to their programmer, and then they have to build it, replicate it, and backtest it. This takes time, sometimes a couple of weeks or even longer. You could be exploiting this strategy for a few weeks with no HFT competing with you until they can deploy the whole thing and be ready to go. Now they're much quicker at this than they used to be. Years ago, a good strategy would last six months to a year. Now it seems that a good strategy lasts only a few weeks, because the HFTs will figure out that its working and exploit it. So you have to be doing even more research to stay profitable.

After decimalization and before Reg NMS, what were your main strategies?

I don't want to get too specific, but I can give you an overall idea. There was the opening strategy that we talked about before, we were doing…

Pair trading?

Yes, we were doing some of that. I would do different arbitrage type strategies. For example, I used to do share-class arbitrage in Viacom. I would arb the Viacom A class shares versus the B class shares. I did that in 2003 and 2004 almost exclusively. Those two stocks would just track each other very closely, because it was the same company. I would just try to scalp a few cents by being on the bid and being on the offer. I think at one point, I was doing 7 to 8 percent of the volume on the class A stock, which was the illiquid one. The B shares were much more liquid. If the B shares were rising, I would just try to get long the A shares or vice versa. I could make markets on the A shares and then quickly hedge with the B shares. But these days the HFTs are all over this strategy. They've written programs to do exactly what I was doing. You don't stand a chance in trying to do that now, at least manually.

You would frequently hedge out your exposure?

Yes, you always put the hard side on first. That's something that goes back to the basics of trading. Put the hard side on, and then take the easy side. The B shares had a 1 cent spread, while the A shares would have a 10 cent spread. I would just pick up the A then hedge out and make 6 to 7 cents all day. If I had to carry it overnight, it didn't matter, because it was the same company, so company-specific risk was out the door. There were a few other stocks with dual classes as well, some more illiquid ones, but that was the main one that I focused on.

Then Reg NMS hit. How did that immediately impact you?

I don't think it affected the market until a couple years later. I think what started to happen, especially in the last two or three years when things got more difficult, was that most retail orders that used to interact with our orders were now entirely intercepted (100 percent) by the internalizers. If I'm getting too deep here let me know, but they're called OTC market makers and they basically intercept any retail order flow so we don't get to interact with retail flow anymore. By retail flow, I mean, for example, the TD Ameritrade traders, the guys sitting in their basements, etc.

For the most part, retail flow is more uninformed with less market knowledge. Now, there are good retail traders too, don't get me wrong, but with all things being equal, the average retail trader won't be as good as the average proprietary trader, because most of these people have day jobs. They're kind of doing this on the side. Their order flow is attractive to trade against. What we see is that the retail brokerages sell their order flow, it's called payment for order flow, to OTC market makers, where they have the first chance of trading against those orders. What happens on the exchanges is that when you place your limit order, it often doesn't get filled. You'll see these subpenny prints going off in front of your order. You'll have trouble getting filled on the bid or the offer because the order of the person who was trying to hit your bid was intercepted and traded against off exchange.

I read your report to the SEC and thought it was very interesting. Do you think that with this subpennying going all around, sometimes it's just better to use a market order and take liquidity?

I would never advise using market orders. I hate using market orders, because it's just a blank check. It's such a fast trading world right now, and I believe that some HFT participants can see your market order coming down the pipe, especially if your order is pinging multiple destinations. If they're on the offer, they'll move the offer back as far as they can to extract as much value from that order as they possibly can. I would rather use a marketable limit order. For example, if the offer was at $94.50 and I really wanted to own a stock, I would maybe put a $94.55 limit or something like that. I'd probably get filled at the $94.50 offer, but if the price changes rapidly, I'm not going to get filled at something crazy like $95. I hate using flat out market orders, because the market moves so quickly right now that you can get some really bad fills. I don't like using standing limit orders either, so I usually just take liquidity. Most of the time, I just take the offer or hit the bid. If you're trading illiquid stocks, that doesn't work as well. You don't want to be paying big spreads, but if you're trading stocks like GE or stocks that are relatively thick, I don't mind paying a 1 cent spread to get into the trade.

You see subpenny prints because the internalizers provide subpenny price improvement to the retail orders that they're intercepting. It's their way of justifying the practice. If you ask me, that subpenny price improvement does not justify taking an execution away from a displayed liquidity provider.

What about pricing your limit order aggressively in illiquid stocks but inside the spread?

Sometimes I do that too. It all depends on what stock you're talking about. If you're talking about a stock that has a 25 cent spread, let's say it's bid at $24.25 and the ask is at $24.50. If I bid $24.26, there's an HFT that will automatically step ahead of me at $24.27. If I go $24.28, he will go $24.29. If I go $24.40 he might not go there. So, if I didn't want to pay the offer, I might go $24.40 and see what happens. That is an aggressively priced limit order and can sometimes be a better alternative to lifting the offer.

If you wanted to sell, could you fool these guys by bidding up and getting them in front of you then hitting them with your sale?

Be careful with stuff like that, because it can be considered by the SEC as gaming or spoofing the quote. A rule of thumb is: if you're bidding for something, you actually want to be a buyer of that stock. The SEC is cracking down on anything like that right now. If you're intentionally trying to drive up the bid, trying to get a higher bid just so you can hit it, the SEC will likely have a problem with that. You never want to do anything gray or illegal.

Let's move on to more recent events. How did you do during the flash crash?

It was my best day of the year.

Did you buy during the panic?

Yes, but you know what? It was still hard to buy during the panic, because there were bots that were automatically stepping in front of my order even during the flash crash. I can remember trading stocks where there were no bids. It was a crazy experience. There was literally a vacuum in some stocks. For example, Accenture was bid at $0.01 and offered at $33. If you watch the trades, it was like one trade at 1 cent, then one at $33, and on and on, due to market orders. I wasn't participating in that one. I knew that if you were buying something that low, those buys were going to get busted and the trades wouldn't stand. But I was trading some other stocks, even some preferred stocks. I was making two or three points in some trades because there was nobody providing liquidity. I put out some low bids, and some of that stuff I was still getting subpennied on, but sometimes I did get filled. I did very well that day just by being a human trader, because the HFTs weren't participating as much. I just provided liquidity and really got paid for it.

Weren't you afraid though of accumulating some kind of inventory and facing an '87-type situation where it just goes from -10 percent to -15 percent to -20 percent?

Well, I wasn't putting myself in a situation where my margin would lead to trouble. At Bright Trading, if your account goes red, you're done. I was also hedging with other stocks, doing pair trades on similar stocks in the sector. I wrote an article on ZeroHedge in January of 2010 in which I was predicting that this could happen, so I was somewhat prepared for it. That's probably why this was one of my best trading days. However, I wasn't just randomly buying everything. I was buying something that was getting killed 10 to 20 percent down, but then I would sell short something similar to hedge, so if the market continued to crash, hopefully my hedge would work out and I would be OK.

So it was similar to the old days with the Viacom market making?

Yes, but not on pure plays like that. That was a pure share-class arb. Here it was more like stat arb through pair trading, a calculated risk.

Did you also do well in 2008?

That was my best trading year ever. That was an unbelievable year. In 2007, it was really starting to get good, but 2008 just blew away every one of my other years. We were just doing a bit of market making, providing liquidity. I can remember on the opening strategy and other strategies, everything was working back then. You essentially had institutions throwing out all their stocks, not caring about anything. They just wanted to liquidate. If you ask any trader, 2008 had to be one of their best years, because every strategy that I had was working.

Do you think that short-term trading is naturally long volatility? It sort of wants the bad times to come?

I think short-term traders do better when bad times come for sure. Do we want bad times to come? No. I'm a trader, but I'm also an investor in the market. I have an investment account, managing my own and my wife's money. I obviously don't want to see my investment account be cut in half from a crash or something. But traders definitely do better whenever there's economic uncertainty, because that's when irrational decisions are made by money managers and big money. Like in 2008, institutions were throwing out the baby with the bath water. We would basically find a good stock that was being thrown out and buy it. From a pair trading perspective, you can buy something and short a similar asset, and by the afternoon, or sometimes even within minutes, the price would converge. So yes, short-term traders definitely do better in crisis situations. I think a human trader is really equipped to do well, because there are so many human traders that aren't even in the game anymore. We live in such an automated HFT world, and when those HFTs say, "We don't want to participate," there's way less competition. Back in 2000 and 2001, I was competing with a lot of day traders, short-term market makers, specialists. Now I just compete with HFTs and a few other day traders. Probably 70 to 80 percent of the time, I'm competing with HFTs. If you eliminate four-fifths of your competition during a market impacting event, you're going to do better.

So essentially, during the opening, you had these big funds, hedge funds, and institutions creating distortions due to human emotions and people like you repricing the assets and profiting from it?

This is exactly what happened. You can vilify HFTs, and I sometimes do that myself, but not all HFT is bad. I criticize the predatory aspect of it, like when programs are written to step in front of your order or take advantage of your order. A lot of HFT is just statistical arbitrage where they're taking advantage of inefficiencies like that Viacom class arb that I used to do. There's nothing wrong with that. It keeps the prices in line. You also need market making type participants, and I think that's the problem now, because most of the market makers are HFTs and they don't have any affirmative obligations. When things get tough, they'll press their stop button, and all of a sudden, you'll have a liquidity vacuum where there's really no liquidity available. Any trader sending a market order at that time is going to get a really bad fill.

How much do you think HFTs make from subpennying as a percentage of their revenue?

For the OTC guys, the internalizers, it's a big chunk. It's their bread and butter, but they have a lot of different strategies. Not all HFTs are internalizing orders. I would say there's probably only a handful that are participating in that game. They're basically your big OTC guys like the Knights, Citadels, and UBSs of the world that have that order flow relationship with retail brokerages and have the ability to trade directly against that flow. Those guys make a lot of money by stepping in front of everybody else's limit orders. They're just capturing the spread, but at the expense of whoever's limit order is not getting executed.

But there are a lot of good HFT strategies out there too. The stat arb guys make a lot of their money by keeping prices in line, not engaging in sketchy practices. I think predatory market making has an unfair advantage over other participants, and that practice should be eliminated. I want a level playing field for everyone.

Besides subpennying, do you think they should change other things as well?

I think the structure has become very complicated. If you look back ten years at NYSE stocks, 90 to 95 percent of the volume used to be executed on the NYSE. Now you have thirteen different exchanges, thirty or forty dark pools, and a hundred internalizing broker dealers/HFTs. You have so many different places where your order can get executed. The market is very fragmented, and this fragmentation can lead to confusion, which can lead to problems. I think the market has become way too complicated in this way. I want to see it simplified. I want to see fewer exchanges, fewer dark pools, and more orders in the lit market where there's pretrade transparency, where you can actually see the quote, as opposed to dark trading where many participants are just free riding off the public quotation. I would like to see the market structure get simpler somehow. I don't think it's going to, but in a perfect world, my wish list would include less fragmentation, elimination of subpenny trades, and more transparency in the overall market. I don't like firms getting a sneak peek at orders and then cherry picking which orders they're going to trade against.

Do you think there's an edge in watching subpenny trades in the Level 2?

Yes, and this is something I wrote an article about for *CFA* magazine recently[13]. Tape reading is more important than it ever was before, especially if you're trading illiquid stocks. You can see when the internalizers are subpennying the offer, stepping in front of the offer. Sometimes it's just market making. On a stock like GE, for example, they're just trying to capture the spread, so I don't think it means anything there. But if you get into the small or mid-caps, it can definitely give you an idea of the direction the stock will go. If the internalizers are willing to step in front of that offer, that means the smart money is placing its bets that the stock will go down, so you might want to aggressively sell it or hit the bid knowing that information. I believe tape reading is very important, and the subpenny trades provide valuable information for traders.

Other than that, did your tape-reading skill come from just watching it a lot and getting a feel for things?

Yes, especially if you're trading illiquid stocks. I don't trade as many of those as I used to, but if you're trading them, you can really get a feel from the tape. You can get a feel when these HFTs have caught everybody short and they're going to try to

---

[13] http://tinyurl.com/paxt6xu

pop the stock. You can almost read it on the tape through the size, subpenny printing, etc. If there's an internalizer that's willing to step in front of the bid all day long, that makes me confident that the stock might be going up. It's not a perfect science, but if it goes up 55 to 60 percent of the time, there will be an edge there. I believe there's an edge in figuring out what the smart money is doing.

Do you pay attention to rebates? Do you try to minimize your costs routing orders?

Not as much. Some of the guys at Bright really do. I know Don is a big proponent of really managing those expenses. I used to be a scalper, but now I've lengthened my time horizon, which is important in this HFT world. Scalping strategies have been taken away from us by the HFTs, but they haven't taken away the longer-term stuff. If you can make smart market calls and hold on for a little bit longer, you can do well. In the past, I used to hold some positions for just seconds. Now, I hold positions for minutes, sometimes hours. Rebates were important to me when I was a scalper, but now they're not as important because I hold longer. Some days I used to trade 500,000 shares, now I trade a lot less volume. So I don't mind paying the take fee, up to 3/10ths of a cent, because I'm making more on my average trade. If I was doing scalping-type strategies, I would be more concerned about take fees and rebates. I'm conscious of them though. If I see BX and ARCA offered, I would take BX because I would be paid to take liquidity as opposed to paying for it on ARCA, but I wouldn't say that I'm concerned about it.

Is that lengthening of the time horizon something you see in your profitable trader friends?

Yes, I think so. I used to hang out with a lot of Bright traders, and the ones that remained profitable all lengthened their time horizons. I think we all used to be scalpers for the most part, but now we've had to become what I call intraday traders, where we are making a call on a stock. Before, we were just making markets. Now we just think, "Wow, this is setting up nice. I'm going to get long some stock here." Then we hold it for a while. You also have to be conscious that there's going to be a shakeout. If an HFT thinks you're long, they'll try to shake you out of your position, so it's critical to position yourself well enough that you'll not get shaken out. You need to be able to take a little bit of heat. Years ago, I never had to take heat, but now the market is a lot choppier. That has a lot to do with decimalization as well. When you had fractions, there were only sixteen pricing increments per handle. Now there are a hundred, so you're never going to be perfect. Sometimes you can scale in a little bit instead of getting in all at once. That can help.

These shakeouts that you mentioned, do you think it increases the value of having a time stop? Holding XYZ based on time instead of a hard price point?

Time stops are scary because what if the market goes into a downturn? I like to watch relative strength. I like to see that if the market is selling off, my stock is not selling off as much as the market. If the market is going up and my stock is not going up, that's a pretty good tell that there's some extra selling pressure in the stock that day. I don't use time stops very much. I try to gauge relative strength. I used to use hard stops too, but I'm probably looser with them than I used to be. Sometimes it helps to be a bit smaller so that you don't get shaken out. That's the key in trading. Don't be so big that you can't make rational decisions on the position. You want to be small enough that you can hold on when you're taking heat, but big enough that it's worth it too. You have to find the sweet spot.

You think momentum is one of the edges that have survived in the markets over the years?

Actually, I think there are a lot more momentum plays than there used to be. Contrarian strategies used to work better, where you would fade the moves. A stock would be going up so you would sell it, or if it was going down you would buy it. That's what market making kind of is, to a certain extent. I think momentum strategies work better now. When these HFTs get a trend going, they keep pushing that trend higher because they can catch a lot of contrarian traders. Let's say a stock is falling hard, there's always that buy-the-dip crowd that's naturally attracted to the cheaper price. HFTs know this and can sense that the stock is still heavy with short-term traders. They'll try to take the stock down further, to shake out those traders before allowing the issue to reverse. So yes, I think momentum strategies are probably more effective than they were three or four years ago.

Do you think the key to those plays is news interpretation? Knowing which piece of news will affect a lot, affect a little, etc.?

I do watch the news very closely. I got Benzinga Pro. I think I pay $99 a month or something, but it's solid.

If the news source lags a bit, is that a big deal?

If I get the news a few seconds after it breaks, I'm fine with that. I'm not going to beat the HFTs in the speed game anyway. If I was getting the news five minutes after it breaks, then that information would be kind of useless. But a delay of a few seconds is no big deal. If a trader doesn't want to pay for news, there are a lot of free sources too. You can just Google the stocks you're trading, go to StockTwits, or Twitter. Social media is a great asset to use.

Can't you just use a Bloomberg terminal to get ahead of everyone?

If you're a news trader, sure you can get a terminal and spend like $2,000 a month, but I just don't need the news that quickly. If Benzinga Pro gives it to me a few seconds after it happens, that's fine for me. If you're an HFT firm, those seconds matter. To a human trader, they're much less important than they were years ago.

Have you ever provided training for traders?

Yes, I do a lot of webinars[14]. A few times a year I do some lectures, usually about something to do with high frequency trading. This is where your book is interesting to me, learning to be profitable in an HFT world. I have a number of PowerPoint presentations that I've made about this stuff. Everybody complains that the market is rigged. Sure it is! I'm not going to lie to you, it's rigged, but you can still beat these bots. There are still successful traders out there that are doing very well. They're finding their edges, understanding who they're competing with, and adjusting their strategies accordingly.

The advantage of the human is that they can think rationally, whereas the computer will just do what it's programmed to do. Take the flash crash for instance. I can rationally think that PG was just trading at $62 and now is trading at $45. This is irrational and makes no sense. I can rationally think the Accenture is not worth 1 cent a share when it was trading at $40 five minutes earlier. That's a nice thing that we have. We can be rational, whereas a computer cannot. The programmer behind the computer can be rational, but we're going to be quicker because we can think and execute. The programmer needs to think, program, and then execute. We skip a step there. So if you can stay one step ahead of the computer like that, you can still be profitable even though the game is rigged against you.

In the case of PG, what would you have done if the stock didn't come back? Would you have held longer?

No, like I said, I was doing a lot of hedging. I don't even think I was buying PG. I was buying a lot of different stocks, so I can't recall which ones exactly. I was buying a lot of them on the way back up. I don't think I even took any heat, but I was hedging with a lot of other stuff. PG, you can hedge with so many things. You can short Colgate, JNJ. They have very similar business models. It's not a perfect hedge, but it's going to have a relationship there for sure. The correlation between a JNJ and a PG over time is very high. Like KO and PEP, they tend to be very correlated over a long period of time.

You prefer to look at correlation instead of cointegration?

---

14 An interesting webinar he made about trading in an HFT world is this one: http://tinyurl.com/lww4tj3

What do you mean by cointegration?

It's a statistical tool that tells you if two or more time series share the same stochastic drift.

I like to keep my trading very simple. I don't have to get into the fancy quant stuff. I just need to understand the basic relationships. I do a lot of crutch trading. For example, KO has some bad news come out. I'll short PEP or something like that. Sometimes those relationships don't hold as well as they used to, but in a market impact event, that stuff tends to hold very well. If PG drops 25 percent and I'm buying it, I can easily hedge with something else.

So you do a lot of sympathy plays?

Yes, but not as much as I used to. But off the open a lot of this stuff still works. During the regular trading session, it gets a little bit tricky, because there are a lot of other factors involved. In the first five minutes, sympathy plays can work. Not always, but sometimes they work for sure. There are hundreds and hundreds of ways to make money in these markets. You only need a few of those that work for you.

How much confidence do you have in your ability to keep making money in the next five to ten years?

I'm thirteen years into my trading career, and I've never had a down year. In May 1999, when I started, I was down until about August, but I think I ended the year up about $8,000 or so. I haven't had a down month since the year 2000 or something like that. I have down days and down weeks, but I haven't had a down month in a long time. So I'm still fairly confident in my trading ability because I'm very consistent. You just have to keep adapting to the new environment. If I started losing money on a consistent basis, maybe I would have to reevaluate, but as long as I can grind out my decent living, I still think this is one of the best jobs in the world.

Do you think this consistency is the result of being good at pattern recognition in the price action?

I think the number one factor that contributes to my consistency is discipline. I'm very disciplined in my overall trading. I'm never letting positions get out of hand. That's the one thing that traders do all too often, especially novice traders. They cut their winners too soon, and they let their losers get out of hand. You also have to be able to make adjustments. You can't keep tight stops or you get stopped out of everything in this market. You have to reduce your size a little bit and adjust your time horizon. I think these adjustments keep me profitable. I'm always adjusting my strategies to make them more effective. Things like scaling back on strategies that aren't working, moving to strategies that are working, cycling them through. I think all of those things are factors that contribute to success. I'm not going to say that I'm the best trader in the world, but I grind out a good living.

Do you keep very detailed records of everything that you're doing in your trading?

I've never been a good secretary, but it would probably be an asset if I could do that. I've been doing this for thirteen years and have done 50,000 or a 100,000 trades a year for so long that it's probably second nature to me now. But for anybody just starting out, yes they should keep good records. I used to have a list back in the day for NYSE stocks with the specialists. In the list I would keep track of the specialists that I felt were screwing me. I would see which stocks were in their posts, and I wouldn't trade any of their stocks. I would put in the list, "This specialist is an asshole." That sort of thing. And a couple of other traders in our office would do the same thing.

So your adjustments come from looking at the P&L rather than record keeping?

It's more on feel than anything. It's mental. I have a lot of records in my head. When a strategy is not working, I change it. OPGs[15] have not been working well for the last two weeks, so I've scaled back significantly in this strategy. I'm still doing some, but I scaled back. If it starts working again, I'll increase the size. By scaling back I ensure that I'm not losing as much money when the strategy is not working. This is probably why I have losing weeks but not months. Continuously making these adjustments keeps me profitable.

What kind of equipment do you use for trading? Do you have the latest processors and hardware?

I just bought a Mac because everybody is saying you have to have a Mac, but I haven't integrated it yet. I'm always pretty up to date. I upgrade my computer usually every other year, so right now I'm using a core i7 from HP, but I'm going to switch it over to the Mac in the next week or two. But yeah, don't try to trade with a really cheap computer. If this is going to be your career, buy something near top of the line. But keep it within reason.

The thing is, because I've lengthened my time horizon and am not competing in milliseconds, I don't have to spend thousands and thousands of dollars on a super machine. It just needs to be fast enough to get the job done.

---

[15] This another name for the NYSE opening strategy.

What is your best advice for average traders that are having to deal with these markets over the last few years?

My best advice is to understand your competition. If you think you can come into this game and immediately make money without understanding how the microstructure works, I believe you're already at a disadvantage. You need to become educated about it. Then you have to adjust your trading tactics to suit the environment. What I say to new traders, and the information that I would pass on to even seasoned traders, is that there are three or four main things I've done to stay profitable in my career:

1. Lengthen your time horizon. I don't want to compete in a scalping trading world. Unless you want to spend millions of dollars developing these HFT collocated systems, it's very hard to compete with them on time, so lengthen your time horizon a bit. I'm not talking about becoming a long-term Warren Buffett type investor, but it's better to think about trading in terms of minutes as opposed to seconds.

2. Never show your hand. If you tip off the HFTs that you want to buy the stock, they'll try to take the price higher on you and vice versa. I don't like putting limit orders out there, unless I'm fairly confident I'm going to be executed. In liquid stocks like GE, it's a little bit different, but if you're trading stuff like small or mid-caps, you don't want to show your hand in any of that stuff, because they'll try to make you pay.

3. Take liquidity as opposed to providing liquidity, for the reasons I mentioned earlier.

4. Try to learn how to read the tape. Take your time if you're learning. Trade small size off the bat, but understand and learn how to read the consolidated tape, because there's some great information in there.

Have you found yourself reading more about rules, regulations, and microstructural issues?

Yes. I knew nothing about rules and regulations five years ago. I knew what I could and couldn't do, and that was about it. Now I'm more active within the CFA Institute, and I'm a member of their Capital Markets Policy Council, so I'm digging deeper into market structure. I don't think any trader has to dive down as deep as I have in the microstructure of the markets, but I find it interesting.

A great book I just read is Scott Patterson's *Dark Pools*. He did a great job of outlining the history of the markets and the microstructure. This book is a good overview. Keeping up with the market structure is also still essential. For example, the NYSE just got their dark pool approved yesterday and that affects me. My limit order that is sent there is now going to be executed even less, so I'm going to use fewer limit orders. It's important to understand where your orders are going and how they're getting executed. I'm a big fan of direct routing as well. If the stock is offered on NSDQ, I'm going to route to NSDQ. I don't want to route to ARCA first and ping that exchange, which would tip off some HFT, allowing them to see my order coming up the pipeline. They can then grab the offer before I can. By understanding microstructure a little bit better, order execution quality gets better as well.

Do you think the trend of lengthening the time horizon is going to continue for five or ten years? Are we all going to become swing traders?

I don't know, maybe. The trend is definitely going that way. If I look back to 1999, I was the scalper. I was the HFT in 1999, scalping the spread. Scalping basically died for me (and for all manual traders) in 2007/2008, so I adjusted by lengthening my time horizon to minutes or hours. Maybe eventually we won't want to deal with the daily intraday fluctuations at all, and we'll move entirely into swing trading where we're holding stuff for days. I think there's good value in swing trading. I argue sometimes that the inefficiencies that HFTs eliminate in the short-term can actually lead to inefficiencies in the longer-term. HFTs are just leaning on orders, stepping in front of orders, momentum buying, etc. When some institutions are buying, they'll press the stock higher, trying to extract as much money as they can from the order. Because they pressed the stock even higher than it would have naturally gone, there's an opportunity there. A trader with a longer time horizon might say, "Look, this stock is irrationally getting bought here, and once the short-term traders stop pressing it higher, it's going to come back down." So maybe he takes a short position as a swing trade.

Do you think it happened in NFLX yesterday?

I don't trade a lot of NASDAQ. I've always been a bigger fan of NYSE issues. But I do think that happens. As momentum traders jump in, the HFTs take it even higher. I'm not saying you should fade every move up. These moves can continue for quite some time, but I do think there are some opportunities there, especially if you can be quick to identify the turn when it happens.

Do you think the HFTs can just tell when these trends are going to take place?

I believe they're very quick at identifying new trends. They can smell the orders. These computers are smart, man. The predatory HFTs can sense there's some institution buying, and they'll make them pay. They have a lot of access to information that we don't have. It's not all HFTs. It's the more connected ones.

Do you avoid mid-day trading?

Yes. If I look back to 1999/2000, I would never take time off during lunch hour. But now during the hours of 11 to 2 EST, I do very little trading. I find it very choppy and unpredictable. You have HFTs trading against HFTs, and when you step into their shark pool, they see your order and try to attack you, especially if you're trading illiquid stocks. I do the majority of my trading at the open and at the close. Those are the best times to interact with non-HFTs. I find that when I trade from 11 to 2, I just trade a lot, pay a lot of commissions, but don't make a lot of money.

What do you do with the money you don't use for trading? Do you buy stocks, bonds, real estate?

That is the big question everybody asks. "What do you do with the money when you don't trust the stock market because of flash crash issues?" You can't stick it in T-Bills when you get less than 1 percent. I do have my own stock portfolio. I like dividend stocks. I like to get paid to be in stocks. I do some covered call writing. I'll buy higher yielding stocks and write calls on them to enhance the yield.

November 2013 Update

Do you think today is one of those days when guys who've been trading for a long time know they shouldn't be doing much? The market barely moved.

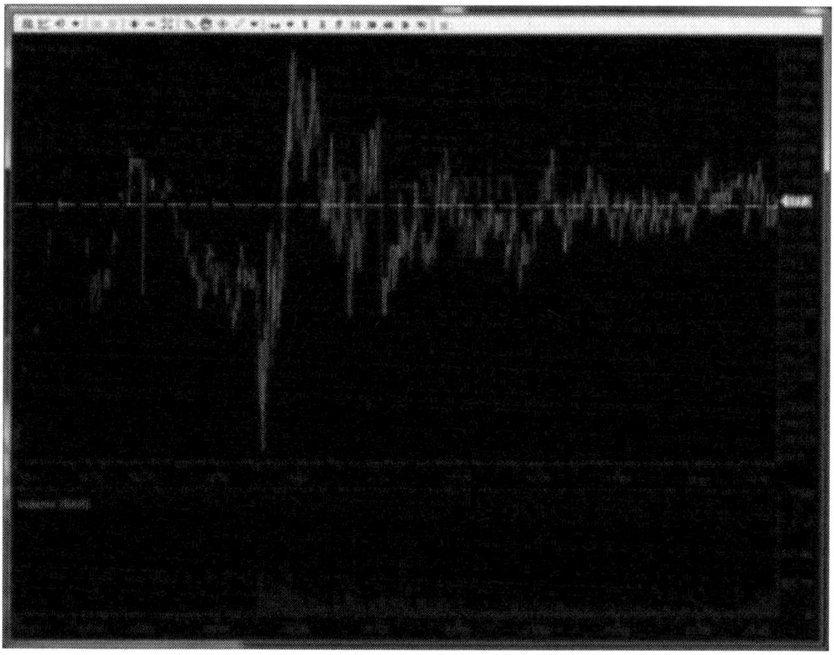

SPY 1 min chart. Source: DASTrader. Veteran's Day Holiday 2013.

The issue is that we're coming off earnings season, so there's no catalyst here. Another issue is that in the first ten to fifteen minutes, there's no liquidity at all, because there's too much risk to the HFTs. As real participants start to place orders and HFTs start to do the same, they start to lean on each other, and that thickens the market up. I know Joe Saluzzi calls it "the HFT vice grip," and that is a pretty good name for it. Because what happens is that the market thickens up so much that stocks hardly move. The HFTs are just scalping for their pennies or rebates.

Is the liquidity a bit like a self-fulfilling prophecy? Is it that if there's some, then there's more, and soon a lot, while if there's just a little, then there's nothing.

Yes, that's exactly it. It's what I like to call dependent liquidity. That's what the majority of HFT liquidity is. I'm not saying it's bad or good, I'm just telling you, that's how it is. The HFT liquidity is dependent on other participants being there. If there's nobody bidding, like in the flash crash, everybody cancels. Once there's one bid, then others start to join. You can see that as a trader when you put an order out there, and all of a sudden two or three orders show up ahead of you. Those are mostly HFT orders piggybacking on you. It might have started as 100 to 200 shares, but because they're all leaning on each other, all of a sudden there could be thousands of shares at the NBBO[16] . If the original order cancels, then they all cancel. It's like a lean party.

How would you rate this year in terms of profitability compared to other years?

I'm actually a little bit ahead of last year in my own trading, but the thing is I'm always moving around strategies. Good strategies don't seem to last that long these days, when people or the machines figure out these edges you have to move on. I'm trading quite a bit in options lately too. I've always traded them, but I'm starting to focus on them more. I feel that there's more opportunity there. You see some overextended moves in small caps a lot of the time, and buying some OTM[17] options can be like lottery tickets. They sometimes pay out.

You're using the options for the leverage or for the staying power that they give you?

Leverage is the number one reason, because I can buy a hundred contracts in something for a dime and it gives me a ridiculous amount of exposure to something. I will often play the weeklys too. I played JCP a few times this year. When it starts to consolidate and you think it's going to have another down leg, instead of shorting the stock, your risk/reward might be better if you buy some OTM options.

---

16 National best bid and offer.

17 OTM - Out of the Money.

Sometimes you can get those options pretty cheap. I don't do a lot of spreads and stuff. I like to keep it simple. Nine out of ten of my options probably lose money, but that 10th one can be very lucrative.

Did you catch a lot of the down move on JCP?

Not really. I just caught a couple of smaller moves there. I'm usually in the options of smaller caps, like some of the biotechs. I was in QTWW and caught a nice trade in that one. I had the $5 calls and it ended up going to $7.

©1999-2016 StockCharts.com All Rights Reserved.

Chart courtesy of StockCharts.com

That goes to show you, many years ago I was a scalper, but now I'm trading in a much different time horizon. I'm looking at options, and exploiting different edges. I always traded options, but I'm still in the R&D stage of my option strategies, I wouldn't say they're my bread and butter yet.

The support and resistance numbers from Premarketinfo, how do you use them? Is that something that you should use to fade those illiquid extremes off the open?

It depends. Joel Elconin is the one that puts those numbers together. He has been doing that since the '90s. It's kind of old school but still works. It's not a simple method where you use the numbers and you're going to make money, but they're another tool. I will be aware that if a stock has bottomed three to four days in the last six days in a certain area, there's probably some institution that's accumulating the stock there, or there's some other reason, because stocks don't normally do that. I become aware of areas like triple tops, triple bottoms, etc. The numbers that Joel puts out are based on things like that. He will put a one-star rating if it's a one-time high or low, but if it has four to five stars, that means it probably has multiple highs or lows in that area. It's a quick way for me to know the important levels instead of having to look over the chart. If I'm long the stock, and it reaches a key resistance level, I probably will sell it or possibly reverse it and short the stock. There are a number of ways to use those numbers, but it's just another tool in the toolbox.

Are you still trading that opening strategy this year?

It has been tough, but like I said, all strategies cycle. It's been very tough in the last few months. I still play around with it a bit. The reason it's been tougher is that the liquidity is so low in the first few minutes of trading. So what happens is, you get short that opening print in XYZ, 50 cents above its fair value, but there's nothing behind you. A lot of other traders are probably short as well. It might be overvalued relative to fair value, but it doesn't matter. Because the trade is so crowded, they'll be scrambling to get out, and all of a sudden it will move up another 50 cents. You can get some really exaggerated moves because there's not enough liquidity in the first few minutes. The original strategy, the way Bright used to teach us, of just getting in when the stock was away from its fair value is not working the way it used to. You have to adjust. For example, instead of shorting that opening print, wait a few minutes, and short the stock when the OPG traders are scrambling and covering to get out. Maybe you can short the stock up another 50 cents.

What you used to see was that the trade would just work. You would put it on in the opening print, and it would go back to fair value. Now you have to think it through. Now the play is to sometimes fade the opening strategy until it gets to a point where it might reverse. All of these strategies still have relevance. It's just a matter of using them differently.

You mentioned that you were trading 150,000 shares a day. Isn't there an advantage there to move from per-share commissions to per-trade commissions in a retail firm?

No, because you lose the access to serious capital. It's not an issue of how many positions they'll let you put on but rather how many orders you can put out at the same time. The biggest advantage of prop is always the capital. I can send a lot of orders without having to think that maybe they won't let me send that many orders due to lack of margin. The prop firms can negotiate commissions too. If you're doing a lot of volume, they're going to give you a good rate. If you'd interviewed me three years ago, you'd have found me doing something like 300,000 shares a day. One year ago, I was something like 100,000 to 150,000 a day. Now it's more like 50,000. In a day like today, I did about 20,000. Obviously, I'll trade more when there's more action, but over the years my volume has come down.

Would you say that the number of trades is also coming down?

Yes. That's mainly due to the transition from being a scalper to holding the trades for longer periods of time. We have to extend our time frame, because we're paying an HFT toll. They have monopolized the spread. In order to remain profitable, you have to make a little bit more in the trade to absorb the extra cost of paying the spread. Scalping is pretty much dead to human traders. I used to sit and scalp all day between the bid and the ask, and that's how I did the 300,000 shares a day. Now I'm holding trades sometimes for hours, maybe overnight, or even for days. So my volume tends to come down a lot. You might be trading the same size, but you're not in and out as much.

Profitability is still not that bad in these markets. We still have Bright traders doing well. I've still had no down months this year. It's not as awesome as it was in 2008, 2009, but that has to do more with volatility than with HFTs. The good traders have adjusted to this environment and they're still making money in it.

What would you say was your best trade and worst trade of the year?

I'm always hitting for singles. I'm never in big and cleaning up on something. It's hard for me to remember.

You're always in for small- and medium-sized bets?

Yes, I'm always going for base hits. In a typical day, I probably trade thirty stocks, make money on twenty, and lose on ten, or something along those lines. Usually I'm in 500 to 1,000 shares in a lot of different stocks, making $100 to $200 here and there. Very rarely I will make like $5,000 in one trade. I never had a day that I lost more than $5,000. Sometimes I'll play the big movers too and make like $1 to $2 per share in something. In AAPL I had one trade where I made $8 a share.

What was your best day ever?

It was in 2008. I made $110,000. It was in October. Every single name out there was getting dumped off the open, and it felt like capitulation. They were just throwing everything out the window.

You played the bounce off the washout?

It was actually a lot of preferred stocks that were crashing. Everything was getting thrown out. I got in stuff like Citigroup, HSBC, and JP Morgan preferreds. Some of these preferred stocks closed the day before at $10 to $11 and they were opening at $5 to $6, down 50 percent on the opening print! We were like, "This is ridiculous." I was buying these preferred stocks and hedging by shorting the common stock. If the company went under, I was going to be OK, because both would go to $0. I remember some of these preferreds were yielding like 40 percent, and they were still paying. It was crazy.

Would you say you use a lot of hedging and swinging for base hits in order to avoid the stress and the worse decision making that comes from big losses and big volatility?

I would say that for sure. The reason I've been successful pretty much every month since 1999 is because I'm very risk averse. I'm always entering a trade and thinking how much money I can lose and not how much money I can make. I'm entering low-risk trades as much as I can. When the trade starts to go against me, I'm looking at how I can get out, how I can minimize that loss. I'm not thinking, "Oh, it's going to come back." I'm never in the "hope trade." I'm out before I'm even hoping. I never add to a losing position. It's a cardinal sin for me. I probably never will. I'm always playing defensive. That's why I'm always looking at base hits. My losses are small and my gains are relatively small as well. Consistency is the key for me. There are guys that do it completely differently. Some guys in the firm will make $30,000, then lose $30,000 the next day, make $20,000, then lose $10,000. Maybe at the end of the week they're up like $5,000 but they had a lot of stress the whole time. Meanwhile, if I can grind out $1,000 a day, that's pretty good.[18]

I believe I noticed that you follow this style more than other traders I've spoken to.

Yes, there are some wild traders out there, but there are guys like me as well. That's how HFTs make money every day too. They're very risk averse. They're very good at getting out of the way when there's danger. They're very good at managing adverse selection risk. I always felt that I was pretty good at that too, but I'm not as quick as an HFT, because I'm still a human being.

Did you trade the TWTR IPO?

I was out of the office, so no.

Would you have traded it?

Probably, but just to play around with it. Maybe 100 to 200 shares. You can lose too much too quickly in these types of situations. It's like going to a casino really. It goes against all my trading fundamentals. I wouldn't trade it with size, because you can't really control the risk.

---

[18] This would add up to something like $200,000-$250,000 a year, which is in the top 5% of US incomes.

You mentioned tape reading in our first interview. A lot of traders I spoke with don't really do it very much. Why are you able to read the tape?

The one thing with tape reading is that now it's different than the way it used to be. There's so much fluff now, stuff that isn't really happening. The tape used to have a lot of information. Back in 1999, when I started, the majority of the information that I gathered from the tape was incredible. It's not like that anymore. You can still get a lot of information from it, but you have to know what you're looking for. Nine-tenths of the trades that are going by on the tape are just short-term HFT rebate trades and stuff like that. You have to be able to read the real liquidity off the tape and the quote window. Find out the real buyers and sellers. Once you figure that out, then it becomes like old school trading. You have to be able to filter through what is real and what isn't.

You have to get a sense of a big buyer or big seller?

Yes, we still do that. In the old days it was all about that. Leaning on the big bids and big offers, that's how you eliminated your risk. There are still institutions out there, and they're the real market movers. When you identify an institution that wants to get the hell out, it's a trading opportunity for sure. The HFTs are doing that. They sense real buying or selling pressure and they trade ahead of that. An opportunistic human trader can do that too.

With regards to small and mid-cap stocks that have wider spreads, I've been playing around with hidden orders and it's really amazing how much better the fills are when you use the native 100 percent hidden orders. Sometimes they'll play games and fill you for ten shares or one share, but these HFTs must hate hidden orders because it prevents a lot of their games.

That's why everybody has gone to hidden orders now, and this is a concern for the overall market. Off exchange volume is 35 to 40 percent, and hidden exchange volume is 5 to 10 percent. The market is going dark, and that's because there are so many games being played against displayed orders. You sit an order out there and everybody leans on it. They're using your order as insurance. When you hide your order, now they don't know it's there, and you won't have as many people leaning on it. It's tricky, because sometimes you want to have your bid out there so that if there's somebody that wants out, your order might get hit. But you have to use both hidden and lit orders. That's what I do. I would say 30 to 40 percent of the orders I place are hidden. Sometimes I do a combo too. I put a lit order out there and put a hidden order in front of that. If someone tries to lean on my order, I'll be ahead of them with my hidden order. Being able to use both of them is essential to traders these days.

Are you optimistic that some of the HFT games are going to get shut down?

Some games are being shut down, but there are always new games being played too. HFTs are here to stay. If someone thinks that the regulators are going to make the environment profitable to human scalpers again, then that's just wishful thinking. It's just not going to happen. Traders have to learn to trade in this environment that we have. It's not going back to the way it was. It's all about making the adjustments. The biggest adjustment for me was to rarely use limit orders. They're too toxic. I prefer to just pay the spread. I play less in the small and mid-caps because of that. The spreads are wide and too costly to pay, but it's too hard to get filled on your limit order. Hidden orders help a bit, but it's still difficult to get filled without paying the spread.

Do you think that with your style, you sacrifice some profits in order to lower your P&L volatility?

I believe my P&L volatility has always been low. Obviously every trader will have a bad day or a bad trade, but I'm shockingly consistent. Over the course of years, I always seem to be able to grind it out. My week-to-week profits are very consistent. I'm a steady climber. I'm usually making money by getting base hits, and I'm probably profitable four out of five days. Before 2009/2010, I was probably profitable forty-seven or forty-eight out of fifty days. I still have an occasional bad day, but it's never terrible. I don't blow out my weekly profits because I'm so risk averse. I think what keeps me successful is that I have so many tools in my toolbox, whether it's reading the tape, trading levels, technical analysis, etc., and I'm always using them in different ways. I rely a lot on my feel for the situation. When I don't trade for a couple of days, I usually lose that feel a bit, because I haven't been watching the trade action. It takes me a couple of days to get that feel back. When I'm in the zone, I can feel the reverses. I can feel that the S&P500 futures are due for a spin. I can feel that we're getting toppy for the day. I even use social media to get a sense of things. All of those tools help to keep the volatility of my P&L low.

When you do trade mid-day, do you wait for breaking news or big setups?

In a day like today, where we were stuck in a two-point range for three hours, the best thing you can do is to sit on your hands, because nothing is going on. For the most part, when there's nothing moving, you shouldn't try to make something happen. I used to do that. I would get bored and try to make something happen when the setup wasn't there. It's all about knowing when to swing your bat. There are only so many balls out there for you to swing at. From 10:30 to 2:00, sometimes it's just a grind. HFTs grinding it out with other HFTs. You jump into that and it's like jumping into a swimming pool full of piranhas. They'll eat you alive. You've got to know when to trade and when not to trade. I like to trade when other participants are trading, not just HFTs, and that's why most of my trading happens at the open. The majority of my money is made in the first thirty minutes of trading.

What percent of your trades do you initiate outside of the opening period?

Probably at least 50 percent of my volume is in the first twenty minutes. About 25 percent is in the last twenty minutes, and 25 percent in the other time periods. I'm very aggressive at the open, aggressive at the close, and just picking and choosing in the middle of the day.

Mid-day it pays to wait for stuff like news?

Yes, I like to play the laggards instead of the leaders though. It's hard to control the risk in the leader, but it's not so hard in the laggard. For example, if there's bad news in an airline stock, I'm looking at the other airline stocks and shorting them. It's amazing how quickly a sector turns. The other day the market whacked the TLT[19], then all of a sudden they started hitting all of the utilities, the preferred stocks, etc. They hit anything with yield in it, because all of that stuff is correlated. I thought, with TLT down $2, anything that has yield is probably going to be weak. Some of the utilities opened flat and then tanked. Knowing and being able to see those relationships creates opportunities for me.

In the middle of the day, if there's news in something, I might get in the laggards and play with them.

How do you prepare for a new trading day?

It starts with the after-hours of the previous day. For example, somebody is selling eBay tonight. There's no news in the stock, but somebody is whacking it down just while we're talking. They hit it at $52.75, $52.50, $52.25, and it's the same guy. I can just tell by the way it's trading. I'm already writing on my sheet for tomorrow, "Somebody was selling eBay after-hours." Maybe there's going to be news that breaks overnight, maybe not, but my point is, someone wanted out of that stock. I'm going to put eBay on my ideas list for tomorrow as a potential short, especially if it doesn't open down much.

Do you come to the open with a full list of stocks you're going to watch, the levels and so forth?

Yes, I'm very prepared ahead of time. The market closes at four, but then you have the after-hours session for four hours, then you have the premarket session for five and a half hours, and then the open the next day. Between today's close and tomorrow's open there are two full trading sessions. There's so much information in these sessions. I'm logging highs and lows from them. I want to know where the stock has been. If something trades like 200 shares away from the close by $1, that's

---

[19] The TLT is the 30-year Treasury Bond ETF.

nothing. But if it's trading thousands of shares then it's important to log the levels that it's trading at, because those levels might come into play in the regular session as well.

Would you say that a lot of the moves premarket or after-hours are an overreaction a lot of the time?

I'd say overreactions happen all the time because the liquidity is so low. If somebody just wants out, they'll have to pay to get out. I've seen stocks like PG go down $4 a share on a headline outside regular trading hours, which is a bit crazy, because it's a thick, low-beta stock. Once the real liquidity comes back in during the regular session these moves tend to reverse. Knowing the average range, the beta, etc. helps too. I won't bet the farm on it in these overextended plays, because the liquidity is so low, but I will nibble in them.

Do you think that at some point we're going to have a volatility expansion and an opportunity like 2008/2009 to short stuff and not have to cover one hour later when the dip gets bought?

Sure, it always ends badly, but maybe we're going to ES 2000 first. But at some point it's going to reverse. I often play these sell-offs through options. If I feel like there's a vicious washout coming because we're drifting down and some people are caught long, I'll often look at the weekly options. Maybe we're trading on a Thursday and I sense that things are heavy. I'll buy some cheap OTM puts.

Do you hold the weekly option no matter what?

No, if I feel like it's not working out and things are grinding back up, I work out of them. I don't want my puts to expire worthless. But it depends on the price as well. If I bought the put at a nickel and it's down to 1 or 2 cents, then I might just ride it to zero, but if I bought it at a dime and I can salvage 7 or 8 cents out of it, I'll close it out. This is just one way to get cheap exposure to a sudden move. A lot of times it won't work, but when it does you can make a lot of money.

I've had options that I bought for like $300 and banked $3,000.

Do you get concerned that these weekly options get manipulated at expiration?

They are, for sure. You have to be aware. If you're at a big level, the options will tend to pin at the major strike price. For example, if JCP is at $8 and there's a lot of open interest at $8, the best way for the option writers to make money is to get the stock to close at $8 or very close to that. Maybe you can even short at $8.10 to capitalize on that. There's also a natural drift to the major strike, because the option holders are hedging themselves using the common stock. For example, if JCP is at

$7.95 and you're holding the $8 puts, you'll need to sell the puts or buy the stock to lock in the profit. A person holding the puts may buy the stock at $7.95 to lock in the gains. If the open interest is quite high, the players hedging themselves will put buying pressure on the stock, driving it closer to $8. You have to be aware of that so you don't get caught off guard.

Lessons from Chapter 6

1. Adjustments. A key factor that enables Dennis to stay successful is making adjustments to his trading. It's easy to get attached to a certain style of trading or certain technique, but in these ever changing markets, without adjustments you'll perish. This is where being humble and respecting your P&L statement comes in. When things aren't working, you have to change. Try different things, do a lot of research and development as he calls it (on small size). One thing that can help in these adjustment-making processes is to be connected with other good traders. I didn't ask him in the interview, but I suspect a key factor that helped him become a better trader and adjust is the fact that he stays in touch with other successful traders in his prop firm and via Skype.

2. The importance of simplicity and base hit trading. I believe having a simple trading method can help in many ways, but the main one is that it enables you to act without hesitation and stress.

Being a prop trader, Dennis must have seen hundreds of traders show up and disappear over the years–many of them with all kinds of fancy mathematics, indicators, and wild position sizes—but a lot of day trading is having mental control and not feeling like you're in a battle every day. I believe this is why he engages in SPY hedging or pair trading type hedging in his positions, as well as why he goes for base hits instead of home runs. Even though these types of hedges are likely to cost money in the long-term (since you're taking a secondary position without an edge but paying the bid-ask spread plus commissions), it's likely to make you money indirectly by lowering your P&L volatility, which will lead to several benefits:

A. You won't have to stop trading early in the day as often because you feel that you're getting too emotional and making poor decisions.

B. Your mental clarity will enable you to make better decisions later on in the day.

C. If you're a prop trader, you might be able to get better deals with your prop firm because they can see you're a low volatility trader that's not smashing keyboards all the time.

D. It makes the overall experience of working as a trader more enjoyable.

The same can be said about trading for base hits instead of home runs. As he says, "That's kind of what this job is, to minimize damage as much as possible."

People like Warren Buffett don't need to decrease their P&L volatility; if he gets emotional or angry, he might quit that day but no harm will be done because he probably wouldn't close a deal or buy a stock that day anyway. But for a short-term trader, it's crucial to be relaxed and in a good place mentally as you have to make dozens of decisions every day. **It's important to protect your "mental capital" as much as your trading capital.**

This idea was hard for me to understand in the beginning, because I come from a blackjack and poker background where you're supposed to take pretty much any edge and avoid any negative expectation move. But in day trading, if you do that and create excessive P&L volatility, your mental game is likely to suffer, and this will cost you other edges later on in the day. In blackjack, the strategy is already set in stone, and you don't have to think very much. It's not as important to be on top of your game mentally. You just have to have a good memory to remember the basic strategy. But in trading, there's a lot of discretion involved, so it's more crucial to be able to think clearly.

Trading offers opportunities for hedges and ways to minimize volatility (such as scaling in or out of a position, using small and medium position sizes). These tools are useful even though they might seem to have a financial cost on the surface.

Low stress "base hit" style trading can be extremely beneficial for traders that struggle with discipline and suffer from extreme emotional swings as a result of losses. Try it out and see if your results improve.

3. Avoid being shaken out by sizing your positions correctly and using wider mental stops. Intraday noise can be quite high in an HFT world. There are all kinds of moves and fakeouts that happen during the day. Having tight stops or a position that's too big can be your worst nightmare, as you get taken out and then the stock reverses and does what you just thought it would. This is a mistake that's very easy to make, especially when you're confident in your position. You have to expect to be "tested" by the price action at some point. If you go with a stop that's too big or too tight, you might end up closing the position at the worst moment.

4. Don't use market orders or passive limit orders. HFTs can game these orders. The market orders can be gamed by well-connected HFTs that can see the order coming and leave you with a worse fill. Passive limit orders will be gamed through subpenny trades. These orders tend to get filled when you're wrong and not filled when you're right.

5. Screen time is crucial. Dennis doesn't do much backtesting or use indicators. He just developed a sense for price action by watching it a lot for more than a decade. This is something that I'm finding in my trading as well. Over the past year, by watching markets and stocks trade intraday constantly, I'm finding myself developing a feeling that something is about to happen. It's not always correct, but when I miss these trades, more often than not I regret it as it would have been a winner.

My theory on why instinctive trades can sometimes provide an edge is that some situations are harder to code and therefore less exploited by HFTs and arbitrageurs. As a result there's more money to be made for people who can see what's about to happen. Our unconscious mind can be a great backtester if we feed it correctly.

Not everybody has the luxury of having many years' worth of market data in their heads like Dennis, so for those that are starting out or looking to improve, it's important to record your observations and lessons about price action, tape reading, etc. In Chapter 15, I detail how I personally write market notes using the popular software Evernote. Research indicates that the act of writing something increases the retention rate of the brain significantly, so it's definitely a good habit to have as a trader.

6. The importance of tape reading. Dennis lists this as one of the top things a trader has to do to adjust to current markets. By watching subpenny trades in the tape, HFTs trying to display fake size in the L2, and a number of other variables, you can start to develop a sixth sense for what's about to happen, and this can be an edge. The main idea is to look through the noise so you can detect a big buyer or seller. This enables you to trade ahead of the big player and profit like in the old days.

7. Hidden orders are an important tool for your toolbox. In larger-spread stocks, you can improve your order execution and decrease your costs by using native hidden orders. They can help you be gamed less by HFTs, especially if the stock is very active. The thing about hidden orders is that they will only be executed for the order flow of that particular ECN/exchange and they can be traded through. (Example: You put a hidden order on BATS for $20.22 when the market has a bid of $20.20 from ARCA. If someone tries to sell at ARCA, he will get filled at $20.20 even though you are offering a better price. This is because your order is resting at BATS.

In this case, you would be better of cancelling and sending a hidden order to ARCA. That way you get filled in all the order flow to ARCA.)

Ask your broker if they offer native hidden orders, and if they don't, consider switching to another broker. In Chapter 15, I recommend a retail broker that allows the use of native hidden orders.

8. Capitulation can be enormously profitable. Dennis had his best day in 2008, making $100,000 when preferred bank stocks that were still paying were being thrown out at ridiculous prices. By accumulating market experience, you'll be able to identify when moves are just too large and unjustified, which can lead to great trades. Even in this situation, Dennis stuck to his risk averse style and hedged by shorting the common stock of the banks.

9. Sometimes the best risk/reward trade is in the options. When you think a stock is about to make a significant move, it might pay to take a look at the options. Depending on what you expect the stock to do, you might get more bang for the buck by buying out of the money calls or puts. Notice that Dennis doesn't get fancy with complex option spreads. He just uses for them directionally, mainly for the leverage they provide.

10. Strategies get crowded. At that point, doing the opposite is what works. The opening strategy lost a lot of its profitability as a result of lots of traders and HFTs exploiting it. This created a crowded trade, which the liquidity off the open can't absorb. The way to adapt to this is to not participate in the opening print but to wait for the shakeout of the opening players and then take the other side. This applies not just to the opening strategy but to other strategies where there are too many short-term players compared to the liquidity available. You can observe this in momentum trades as well—when they reverse you will see the "trading herd" trying to get out and a large move in the other direction. You also can see this in some of the news plays, right after a piece of news comes out, often, a lot of people will be on the same side looking for a quick gain. Frequently you will see a shakeout as the stock moves in the opposite direction. HFTs and smart players like to take advantage of crowded plays. Try to always be aware if the trade you are in is crowded or not.

11. Play the laggards instead of the leaders. In news plays, even if you miss the initial move in the stock with the breaking news, you can still profit by going into the laggards, sympathy plays, etc. Try to think of the ramifications of the news and how it will impact other stocks. The example Dennis gave of the TLT and utilities trade is a great one.

12. Last but not least, discipline. Dennis says he always remained fairly disciplined in his trading and has no issues taking losses. Given that taking losses (by being disciplined) is such an important factor in short-term trading success, how do you improve your discipline and make it easier? I wrote a quick, practical course on how to boost your discipline in Chapter 15 titled "The Boost Your Discipline Mini-Course." You might find the advice different from what you are used to reading. It is based on recent findings and studies in the field of neuroscience and psychology.

Chapter 7

Jeffrey Goldman—Market Maker Turned Prop Firm Trader and Manager

Jeffrey Goldman (Twitter @jeffg44) is a veteran former market maker who manages the prop trading firm JC Trading Group. Over the years, he has seen literally hundreds of traders in his firm, some successfully becoming full-time traders, many others losing part or all of their trading stakes. He's the voice of experience, having watched markets and traders for a really long time, which allowed him to develop a strong opinion of what it takes to succeed. In the pharmaceutical industry, there are all kinds of large empirical tests that can help shape someone's views of what works and what doesn't. Think of him as someone who has overseen a large empirical study of traders by managing his prop firm and seeing pretty much everything under the sun.

Even though he manages JC Trading Group, make no mistake, he's still a trader at heart and trades quite actively. "It's in my blood," he said in the pre-interview.

This interview was conducted in August of 2012 and updated in November of 2013

Why did you decide to get involved in the markets and become a market maker?

My first job after I graduated from Michigan State University was at the Chicago Mercantile Exchange. It's always been my passion, always being my interest to trade.

You started as a market maker?

I started at the CME doing research and running trades. I did that for a couple of years. I became a market maker in 1992 for a firm called Olde Discount, making markets in NYSE listed stocks.

Were the profits you made just for the firm, or were some of those profits for yourself?

Olde was one of the first firms that internalized the order flow of their customers. I would take the opposite position, like all the market makers did. If a client sold a stock, I would buy it from them instead of the trade going to the exchange, and if a client bought a stock, I would sell it to them either by shorting it or selling from my inventory. I was definitely trading for the firm, and I got paid out a percentage of the profits.

How did you deal with having to make markets when there was a lot of volatility and news?

As a market maker, you had your book to trade against. You always have buyers and sellers lined up. For example, if a stock was trading at $10 and you had many buyers at $9 7/8, you could buy all the stock you wanted at $10, because you always knew you could sell at $9 7/8. You actually wanted volatility as a market maker, because you wanted the price of the stock to go through your book. For example, let's say I had sellers in my book of 25,000 shares at each level between $15 and $15.50, and the stock was at $14 ⅞ x $15. Once the stock went through the $15 offers, I would automatically buy the 25,000 shares. Once it went through the next offer at $15 ⅛, I would buy another 25,000 shares from our clients. So as the stock was going higher I would get longer and longer! My job was to manage that position and determine when to sell the position to another market maker or to the NYSE.

For some stocks, you didn't mind that it just sat there if you had a lot of customer order flow, but for the most part you wanted the stock to move. As a market maker there's a lot less trading and more just managing your inventory. Sometimes the position was just given to you instead of you going out and taking a position because you felt that you had an opinion on the stock's movement.

So you were able to make steady and frequent profits by just trading around the book?

Correct. I traded a lot of K-Mart, because the company I worked for had their employee stock option plan. I probably traded one million shares of it every day, and it rarely moved. I would buy and sell stock all day long. I would buy on the bid from the firm's clients then sell to other clients on the offer, thus capturing the spread of 12.5 cents every trade. It was easy money. I wasn't really doing anything unless my position got too big, either long or short. And, when that happened, I could usually liquidate my position in the middle of the spread on Instinet and still make 6 cents.

Did you do any directional trading for your own account?

Well, you would add value if you could position yourself correctly. For example, if you thought a stock was going to go higher or you anticipated the firm's clients wanting to buy a stock, you could go long the stock by going to the exchange or other market makers and buying some. Once the stock went higher, you could sell your inventory to clients who wanted to buy the stock, or sell it back to the street.

So anticipating demand and supply for a stock definitely helped with your profitability.

You stayed as a market maker for how long?

I worked as a market maker at Olde from 1992 to 1998. Then I worked as a market maker with Knight Trading in Chicago from 1998 to 2001.

Do you think that by watching the markets for so long you were able to develop a sense for price action?

That is definitely the case. Watching stocks over and over again act the same way definitely helped me transition from a market maker to a prop trader. I left the market making industry because I knew computers were going to take over my job. Eventually they did and these days there are just a few market making firms, and most are automated. Guys who were able to watch the markets and learn from them have become better proprietary traders than the guys that didn't.

I also think my years at the CME helped. When you're down on the floor and by the pits, you're literally in the middle of the market. You get a great feel for the ebb and flow of markets just based on the excitement and noise level of the pits.

Did you decide to leave Knight Trading because of the decimalization rules?

You're 100 percent right. When the exchanges went to pennies, there was no longer an advantage for me to be a market maker. The spreads are your margins. So basically our margins went from 12.5 cents to 6.25 cents, then down to 1 cent. At Knight, we took the opposite side from pretty much all the major online brokers, so when there was news in a stock, we would get bombarded by orders. For example, if there was negative news on a stock, we would get inundated with sell orders that we would be forced to buy. So basically we were forced to buy stock while it was going straight down. As a market maker, we took the good with the bad and accepted these situations. But when spreads went to a penny, the bad was much worse than the good. Fortunately, I was able to make the transition to prop trading, but yeah, when they changed the rules I left, and the writing was on the wall for all market makers at that point.

Couldn't you back out from orders or drop down your bids?

Some market making firms would do that but not Knight. They had agreements with customers that they would fill up to 5,000 at the best bid/offer, even if they were displaying just 100 shares in the quote. If the stock went non-firm you could pull your quotes, but that was a last resort and didn't happen often. There was one time I had to buy 20,000 shares of Celera Genomics on a 100 share bid. The stock was $200 and extremely volatile. The stock was even halted for some of the executions, but for some reason our system was still filling sell orders. The stock opened down $20 after the halt, and I lost $400,000. We wouldn't cancel any of the trades. Once we reported a trade to a firm, we didn't cancel that order, so it was a real loss.

When you started trading prop, were you directional right away or did you trade scalping strategies?

When I became a prop trader, I was mostly directional and also looked for inefficiencies of the NYSE specialists that I could take advantage of. One of the easiest ways I would make money was when specialists went wide. For example, if a stock was trading at $28.00 x $28.01, and all of a sudden it went to $28.00 x $29.00. The specialist would go wide because there was news out or the specialist received a big block of stock to buy or sell. In my example, you could just throw orders out to short all the way up to $29. When the block would print, you would be short at that high price, and 95 percent of the time the stock came back down. It was the easiest money you could possibly make. These days the specialists just don't do that anymore. Most big orders are thrown into a time slicer or worked more efficiently by a trader.

That was like the opening imbalance trading?

It was the same philosophy of the specialist opening the stock too high or too low because he took some of that side as well and wanted to make money on it. It was similar, but it was a lot easier because in the opening strategies you had to put hundreds of orders out. You didn't know which ones were going to get done. In this strategy, you knew he was going to put a print up. If he didn't put up a print far enough away from the last sale, you wouldn't get filled and you didn't lose anything.

Did you use momentum strategies as well?

I mostly trade breakouts and breakdowns. I was always the type of trader that would buy new highs and short new lows as opposed to what most traders do.

I noticed a lot that at those key levels the HFTs tend to widen out their spreads.

I mean, they could, but I'm a big believer that at the end of the day a stock will go from whatever it is now to whatever it's going to go. There might be a lot of noise. That's what you're seeing in these markets lately. That's what's getting a lot of traders in trouble. It's definitely real now. It's coming from the HFT guys trying to make fractions of a penny. So you see a lot of movement in the quotes of the stocks and movement in a 2, 5, or 10 cent range. Like I said, I'm still a big believer in the idea that at the end of the day a stock is still going to where it's going to go. I try not to get caught up in all the noise.

For example, if a stock makes a new high, it made a new high for a reason. A stock that made new 52-week highs usually goes on to make higher highs. It's just the way it is. In that first breakout, there might some games being played, and that's all I think they are. But at the end of the day a stock is going to go where it's going to go, and I try to capitalize on it.

Did Reg NMS have an impact in your trading or did it take some time?

It definitely took some time, like any other rule or change. I can remember back when I was a market maker and they passed what they called the Manning rule, which limited how we would interact with our book. Basically if we had buyers in our book at $10 and the stock was $10.00 x $10.01, we had to cross the two orders for our clients. Before Manning, we could buy the stock for our own account at $10. Everybody said, "Market making is dead. No one will ever make a penny again." That turned out to be wrong. When stocks went from 1/8ths to 1/16ths, everybody said the same thing. When Reg NMS came along, you had to change the way you traded. That's why you're seeing a lot of traders struggling now. They're not changing with the times.

What is the biggest difference that you notice in these new markets?

I notice that it's a lot harder to trade off the Level 2 window now. You have to concentrate a little more on charts and where the stock is eventually going to as opposed to looking at the Level 2 and time and sales. You have to take a longer-term perspective of where the stock is going to go.

Is that something that you notice in other traders in your firm as well? I mean the successful ones?

Absolutely. Traders have to adapt. In my opinion you have to move to a longer timeframe, and when you do that you inherently are taking on more risk. That's one area that some traders just didn't get. If you were trading in a small timeframe and trying to make a penny or two, that was great, because you were only going to lose about that much as well. Once you start expanding your timeframe, you have to make a little bit more money per trade, and you're also in a position where you can lose more per trade. The prop traders that didn't adapt and transition well to that didn't make it.

The noise that you referred to, do you think the HFTs do stuff like triggering stop points and then they bring the stock back just to create more activity and profits for them?

I hear that a lot, but I don't think that takes place that much. I don't think there's enough money in it for these computers to try to fake out the retail trader or the prop trader. I'm always in the conspiracy theory camps, but I don't think that's one of them. I believe what you're seeing is the noise generated by the algos and the HFTs trying to make their fractions of a penny.

You mentioned there's less of an edge in the Level 2. Do you think there can be an edge in watching subpenny trades in the tape?

Depends on your style. Some guys are doing a lot of rebate trading right now. For those guys, yes, but for the typical trader that's trying to make more than a fraction of a penny I don't think that makes that much difference. Personally, I look less and less at the tape than I ever have before. I very rarely look at time and sales or Level 2. I used to, but I don't use them much anymore.

Do you try to take advantage of rebates when routing your orders?

Nine times out of ten I take liquidity. I rarely add liquidity, I might if I have a winning position and I'm scaling out of it with limits. I never use a passive limit order to get into a trade. I'm not the type of trader that will pick a point to get into a trade. If I want to get into a stock and it's at $20, I won't say, "Well, I like it here, but for some reason I feel like I should be in at $19.90, so I'm going to put a limit there." I don't trade that way. If I feel like a stock is going to make a move, I just go ahead and initiate a position in it. Some guys can trade that way, but I just don't.

Do you think these limit orders are a trap because of subpenny trades?

I know some traders that do use them successfully. They pick their points well. Let's say a stock is trading from $19.80 to $20 and the trader identified some kind of range or channel. That's their edge. Guys who can trade like that should use limit orders. Will they get pennied sometimes? Yes. But if you pick your spot in that range well enough, you're going to get it filled. That's not how I trade though. I would never knock someone who can trade based on support and resistance like that. I just don't trade that way. I buy when resistance is being taken out and short when support is being taken out.

Did you trade in the flash crash?

I was on vacation, believe it or not. I was in Vegas and had my partner call me saying that the market was crashing. I wish I was trading that day.

Do you think that day showed a lot of the weakness in the market?

I really do feel that way. The HFTs are now the new market makers and liquidity providers. There are no old style market makers anymore. When you look in the

Level 2, you're not seeing Merrill Lynch, Goldman Sachs, UBS, etc. You just don't see market makers anymore. All you see are ECNs, and for the most part they're HFT orders. When the market decides to go down like it did in the flash crash, and everybody pulls their bids, you see a vacuum like the one you saw that day. I do think that's a problem, and I think it can happen again. The HFTs are out to make a fraction of a penny. They're not going to stand in the way of a market that's free falling. That's just not their game.

In the old days when you were making markets, were prices more stable because you had to put real quotes out?

Yes, absolutely. You had to quote a real, two-sided market. There were actually rules with regards to how close you had to be depending on how much volume you did in the stock. You couldn't just go really wide without facing a fine. Also, your retail book became part of the inside market, which doesn't happen anymore, because they're just not displaying anymore. Now they're mostly sent to dark pools and are not displayed. Again, that's one reason I've moved away from trading based on the Level 2.

A lot of traders say their passive limit orders only get filled when they're wrong. What do you think about that?

I do think it happens a lot. The traders that complain about that are the ones who have strategies where limit orders are important. They might be rebate traders or a trader that's waiting for a stock to come down to where his limit order is resting. That doesn't really affect me, because I don't trade that way. The one type of trader that is affected by this is the type of trader that tries to play market maker in thinly traded stocks. They look for stocks that might have a wide spread, like 50 cents, and improve the bid for a couple cents with a buy ticket. Once they get hit, they'll offer the stock out higher and improve the offer. HFTs are really hurting these guys because you have the subpenny trades as well as the computers that will go 1 penny in front of you. I do know of a few traders in Europe who took advantage of that. They figured out the algorithm to fool these penny jumping programs and made a lot of money. They actually got in trouble for that. For me this is not a problem, because if I want to buy a stock I just go ahead and buy it.

So you just use marketable limit orders most of the time?

Yes, I will never do a market order. I just use marketable limit orders. If a stock is 19.99 x 20.00, I will buy it at 20.01 or something like that. I don't use market orders, because there will be a few times where you'll get really bad fills on that.

Do you route directly to the exchange displaying size?

I will usually use a smart order route that will route the order automatically to the exchange or ECN with the most liquidity and the lowest cost.

How did you do during the 2008 crisis?

I did very well. That was my best year as a prop trader. If you were able to capture the trend, you did very well. That was a really big year both ways for traders. Either you got washed out or you made a lot of money. Either you couldn't identify and/or fought the trend or you went with the trend and made a lot of money.

Do you think that was because day trading is inherently long volatility?

It was because the market trended hard. It was a huge downtrend. I was extremely bearish. I put my money where my mouth was and I made a lot of money. Then it looked like the markets were going to bounce. I waited for it to settle down and I got long and made money on the upside after. It was extremely trendy as opposed to being choppy. It was a good market for somebody like myself who plays breakouts and breakdowns.

Did you catch the trend in a day trading timeframe, or did you do a lot of swing trading as well?

It was all day trading.

So flat every night?

Yes.

Are you always flat every night?

Yes. I like to control the risk, and I can do that when the markets are open. I've found that when I see a trader take a position home, he's usually down on it. He's usually taking it home because he doesn't want to take the loss. And 90 percent of the time it's just as bad the next day if not worse. It becomes like that saying where a trade becomes an investment. If you make that conscious decision to never ever take a position home you'll never fall into that trap.

What are the main characteristics of the traders that do well in your firm?

The ones that do well manage their losses well. That is the most important thing you can do. When a trade is not going well, you get out. For me, a good trader will always get in a stock with some sort of target on the positive side and on the negative side. That's where a lot of traders fail. It's very easy to get into a stock, but it's very difficult to get out of a stock. Traders are so fixated on the perfect setup that they don't take into consideration their exit strategy.

Another example of managing losses is the ratio of a good day to that of a bad day. What I see so often is that a trader will make $300 one day, then $500 the next day, then $400, and then he'll lose $6,000 the next. They'll make a lot of small gains doing the right things, and then they'll have one big trade where they just lose everything. The best thing you can do is take the losing trade. Every trading psychology book talks about discipline, and that can't be overstated enough. You have to avoid that career-ending trade. You can be right on a thousand trades, and in one trade you can wipe out everything because you hang onto a position. If your losing days are several times the size of your winning days, the math is just not going to work for you.

Have you found a way to predict if a guy will do well or not?

Yes. Like I just discussed, if a guy has bad days that are so much worse than his good days, he probably won't make it. If a good day for you is $500, a bad day shouldn't be $2,000. If you see that happening a lot, then the writing is on the wall for that trader. It's a sign that the trader doesn't manage losses well. Consistency is the name of the game. Another bad sign for a trader is that he always holds a losing position until the last possible second of the trading day, and that's when he gets out. It's good that he's getting out and is not taking it overnight. But it shows that he didn't have an exit strategy and his only strategy was to wait until the last possible second.

What kind of computer do you use to trade?

I just have a midrange DELL computer. In this day and age I don't think you need a super computer. The biggest thing is your bandwidth. You need high bandwidth like a DSL or cable modem. Also you need a good graphics card and extra memory. You can get a really good computer for $1,000 these days.

What is the speed of that Internet?

I have DSL, it's 14MB down and 3MB up.

What do you use for news source?

I use Briefing.com.

Do you like to trade news events?

No.

What is the best advice you can give to the average trader?

Don't get caught in the noise. Always have a plan when you get into a trade. Know where you're going to get out, especially on the losing side of the trade.

Do you try to stay on top of rules and regulations in these ever-changing markets?

Yes. I definitely try to read about the new rules and things like that. I follow it more as a general interest rather than something that will impact my trading.

Do you avoid mid-day trading?

No. Mid-day is usually a little quieter, but I don't avoid it.

Lots of traders say that it's difficult, that the bots are all over the place and it's choppy.

I agree that it's not as profitable. If a trader says he only trades from 9:30 to 11 EST and then from 2:00 to 4:00 EST, I won't knock him for it, because I do feel mid-day is more difficult to trade. But I still find profits in there. In trading there's only one right way to trade and that's the profitable way. My way of trading might be different from your way of trading.

You manage a group of traders for a proprietary trading firm. For those that don't know, what is prop trading?

Proprietary trading is where you're trading the firm's capital, not your own. You're then paid out a percentage of your profits. This is different from a retail account where you're trading your own money.

Why would someone trade with a prop firm?

The three main reasons are the ability to utilize a professional trading platform, professional pricing, and professional leverage[20]. Using a professional platform allows you to have direct access to the exchanges, ECNs, and dark pools. Your orders are sent directly to the destination without first going to a middleman like a retail account does. Orders and trade reports are sent and received in milliseconds.

Next is professional pricing. Most prop firms have very low clearing rates and are on a per-share basis (as opposed to per-ticket pricing). This allows a trader more flexibility to scale in and out of positions. It also allows a trader to trade strategies that rely on ECN rebates.

Last is professional leverage. Trading through a prop firm, a trader has access to the firm's capital. Usually a trader is assigned a certain amount of the firm's overall capital to trade. For example, a trader might be given the ability to have $1,000,000

---

[20] You can also avoid the PDT rule by trading through a prop firm. You do need a "Series 57" or "Series 7" license to be able to trade. Also, as professionals, prop traders are subject to professional data fees.

of positions on at any given time. It also allows a trader to trade strategies such as opening and closing imbalances that require hundreds of opening orders, but only few get executed. Those can't be done in a retail account.

What are the drawbacks?

Prop trading isn't for everyone. It's geared toward the person that wants to be a full-time trader. Also, traders are attracted by the leverage aspect of prop trading. However, there's an old saying that leverage is a double-edged sword. A profitable, well-disciplined trader might benefit from increased leverage. But an undisciplined trader will just see his trading career end quicker with increased leverage. A prop trading firm needs to be responsible in allocating the buying power, and a trader needs to be responsible for using it in a reasonable manner.

November 2013 update

How would you rate this year's profitability compared to the previous year's?

2013 was a very profitable year, especially the second half of the year. We had some very profitable traders. Some of them weren't making money, but now they're making it.

Would you say that was because of the Fed starting to scare the market a little bit and creating volatility as a result?

No, I would say there's a little bit more volatility, more volume, more predictable moves, more follow-through in some of the moves. We had a lot of guys trading Facebook. That was a nice move. If you aren't that type of guy who's fighting every trend, which a lot of guys do, you could make a lot of money on FB. Looking back now on the FB chart, that was a great stock to trade. It went down then sideways, and then it had a really great up move. We don't have a lot of guys who trade the high flyers like GOOG and NFLX, but we did have some guys making money on that. TSLA too. A lot of money was made on that stock, the long side and the short side. Again, looking back you can see that those were some really good-looking charts. There were some predictable moves with follow-through.

What are your thoughts on futures trading and why is it not offered in prop firms?

It's so hard to trade futures. In my opinion, there are only five or maybe six futures contracts you can trade. There are so many people trading them that they become very efficient. You can't find an edge trading futures in my opinion.

Which are these six contracts?

You can trade the NASDAQ, ES, gold, oil, maybe the bonds.

Maybe the Russell 2000?

Yeah, they move a little bit. The thing is, the edge is just not there. It's like Forex. Everybody just trades the EURUSD or the USDJPY and that's it, that's like 90 percent of all trading. It's hard to profit because of that. That's just one of the reasons it's hard to trade Forex. A lot of the time everybody is underfunded to begin with. One whipsaw and they're completely out of money.

In the first interview we didn't really go deeper into your strategy of buying breakouts and shorting breakdowns. Would you say that, in this style, reading the daily charts is one of the biggest components of the strategy?

Yes, not necessarily reading the chart but knowing where the key levels are, like today's highs and lows and yesterday's highs and lows.

If you buy every breakout and short every breakdown, that's probably not going to work. Do you filter out by instinct or a criteria?

I will usually just trade the active stocks of the day, the news stocks. I'll also trade some of the recent momentum stocks, like the TSLAs or the FBs of the world. You always want to be trading stocks that are moving for a reason. You want stocks with volume. Those are the stocks that usually have follow-through. I think that's something some traders fail at. They'll find a stock they like and they'll always trade that stock. The issue is that in a particular day, that stock might not have any catalyst or reason to move. You'll just have some random buying and selling. The real stocks are the stocks that are moving for a reason and everybody is trading them. That's where you want to be. I would say it really pays off just to trade the most active stocks of the day, some people just keep going back to the stocks that they're comfortable with. Lately that has not been paying off.

Isn't TSLA a little tricky to play the breakouts and breakdowns? I noticed that a lot of times it just runs one way and then it reverses all the way back. It just shakes everybody out before making the move.

I definitely agree with you. Of all the momentum stocks, TSLA is a little trickier. That's sort of because of the new trading world we live in. There's a lot of noise out there, depending on the price of the stock. In a cheaper stock there's a lot of noise in the 5 to 10 cent range. In the more expensive stocks like TSLA, maybe that noise is 50 cents to $1. You have to just ignore the noise, the HFTs and the back and forth battle between them. At the end of the day a stock will go where it's going to go.

The better traders are the ones who can see that and capitalize on it, but I'd agree that TSLA does whip around a little bit.

When a stock like TSLA is up like $7, it's usually going to go to $9. I don't know it for a fact, but the chances are that it will keep going. You can wait for that pullback and get in.

Did you play that back on MSFT? It had a nice multiyear breakout.

I played MSFT a little bit, but that stock doesn't move enough for me.

When you play your strategy, how do you decide how much you'll let your profits run?

I always put stops in. Usually it will be in a relationship to where I got in. When you're doing breakouts and breakdowns, you have to assess how much that stock is likely to move. If I'm playing a breakdown of $30.25 and I think the stock will go to $29.50, that's a 75 cent profit potential. I can then tell myself, "OK, maybe I can give myself a 25 cent stop on this one." That's a three to one ratio. I get out of my trades when they're not working. I'd rather get out at $30.40 or $30.45 and get back in when it goes back to $30.25. If I'm right, I only have to be right once, but I can be wrong three times.

Are the profit taking exits based on support and resistance levels or just a feel thing?

It really is just a feel. When you're playing breakouts or breakdowns, there usually won't be a current-day or previous-day high or low anywhere, because it's a new level that's being reached. A lot of times it's just a feel. I'll also protect my profits by lowering my stop. The best trades are the ones that become profitable really fast. Then you move your stop, so even if you get hit you're still in the money. It depends on the stock, on what the Average True Range of that stock is that day. That really determines how far the moves can go. If there's news in a stock, you can just never know how far they can go. In the last couple weeks we have seen some stocks double, some cut in half. There was that NQ, don't know if you watched that.

Yes.

I mean that thing is just crazy. Who knows where these moves stop. I shorted it. It was a perfect example of a breakdown.

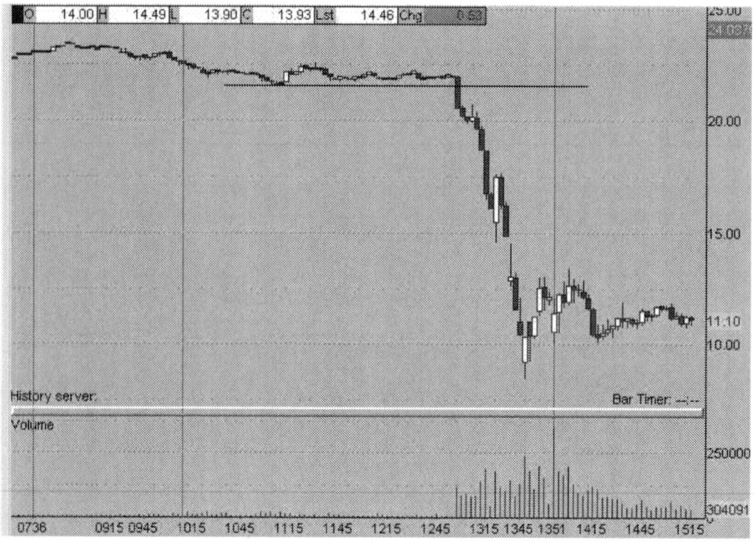

NQ Mobile 3m chart. Source: MBTrading Desktop Pro

So you play these 2- to 3-day breakdowns and breakouts. How about 52-week or all-time highs?

I usually only will play them if there's news out.

Would you recommend this strategy for people who have issues letting profits run?

I wouldn't say I do or don't recommend it. I would say it's definitely a strategy that has to fit the person's personality. Some people see breakouts and they immediately want to short it. Some people want to buy them. Both can make money.

Would you say that in your criteria, there's a lot of feel to it and it's not scientific with a lot of scans, filters, and things like that?

I keep an eye on fifteen to twenty stocks in a given day. I do use trade-ideas[21] to find intraday highs and lows. I also use our Fusion software, which has a scrolling list of stocks making highs and lows, so I keep that up as well. I will also watch big cap stocks that trade a lot of volume. I'll keep the one-to-two-day highs and lows on watch.

If you keep that type of watch list and you keep seeing the same stocks all day long making new highs/lows, you know there's something there. You look to see if

[21] Trade-ideas is a paid service.

there's a logical place to get in, like yesterday's high/low or today's high/low. You assess and take action if there's a play there.

Is it fair to say that you don't really care about what the news is? That you just want to know that there's some kind of news behind a play?

Exactly. I don't really try to interpret news. I let the market do it for me. I have a friend that makes maybe one or two trades a day. He's not very active. He holds core positions for quite a while and trades around them. After an earnings report comes out, sometimes he asks, "Hey, what did you think of that earnings report?" I say, "I don't know. Who cares what I think? I care about what the market thinks." The market will tell you what it thinks. I don't try to interpret news, economic numbers, or earnings.

Lots of times traders will try to interpret news or numbers. I find that more often in traders that are failing. Once you interpret something and you have that in your head, "That's bullish," or, "That's bearish," and if the market does the opposite, you'll fight it more, because in your head you're right and the market is wrong. That doesn't usually end well.

Do you trade more NYSE or NASDAQ stocks?

It's probably equal. I don't differentiate one way or the other.

Did you trade the Twitter IPO?

I did, not successfully.

Yeah, most people that I know lost money that day.

I kept buying the new highs of the day. I mean, you couldn't short it.

Actually, I got a borrow of the stock.

Did you?

Yes, but it was really expensive. 40 cents a share.

The way I was playing was, I had my finger on the button to buy at $50. There were about 250,000 shares for sale there. I thought if it broke $50, it would rip to at least $50.30. It broke out, but it stopped at $50.09 and quickly tanked back to $49.40. I played it small though just for fun, just to say I was a part of it. I lost like $600 in the stock for the day. It was a day that I had a lot of good things going on. I was up a lot of money. I just wanted to play around a little bit.

So you wanted to buy a big level break and quickly scalp out a profit? Is this one of the ways that you play breakouts?

Yes. For example, GOOG. When it broke $1,000, it went to $1,000.60. I don't know if anything printed in that 60-cent move. I don't do it often, but when you see something like that, a big number, a big offer, or big bid for a breakdown, you can profit like that. GOOG was a perfect example. I think there were at least 150,000 shares on the offer there. You could see them slowly going, and then all of a sudden they were all gone. If you were quick enough, it was easy money.

You have the finger on the button. You have to have direct market access with lots of different routes, preferably a smart router that will go to all the ECNs and dark pools. You have to be fast. You have to see them start to go, take it, and see where the bid pops to, then get out. It's that quick of a play. We used to do it all the time back in the day. The thing is, everybody is looking at the same thing, so you have to be faster than others. That GOOG breakout was very predictable. The TWTR one wasn't, and there was no money to be made buying the $50 break. There were definitely lots of people taking profits on the stock at that point.

What would you say was your best trade this year?

I don't think I can pinpoint one particular trade. I can say that playing the gold ETFs and stocks was more profitable for me than any other instrument or any other stock. Whether it was the GLD, the GDX, which are the miners, or the DUST/NUGT, which are the triple ETF of the miners, that's where I think I made most of my money. If you look at the charts of the miners, there are a lot of breakouts and breakdowns. I like to trade the miners, because they trade off something. Some people say the price of gold moves the miners. Some say it's the miners who move the price of gold. One way or the other, if you see something moving, the other ones will move too. I like them because there are just more signals and signs of where the market is going based on something else.

What was your worst trade?

I would say it has been the last month of this upmove in stocks. We are pretty much at all-time highs in the S&P500, Dow, and ten-year highs on the NASDAQ. In the last month I started to short NASDAQ, using the QQQs. I would build a short position and then cover because it has been going up nonstop. That's probably the worst trade I made, shorting the QQQs and having to cover it. Thinking that maybe this bull market in the NASDAQ has gotten a little tired. Definitely, it has not been working out.

It's like the opposite of your normal strategy.

Yes, I just feel like the NASDAQ market is getting a little overbought here and losing some of its steam, and we are going to roll over a little bit.

When you get new traders in your office, what kind of advice do you give them?

Very easy to answer, because I give this all the time. I always tell them, "If a trade is not working out, get out of it, because you can always get back in." You can't fall in love with a position. You can be right in a thousand trades, but all it takes is for you to hang on to that one trade, feel like you're right and the market is wrong, and then it becomes your career-ending trade. I've seen way too many times where guys will be right many times in a row then get stubborn and lose everything. If a trade is not working out, get out. You can always get back in.

In my opinion, that is the most important rule. In my strategy of breakouts and breakdowns, if a stock breaks down and I shorted it, if it comes back up, the trade is not working. I'll find a spot and get out. Traders just don't do that. They get into a position and they just stay in it. It goes 20 cents against them, then 40 cents, then they think they can't get out because they're down 40 cents. Then it's 60 cents. Then it's $1. Then it's four o'clock and they think that it might come back tomorrow. Next day maybe it goes another 50 cents against them. Next thing you know, the next day they can't even trade, because they got this big loser sitting on their screen. It just never ends well. Maybe one time it does come back and they get negative reinforcement. They think it will always come back, but the next one it might not and it's all over.

My best advice is to get out. You can always get back in. Especially these days where clearing rates and commissions are so low. It's not like you're going to get eaten up in trading costs.

You have to balance that with not getting caught in the noise, right?

Right. That goes back to the other point. When you get into a trade, you have to know where you're going to get out. You need that pre-established exit. That exit should be at a place where that noise isn't going to affect you.

Do you use a number from the Average True Range (ATR) to stay away from the noise?

No, I guess you can say I pretty much just eyeball the chart. It really depends on the momentum of that day of the stock. I don't use the ATR, but I will go back and see how big a big bar is in that stock. If I see a stock that has a big bar of 70 cents, then I know that it can move 70 cents that day. I won't use ATR, but I'll eyeball a chart to see where that stock can move, what type of volatility I can expect.

Another thing I will do is, if it's a stock that just made a really long move, maybe one of these crazy Chinese stocks or biotechs that go from $2 to $22 in six months, I know that even though it's at $20, it can move $3 in a day, as opposed to a typical $20 stock that can move 40 to 50 cents in a day. I always like to look back to see where the stock came from. If a stock is breaking down after it just made a huge up move, there can be a lot of action there.

Lessons from Chapter 7

1. Avoid and respect the noise. As Jeff explains, there's a lot more movement in the 2, 5, and 10 cent range in cheap stocks and 50 cents to $1 in higher-priced ones. HFTs play all kinds of games with investors, traders, and other HFTs. I can't tell you how many times I paid too much attention to this intraday noise and ended up closing a position that would have turned out to be a winner. It's important to keep yourself out of this noise so you can actually have a shot of having your day trading strategy working out. Jeff's choice in dealing with this was to move away from staring at the Level 2 so he doesn't even see that noise anymore.

2. Extend your timeframe. As he says, they used to play for 5 cents or something like that. Now you have to gun for at least 15 to 25 cents, possibly more. If you try to capture smaller profits, particularly in illiquid stocks, then you're stepping in the HFT shark pool. They're better equipped and connected than you, so your chances of long-term success are low.

3. Take liquidity. Jeff takes liquidity most of the time. He realizes that the game has changed the way orders are executed and that passive limit orders are being taken advantage of more. I wrote about how to improve your executions when taking liquidity in Chapter 14 in the section called "Improve your order execution by using IEX as a smart order router."

4. Avoid taking positions home. In his experience, most traders taking positions overnight are simply stuck with a loser that they don't want to close out. It's easy to fool yourself into thinking it's overdone, but in his experience it's just as bad if not worse on the next day.

5. Buy breakouts and short breakdowns. His bread and butter strategy is to bet on follow-through and continuation of a trend. The key to trading this style is to only get involved in stocks that are in play, have lots of volume, have news out, or are being traded actively due to momentum. You have to be able to assess how much the stock is likely to move after the breakout/breakdown, then you decide how large your stop will be to avoid the noise. A good reward to risk ratio is three

to one. Ultimately, you have to be comfortable with the idea that stocks that are making new highs are likely to continue to make new highs and vice versa for lows. TSLA is a good example of a stock that tends to keep going when it has a breakout or breakdown.

6. Avoid holding losers until the last minute of the day. Jeff has seen hundreds of traders during his years managing his prop firm. He says that this behavior is a bad sign for the future of a trader.

7. Managing losses well is the number one characteristic of winning traders. Over the years he found that this was the number one factor in determining the future of a trader. You probably already read about that in different trading books, but how can you actually develop your ability to take losses and make it easier? In Chapter 15, I provide a different perspective with practical actions and exercises that you can do to improve in this area.

8. Your win/loss math has to make sense. If you tend to make $500 a day in your good days but then lose $5,000 in your bad days, it's important to fix your loss control in order to have a good trading career.

9. Interpreting the news can be dangerous. When you read the news and develop an opinion about it, you'll find yourself fighting the market more often. You'll ignore price action signals telling you that you are wrong, because your ego will get attached to a particular view. This can lead to some big losses. I know I've been guilty of this several times in the past due to my background in macro trading. Once you build up an opinion on what the data means, letting it go can be the hardest thing.

10. You can scalp big level breakouts and breakdowns for a quick profit. The GOOG $1,000 break was an example of a quick scalp profit off a level that everybody was watching. This made it likely that there would be some follow-through pop in the move. This kind of situation presents an opportunity for the trader to make good money very quickly if he has his finger on the button and can act faster than others. It's tricky to do this, because the HFTs will take out an entire level in milliseconds when they realize the level is going to be broken, but it's still possible to profit from this in select instances. This trading style is not perfect though, and in some situations, like in TWTR, you have to be ready to take a quick loss, because if the pop is not strong enough, a lot of traders and HFTs will be heading to the exit at the same time.

11. Always check the level from where the stock came from. A stock that has risen from $2 to $22 in one year will behave very differently than a stock that has been trading in a $20 to $24 range in the last year. The first has many people with

large profits who will potentially sell once a stock breaks down, has bad news, etc. Also, potentially there will be more people short the first one (and people looking to initiate a short) then the second one. NQ provides a great example of that type of additional volatility.

This additional volatility has to be taken into account when deciding when to take profits and where to put your stops in.

12. Don't be afraid of getting out of a trade. You can always get back in. Jeff talks about how he can short a breakdown, take a loss if it rallies back up, but then reinitiate when it drops back down. His three to one reward to risk ratio assures him he can be wrong more than once and still profit from the trade. It's key for trading in general to look for situations where your payoff is several times your risk. This usually happen in major support/resistance levels, when a catalyst hits a security or when momentum shifts.

Chapter 8

Eric Scott Hunsader— The Market Structure Expert

Eric (Twitter @nanexllc) is not a trader. He makes that very clear. He is, however, one of the most informed and innovative market structure experts in the United States. Through his company, Nanex LLC, he monitors market data and shows the world alarming occurrences that routinely happen in the US stock and futures markets.

After the rise in electronic trading and the HFTs, understanding market structure and how things work behind the scenes has become more important, which is why I decided to interview him for this book. A lot of the things he knows about HFTs and how they squeeze every dime out of orders would have helped me tremendously when I was starting out. In fact, to this day I have to keep reminding myself to cut back on scalping. I find that my toughest days in the markets are the days I'm taking HFTs head to head, trying to scalp stocks for a quick profit because I think its "obvious" that it's going higher or lower. The problem is that for a variety of reasons that he explains in the interview, it is not that easy. If it were, the HFTs would have acted already.

Eric is known for his innovative charting methods that can explain price action in a way that aggregates all the information in one chart. If you browse around his website, it's not hard to see why the US regulatory agencies like the SEC aren't aware of a lot that's going on in the markets. It takes quite a bit of intelligence to figure out how to process the data and understand it. The SEC has too many lawyers in their staff who are not prepared to have to figure out modern markets. Maybe they should consider significant personnel changes.

This interview was conducted in September 2012 and updated in November of 2013.

What made you interested in markets and market structure?

I started back in 1986. I was trading S&P500 futures. I started collecting tick-by-tick data. I taught myself how to program, and I found that was what I really liked doing. I started processing, compressing, normalizing, and understanding market data ever since. I got involved in the market structure from the monitoring of our feed and seeing the explosion in market information. Having just from lived through options going from a 100,000 updates per second to six million, with the projection going to the stratosphere, I saw the same thing happening in equities. It made me realize that there were not going to be many people who would be able to get real-time data. That's when we began to investigate market structure.

Back in the '80s and '90s, were you up to date with all the rules and regulations, or is it something that only recently became more important?

We only tried to understand more of the rules and regulations side after the flash crash. We wanted to figure out how it related to the market data. Before data, we would look at regulations to see how it would affect the data that we would have to process.

So your company, Nanex, has been in business since the '80s and '90s?

No, I started this one only in 2000. There was a project at quote.com called qcharts, which was really the first source of streaming charts on the Internet. I realized the Internet was perfect for what I'd been doing. We were watching real-time streaming charts of S&P500 futures back in the late '80s on a Motorola cell phone connected to a Compaq laptop. When the Internet came along, it was a no-brainer to get involved there. While at CQG, I started my own company. We wrote software to stream data on the Internet. It quickly got bought out, and then it became part of quote.com. I needed to find something to do for the rest of my life, so I came back to this field.

Were you monitoring the markets in the '87 crash?

Actually, yes. When the *Wall Street Journal* was doing the twenty-year anniversary of the crash, they were looking around for intraday data, and I still had it on floppy disk.

What was the main difference between the '87 crash and the flash crash?

Well, the '87 crash was in slow motion. The flash crash, I mean, if you went out for coffee you missed it. In the '87 crash, I remember the open. It was very jarring. It really made you want to buy it, because it was such a large drop, but then it just lasted the whole day. I remember that it wasn't until the end of the day that I looked at a daily chart and said, "Wow! That's a pretty good drop there."

In that crash, were there a lot of glitches in the system and things breaking down, or was it orderly selling?

Well, at the time I was only looking at futures, so I'm not sure what was going on in the stock side. I don't recall problems with the data in the futures side. It wasn't something that went really fast. When it opened down so much, it really kept a lot of people on the sidelines. It wasn't something that started rolling down and gathered steam. That might be why there didn't seem to be a frenzy of trading activity, unlike the flash crash. That one was a whole different league, because you had so many systems that were either broken or way behind. Like the Dow Jones calculating their DJIA, for instance. It was forty-five seconds behind the data that it was processing. You had all kinds of funky delays. Clearly the systems were overloaded. They hadn't been upgraded in a long time, and we broke into this new territory of higher volumes.

I believe I read that you said the hardware needs are going up a lot to meet the needs to process the data. What kind of equipment do you use to monitor the markets, and is that available to other folks?

Part of what I did was the NxCore product, which I started in 2000 with my company, Nanex. I wanted to solve the problem of having to deal with an aggregate of real time data and be able to process it without needing to have a large number of machines. A lot of firms will dedicate eight, twelve, or sixteen computers. Each one does a subset of symbols, but the way I structured it made it possible to process the data in any computer, really. It's hard to find a computer that doesn't have the specs that can process our feed. It doesn't take a whole lot of horsepower to monitor the markets. We use $500 Dell boxes, actually.

If a trader is at home looking at the Level 2 or Total View, is that a bit like looking at the past?

The biggest delays tend to be the speed of light. If a trader is using his eyes, that's going to take at least 50 to 100 milliseconds just to receive the data. Then you have brain absorption and being able to react. You're really losing 100 milliseconds just to go from screen to human. Getting the information to the machine itself at the speed of light has been the number one source of latency for a couple of years now. As a rule of thumb, 180 miles will cost you 1 millisecond. If you're in Chicago and you're getting the Total View data from NY, you're looking at least 15 to 20 milliseconds. That's how long it takes to send the information. A lot of times we see that the number of messages easily will exceed a 1,000 per second, which means each will last less than 1 millisecond. So yes, a lot of information that you see, especially in the active issues, doesn't exist. The orders don't exist anymore. You don't want to compete at that level. You want to compete at a higher time frame, knowing all the weaknesses of the algos, how they're all reacting to each other.

You want to play at least in the ten-second to one-minute range. My successful customers are not super short-term. I used to have some that were pretty successful arbitraging options, but when the market message rates climbed over a few million a second, it was impossible for them to compete anymore. They would need special feeds to do that, and you have to be an exchange member to get that top tier. Things have changed, and you can't really scalp off the screen, but there are successful traders that were able to extend their timeframe a bit.

What is the main flaw of HFTs and algos?

They follow each other. Because they're based on speed, they really react a lot to current prices. They tend to be like lemmings and just follow along in a short-term trend. They tend to cause the market to move swiftly in one direction, then the move burns itself out and comes right back. You can see 1 to 2 percent moves that can start and stop in just two seconds.

Do you think these HFTs have special treatment, and if you take it away they all go bust, or would they make money even if stripped of special advantages that other people don't have?

I think the SEC should enforce Reg NMS, which is what it looks like they're doing now with this recent ruling against the NYSE.[22] But that's just the tip of the iceberg. They affirmed what the NBBO was and how it was supposed to be used and calculated and protected. If they go all the way to enforce that, which is likely because they wrote it out in the order against the NYSE, a lot of HFTs will be in a world of hurt. They'll no longer have that advantage, which is a significant one. The direct feed and colocation advantage is significant. In the end, there's only going to be one or two large HFT firms that are going to be making a market. There won't be room for somebody else to come in there and participate. A lot of what they're doing now are games. They're not really market making, they're working around this latency arbitrage between two data feeds. If the SEC goes down this path, that game will disappear.

When you look at your stock data from before the rise of HFTs, do you have evidence that intraday stock volatility is now higher than in the past?

---

22 NYSE Penalized by SEC for Giving Head Start on Trading Data - Joshua Gallu – Bloomberg September 2012.
In 2016, Eric won a $750,000 whistleblower award from the SEC for his work in exposing this practice.

Yes, actually we just did something that looked at the number of price ticks in SPY since 2004[23].We put the study up on our website. It's interesting, because right after Reg NMS came in, the number of price ticks in a day, and this takes into account the daily range and things like the VIX, rose by at least twice, if not much higher. There are more different price ticks during the day than before Reg NMS, which started in 2007.

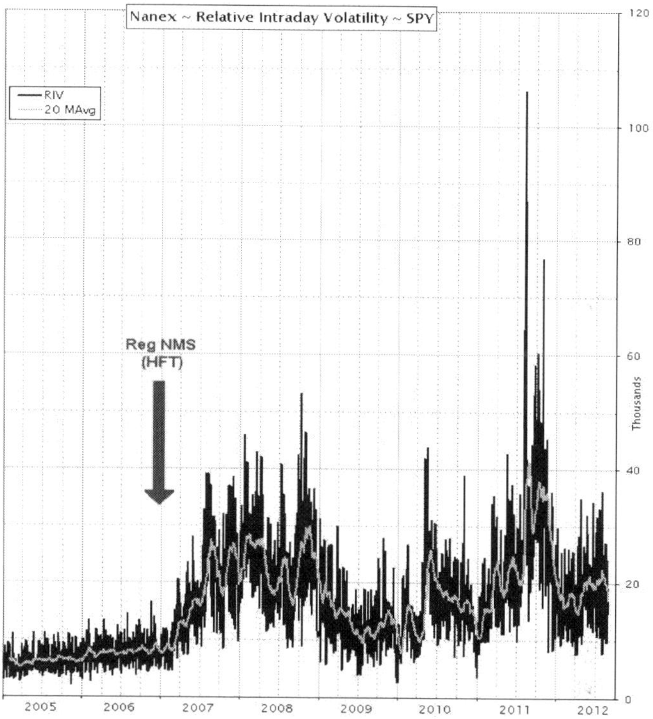

Source: Nanex LLC

It's quite noticeable in the chart that there was a fundamental shift and change. We see it in the data all the time, but it was really very hard to quantify until we came up with this method. The ticks will go up and down a lot more than they used to.

Doesn't that create an opportunity to fade the extremes of those moves?

Yes, it sure does. You would think that people who jump on activity would dampen it out and you wouldn't see this much. It could also be because there are so many

23 http://www.nanex.net/aqck2/3563.html

ETFs out there that there's something else going on that prevents it from dampening. Or maybe there's just not enough profit in it. Hard to say.

Another thing that's interesting is that we looked at quote rates back in the 1999 bull market when tech stocks were going crazy. The NYSE had just upgraded in 1999 to be able to process 1,000 quotes per second. And this was for all stocks trading at the time. Now we're at 1.5 million quotes per second. This is the capacity difference between when we had a bull market in 1999 and now. Maybe we're in a bull market, but it's not close to what it was then.

Do you think market orders are a sucker play?

They definitely are, because market orders for more than 100 shares usually will get filled for the first 100 shares, where you're expecting it, but the rest of it won't. This is because the HFTs can see orders coming in the exchange, and they withdraw the orders. Or they'll just pull back before the router is able to spread it out. If you're trying to do 1,000 shares and you have ten exchanges and each one has 100 shares, the order has to be split up to be able to go to each exchange. The router simply won't be fast enough to get it done.

They're able to see the orders in one of the exchanges and cancel their orders faster than that order router will be able to send them to other exchanges. This is why the first 100 shares will be filled but the rest will usually have inferior prices. There are strategies that they developed over the years. One is called Thor.[24] They try to time it so it won't show up in one exchange faster than it shows in the others.

What about limit orders? Is trying to post them and collect a rebate a sucker play too?

That's the other problem. They'll run right in front of you and wait you out. They jump in front of you, buy, and see if they can make the spread. If they can't, they'll dump the stock on you. Now, this is in an inactive stock. In an active stock you won't run into this problem. In NASDAQ stocks, I've heard this time and time again from my customers and I've investigated several of these instances. These internalizer or wholesalers will buy and sell at subpenny prices. They can go 1/100th of a penny above you, and that's their total risk. They'll just dump it off on you if they can't make the spread.

What about using hidden orders to avoid that?

---

24 Thor is a smart router type algorithm that tries to make sure all the broken down orders from the larger order hit all the ECNs and exchanges at the same time.

Oh, that's fine. If you put that in there and see no reaction then it really is truly hidden. If you put that in there and you see the market move, then it's not truly hidden.

Do you think some exchanges might be selling the hidden order books to HFTs?

According to Scott Patterson's book, *Dark Pools,* it could be true. There are all kinds of special order types that have been created to accommodate the HFTs.

Do you think stop books are also being sold?

There's no way for me to know. I can only say what I've heard. It could be that they just use the conventional wisdom that people tend to put stops around even numbers prior support or resistance.

Sometimes I use hidden orders and I get hit for one share many times in a row. They discover where my order is. Do you think there's any reason an HFT firm should be allowed to use odd lots like that?

No, of course not. When there's a perception of unfairness or a two-tiered system, which Reg NMS says should be strongly discouraged, you end up losing a lot of participants. They don't want to play the game anymore. They feel like it doesn't matter if they're right on direction if they're going to get hurt in the entry or exit to the extent that makes them unprofitable. All you have left are these machines with special orders that are all going to react the same way when there's some unexpected news.

Do you think it's possible to look at subpenny trades and predict where order flow is?

Yes, you can tell what the retail is doing by looking at the subpenny trades in aggregate. Anything that's priced 1/100th to 49/100th is almost always a public retail trade sale. The 50/100th to 99/100th is a retail buy. If you can aggregate those, you can tell what retail is doing.

So you can get an advantage being on the same side as the internalizer?

You always want to be on the opposite side of the retail. Almost always, the retail is wrong.

When you personally invest your money, how do you work your orders?

I don't trade. I'm a very long-term trader. My last long-term trade was buying Apple in 2000. When I have positions and I worry about them, I can't get anything else done. I don't have the temperament to trade.

How do you see the market evolving over the next ten years?

Up until last Friday, I thought that the HFT issue would play itself out by having a lot of the retail traders just die off. After the SEC ruling last Friday, I'm very encouraged that we may have seen the worst of it. We might get to equality between HFTs and other traders. I just hope the SEC is not going to back out of what they've said in these orders against the NYSE.

What do you think is the best change they have to make right now?

They have to look at how order routing works. They have to ensure that the exchanges are using the consolidated quote to determine where to route the orders, not the direct feed like they're doing right now. Once they get past that hurdle, a lot of the latency arbitrage games will either completely disappear or greatly diminish.

Without this arbitrage, you don't think they have a lot of additional advantages to remain profitable?

No, it's all speed. A lot of what they're doing has nothing to do with economics. They're just trying to flush out or fool another algorithm into doing something stupid. So 99 percent of this type of code is antieconomic.

I've read about quote stuffing in your articles.[25]

That continues to happen, in spite of all. We used to think it might be stupidity or that they were unaware, but that time has long passed. The reason they do it is because the law of averages will tilt things in their favor. It allows them to see the Thor-like programs that are trying to time the orders that are trying to reach the exchanges. They want to tilt these orders and the order routers out of balance so the order router might misroute to one of the other exchanges. It's all about discovering which orders are real and which are not.

Do you think they're also trying to slow things down for other people?

Exchanges assign groups of stocks to different machines. Let's say stocks A through C are in one machine, and the network that carries that traffic into that machine gets stuffed. Basically, any stock in that group that has slightly higher quote rates will cause that machine to slow down in processing them. A Thor-like program is trying to time something so that order appears in all these exchanges at the same time. NYSE computers take 100 microseconds from the time it receives an order to the time it displays an order. Let's say BATS computers takes 50 microseconds to do

---

25 Quote stuffing is essentially spamming an exchange or ECN with orders and canceling them immediately. Could be also constantly changing an existing order millions of times in a row.

that. The Thor-like program will time the order and will wait 50 microseconds to send it to BATS. That means it will appear on the NYSE and BATS at the same time so nobody can detect orders on them.

But that only works in the ideal case. If you have a hundred quotes going through one of those stocks in that group during that time, now it's now longer 50 microseconds, it's 75 microseconds, and it's just enough that with the law of averages it will expose some orders every once and a while.

It doesn't work 100 percent of the time, but it works enough that it slightly tilts things in their favor, and because there's no cost to send that extra information there's no reason not to do it. You don't have to send thousands of quotes to cause it to happen. You only need to send a few more than whatever threshold exists. Back in July 2010, we were looking at the NYSE system, Open Book, and we noticed that whenever any stock had a message rate of more than a 1,000 in one second, it would immediately cause a delay of 16 to 20 milliseconds in the consolidated feed versus Open Book. If you take six random symbols and just put 5,000 quotes a seconds in those symbols, you effectively delay the entire NYSE consolidated quote update.

And you don't have to do it for a full second. You just have to do it for a few milliseconds. If you do it randomly like that, you cause these Thor-like programs to fail. It's kind of like an antistrategy to prevent people from executing large orders simultaneously in multiple exchanges.[26] Does that make sense?

Yes. The consolidated quote slows down, but the proprietary feeds work just fine?

Time is money. You can definitely slow down any feed, even a direct feed, whenever you want by simply putting a heavier load on them. The load doesn't have to be that high. Even NYSE's Open Book starts to have serious delays at 200,000 a second. You can do it for 15 milliseconds and knock out substantial information.

Do you think the exchanges have to update their hardware?

---

26 This allows HFTs to cancel their orders from other exchanges when they see the executions going on in another exchange. When the Thor-like program misfires because of all the quote spamming, the HFTs now see that there's some buying or selling interest going on and they can extract a few more cents out of that order. Without the data spamming, the Thor program would execute in all the exchanges at the same time.

Yes. That's why we have these high quote rates. People are testing to see what the latencies are. You can tell when machines get upgraded or circuits get upgraded or get fixed by simply doing these tests at random times. A lot of what these guys do is that they build these tables. In a specific set of symbols, they know exactly what kind of quote rate translates to in terms of latency. A lot of the software engineering and expertise and brain power is going into this kind of activity.

I believe I've read that you think the BATS IPO was an act of revenge by the exchanges.

I just can't see how it couldn't have been. These were all ISO trades[27]. It wasn't one big one. It wasn't somebody selling. Who would have that stock to sell? Somebody who understands how markets work or an idiot? You put this all together and you see how the trades were executed. It just didn't hit all the bids on the way down. The algorithm would sell a bunch, and it would pause a little bit. Then it would wait for the bid to perk up a bit, and it wouldn't hit a single one. Then it would resume selling into it. It was something that was clearly meant to sell indiscriminately. You look at the people who would have the ability to sell. They used ISO orders, which means it was a broker/dealer. It rules out stupidity. To us it was pretty blatant. I guess it could have been some supreme stupidity, but I just doubt it.

[27] An ISO order is allowed to trade through better prices bid or offered somewhere else as a long as it respects the initial inside quote. After that, it can theoretically be executed at any price even if it doesn't make financial sense.

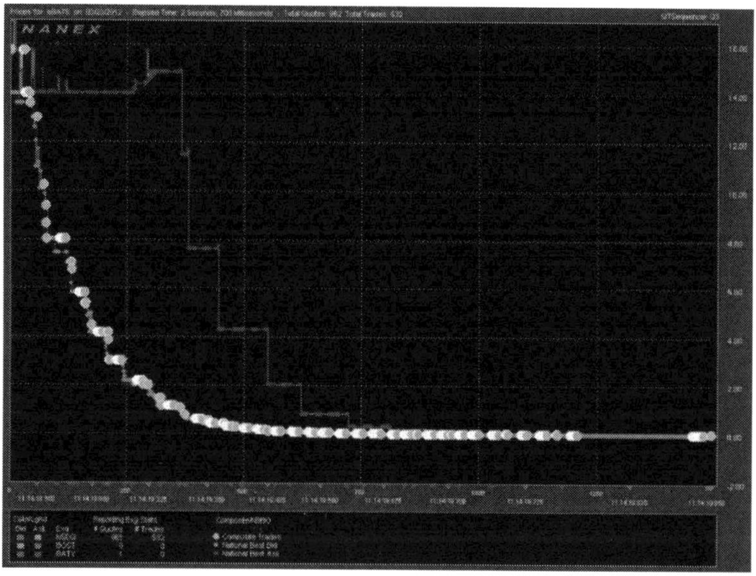

BATS IPO. Source: Nanex LLC

The NYSE and the NASDAQ had a lot to lose. They enjoy pretty nice listing fees, and BATS was coming along offering to list for free. So they were definitely big winners on that day when BATS's IPO failed. Unless someone confesses that they did it, we'll never know. Over the years we've seen people do this sort of thing. For example, I think it was in August of 2010 the AMEX just started trading NASDAQ stocks. In the first or second day, they open up a quote on CSCO. It was really wide. Somebody decided they wanted to pay more than 5 percent to the market price on AMEX. He sent an ISO order to AMEX, which caused it to execute on AMEX. That halted CSCO for five minutes. That sort of gave AMEX a black eye.

I heard later on from someone on the board of directors of one of these exchanges that the NYSE called up the guy who made the trade and asked if he wanted to bust the trade, and the guy said no.

Until I hear otherwise, I believe the BATS IPO was somebody intentionally trying to crater BATS stock on the open.

How long did the whole collapse last?

It was like a second and a half.

So there was no time for someone like a value investor to try to buy the stock?

The problem was that BATS couldn't get their quotes out. The only one quoting at the very beginning was NASDAQ. We don't know for sure, but if BATS had gotten a quote out there, it might have been different. But we can't be sure, because these were ISO orders, which means "do not route."

These ISO routes mean they're allowed to trade through better quotations somewhere else?

Yes, the trade-through exception of Reg NMS applies to ISO orders.

So the guy knew it would only execute on NASDAQ?

Yes, whoever put it in did not want better prices. It was either supremely stupid or supremely wise. It wasn't a random fluke.

How many shares got sold on the way down?

It was a 100 shares each with 500 or so trades, so about fifty thousand. The total value was pretty high, something like half a million dollars.

Do you think IPOs in general are way glitchier and investors should avoid them?

Yeah, I'm really shocked at how they botched that stuff. NASDAQ was just asking for trouble when it used its order book for dual purpose. Before the open, the order book was used to compute an opening cross in a Dutch action. After the open it was supposed to be normal. What this means is that before the open NASDAQ would allow buy orders that were higher than sell orders. In a normal market those were going to cross and be executed. NASDAQ's problem in the FB IPO was that it couldn't clear out the book and it transitioned from before open to after open. It had these buy orders in for $70 or something for a couple hours, until something like 1:15 (EST). Its whole order book was crossed. That's what I think caused Knight and the rest of these guys, like the internalizers, to lose money. The software didn't properly handle it. Why NASDAQ did that was beyond me.

Do you think that because NASDAQ doesn't have a long history of handling auctions it suffered from inexperience, whereas NYSE would be unlikely to mess it up like that?

Yes, you're right. NYSE doesn't use the same order book for two different things. It doesn't do anything stupid like that.

So NASDAQ IPOs are a little riskier than NYSE IPOs?

The linkages between exchanges in an IPO always seem to have really wild quotes. One exchange can be way off from the others. I don't quite understand why. At the very beginning of the FB IPO, there were really wide bids and offers. If somebody wanted to, they could have caused FB to print at way higher prices just by hitting some of the quotes that were out there at the time. There's always the possibility that someone is going to come in and do it. It doesn't cost a lot of money, and it can significantly impact the overall psychological feeling of that market.

Are you a fan of ISO orders or not?

You know, if they were used for their purposes I would be fine with them, but they're so abused. They were supposed to be used to try to mop up liquidity, like if you're buying more shares than exist in one particular exchange. The ISO order prevents the order from routing the balance to another exchange. The ISO orders are used a lot now by some HFTs that don't want to get direct feeds from other exchanges. They only want to get the direct feed from say NASDAQ, BATS, and EDGE. They just use ISO orders all the time so as to ensure it will only execute in the exchanges where they know the prices are.

With regards to the Knight trading glitch, did you have a lot of clients who were able to capitalize on that?

I know people that saw the obvious in large cap stocks that were completely mispriced and they just jumped all over it.

I read about people complaining that sometimes they try to hit a specific ECN or exchange for, say, 500 shares, but they only get a 100 shares, the rest just moves. This is a little different from the routing issue we talked about earlier. What is going on here?

A lot of things like that go on. I hear that a lot.

I understand that they can pull away when the order needs to be routed out. What happens when it's the same exchange?

According to the book *Dark Pools*, there are special order types that allow them to do that. When you see 500 in one exchange that could be five different lots of 100 share orders. It might be that they're flickering in such a way that the 400 is not always there, and it happens to be when your order got in there. Or they saw your order coming in for 500 and they just canceled the 400. I've seen that looking at order book data, where all of a sudden a big order comes in and a lot of orders, even some that were there for a long time, for some mysterious reason, get canceled. It leads me to believe that they're seeing that order somehow.

Some traders I know use some ECNs or exchanges like EDGA or BX in order to sit at a limit order and get hit first, because they offer a rebate or low fees for liquidity takers. That way you can get ahead of other people in the same level. Do you think it's a good idea?

As long as it holds, yes. But I've never seen something with more footnotes in my life than in these fee schedules from the ECNs and exchanges. The fees depend on the order that's routed, where it's routed to, the size of the order, the type. If that changes all of a sudden, you'll have to adapt.

To me this looks like a way for retail or professional traders to subpenny everybody else at the same price level by offering a rebate for liquidity takers and thereby getting some type of price priority over others in the same level.

That sounds like a good idea.

What are the main differences between the open and close periods?

Oh, the open has really wide spreads. It really doesn't take a lot of capital to affect the market open. We saw that on Knight Capital when they had their error on August 1. What I believe happened was that their test algorithm was randomly buying and selling all kinds of stocks. Some stocks opened down 4 to 5 percent and stayed down and vice versa. If it had not been random and it were all to the downside, for example, it could have brought the whole market down. In the first fifteen seconds of the open, the bid ask spread is just phenomenally wide. At the close, there's a whole additional liquidity there, especially in the E-mini contract and the larger contracts. They do game that last millisecond of the day. People that are not collocated and don't have speed the last ten seconds probably want to be out. But there's a lot more liquidity in the last fifteen minutes.

What are the games that they play right before the close?

The last millisecond of the day belongs to the fastest player. They can affect the set the close of the market and affect things like options that they want to get out of. I've seen them flood the SPY at the very close and send it down by 15 cents. They'll get it back and forth by 15 cents in the last milliseconds of the day. In that very last millisecond, anything goes.

It's like massive tape painting?

Yes, there's such a huge volume of messages in that last millisecond that sometimes it takes a few seconds to print out on the tape. You don't really know what happened in that last millisecond unless you have absolute state-of-the-art processing. You get an immense flood of information.

Some people say that at the open the spreads are really wide because the HFTs don't like risk, but I also think that maybe they're trying to make more money off the retail orders, market orders, that are hitting the market.

I think you're right. We see the bulk of these flash crashes happen at the open. In the first minute of trading, there's a high percentage of them. I think they know that some people don't know the dangers of market orders. They don't have time to worry about it, and they get their market orders or even limit orders taken advantage of. We did a study and found there was a gradual erosion in the first fifteen seconds since 2006[28]. Spreads have gotten wider gradually, and things have become much less stable. If somebody really wants to affect the market, that's the time to do it.

What are your thoughts on the mid-day period?

We see a lot of algo testing going on around eleven in the morning and one or two in the afternoon. We see significant market moves during that time on no news at all. Maybe they're testing to see what it takes to perturb the market. And they come out of the blue.

What do you think happened today in crude oil? It had a tremendous sell-off.[29]

It wasn't an algo gone wild. It wasn't somebody trying to scare the market. Maybe there's some kind of news that slowly got disseminated and nobody had an advantage there. It was a very slow rolling move. It took a minute from when it started to when it reached the bottom. You didn't see any spikes or any telltale signs of anything other than a large number of participants shifting their opinion on oil.

---

28 http://tinyurl.com/7n597w7
29 Nanex ~ 17-Sep-2012 ~ Crude Oil Drops www.nanex.net/aqck2/3586.html

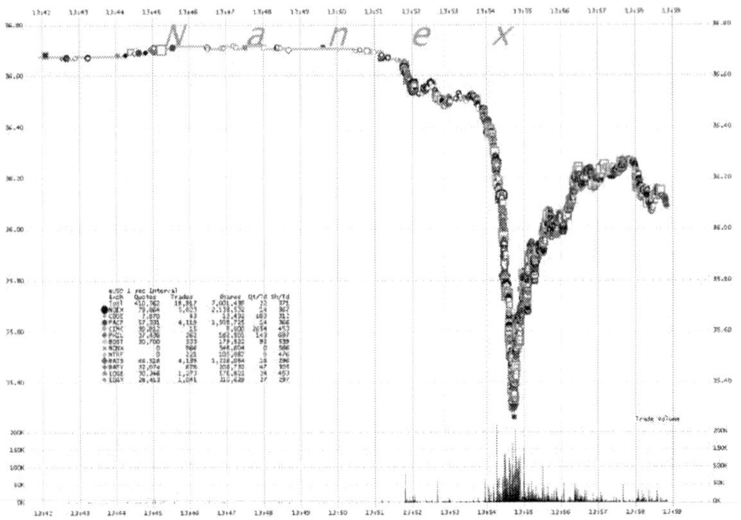

Crude Oil. Source: Nanex LCC

With regards to the flash crash, who do you think lost the most there?

Probably Waddell and Reed. They took a pretty big hit. They got substantially lower prices for those E-mini contracts than they would otherwise. Some retailers definitely got hurt. The ones that had drops in their stocks that weren't big enough to get canceled. There was a lot of frustration that day, people trying to get executions. I know somebody that was trying to get SPY fills from Fidelity and it was hours before they were finally filled. I heard that Goldman Sachs made a lot of money in that afternoon.

Do you know how? They bought the S&P500 E-mini at the lows?

Yeah, trading the E-mini.

Some people say that the old market makers would back out from chaotic times just as the HFTs did on the flash crash, so there's no difference. What do you say?

Well, I'm not so sure. When we reopened from 9/11 a week later. That's when you had market makers stepping in there and holding the market up. You had the expected gap down open and then it traded higher. It wasn't like in the flash crash where there just wouldn't be any buyers at all.

Do you think the exchanges and ECNs should make the special members have some kind of firm obligations instead of just making whatever market they want?

I believe they just need to stop this nonsense of being able to cancel orders when they see real buying or selling interest. There's a big difference between requiring them to step in front of a moving train and making them step away every time there's a slight breeze because they know they'll be a little bit more profitable. Just require them to honor their quotes, for example. If they tried to pull this type of trick in the pits, nobody would trade with them anymore, or they'd get a black eye, or both. This game of hiding behind being anonymous and pulling quotes because they can, especially with the speed of light in their favor, is just wrong. If the exchanges were too look ahead to the future, they'd realize this.

What kind of advice do you have for traders and investors dealing with these crazy markets?

Learn as much as you can before you jump in, and don't try to compete with groups that you're not on an equal footing with. Don't try to compete with HFTs.

November 2013 Update

The last time we spoke you were optimistic that regulators would crack down on a lot of the advantages that the HFTs have. How's your assessment now?

It's like a roller coaster. It really is hard to say. Every once in a while I'm hopeful, but it seems like they take one step forward and one step back. The last big hope was when the CFTC fined Panther Energy Trading for placing large fake orders, but they didn't follow through with others, so...

What do you think of the SEC getting the Tradeworx system with that whole MIDAS thing?

What they put out is an abomination. You're averaging data for the whole day when lots of events happen in less than a hundred milliseconds now. Even if you average for a whole second, you won't see a lot of what's going on. I remember Greg Berman saying that these flash crashes weren't caused by HFTs, and he was going to show us with the data. They still haven't shown us anything. And they won't, because the data can't back up his claim. They also haven't updated their site in six weeks. That's a long time.

This year, you've brought attention to the fact that HFTs are getting economic news before everybody else. Do you think they've been doing this for a long time and they only got caught now?

Yes. The thing is, I don't have a problem with that. I do have a problem when they're doing it in secrecy. In fact, what we found was that once people knew that Thompson Reuters was supplying the Consumer Confidence Index earlier to some folks, the explosion of market trading stopped. It went from hundreds of thousands of shares traded in milliseconds to less than one thousand. It was like night and day. Nothing changed with the news. Nothing changed with them getting it faster. The only thing that changed was that everybody knew that it was happening.

So if there's a perception of unfairness, the volume just disappears, and no one wants to play anymore?

That's right. They won't participate when they know it's unfair. Take what happened with the Federal Reserve in the FOMC no-taper announcement, for example. That whole thing was about doing it secretly. It was so secret that the Fed didn't even know it was going on.

Do you think they did this because the time difference was so small that they just thought nobody would notice?

Yes, I think they thought nobody would notice it.

You rated the NYSE Twitter IPO an A. I noticed that the OTC markets were shut down that day. I remember you said that the BATS IPO was manipulated. Do you think they shut down the OTCs because they wanted the retail volume going into Twitter stock, so it would look better to the investment banks?

No. The OTC is so small. It's a rounding error compared to the listed markets. There's not enough going on there to make any difference.

Lately there have been some fines over layering the quotes and showing fake sizes. Do you think that game is going to end? I still see that a lot in small-cap stocks.

It's happening more. This is the roller coaster I was mentioning earlier. When the CFTC investigated Panther Trading in July for doing just that, putting large fake orders in one side to drive the market to their orders in the other side, they were fined so much that they were shut down for a period of time. That would be disastrous if it happened to, say, Goldman Sachs. It was a monstrous fine and totally unexpected. The natural thought was, "Well, they're going to do this with everybody. Now that they have this hammer, they're going to find some nails to use." For a period of time after the Panther fine came out, there was a definite change out there, but after a month or two it just started to creep back in. Just last week we saw somebody putting this order of 20,000 in one natural gas contract. Normally, anything over 100 is big, 1,000 is just huge, 10,000 is unprecedented, and this was a 20,000 contract order! I didn't see any fine for that. If I was the regulator, I could find out who did it within one hour.

Do you think this game will ever stop?

If I were the regulator, I would fine the bad guys and that would be it. Right now, it almost seems like the bad guys are too big to jail, and maybe that's what is going on. I can't answer the question because the whole thing just defies logic.

Do you think the Twitter IPO was smoother because it was in the NYSE, and they have a better system compared to the NASDAQ?

NASDAQ was trying to use the same order book software logic to do two vastly different things. They were trying to use it to do, essentially, a Dutch auction in the opening cross then instantly switch to the regular auction system for regular trading. When they couldn't make the switch from one to the other, that's when it failed in the Facebook IPO. NYSE doesn't do that.

Does NASDAQ still do that?

I don't know. I haven't looked close enough. There hasn't been a big enough IPO on the NASDAQ in quite a while. So I don't spend time looking at this.

What are your thoughts on SMART routers from retail brokerages?

Well, I've seen the results of them. I've had large institutional firms share their trade date with me. These SMART routers are not as smart as the HFTs that are trying to trip them up. When the NBBO flutters, say, a hundred times a second, some of these SMART order routers get shutdown. Some get delayed.

We spoke a little bit about that the last time. The HFTs try to overload the servers so that the time it takes to send an order to different ECNs and exchanges changes, and since the SMART router is counting in a stable relationship they kind of misfire and are exposed. The HFTs can cancel and make the person pay more.

It kind of builds a momentum train longer when you've got pent-up demand. The more pent up you can get the demand, the bigger the bang when it comes out. This is just one of the many strategies going on. Another one is just to try to detect if there's a large order coming. If somebody is trying to split up a 10,000 share trade and hit ten different pools of liquidity, if they can trip it up and expose the order, they can pull their bids and offers in the other remaining pools. If you think of these milliseconds of delays in human terms, it's like a whole hour. A lot can be done in that period of time.

So, instead of using the SMART router, a trader might be better off using direct routing to a specific pool, taking that and then assessing if he wants to buy and sell more?

You really have to experiment a little bit. You have to be very careful of never really exposing your order size if you want to buy or sell a lot. You can use time too. Algos can forget about things after a couple of seconds. I've seen one algo that was trying to sell a lot. He hit the market hard, and after a couple seconds that bid book was almost completely recharged. Now, things change. After a while the algos get smarter and that might not work anymore. So you might have to change it up.

You mentioned that you have some products that you sell to your clients. I didn't understand exactly what it is that you offer. Is that like a direct type feed of market data?

A lot of our traders are not trading in the subsecond time frames. They're longer-term, so we provide a real-time data feed that contains almost anything traded in the United States. Options, futures, equities. We also have archived data for people that want to go back in time and check how things traded. Pretty much all of the statistics that we publish comes from that.

What is the advantage of your data compared to other places?

The advantage is being able to use the data immediately. As a programmer, sometimes you do all the hard work of dealing with different types of data, APIs for futures, equities, options, etc. They can change over time too. We normalize that so you don't really have to think how to decode. That's all done. We do it in a way that allows you to write an algorithm that works on historic data and uses the same exact algorithm in real time. We also compress the data about twenty to one, which allows much faster work with that data.

How did you come up with your charting style?

Two of the things that I specialized in are compressions and graphical display of the information. I've been doing this since '86.

You had to come up with a whole new charting system because regular charts just wouldn't do it?

Yes, it's a big challenge trying to put all the different kinds of information together in a way that's not just a cluttered mess. With these charts, we tried to bring out information that wasn't apparent.

Last year the *Wall Street Journal* and Haim Bodek exposed a lot of the special order types that the HFTs have. Which do you think is the most abusive order type out there?

Given that I'm not in the trading side, I'm really not an expert on that. I would rather rely on what I've heard from other traders. Again, like the stuff about early news releases, it's not so much the fact that it exists as the fact that's done secretly and not widely disclosed. If the way they roll out these order types is requiring people to look for fine print, or they're not disclosing it unless you belong to the club, I would have a problem with that.

You want them to disclose and be transparent about this stuff so that the people who participate and don't use these order types can avoid playing that game?

The best markets are the ones that are the most transparent. They have the most diversity of participants. People trading on different time frames, methods, news sources, etc. The only way you'll get diversity of participation is if all these different players know exactly who's doing what and who has what advantages. It's OK for some groups to have advantages, as a long everybody else knows what those advantages are. It's fine for people to get the Fed news early, as a long everybody knows what's going on.

In that day of the Fed FOMC no-taper announcement, gold was moving way before everything else. What was that about?

My best guess is that this information got leaked out of the Fed. It had to be a leak, because the machines bought with such abandon that they had to know. They were all-in, and in Wall Street they rarely do that. Quite a few people had to know that information. It wouldn't surprise me if some of those leaked to someone else, and that's how it ended up in gold. In other words, there were probably a dozen people who knew it. It probably wasn't as closely guarded as it should have been. One of those people leaked to someone else.

Why do you think they chose gold specifically?

Because it's international. It trades around the world. They might not even have bought the COMEX or CME gold. They might have done it in Europe or in the Middle East. Then it was arbitraged into our market.

Do you think they did this because if the leakers got caught it wouldn't be easily traceable to whoever was behind the trades?

Yeah, they probably went to the place that was the easiest and most anonymous. It only showed up in our markets later. I haven't looked closely at that. Maybe it's something to investigate one day. That's my feeling. Gold always seems to be involved. If anything is going to have a tell early or have a fake-out early, nine times out of ten gold is going to be a part of it.

If they'd bought the S&P500 futures, it would be so obvious that everybody would want an investigation?

Yes, and you can only trade the S&P500 futures in one place.

And it's easy to trace the orders and trades too, correct?

Yes, it's quite easy to trace.

According to some reports, the profitability of HFTs is going down. Why do you think this is happening right now?

Part of this is the fact that the rules are being followed closer now. For example, we don't see as many locked or crossed quotes as we used to. But a big part of this comes back to the issue I talked about earlier, which is that people are becoming aware of what is going on. If people know the advantages that are going on, they're going to adjust accordingly.

The low hanging fruit's gone. Their costs skyrocketed too, because every time you move things faster, your costs go up exponentially. You have to have really talented people to run ten-gig networks, for example. We are getting to the cutting bleeding edge, as we like to call it. It's extremely expensive all around, and the cat is out of the bag.

Do you think there's hope for a fairer market, because they're going to start to go out of business, and they'll be unable to do as much lobbying and pushing for advantages and things like that?

Yes, you could be right. The market's becoming aware of all this might end up doing more than a regulator ever could. It's a shame that we pay for these organizations, the SEC and CFTC. We've got these rules that are clear and easy to follow, and it's frustrating when they don't apply them evenhandedly. Capitalism doesn't work unless you have the rule of law.

In the OTC markets, the SEC has been very aggressive in stopping frauds and scams this year. What do you think of this new chairwoman of the SEC? Do you think they mean business this time?

I think the new boss is the same as the old boss. If she wanted to show us she was serious, I would have expected a lot right away. Take the whole Mark Cuban trial, for example. I actually looked at that data very closely. I spent a couple of days investigating it. My take away from it was that the stock manipulators who were behind mama.com were complete frauds. They should have been investigated. Mark Cuban was just a victim of all that. The SEC went after the victim. It didn't make any sense to me at all. I was surprised that it was allowed to go on like that. It didn't take much reading to realize that they were going after the wrong people. They essentially gave the mama.com people immunity for their weak testimony against Mark Cuban.

They fined the NYSE over the fact that they were delaying the data on purpose. Is that still going on?

Yes. I published a paper after the SEC had the rollout of MIDAS in which I said that the one thing they should look at immediately was the quotes from the consolidated feed. Then they should find their counterparts in the direct feed and compare the time stamps. That's how we found the NYSE delay. That's how they're going to see that the delays are much more frequent than anybody realizes.

Do you think the SEC doesn't understand a lot of this stuff because they have too many legal experts and lawyers on their staff?

No, they have the trading and markets division. Greg Burman says he knows what's going on with markets much more than Nanex does, for example. He told a group of institutional investors that Nanex doesn't know what they're talking about. That would seem to imply that he does. I would say that they're very aware of what's happening, which makes the next question even more difficult: why let it happen?

If you were asked to take his job, would you take it?

I would do it for free for a year, but only if they applied the law to whoever I found to be the bad guy, no matter who it was.

So if you accused Goldman Sachs and they didn't fine them, you would step down?

Yes.

What about that Goldman Sachs issue with the options in the NASDAQ. How come they had their trades busted?

What's so odd about that is that when NASDAQ had their outage one week earlier, one of our customers was arbitraging equities and options. The BBO stopped, and he was thinking the price of the stock was X. He'd gotten on in the options side and was working his order in the equity side, and it kept coming back—failing because the price actually moved. NASDAQ wasn't printing out the quotes anymore. He ended with only half the side of the arb. He immediately requested the CBOE to cancel his options side because of the equipment failure in the equity side. They didn't let him out. They said the equity didn't go out until 12:20, when in fact the trading stopped at 12:20, but the quotes stopped at 12:10. It was a small trade, less than twenty contracts, but two weeks later they helped out Goldman Sachs, who obviously should have known better, get away with destroying with the whole price discovery process. That got them all busted. That makes no sense.

If it was Knight Capital that had done that, would they have busted it?

In my opinion the only reason they didn't bust Knight trades last year was because they weren't cleanly delineated. You couldn't say, "All trades above this price, or below this price." It was a mix. It was impossible to say they were going to cancel some trades but not others. That's why they didn't cancel Knight's trades. I believe they would have if Knight had done all the trades in one side above or under a certain price. The CEO even called Mary Shapiro's private cell phone that evening. He wouldn't have made that call unless he thought there was a chance of a cancel there.

Do you think the exchanges are in urgent need to update their systems?

Yes. The thing is they spend all their money on the direct feeds, not enough on the consolidated feeds, which is the one that retail and dark pools get access to.

Lessons from Chapter 8

1. Don't try to compete in ultra-short-term timeframes. As Eric explains, the delays both from the data feeds (most people get the slow consolidated feed instead of the fast direct feed) and the human eye (along with brain processing) means that by the time you hit the buy or sell button you're already trading ages after the HFTs have. If there's any kind of opportunity for profit in excess of trading costs, it's likely already been taken by the HFTs by the time you act.

2. Levels of intraday noise have increased significantly since 2004. As Eric's study shows, prices have become more noisy and volatile since then. This makes it important to have wider stops. Lengthen your time horizon to avoid getting caught in that noisy chop.

3. Market orders are gamed because the order routers can't send out the order to other exchanges fast enough. The HFTs can quickly cancel their other orders, leaving you with a partial fill in your intended position. Anything more than a 100 shares is a risky size to be used in a market order. This doesn't apply as much in

liquid ETFs such as SPY, but it does in less liquid issues such as small, mid-cap, and certain big-cap stocks.

4. Passive limit orders will be gamed in illiquid stocks. In more illiquid names with a bigger spread, if you try to avoid paying that spread by posting a limit order on the bid or ask, your solution might be worse than the disease. Assuming you don't get penny jumped by a market-making HFT (which is likely to happen a lot of the time), you will still get subpennied by internalizers and wholesalers. What is the solution? **Only trade in these more illiquid issues when they're in play** (when there's big news going on with a lot of retail or big money participation). If they're not, don't trade them at all. Avoid scalping on them because fills are really difficult. If you do trade them, use native hidden orders—that way at least you won't have some of the games played against you.

5. Retail flow can be inferred through subpenny trades. Eric points out that aggregating subpenny trades can tell you what the retail is doing. This might serve as an indicator of which side is likely to be a good fade down the line or what kind of interest is behind the current move of a stock.

6. Lots of HFT games in stocks are about trying to find out which orders are real and which are not. This is why you should never show your hand. These guys make a living off making you pay a few cents more after they know your intentions.

7. The open has significantly wider spreads. It's very important for you not to misjudge your liquidity at the open. If you take a big position through the NYSE opening auction or NASDAQ opening cross, you'll find that it's impossible to exit without materially affecting the price. You can bet the HFTs know this, because they have access to the opening print volume and the current liquidity level. At the mere sign that some people are trying to exit their positions, they'll make these traders pay. This also applies to overnight positions and trades taken after the opening.

8. The importance of position sizing and knowing how big you can get in a trade. This lesson is related to the last one. In an HFT-driven era, liquidity is really scarce; lots of firms have strategies to try to detect big orders and then make these orders get executed at worse prices. **Always know how big a position you can take and try to be on the safe side because you are harmed asymmetrically by mistakes.** You will hurt yourself a lot more by having a position that is 4 times what it should be (given the available liquidity) than one that is 2 times what it should be. You are likely to be harmed by more than 100 percent in comparison (it would be 100 percent if there was not asymmetry) by making the larger mistake due to the efficiency in which HFT firms can detect bigger orders and the mechanics of auction

markets[30]. It's a much bigger problem to have someone discover your intention to liquidate your position if you are several multiples of the available liquidity because now they can "squeeze" you (whether you are long or short). They can now find the highest price you are willing to pay or lowest price you are willing to offer (your "squeeze price") and get your order done there. With bigger positions there is more time for you to be detected (as you work your order) and more volume to be done closer to your maximum squeeze price.

9. Never show your hand. Be careful with "smart" order routers. A lot of the time these routers don't even have a Thor-like system behind them, which means they constantly give HFTs a chance to cancel orders and make you pay more to get your orders done. The issue is that even if they do, these routers can be gamed by HFTs because they have a set criteria of how to route to multiple pools of liquidity all at the same time. Lots of times they count on a stable relationship in the time that it takes to send the orders from the broker to the ECNs—exchanges. It will try to send the multiple orders in the exact time difference between them so they all hit those pools at the same time, taking all the displayed liquidity without allowing the HFTs to cancel their orders. When the relationship changes (due to tricks such as quote stuffing, essentially bombarding an ECN or exchange with orders and modifications), the router can backfire and end up exposing your buy or sell interest. Another issue with these smart routers is that they sometimes will hit dark pools first before going to displayed exchanges. Some of these dark pools might be tipping off HFTs about incoming orders and this will allow them to cancel and make you pay more. How can you deal with this issue? That's where lesson 10 comes in.

10. Direct routing can be effective when trying to move size. If you're trying to work out a larger order, try directly routing to an ECN or exchange that's displaying the larger size. Take it out and see how the price reacts. As Eric says, sometimes by waiting a bit, you will see some recharging of bids and asks, which allows you to continue to work your order. It can be a costly mistake to try to get out of size all at once with a regular smart router. **An even better solution, though, can be routing the entire order using IEX (The Investors Exchange)**. Although it was not mentioned in the interview, Eric says some of his clients report better fills using IEX when trying to work out big orders. I wrote a guide about how traders can use IEX to their advantage in Chapter 14 in the section called "Improve your order execution by using IEX as a smart order router." Using IEX and their proprietary routing system (which is much better than the average broker smart router) can stop the

---

[30] In an auction market, the price is set by the highest price a buyer is willing to pay and the lowest price a seller is willing to offer.

problem of having quotes being cancelled as soon as you try to take out an entire level. This can be quite useful for big orders.

11. Gold can provide you with tells or clues of incoming economic releases. Due to its international nature and liquidity, gold is used by people who get leaked news. It's likely to have happened in the FOMC no-taper announcement. The folks who get the data ahead of time, in an effort to hide their activities, will buy gold in Europe, Asia, Middle East or any market where they have anonymity. Due to arbitrage, that buying will show up in GLD, CME Gold, etc. Anyone who correctly read the gold rally on the FOMC no-taper day could have made millions buying the S&P500 futures, all legally, since this is simply a speculative opinion about a public price.

Chapter 9

Mitch Semon—The Veteran Stock Operator

Mitch (Twitter @mitchthemoney) has been trading for a really long time. He has a lot of experience dealing with all kinds of markets and has pretty much seen it all when it comes to stock trading.

After working for a decade as a market maker, he made the move to prop trading, initially using other people's capital to trade. I didn't notice it during the interview process, but as I got into transcription and editing, I realized that he'd been a bit guarded about sharing too much information about how he trades. I suppose this is normal during tough times in the markets, and it further reinforces the main lesson from Chapter 12. Even being a bit guarded, he did provided significant insights and lessons that I found helpful.

This interview was conducted in January of 2013.

When did you decide you wanted become a trader?

I'd just come out of college, then I got hired at OLDE Discount, which was a discount brokerage firm. I worked at OLDE for maybe ten or eleven years until I got moved to H&R Block, and then we got bought out. After 9/11 they didn't like the risk of that firm, so they eliminated their trading force. I was a market maker, like a New York specialist, with them for ten or eleven years, and I was actually the head of the listed equity desk for last year before they shut it down. Then we got laid off. I didn't really want to move to New York, Florida, or Texas. I decided to start trading on my own. So I've been doing it probably for eight or nine years on my own now.

So you were a standard market maker back then?

Yes.

How do you see the computers that do that job right now? They seem to make the markets, but they don't have the obligations that you guys had.

That's the problem. The spreads used to be large. Then we went to teenies, then to pennies. Once it got there it just wasn't worth it for the New York specialist anymore. So what that did was to make the market thinner, take volume away, like the NASDAQ now. These computers put bids and offers in, but they're not really making markets. They're not ready to stand by whatever they're showing. The computers now are just throwing stuff and moving it, putting the bids and taking them away really fast. That's why we have more things like flash crashes now. There's no one ready to step up when liquidity dries up. Before, a market maker would step up. These days there's too much risk and not enough profit. It's not worth it. For me, that's the biggest problem with the electronic trading now. They're not there to stand by a market. They're interested in making a profit. But a market maker's job was not only to make money, but also to make a good market.

Back then in the '90s, was it easy to make the markets and make money every day?

For the most part, yeah. When we made markets, we had order flow also, which helps make you money, because it helps in capturing the spread. And we had somewhat bigger spreads, especially on the NASDAQ where they had different rules. They could do whatever they wanted. In New York, it was pretty well written what you had to do. It was pretty easy to make money every day.

When markets went to decimals, did you immediately give up on the idea of making markets and try to develop a new strategy?

No, because I was with the company. We were still making markets, and it was still pretty profitable. We did a report from before they shut us down, and it showed how profitable we were. It was still profitable business, just not as much as in the past. And, like I said, we had 9/11 and a few things that made the risk outweigh the rewards, because there were lawsuits starting to happen at that time due for people not getting prints or people doing funny things with the orders. Not necessarily at our firm, but just street wide. H&R Block bought us out, and they didn't know the risks involved. They didn't want to delve into it and figure out if it was risky or not. You still could have made it in market making back then, but it was getting harder, and the profit margin was getting squeezed big time.

And what college did you attend?

Oregon State. I was in finance.

Do you think the knowledge there helped you?

It helped a little bit, but I think it's more of a personality trait than anything. I think you can't really learn how to trade. You know, it's kind of in your blood to trade or it's not. I don't think it's something you can pick up by reading it in a book. It takes a certain type of temperament and frame of mind to be able to do this.

After they closed down the trading division there, you moved immediately into a prop firm?

I traded on my own a little bit with Ameritrade. I had a no-compete clause for one year, so I couldn't go anywhere else. I traded in that period, taking longer-term views of the market. And when that time expired, I actually went to two other firms. Short-term trading prop firms.

What was the main reason that you wanted to go prop? Was it the leverage or being able to be next to other traders and learn from them?

We were working for companies at that time, prop firm for the company, trying to make money for them. So we were using their money. And that was the main reason. If you do blow up or you do have an issue, it's much easier. It's not your own cash.

How long did you have the advantage of trading on their cash?

Probably a couple of years. I did it with two different firms, and it probably lasted a total of two years, probably about a year each.

And back then, what was the way to make money?

A lot of time, I pull up a lot of stocks by sector. And whatever news is out, you find a hot stock and you find some of the laggards and the others in the same sector. So if somebody had good news, you pulled the whole sector and just traded off the stocks and didn't quite pick up the same momentum that they had.

Like sympathy plays?

Right, yeah. Sympathy plays. It was a hot news of the day strategy. I was basically a high frequency trader back then. The market is very different now. It still wasn't as computerized as it is now. A lot of big levels would have a sell stop, so they would blow through whole numbers. You could put these sized bids in. When it hit the number, it would gap. We still had gap prints, which we don't have anymore. So that was an easy trade to make, quick money.

When did you start to notice that the markets had become more difficult?

Markets became more difficult in the last two years for sure. Two and a half years.

So you had a ten-year period in which it was good for you?

Seven to eight years.

Why did it become more difficult?

Two reasons: the computers and the volatility. Volatility is what all day traders live for, and when the volatility has just gotten killed like it has, it's really hard. And then you add the computers on top of that. It seems like they're controlling these thin stocks out there.

So after Reg NMS, you didn't notice anything. It took a few years for things to get harder?

Right, yes. But like I said, we had huge volatility at that point, which still made it easier for a trader to make money.

Was what you were doing mostly momentum trading?

No. I usually did revision to mean. So when something got too far oversold one way or the other, I used to trade.

Is it like STZ today?

Like RIMM this morning when it just sold off hard. When it accelerates in the downside, I start buying small, and as it gets lower you buy more and you profit on the way back up. That's how I used to trade a lot.

Source: Thinkorswim platform

A lot of traders say you're not supposed to trade mid-day, but sometimes I find that if there's news, it becomes a good opportunity, like STZ. It's mid-day, but it's down a lot, and it's probably going to bounce.

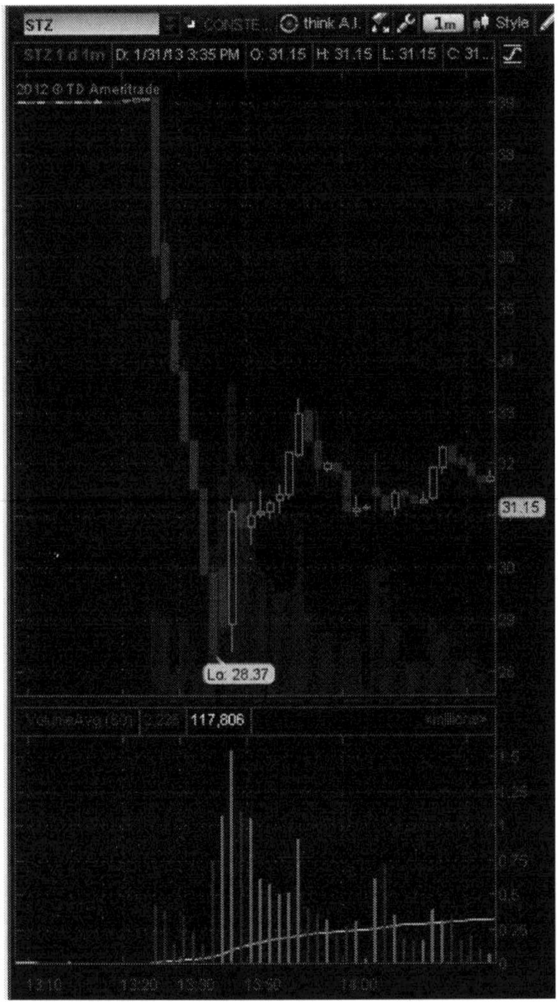

Source: Thinkorswim platform

Yeah, I played that a little bit today. A lot of it these days is picking news stocks because you need the volatility. If you don't have it, it's really hard to trade in this market, because these computers can just move the stock back and forth. Unless you have strong conviction about the position, it's hard to keep it. I'm trading more now on breakout levels, 200 moving average, finding levels that will give me more conviction in what I'm doing. Before I used to trade the momentum, oversold or overbought stuff and took the other side. With the computers, it's more of a trend thing. You have to go with the trend more.

Given that you do these news plays, don't you find that it's worth it to invest in more expensive news services?

When I'm trading the news, I'm trading more to see the stock. I'm not quick enough to see the news and understand it. As soon as the news hit STZ, they already moved the stock a ton. Same thing with earnings. As soon as it hits, they move the stock and you have to figure out if it's overdone or not. Hearing the story first is great if you can do it, but everybody gets the story at the same time, and the computers are already doing what they're programmed to do.

So you're not trying to compete with them in that game?

They're way faster than I am, and they're going to understand it faster. What I'm waiting for is for the computer to make a mistake, like in STZ today, where they just take the news and keep beating a stock down. The computers feed off themselves because they don't know what's going on. They just follow the momentum.

Do you use Twitter a lot to get a sense of what is going on?

I follow some people on StockTwits to get a sense of what they're looking at, what they're doing. I don't tweet anything, but I do follow some people just to get an idea of what they like in the market. Helps me find some trading ideas. It also helps me with research so I can piggyback on other people's research. If someone says some levels are breaking out, I'll pull up on my chart and see if it's something that I'd like to pull into my watch list for that day.

When you gave up on market making and moved to retail or prop, were you profitable right away, or did it take a while?

No, I've always been profitable. Of course, there are days that you're not. I've probably had a couple of months in my ten years that I was not profitable, but the rest of them I made money.

Do you think right now is probably the toughest time for someone to start?

Yes, this definitely has been my toughest time in twenty years, mainly because the volatility is low and the markets are being run by the computers. It's a double whammy. As I said, right now you have to play news stories, and it's hard to decipher exactly what the news is and how it will impact the stock in real time, so you're taking a little more risk.

So you found that your timeframe had to be widened out a bit? You can't get in and out so quickly?

I do both. I try to not carry stuff overnight, because you never know what can happen, but I definitely do sometimes.

Do you backtest your strategies?

I don't do any backtesting.

You just learn on the fly?

I traded as a market maker for ten years and did it on my own for another ten, so I know what I see when I see it. It's hard to teach somebody. It's a matter of being in the market for so long.

Are there any similarities between the current market and the markets back then?

This is kind of like what we saw in the NASDAQ during the tech boom. Back then the market makers would just keep stepping away, because the stocks were just going nuts. Everybody would just keep buying and the market maker would just keep moving his bids and offers up so the stocks would just move insane amounts. I think we see some of that in stocks these days.

Do you think because you had all those years watching the markets, you built up an instinct that tells you when something is overextended, it's too low, too high, etc.?

Right, just watching, you can get a feel for the market. You have to put in the time. If anyone is thinking of getting into day trading, they have to just sit and trade a dummy account for a long time just to get a feel for it. The people that are jumping in right away, they might get lucky a little bit, but it's hard to be right consistently.

Do you make most of your money at the open?

Open, the close, and the after-hours.

After-hours for earnings and things like that?

Earnings, news, or just market making. Sometimes you find people who have to get out of positions, and I'll take the other side. I do it in stocks that don't have a lot of risk.

With regards to executing orders, do you find yourself being screwed over by the computers many times?

You can see that if you put an order in, you get front run a lot, usually before the open and after the close. Sometime they'll penny jump you.

Do you use stuff like hidden orders?

I will use a hidden order if I want to buy some stock and there's an order in front of me and he keeps penny jumping me. I might go ahead and put a hidden order, but I don't do that a lot.

Do you take liquidity most of the time?

I do both. We get paid to post an order on most exchanges, so it's more beneficial to post instead of lifting, but obviously in the news stories and trades like that I will lift, or if I want to get out of something I'll just hit what I see. In other types of trades I'll post.

In these news stories, sometimes I find that it's good to post. Like in STZ, it was already down so much that sometimes it dropped more, hit you, and then bounced right back.

Right. Another thing I do because the market is more momentum driven is to use buy stops or sell stops.

In those days where the markets just keeps going, it looks so easy to make money. You just buy the dip and cash it. Is it really as easy as it looks?

It's easy if you can do it. As I said, I tend to be more countertrend so it's hard for me. I'm having a harder time in the last year. It's a slow creep up, and I'm just not used to doing that. It does look easy. You see a lot of those people on StockTwits, or whatever, that do go with the momentum. They're just buying with small size, so they don't get rid of it if it does pullback, and then they let it run.

Do you think this is a sign of complacency? That everybody is so comfortable with the markets and buying the dip that we're headed to a crash or volatility expansion?

I think we could be, but a lot of that has to do with the Fed just pumping up money. All the stocks are just propped up by money. When the Fed puts that much liquidity in the economy, it has to go somewhere. It's going to bonds, which are headed to a crash, and they're putting in stocks, which over-inflates its true value.

In 2008, when there was a lot of volatility, did you do well there?

Yes, that was my best year.

You just shorted bounces?

I bought sharp moves down and shorted large up moves.

You believe it was easy in that year because there were so many fund managers in the market distorting prices?

Right. It was the movement for one thing, and because there were so many different players and lots of disparities in the market.

These fund managers seem not to care about a few cents. Does this benefit the day traders?

Yeah, these fund managers just don't care about a few cents. The machines are different. That's what they're playing for.

Sometimes I see intraday that, at a key support or resistance level, a fund manager will be sitting there with a huge order. Aren't they just giving money away doing that?

No, because if they have a level that they want to get in or out at, they don't care if they're wrong in the short-term. For instance, if a manager wants to get STZ at $32, he doesn't care if he buys it. It goes to $31.75, and he had to overpay a bit. If he wants to buy a million shares, he can just post at $32 and sit there all day until he gets his size done. He knows where he wants to enter the stock. He's giving away a little bit of money, but he's also happy he got the price he wanted. That's what his goal was. In the long-term, 20 cents doesn't make a difference for hedge funds.

Can a human take advantage of that, or is it just for the computers?

If you know the guy is there and he has an order, he's usually not going to show that kind of size. We used to have people on the floor that would give us an idea what the order books looked like.

What is your take on subpenny trades?

They need to get rid of that. There should be no off-exchange trades. It's hard enough with a one-penny, and it really doesn't provide much price improvement.

What other advantages do you believe should be stripped away from the HFTs?

Off-exchange trades is the main one. I can sit in a stock as best bid and ask, and I still see plenty of volume going through off exchange, and I don't get those fills.

Through all of the years in your trading and in prop firms, what's the biggest characteristic you noticed in winning traders?

The biggest characteristic is that they know how to take losses. It's easy to make money, but it's hard to take a loss. If you see something going up and you like it, you buy it, but what do you do when it turns? Do you double up? Do you ride it? That's the hardest part. Knowing when to cut your losses and limit your losses.

Do you think it's easier for you because you have a long history of making money? A new guy doesn't have that confidence, and he might have bills to pay, so he has to deal with a bigger psychological pressure.

Yeah, I had ten years as a market maker and many years using other people's money before I had to use my own money, and by then I knew I was a successful trader and I could do it. If you're starting out, if you make money, that's fine. But if you lose, it puts you in a hole and a bad mental frame. It does make it a lot tougher. You might step off what you normally should do, trying to make it back. It's similar to what a gambling addiction would be. If you're behind, you might start pressing your bets, and that's a bad way to trade. If you have a big loss one day, that's life. You just have to go back to your normal trading and not try to recoup it all in one big swing.

Are you confident that you'll continue to make money in the next five and ten years?

Yes. It definitely has gotten worse, but I assume the volatility will pick up some. I don't think it will pick up anytime soon, but I believe the markets will get a bit shakier if the Fed will quit flooding the markets with money.

Are you concerned that the computers will get so good that they'll start to take profits away even in longer-term timeframes?

No, value wins out always. If a stock is worth X, it will get there. If you like a stock and do your homework, the value will shine through eventually. What the computers do is take stocks that people like, such as Apple, and when everybody is pounding it higher, the computers extend that run a bit more than what it should have been. You essentially have a bit more boom and bust.

So they just exacerbate daily volatility?

In certain stocks, yes.

And the edge lies in fading these extremes?

Yes, it's hard now without other people in there, because liquidity is thin. The computer doesn't know that. It just knows that it went up, so it wants to get long. And then it goes up more, and then others want to get on. You can see that when it's really thin and nothing else is happening, the computers control the stock. They'll throw fake bids and fake offers to make it move around a little bit, but for the most part, there's not a lot happening. Most people take lunchtime off, because there's not a lot happening, but when there are news plays, its worthwhile trading. It's the same thing with the market in general. Back then the down period during lunchtime was like the whole time today. We used to have a lot more volatility in the open and the close.

Some people are concerned that the computers can tell when there's an area full of stops and they can trigger that to mess with people. Do you think they do?

They do.

Do you get stop hunted sometimes?

Yeah, they'll go down to trigger something they see. I believe they pay for that. I think they see that ahead of time. That's for sure something they're doing.

So you don't use hard stops?

I do use some ARCA or NSDQ stops, and they'll still trigger then, but sometimes you have to use them. In super thin stocks I don't use them, because they'll go there and trigger them on purpose. In more liquid stocks it's not a big issue.

How much of your trading is instinct compared to logic?

Probably 70 percent are breakouts, moving averages, news, etc., and 30 percent is just gut.

Do you use moving averages to figure out what other people are thinking?

I use them to know some breakout levels. Whether it's right or wrong, they do move the stock. Fundamentally it doesn't make a difference, but technically it does. Stocks react to that, the computers react, Twitter and day traders do too. It's a self-fulfilling prophecy kind of thing.

Which MA are most people paying attention to?

I don't know. 30, 50, 200 day.

So you don't use intraday MAs? You only use daily MAs?

Yes, for important support and resistance levels. I have friends that do use intraday MAs, but I don't.

Some traders I know found that moving away from one-minute charts was useful in an HFT-driven market. Is that something that you found as well?

No, I just use one-minute charts.

Do you pay attention to longer timeframes?

I'm watching basically the same stocks every day so I don't need to, except for news stocks. For those I will pull up a longer-term chart, because you don't want to be in the opposite side of something that's a big move. For the ninety stocks that I watch regularly, I just know from watching them every day and seeing what their ranges are.

So you have a set of stocks that you watch every day and try to learn from. Then every once in a while you'll put a trade in?

Yes. I'll also trade whatever the news is, whatever is hot or is moving. These stocks I'm not as familiar with, so I'll need more information from longer-term charts.

Do you think that by watching those same stocks every day you accumulate knowledge that gives you an edge over other people?

Yeah. You know the general range of what the stock does. If $1 or $0.30 is the normal for it, you get more comfortable taking positions when it reaches one of those two bands.

For instance, on the Knight debacle day, REE, which normally trades in a narrow range, just quickly dropped over a dollar and kept bouncing 20 to 40 cents and selling off. I liked being long down there and made really good fast money without much risk.

Do you use the Level 2 to predict, to make decisions? Or does it not matter anymore?

It doesn't make that much difference. I do use it and watch it, but there's a lot of BS too. They put stuff then take it away. I use it, but it's not as indicative of what it used to be.

In the old days you could use it to predict a lot of moves, right?

Right, that's what the computers are doing now by paying to see all of our orders ahead of time. They see the orders, and they're front running. Back then, if you saw a big bid or offer somewhere, you'd sit in front of it and have a stop to lean on. You could make money if it went up, or lose a penny if it went down. Now the books aren't what they used to be.

Would you say the same thing about tape reading?

Tape reading is more of a feel thing.

Do you think there can still be an advantage there?

Yes, there's definitely an advantage there. You can see if someone keeps refreshing and the pace at which they're doing it, and you can kind of see when they get cleaned up. Let's say a stock is down a lot. When you feel the seller has been cleaned up, you want to be back in there, because it will probably bounce.

So you try to get a sense if there's a big fund that's liquidating or accumulating?

Yeah, it used to be a lot easier. It has gotten a lot harder in the last couple of years.

Sometimes it seems that you can tell a big fund manager is liquidating just by looking at the chart. You see a stock with bad earnings going down over quite an extended period of time, and it hardly bounces. Could that be an indication?

Right. Like I said, most of the fund managers, if they have a target or something has changed in their perspective, they don't care what the price is. They'll just get out of their position. If they don't like earnings, or they were expecting a certain amount of growth, if it doesn't achieve what they want, a lot of times their whole view on the stock changes, and they just want out.

I think I saw that the other day on AAPL after earnings. In the middle of the day, it just went straight down with hardly a bounce. It looked like easy money. Just short, and these guys will continue to sell.

Yeah, before it used to be different. Now it's easier to go with the trend, because you got the computers, the funds, the day traders. Everyone is doing the same thing. It becomes like a self-fulfilling prophecy. I'm not as used to those plays, so it's harder for me to get onboard with that. I'm more of a countertrend guy. I'm trying to adapt to that a little bit. You have to keep adapting to these market changes. You have to try new strategies, new ways to trade.

During earning season though, it gets a bit better, right?

Yeah, there's more news, volatility, a little more movement in the whole market. Earnings season definitely helps.

With regards to reading the news and interpreting it, doesn't your finance background help on that?

It does, but I don't try to pretend to be smarter than all the funds out there. I'm probably better than most of the day traders, but for all the mutual funds and hedge funds that have positions and are reacting to that news immediately, I assume they know more than I know. Also, the news we see is not exactly the real news. You can see news stories that are wrong. Some are fraudulent, and some are stated incorrectly.

What kind of machine setup do you have?

I'm not really tech savvy. I have three computers, eight monitors.

Why so many?

I have my platforms that I trade on two, six have charts, and one of them has news as well. I have Fly on the Wall, Briefing, StockTwits, so I can see what news is coming.

Do you trade inside a prop firm or do you trade from home?

From home.

You don't find that it's worth it to go to the prop firm?

I'm on Skype all day with people that I used to trade with at OLDE, so it's like sitting next to them. It definitely helps to have people to bounce ideas around. It's also good to have more eyes to see when something is moving. If I didn't have that, I'd probably prefer to go to a prop firm.

In the period that you were in the firm, did you learn a lot from others?

You definitely learn, but everyone has their own style and their own risk tolerance. You can see someone make $100,000 every day, and you think all you have to do is to mimic him, but you have a different risk tolerance and it just doesn't work. Sometimes you try to do what others do, and you just don't have the same feel for it, because they have a different style of trading. You can learn stuff from others, but you can't just trade like somebody else.

Why do you think you were able to adapt to changing conditions while lots of other traders weren't able to do?

The biggest thing is that you don't want to get too stubborn. Take your losses and move on. The markets are constantly evolving. There will always be something new. You have to adapt, otherwise you'll be left behind.

Do you think it helped that you were humble about the market?

Probably, because I've seen it all happen. I've seen plenty of people blow up, have big losses, and end their careers. Seeing that definitely makes you more aware of what can happen. It also makes you a bit more risk averse, which can hurt your profits too. During the Internet boom, I didn't care to play any of those stocks that people were making a killing on.

What's the biggest loss you ever had?

My biggest loss was working for a firm. A big loss is usually something that moves really quickly, so fast that you can't logically get out of it. Like on STZ, if I was long at $39 and the news came out, and it was at $34, $33, and then I bought more and it then went to $32, $31, $29. It's too fast and I wouldn't be able to take a loss at that point. I'd be stuck playing my average instead of doing what I should be doing, which is cutting the losses after a certain amount no matter what. If a trade blows through those limits, it's hard to do that. You're nowhere near where you wanted to take your loss.

I believe I lost $200,000 for the firm once. We had a minicrash. I was long on big name stocks, but the market makers were backing away. These big name stocks were dropping a buck or two bucks with every print, kind of like a flash crash.

During these flash crashes these days, I find it hard to trade, because you don't know if there's news out that you are not aware of.

Right, right. If it's an individual stock, it's a lot more risky. If it's market-wide, it's a little easier to handle, because you know it's probably an exaggeration or a matter of computers chasing computers. In a single stock, you just never know what the news could be.

Do you step in every once in a while in a specific stock in a flash crash type decline?

Yeah, like STZ today, you have to pick your spots and start small. Normally you shouldn't average in a bad position, but in this case you're just saying it's an overplay on something and you average in. You just don't want to get too big too fast.

During the mid-day, do you just sit and wait for the news plays?

I actually try to walk away from my computer. I trade from 7 to 11 in the morning (EST), then come back at maybe 2:30. I try to take that mid-day off unless the market is active with news, maybe the Fed or something. I find that I get in trouble if I sit at the computer during the mid-day.

In the premarket, do you trade the ARCA/NSDQ premarket or mostly after BATS and everybody else comes online?[31]

I trade right from the start, the ARCA/NSDQ premarket.

---

31 ARCA and NSDQ pre-market session start at 4AM EST while BATS, EDGX and a number of ECNs come online at 8AM EST.

Usually news plays as well?

Yeah. I'll put bids in stocks that I like. In premarket, some people can get nervous, and sometimes they'll sell it quite a bit away from where the real market is simply because there's no liquidity. In that case, no liquidity is a good thing.

You just try to capture the spread a little bit there?

Yes, try to capture when somebody gets nervous about the market or they don't like their position. Every once in a while I'll get hurt because there will be news coming out that I didn't know about, but for the most part I just try to capture a wider spread than there is during the regular trading day. Same thing with after the close.

Sometimes you can catch people in the ex-div days, if a stock goes ex-div for $1 and you put an offer at where it closed and get hit while in theory the stock should trade $1 lower than the close.

What kind of advice do you give to a novice or struggling trader right now?

My biggest advice is just sit down and study the market for a while. Do test trading. Don't put real money until you're comfortable with what you're dealing with. When you do go with real money, start small and learn to cut your losses. Take whatever you can afford to play with, and don't use more than that. If you want to be around, cut your losses well before you hit your personal limits.

Why did you decide that you wanted to trade equities instead of something else?

I don't know. I wanted to be an investment banker when I finished college, but then I got into trading and I liked it. It fits my temperament and my style. I enjoy what I do. It doesn't feel like a job. It feels like fun for me.

Over the years that you traded, did you have a lot of strategies that you discarded?

Yes, like I said, the markets are constantly evolving. As long as it's working, I don't try to change it, but when it starts to slow down, like right now, I try a few different strategies.

Do you use top-of-the-line, expensive software for charts and everything, or will anything work?

I use QuoteTracker, which is free, and it does a pretty good job for the charting. I use Bigcharts for longer-term, but you definitely need good charts and good news services.

US markets have pretty low volatility right now, but have you ever thought about trading different global markets where volatility is higher? Maybe Europe or somewhere?

We thought about that, but I've watched this market for twenty years. I know it pretty well. I'd be open to that, but I'm not there right now, because I don't have the need for it.

Lessons from Chapter 9

1. The ability to take losses is the most important characteristic Mitch noticed in winning traders he saw over the years, and he's been trading for over twenty years. Chapter 15 provides some advice on how to improve your loss-taking abilities.

2. When the markets are not really providing good opportunities, you have to focus more on news plays. They tend to attract retail traders, fund managers, etc. This provides you with an opportunity to interact with non-HFT order flow. They cause volatility to rise as well.

3. After a big loss, don't try to make it all back in one swing. Go back to your normal trading, and build your account back up. I know it's hard to do. People get addicted to progress and growth. Having a big loss is quite a setback to a rising P&L. The natural human instinct is to try to fix that by continuing to play larger. That's a mistake, because you will be trading bigger when your mental capital is the most depleted. (Large losses are mentally destabilizing even for great traders.) Your judgment will be at its worst, but your risk exposure at its highest. This combination simply doesn't make sense.

4. Try to develop your trading style so it becomes more robust. This lesson applies to solid winning traders only. Mitch mentioned how he is more of a counter-trend trader and was struggling to just jump in trends and ride them out. He was making an effort to adapt to that, however. The lesson is to try to develop your trading skillset so you can be great at a few things (your main strengths – these are the ones you nail with large size) and at least good at the rest (where you play with small to medium size). If you are a short seller, try to push yourself to buy more stocks even if it feels strange; if you are a long based trader, try shorting more. The same can be said about trend following and reversion to the mean traders. We all had setups and trading situations where we highly suspect something is about to

happen but have a hard time getting in because it's not how we are used to trading. By pushing yourself to trade in these situations you will get more comfortable and develop a more robust trading skillset. You will be ready for different market conditions. The stability of your trading income is likely to improve as well. There are plenty of periods where your main strengths don't come into play due to market conditions. By having a robust skillset, you can still make money while you wait for these conditions to improve.

5. HFTs and electronic trading cause momentum to be more persistent and overshoot. Computers can exacerbate these trends. You can profit by jumping into these trends and using a trailing mental stop, or you can wait for them to get really extreme then fade them. For fades, the ideal entry point is when the price action starts to accelerate in the direction of the trend, like in the RIMM trade.

6. Avoid stocks that are controlled by HFTs. They tend to be small and mid-cap stocks that aren't news plays. They have larger spreads and tend to be illiquid. The price action is much noisier. You will get tested a lot, and it will be hard to keep your position.

7. Be careful with hard stops. Mitch believes HFTs can see where they are because they have access to the order books. They're OK in liquid issues (like GE or liquid ETFs like SPY).

8. Have a set of stocks that you watch regularly. This will help you get familiar with their ranges, typical behaviors and patterns. You'll develop a sense of how they'll act on a particular day, and you'll be able to tell when they're overreacting or when they're cheap compared to everything else. This can be quite profitable at the open, because that's where a lot of the temporary price distortions occur.

9. Leaning on big orders is a dangerous game these days, since HFTs will often put fake size on the Level 2. In the old days you could try to be in front of that order, knowing it would provide an out for you. These days this game is way more dangerous. Even if the order is real, the HFTs will know when that order will get cleaned. Then they'll take out the rest of that order and several levels below that before you even have time to blink.

10. Big money managers usually don't care about 20 cents or so, and this provides an opportunity for day traders. The key is to put yourself in situations where you're interacting with them more and with HFTs less. Since these guys have to get their orders done, if you can anticipate how they'll act, you can profit. This is what academics miss about winning day traders when they claim they are just lucky coin flippers. They are actually really good at extracting profits off these big money managers by using tools like charts, L2, tape, orderbooks, etc.

11. Try to keep contact with a group of traders through Skype so you can bounce trade ideas off each other, share breaking news, and learn from each other's mistakes. You might also notice some methods other good traders are using to adapt to changing market conditions, and this can speed up your own adjustments.

12. In bounce plays, average in slowly with small size to start. The computers can exacerbate these trends, and if you get in big too fast, you could face a devastating loss. The STZ trade provided a good example of that. The stock declined from $39 to $28 in about ten minutes. This is different from averaging down, because it's all part of your plan, and it respects position size and loss limits. By averaging in, you can make a mistake or two in terms of timing and still be ok; when you buy all in one shot, you leave a lot of room for yourself to get hurt.

13. Walk away from the computer mid-day. When there are no great plays around, try to leave your computer. This is especially important to struggling traders or people who lack discipline.

Chapter 10

Wayne Kulcheski—The Trend Fighter

One of the first things I noticed about Wayne's (Twitter @trendfighter) trading style is how his mind seems to be immersed in the idea of mean reversion. It's as if his mind works in such a way as to give him the confidence that price contrarianism is the way to go. He frequently uses terms like *never, it's ridiculous, always,* and *forever.* These types of strong opinions seem to support him mentally when he has to fight trends in the markets and put a big position against the price action.

Trends can be powerful. They can capture people's imaginations and greed, which can frequently result in financial ruin when they reverse. It takes a certain mindset to resist falling for them. Wayne possesses that mindset, and he's a true contrarian.

At the same time, he's a longtime winner at trading, and anyone trading for so long is also mindful of risk management and the importance of knowing when to get out. Wayne balances the strong mindset and beliefs necessary to be skeptical of certain trends with the ability to pull back, protect trading capital, and live to fight for another day.

This interview was conducted in August of 2012 and updated in November of 2013.

What made you want to become a trader?

I guess the initial attraction to trading was to make as much money as humanly possible. I guess the sky's the limit if you can get a handle on it. I was always fascinated by the markets themselves. Of course, being able to create your own schedule was quite appealing. It gives me the chance to have a life other than working nine to five every day.

Which year did you start?

I started in 2001.

So you came after decimalization?

Yeah, they just switched to decimals, and they had the big NASDAQ bubble collapse, and we were just close to the bottom of that.

When you started, were you comfortable with short selling right away, or did you have to adapt to that?

No, I was comfortable right away. I just considered it the same as buying, really. I started at a prop firm in Canada, and they didn't really educate their people a lot, but they gave us very strict guidelines. We were only allowed to lose a few pennies per share. We just tried to make a few cents every trade, over and over again. At that time it was a little bit easier because, even though it was decimals, there were still spreads, and on top of that there was a lot of activity in both sides of the market.

Were you profitable right off the bat or did it take some time?

It actually took two months for me to become profitable. In order to get a full-time position in this job, a person had to make $5,000 net. I believe in my third month I ended up making $10,000 or $11,000, and I've been profitable ever since. I worked at that firm for maybe three years, but the profit split just wasn't enough. We were making between 35 percent and 50 percent of our profits. It was much better for me to go off on my own and get a better deal where I would keep more of my profits. That's what I did, and a bunch of other people in the office did the same.

Why did you go to a prop firm in the first place?

Primarily because I was twenty years old and I didn't have a lot of money to get started. The $25,000 minimum required and all that. I saw an ad for a prop firm that didn't have that many requirements, because prop trading was new at the time. I applied to all of the branches in my province, and I got a call the next day from a branch that wasn't in my hometown but I moved there. If I was older and had more money I would probably have started on my own, but at least this firm provided access to the market without me having to pay any commissions, so it was helpful.

Do you think that starting at prop and having contact with other traders helped you gain a sense of what worked and what didn't?

Well, because we were all new at this and no one had that much experience, it did help to talk and brainstorm with other people and trade off other people's ideas. It did provide us a good base to start to trade in our own styles and help each other. It was beneficial, for sure.

And back then, the main strategy was just scalping?. Buying at the bid and selling at the ask?

Yes, that was basically all we did. I started trading simple stocks too. I didn't go around on different stocks or follow trends or currencies/commodities. I just stuck with trading Cisco, Sun Microsystems, Intel, stuff like that. It was relatively easy to make money scalping, so there was no reason to venture into anything else.

When did you notice that this type of trading stopped working?

You know, even to this day I still do a lot of scalping. I have a few different accounts that I trade by different strategies. It's harder now, because the market has completely changed. There's not as much liquidity in the market. There are a lot more institutional orders and dark books that I can't really take advantage of. We can't get access to those fills. Whereas before all of those fills would have to be delivered through an ECN or through the NYSE, now they're just these big blocks of stocks that just go off at these crazy prices. It's very hard now to get in and out of decent sized positions.

Yeah, just today I had an issue with a stock. I put a hidden bid, and a bunch of orders were going to hit me. Before they did, the HFT filled me for like twelve shares. He found out where I was, and he went to the level, got filled for all the market orders, and I was stuck for twelve shares.

Yes, that happens a lot of the time. You get pinged for 12 shares or 100 shares. It's hard, because I can tell you that so many times during the day I have a decent size position, and let's say I have an offer there to sell at some level. The number of times it comes right to my price and stops there, it's ridiculous. It's almost as if your order will not get executed unless the HFT guy can get a better price than your order. It's like no one is going to buy your 10,000 shares at $9 unless they know they'll get $9.02 or $9.05 or whatever, because they know the order flow.

Can't you use native hidden orders to try to disguise your hand?

I use hidden orders all the time. I use iceberg orders all the time. I also have access to a few dark books. I have NITE dark book and Credit Suisse dark book. These two are excellent sources of liquidity because, essentially, if you're trying to sell a stock, if you're trading Apple at, say, $600, and the spread is 20 cents, what you can do is put an order on the cross finder to sell. You're not displayed anywhere. Apparently nobody knows you're there, and you can get price improvement. You can get filled on the far end of the spread if you have the order in. Sometimes you'll see trades going on the offer in the ECNs without filling you in the dark book, but almost every time you get an even better fill in the dark book.

Is this solution of accessing dark books available for most people?

No. For anybody who trades through retail, through IB or Scottrade, there's no way to have access, but through one of the platforms I use, I can route through the dark books, but I only have access to a couple, and there's a lot of action going on in the market that I don't have access to. Lots of action.

So how are you able to scalp these days? Lots of traders say they moved away from that in recent years because they just can't compete with the HFT programs.

Over the last three years, a lot of the traders I know have stopped trading, mostly because they can't make money or they consistently lose money. I would say scalping has become tougher, but I'd say all types of trading have become a lot harder. The usual technical patterns and indicators that we used to use don't really apply anymore, because the problem with the HFT is that if you're in just a random stock, making a market, trading it, and let's say some news hits. By the time that happens, the HFTs have repriced the stock, deciphered the news, and know what the new price is. So if it was trading at $14, it will just trade to $15 instantly and then trade millions and millions of shares. This all happens before I even get the news or know what's going on.

I've got news feeds, I've got Squawk Box, I've got everything, but by the time I get it, the HFTs already know how much things are now worth. Before, you'd have news and it would slowly get disseminated, you'd see gradual buying, you could jump on and ride the wave. Now there's no wave. Just a big spike, and that's it, done. Sometimes the HFTs overreact, so you can make money taking the opposite side of the trade because there's no time to get on the trend. A lot of the times you have to bet the other way. I have a scanner that scans for HFT programs. That gives me a bunch of stock symbols and tells me how many trades and how many quotes were put in that stock at that second. I can see there were 250 trades in that last second, so I know there was HFT activity there. I can go to that stock to try to figure out what's happening, but it's difficult. Another problem is that all of the news that's been driving the markets in the last six to eight months is from Europe, so there's no possible way we can get the news before somebody else does.

You mentioned that scanner for HFTs. That must have triggered a lot during the Knight trading debacle, didn't it?

That scanner is separate from my platform. All it does is give trade counts. It doesn't tell anything else about the stock. If all of a sudden I see the lights in the stock, I know there's something going on. I can immediately go over there, but by the time I do, I still don't have the news. But at least I have an idea of what's going on.

The Knight trading issue was the best thing that happened to human beings. That day was great. I had it on that day, but I didn't use it. I didn't even have to, because when it happened I was on Skype with about four other traders. I had an overnight position in NOK. The market opened, and I was watching NOK. I was seeing millions of shares going through the buy side and I was thinking, "This is crazy. What's going on here?" Then my buddy told me the same thing was happening in DD. So I looked, but I thought he said DE. Well, when I looked at that, I noticed it was happening there as well. So all of a sudden, we started finding all these stocks. We had a list of ten or so.

We knew within about thirty seconds of the open that there was something wrong. After thirty seconds we started shorting these stocks. After a minute we shorted more. We shorted for the first five minutes, and I said to these guys, "There's something seriously wrong here. Why is it this not turning off?" Because most programs have a stop button, something that will turn it off if it goes wrong. You never have a program in which there are twenty-five or thirty minutes of constant buying. Usually, if a program screws up, within ten seconds or even two seconds it stops. There's no opportunity to make money, but for whatever reason, this thing was just buying forever.

All of us shorted every single stock because we've been trading forever. We knew these were not correctly priced stocks, and they were going to come back down. We were all pending negative tens of thousands of dollars, but it didn't really matter. If I'd had more money and more buying power, I would have shorted more because it was free money. After thirty minutes, they finally shut this thing off. Everyone started to learn who screwed up. The second that program shut off, all of our stocks collapsed, and we all got paid.

The problem is that if you've been trading for as long as I have, if you've lived through trading halts and all of this other garbage, if you cover those positions, you run the risk of having a serious problem. In a lot of cases the exchange will break the trades, but they'll only break one side of your trade: the entry. If you cover on the way back down, on every single stock you were short on, you're going to be long. So that day I had no choice. I had to sit in all of these positions. I had to stay in short DE, NOK, etc. I took some profits, but I had to wait the whole day for the NYSE to say it wasn't canceling any trades. As soon as I got that OK, I covered everything.

Couldn't you hedge with an ETF or SPY?

You could always hedge, but why hedge when you're up thousands and thousands of dollars with zero risk of going back up?

You started shorting those stocks even without checking the news? You just knew it was wrong?

I knew there was no news. Everybody knew. Every single stock was printing millions and millions of shares, a hundred shares at a time, nonstop. And the market wasn't moving. It was flat at the time. There was no movement except in these hundred stocks. You had zero risk of losing money, because if these stocks were priced $2 higher than where they should be trading, even if the market had a small rally during the day, it would never go enough to make me lose money. I was up so much money per share that it didn't even matter what happened to the market. So there was no reason to hedge, no reason to trade. In a situation like that, one second you'll be down fifty grand, and as soon as the program stops, you will be up one hundred grand. That basically happened in a matter of seconds.

Did you do well in the flash crash as well?

The flash crash was a different type of animal. I was not at my trading station at home that day, but I was trading. We did well, but nothing like on the Knight day. The flash crash was a little bit scarier. I kind of sat back because the whole market was collapsing, so I didn't put the type of risk on that I normally would. Fear was the big factor. I still held some stuff against me and made money on the way back up but nothing special.

The last few weeks are the best example. I don't know if you read ZeroHedge. It talks about how the market has been the least volatile it's been in ages.[32] We're in the S&P500 with a four-point range, which almost never happens. What happens in any stock is that it becomes so efficient by the programs that it doesn't even move. It just consolidates into nothing. They'll keep it in the range of 5 cents or whatever. I often question how a high-priced stock can stay in a 10 cent range all day. It's impossible.

Even if PCLN or CMG had earnings, they gap down like $90 a share, and then they don't move after that. It just sits, and it has a $1 range all day. That would never ever happen before. There's no way a stock would gap down a lot and not move the rest of the day. Now it's a matter of all these programs going through the earnings. They now think it's worth X, and they're all in agreement that it's worth X, so by the time everyone goes for lunch, the stocks don't move anymore. It's almost like the people are happy losing $90 a share, and there are no new buyers or sellers. Things are so efficient that people like me disappear, take time off, etc. Then everything becomes very illiquid. It's very difficult to get out of positions, so you get a massive move to the other side where everything gets very inefficient. All of a sudden you'll be down eighteen points in the S&P500 in one afternoon and no one

---

32 http://www.zerohedge.com/news/complacency-5-year-highs

knows why, and there's no reason other than that somebody needed to get off some stock. Before it was easy to sell that stock. Now it's not so easy.

Another problem is the fact that what's moving the market is in Europe. By the time it opens here, the market has been repriced. It opens down six, seven, or eight points, and then there's nothing for us to do. That's a change from 2008 when everything was US based. Now I almost wish I was trading somewhere in Europe, because I think there would be much more opportunity. Basically, everything I learned about reading charts still exists. I base a lot of my reasons for getting in on charts alone. So even though the moves in the market are far more extreme and far more violent than they were before, and a lot of the times things get overextended, I find myself doing a lot more scaling into positions now rather than just getting in at one price, because a lot of the times I'm too early. If something is going down, I'm too early buying. I'm countertrending almost all the time.

I believe that if I missed the down move, all the moves will be overextended. Same on the upside. The more violent the move up, the more I short. Today I was trading BIDU. This stock got downgraded this morning. It was trading at $120. It was $134 the other day. Someone downgraded it, and now it's down $118, $117, $116, $114, $110. That was the low. There's no choice but to buy the stock. For someone like me there's not even an option. You have to buy that stock. I'm not going to market make it. I'm going to hold it because the move was way overextended.

Do you find that sometimes the time of day matters? You'll see these extended moves off the open and they reverse in the afternoon?

In this case, the news came out in the morning after the market had already opened, about two hours intro trading. Throughout my entire trading career, what I've seen is that if I look at one hour increments of the entire day, 90 percent of my money is made in the first hour of trading, even more so these days. What happens in the first hour is that you have all these imbalances, all these buy and sell orders. All these people come together to have a party, but the problem is that it ends very quickly, so everything quickly reprices. The HFTs reprice things, then by 10:30 EST things start to slow down. Then I just sit back on my Skype with my buddies and wait for random events. After the first hour, there's really not much to do until the last hour of trading.

Do you find that when there's news, there are opportunities even in the mid-day timeframe?

There are always opportunities when there's news, always. But a lot of times it's hard to make money, because the programs have already gotten the news and repriced the stock. But sometimes we do really well. I'd say almost every day there's a takeover rumor of some kind. And as soon as the news hits, the stock rallies, and I short the stock. One time you're going to lose because it's going to keep going and going, but 90 percent of the time, the stock just comes right back down for the rest of the day. The other day we had the BBY news. The CEO was going to take the company at $24. The stock opens at $23, and that's simple. You just short it, done. That is nice. We do have these simple trades every once in a while in which it's a no-brainer.

How did you do during 2008?

Best year ever. It was great. An extremely volatile market. In any type of trading, you could make money hand over fist. At that time I made most of my money in Bank of America, cheap stock, huge thick levels. It doesn't take that much to make a lot of money if you have 250,000 shares and you make 5 cents. That's 12 grand. You could do that in five minutes. I wish every year was like that. Even though there was HFT in the market, there wasn't as much. On top of that there were hedge funds, institutions. I mean everyone was in the market. The volume was super high. The liquidity was there. You could get in and out for as many shares as you wanted. Will it ever come back? Of course it will come back, somehow, sometime. Everybody is worried about the programs ruining the market. I'm not saying they haven't, but if you think what happened last time will never happen again because of lack of volume and lack of liquidity, no, it will happen again. It might be even more violent and extreme than last time, because every time you have a superefficient market, no movement, nothing, and everything is fine, you always break out of that range. The more efficient it is, the more inefficient it becomes when something does happen.

So I'm hoping in the coming weeks and months it will happen. Everybody's got debt up to their eyeballs, and if the market goes up because of inflation or down because everybody's got so much debt, makes no difference to me. Either way it's not going to stay like this forever. Another reason the market is so crappy is not because of HFTs. The entire world is flooded with money, with 0 percent interest. It doesn't create that much volatility in markets because everybody is at 0 percent. There's really nothing to do. For bond traders, there's nothing to do,[33] and you just buy and hold forever. Once things shake up a bit, things will start to move. I'm not worried about that at all, because I have a good grasp on what these HFTs do, how

---

33 An interesting piece of data that demonstrates what he is referring to are fixed income margin requirements. Requirements for Fed Funds futures went from a little over $1,000 in 2009 to about $300 or so in 2013.

they work. I'm pretty sure that even if I'm one of the 15 percent of the traders left, I'm going to do fine.

You mentioned your great results in 2008. Were you just riding the trends or doing something else?

I was just riding the trends, the news. I do like to go countertrend trading. One day they banned short selling. It was the best thing in the world. The market would gap down four hundred points, and it's the best buy ever. That's the morning you just come in with your full buying power. You buy everything and just wait fifteen minutes.[34] Stuff like that would happen all the time in both sides of the market. You just had random financial stocks in the middle of the day start to get sold off for no reason. Mid-day, you could just sit there and buy. If you had a large account and were willing to put some risk on, that was a free money year. All of us knew that the government just wasn't going to let this slip away. The market wasn't going to go to zero. Right when they announced that they were going to do QE, you had to buy it. You had to invest all your money in stocks. It was a no-brainer. There were stocks, so cheap it was ridiculous. I look back now and think, "Why didn't I do this or that?" I regret so many things, but what can you do.

So you made quite a bit of money buying in 2008. Were you doing bounces and stuff?

Yeah, sure. Obviously if you were positioned short before this happened, that was great. We participated on both sides. I start every day at zero, so I'm ready to go. It doesn't matter on any given day if that market is going to go up or down. Yes, I have some position on the side, but even though the market is coming down as violently as it was in 2008, there was a lot of money to be made on the upside.

Did you max out your buying power in October 2008 when things just kept falling and falling?

October 2008 was probably one of my better months. During that time I tried to get as much buying power as I could. I can't say I caught the bottom. I wasn't long at the bottom. I wish I was, but I did start to put a lot of money in the market shortly after the bottom. Even though I might have missed the bottom by 10 percent, it didn't really matter.

Do you do a lot of backtesting?

---

34 What Wayne is probably referring to here is the fact that without short sellers, prices will frequently overshoot to the downside due to absence of short covering. This provides traders the opportunity to buy highly mispriced assets.

I don't do any backtesting. All I do is look at my charts, and they're all one-minute charts. I keep everything super simple. Everyone looks at a million indicators. I don't use any. The only things I have are a couple of moving averages. Volume and one-minute candles. I have a few longer-term charts, like sixty minutes for another account that I do some investing and swing trading in, but for my main trading I use one-minute charts. All I look for are price and volume and similar technical patterns. Double bottoms, triple tops, breakouts, simple stuff. A lot of the times these days you get these ridiculous fluctuations off the open, so if that happens I'm there always countertrading. Literally within two minutes you can be out and make a decent amount of money, because there are some wide ranges off the open. You're fighting with programs to get in the position, but as a long you're not in super big size, you can get in and out all of the time. You tend to look back and think, "Why didn't I hold?" or, "I could have gotten a better price," but you're still going to make money.

Do you find yourself taking liquidity more often that adding it?

Yes, I probably do about 500 or 600 trades a day. I probably take too much liquidity. I do around 1.5 million shares a day. In 2008, I probably did about 5 million a day, but now there's no volume. I do take a lot of liquidity to get into my positions, and I try to scale out of my positions by adding liquidity. Unless I'm in trouble, I do try to provide liquidity. But I do pay a hefty price in ECN and SEC fees and all that.

When you try to get out by adding liquidity, do you try to choose the best ECNs for rebates and things like that?

A lot of times now, because there's nothing going on in individual stocks, I trade a lot of SPY. There are some ECNs that get hit first in every stock, no matter what, and the reason they get price preference and hit first is because of their structure. There's no other reason. The HFTs know this. If you're an HFT program and you're not providing liquidity to the dark pool, you're going to hit EDGA, and you're going to hit BX first, because you get paid.[35] Then you're going to hit the rest of them. If you're sitting there, you have a much greater chance of getting hit because you're using them, and they pay others to take liquidity, as opposed to the situations where people have to pay $3 per 1,000 shares. In SPY, because it's attached to the ES futures and because it's the entire market, of course I'm going to throw out BATS or EDGX or something that will throw me a credit. In the SPY, if they're going to take a price level, they're going to take anything and everything

---

35 These ECNs have an inverted model where they pay or cost nothing to take liquidity but charge for adding liquidity.

that's there. They don't care about .003, but in some stocks you have to be very selective in which ECNs you use now.

You said you do 500 trades per day. Is that all manual, or do you have some automation going on?

No, I'm completely manual. I trade fairly large positions, and I usually only carry maybe two to three positions at a time. I don't trade thirty stocks at once. I'm usually focused in one or two stocks. My favorite situation is a stock that's $3 to $10, fairly big float, news play, and I can trade in and out all day. Those are a bit hard to find these days, but that's the ideal. There's nothing better to me than that stock that I can get in and out of with 10,000 to 20,000 shares over and over again all day and make 5 to 10 cents.

You usually make 5 to 10 cents?

Depends on the price of the stock. Like today with BIDU, obviously I wasn't trying to make 5 to 10 cents. I was trying to make 2 bucks, but when I'm trading the spiders, 5 to 10 cents all of the time. Just over and over again.

So you didn't find it necessary to expand your time horizon due to the HFTs?

It all depends on the situation. I'm not going worry about the HFTs, because if there's liquidity and there's volume, I'm just going to continue to trade the way I always do. I've just got to be a little more selective in my entries and exits, because no programs are going to front run you for 1 penny when they can make 30 more cents. You're going to get your fill no matter what. If you continue to scalp in something that's not very liquid, you're never going to make money. You're going to lose money for the rest of your life, because you can't get in and out, and they know you're there.

Even with the hidden orders?

Oh yeah, even with hidden orders. Doesn't matter.

Do you think they're selling the hidden order books to the HFTs?

Because I use dark books, and because I use hidden orders, nothing would surprise me. One thing I really hate are flash orders. I use a lot of EDGA because it's essentially free, but they do what we call flash orders. Do you know what they call a flash order?[36]

Yes.

That I have a serious problem with, because, by the time I blink, they show my hand, and they can choose if they can fill it or not. Many times if they see the order coming for a large amount of stock, the level just disappears, and it reprices and I get no fill. That bothers me a lot. If you're going to get filled, and if you have 25,000 shares and you hit sell and they buy it all in one shot, you know you just screwed up. Because if it wasn't going to go up, they'd never have filled you. You get filled when you're wrong.

By the flash orders, they know the order flow. So if I've got a big position, a lot of times I'll never try to get out of all of my position, but sometimes I do. That's why at the end of every decent sized move, you see big candles and big volume. Everybody's panicking to try to get out. Then you will get an effect like a railway track. One big down candle and one green candle side by side. It's all order flow. They know what people are up to, and they just back off. That's how the flash crash basically happened. That's how those stocks during the Knight debacle started pushing up that morning. They got so high because everyone would just back off. No one will give a fill when somebody is trying to buy millions of shares 100 shares at a time forever. No one will sit there and sell. They'll just ask for a better price.

Does stuff like subpennying hurt you too?

Ah, subpennies are horrible. If I could participate in it, it would be great, because when I started I used to be able to shave on the Level 2 on NASDAQ and ARCA and everywhere. This drives me crazy. If I'm trying to buy 10,000 at, let's say, $25.30, so many times I'll hit my hotkey. I'll buy at $25.30. The thing will print two times my exact share lot at $25.295 and $25.30. I get the thirty print, but somebody else made the half cent, and that's what they do. That's their program's job, just to make the half cent over and over all day long. That drives me nuts. In stocks with very large levels, like Bank of America, it's very hard to sit there at the whole number with your order pending watching halves go off all day long. And it's not even just halves, it's shaved to the 99/100th. It's ridiculous. So, yeah, I would say that hurts. I hope sometime, somehow, we're able to participate in that again. I'm able to participate a little bit on the shaved prints using Credit Suisse, but not like these guys can do.

---

[36] A flash order is the controversial practice where some ECNs will allow some HFT firms to see orders coming down the pipe in a ECN or exchange. This allows HFTs to change their quotes, cancel orders, or trade in a way that benefits them.

Do you think there's an edge in being able to watch the subpenny prints going on in the tape and predicting the order flow?

You know, you can definitely predict where the order flow is going by watching the tape. There's no doubt about that. It's very easy to do, very simple to do. But the problem is that it changes in the blink of an eye. One time they'll be swiping all the midpoints orders and the offers at the same time, so you know there's buy side going on. Then, seconds later, it will be all midpoints, and then all orders will be on the bid, so it's very hard to determine even what side of the market the bids are on, or the midpoints or the shaves. It's very hard.

One thing that does happen very often now, way more often than ever before, are block prints though ADFN. If you look at your time and sales, you have all the prints, and there will be ARCA, NSDQ, BOSX, and there are these prints that go off as D or ADF or whatever. ADF is *alternative display facility* network. It's every other system. All the dark books are ADF prints. They're basically outside of the exchanges, outside of the ARCAs, anything that you can't see.

So now you'll see these block prints. For example, today on BIDU, it went from $120 to $111, and all of a sudden, and this is the best thing ever, you'll see that there's a big print at $111.70 for something like 50,000 shares. How the hell did somebody get 50,000 shares? There's no market for anyone.

I can't get even 3,000 and this guy gets 50,000. And this is another reason why I bought BIDU today, because I saw big prints at $111. There were no big prints before $117 today. There were some of these at $117 or whatever, but when somebody is taking positions of 30,000 to 50,000 of BIDU at $111, and the stock is down $10 on the day, no one in their right mind would short the stock there, and no one would sell either. You have to be an idiot to sell down there. So you got a pretty good indication of a good trade on your hands, even if it went $1 against it or even $1.50 against me, it wasn't going down much more. I mean, it could. Anything's possible, but you got a good indication when somebody is putting 50,000 blocks in there and there's no market to get in and out of that much.

If you really wanted to get out of that much stock in the market, you would be dead. Big prints happen a lot now, and they usually signal some type of momentum shift in the market or in that particular stock. That's another thing I never used to use but that I use a lot now. I have a time and sales window that only finds big prints. You know that almost every trade these days is 100 shares. It's stupid. Nobody buys more than 100 or 200 shares. Ten years ago, the average trade was something like 900 to 1,000 shares. HFTs and HFT programs don't trade at 10,000 to 20,000, so when somebody's trying to buy at that amount, the HFTs know, because all they do is put 200 orders for 100 shares.

So in that situation, with the block trades, you had someone panicking, trying to get out, and somebody who knew something just took the whole thing?

You know, that's the thing. I don't know where these prints come from, because I don't understand who would take the other side of the trade. One thing I know is that if the market is super illiquid, and it's a hedge fund trying to move a position, that's a different story, because if they lose $1 or $2 in a stock that's plummeting $12, they don't really care, especially if they're long forty points lower. They couldn't care less. I never really understand who takes the other side of the trade, because somebody has to sell that. They have to match those shares somehow. Even yesterday, this was the best ever, we had a big correction in AAPL. It was down something like $20. I'm sitting there at the open, and I like $650 to buy the stock, because it was just at $674 the other day.[37]

I like the stock there, so I'm looking at the Level 2, and there's a guy sitting on the L2 at $648.50. He's sitting there and displaying 65,000 shares, and if you ever looked at AAPL, nobody displays anything. It's mostly a 100 to 200, maybe 1,000 the odd time. But I swear to god, a lot of the time these guys put these orders because they know they're going to get filled. I see this every day. 65,000 shares, relatively close to the open, and he's filled 648.50 for every share. All at once, he gets filled on everything. The low of the day is 648.13, and then the stock goes up $20 in a straight line for the rest of the day. This happens all the time. So I look for these types of trades as well.

So tape reading is a key part of your success?

Yeah, I believe it is. It's a lot different from the way you use to read it. I don't understand how these guys do it. It has to do with accumulating and distributing shares. That guy put that order there knowing he was going to get filled, I'd say 90 percent of the time I see these orders, they get filled. I don't know how, I don't know who fills them, but someone does. Before, when these orders used to get filled, you would think, "Oh, my god, the guy got taken, the stock is going to collapse." And it would collapse. Now it's not like that. You never ever short a stock with somebody showing a huge order. You always go with that order. Before it was different. There was some follow-through.

How were you able to adapt to the changing market conditions and make these adjustments over time?

---

37 This is a good example of his mean reversion mindset.

I don't know. Trust me, I'm not making nearly as much as I was making before, but I'm definitely not losing, and I have no intentions of finding a new career anytime soon.

I've got a good group of traders that I'm constantly in touch with. We have a Skype chat that we're on every day, so even though I'm trading by myself at home, I still have the influence of other traders that are really good and that have made money in the last ten to twelve years just like me. But it used to be that traders would make $5,000 to $6,000 a month, or $10,000 a month. Those guys are all gone. They were only making that because it was so easy, not because they understood the market or because they understood what was happening or could read charts very well.

When I started trading, our office would hire ten guys at a time, and eight guys would make money. Toward the end of my stay there, four years in or whatever, three or four would make money. And honestly, now if you get ten people to start trading the way I learned to trade, I guarantee you there would be zero that would make it. You might get one the odd time, but you're not getting anyone making consistent money. It's impossible. From the beginning I liked to take risks, but I would always keep my losses very tight. The main reason I'm still around is that I don't mind punching out of the stock when I lose $20,000. I have no problem with that, but someone else that's looking at this loss will let it turn into $30,000 or $50,000. They'll lose forever, because sometimes these stocks never come back. You get into a position, you think you're right, and you never give up. The guys who trade like that are all gone. I do believe that as long as you know how to manage your losses and take them, the profitable trades will be there, and they'll take care of themselves.

That's characteristic of your Skype friends as well?

Yeah, for sure. I have another good friend who's going through a rough patch. In 2008/2009 he was making money hand over fist. He's never been as strong as other people, but he understands the market. He's a very good trader. But what happens is that our nice free money, our easy trades, are not there anymore. So what happened to him was that he got into trouble, only because when he gets into positions and the stock goes against him, it will go by so much that there's no chance he can ever make money on the trade. If he just stuck to what we were always taught, get out of the losers quick, he would be fine. On a day-to-day basis, he'll make money. He'll make $1,000 a day, but the problem is that when he loses, he'll lose like $6,000 to $7,000, so it takes him quite a while to make it all back. One trade can cost him two weeks' worth of work. He's not making the big trades. He's making small profits because we went back into making smaller profits as a result of these markets, but he still will not get out of the losers.

You mentioned swing trading. Is that a big part of your profitability?

I have another account that I do a lot of swing trading in, and last year (2011) was the first year that I didn't make a penny day trading. I made up for it by swing trading. I have a million excuses for it. I didn't really have a house. I was building a house. I had no office, so I was trading from my laptop, and the markets were garbage. This year, I'm in the house. I have an office set up. I'm having a good year, but I think last year I learned a lot about swing trading and the differences between that and day trading and the mentality it takes to do it versus what I'm used to doing. So I got a lot of education and experience, and I'm actually doing really well with the swing trading these days. These positions I hold from two hours to three days, something like that. That made up for my other account last year that I made $0 on. This year, both accounts are doing really well. When I do swing trade, I prefer futures, I really like to trade gold and silver. The odd time I'll trade stocks as well. Like today I got some BIDU options. I like to trade AAPL. I like the bigger stocks. For scalping I prefer the lower-priced stocks.

Did you find that as the HFTs started to suck liquidity out of the market, you started to trade more big caps and avoid the small cap stocks?

When the markets were really moving, I was trading all of the financials. I like cheaper stocks with thick levels. I'd say more than going to big stocks, I've gone to ETFs. I much prefer trading the SPYs, IWM, GLD. If I'm trading stocks and there's not much going on, then for sure I will be in the big caps.

How important would you say are your instincts compared to reading charts?

I'd say probably fifty/fifty. I do take almost all of my trades based on charting. That's the only thing I know, the only thing I use. But sometimes, like today on BIDU, I had to go with my gut. I've been trading long enough to know that if someone comes in mid-day with a downgrade, and the stock is down $10 bucks before the downgrade and $10 bucks after, there's no way I'm not going to buy it every single day every single time. There are things I've seen happen over and over again that I don't need a chart for. I don't need anything. I just know that it's going to work out.

Do you think these downgrades and upgrades are similar to the takeover rumors and things that you can just sort of fade?

They're very similar. It depends on the situation too. Now that I've been trading a long time, I know all of these companies too. If it had been a different company, or if the guy had a better explanation of why he was downgrading it, I might have thought differently about it. I do try to read into the news to understand what's going to make a stock move to a certain extent. Takeover rumors are a little better because there are random takeover rumors every day. It's ridiculous. You get these and you know it's never going to happen, so you just short and that's it. How many of them work out? And how many of them work out that day when somebody calls it? So when something goes up ridiculously on that kind of rumor, of course I'm going to short it. It's an easy trade. Upgrades and downgrades are a little bit tougher. I need to read in and see what's going on.

What do you think happened in the BATS IPO?

I don't know. I really don't have an opinion there. Maybe sabotage? I like BATS, but I have no idea what happened.

Do you trade IPOs at all?

Oh yes, of course. I love IPOs. Unfortunately we only have the opportunity to buy IPOs, which really sucks. I only scalp them though. I don't try to swing trade them. A lot of the time, what happens in IPOs is that there will be violent candles in there, but there will be a whole number where there will be support. So let's say an IPO price is at $17 and it opens at $18. There might be support at $17.50, and of course at $17 they'll buy it forever[38]. They have to defend the IPO price. When it breaks the IPO price, it's very weird the way they trade, but it's very methodical. It will go down 50 cents. You buy some, then it bounces. It's very strange, but you can make a lot of money trading them, especially if you get in a good one. But I can't think of one that's gone up a lot since it opened. What I like about them is that there's a lot of volume, and if there's a lot of volume, you have a much better chance of making some money.

On the other hand, the Facebook IPO was a complete disaster. Probably the second best day I had this year. It's amazing how much money you can make in these things.

---

[38] Wayne is referring to the underwriters who will frequently support the IPO price.

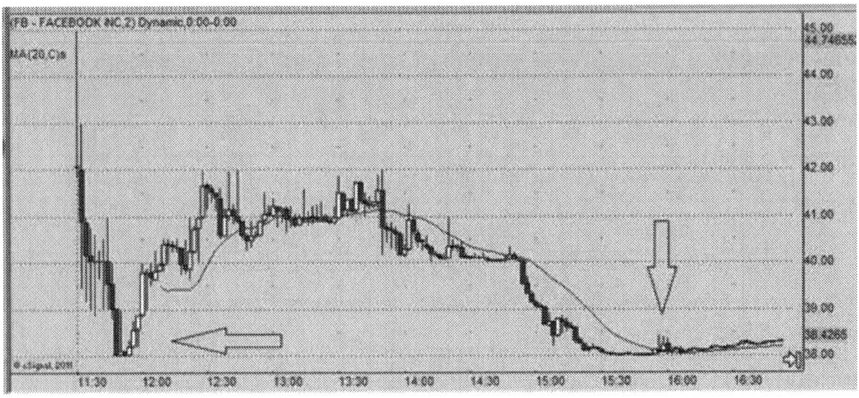

FB IPO. Source: Esignal.

Buy at $38.01 and sell higher?

Yeah, that's what I did. I bought something like 60,000 shares at $38.05 and sold higher. It opened at $40s, or whatever, but it was a total mess. It was supposed to open, but it didn't open. One thing you could do on FB that a lot of people didn't know was that you could route orders through Chicago 20 to 30 cents lower than the best bid and get filled. You could immediately flip it out for 20 to 30 cents, over and over again, until it got close to $38. When it got there, that game was over. For some reason that was one system that was taking orders and giving fills out cheaper than the rest of the market. For whatever reason, when they trade through the Midwest or Chicago, there are always block prints and orders that go through outside the market. I don't know why. It's not outside of what the trading range would be. I believe the reason this happened in this case was because there were a lot of people who had millions and millions of shares of the stock, and these institutions didn't care about 30 cents at that time, because they were trying to get off 10 to 20 million shares of stock or even get short. Don't think that people can't short IPOs. That's bullshit. As this was happening, they didn't care about 20 cents, because they knew they were going to get out lower. As you can see now, the stock is worth much less. It was free money for them.

Does this underwriter strategy of supporting a price create a lot of free money situations? I saw something like that the other day in the MANU IPO.

I didn't trade the MANU IPO, because I was out of town, but my buddy did a similar trade at the $14 level. Manchester United is the biggest pile of garbage ever. I don't know why anyone would ever buy that stock. I don't even understand why it's even listed. I don't know how, but my buddy got short the stock. He borrowed from I don't know who, and he was shorting every time it went up and covering at $14, but he was hoping for the big move through $14. I don't know if you were watching, but when it broke $14 in the first day, it dropped something like 50 cents really fast.

Which news source do you use?

My main news comes from Briefing. One of my buddies on Skype uses RanSquawk audio and also Benzinga.

You have the kind of setup with five monitors and stuff like that?

I actually have twelve.

Twelve?!

Yeah, I've got two different trading platforms going: my swing account and my main trading account. And a third for Briefing. Also one for imbalances, HFT alerts, and then eight monitors for charts.

What kind of hardware you have?

My computers now are about two years old, but when I bought them they were the best of the best. Monitors are standard. They're fine. What's funny is that I actually use the oldest keyboards in history. I don't use anything wireless, because I don't trust it. The keyboards I have are the old clunky ones with F keys, because those are the keys I use for entering orders, now they have these fancy ones without F keys. I probably should buy half a dozen more, because sometimes keyboards around here get broken. Sometimes anger gets the best of me and keys go flying.

What kind of advice do you give to new traders?

Start out small, something like 100 shares. Don't worry about the money you make in a day. Just try to make 20 to 30 cents a day, something like $20 to $30 a day after commissions, whatever. But the only thing that will ever save your life is how you manage your losing trades. You have to exit the losers. It's tough out there. Everyone is trying to go after profits that are super small. Spreads are small, and volume is light. There's not as much money available to be made. It's not just us, it's the HFTs, the specialists, the hedge funds, everyone's profits are down. Any trading firm, any timeframe, profits are down. So it's a very hard environment to get into trading. Anyone who can get into trading at this time and make money will do very well in their career. It's the hardest time to get in. To have a future in trading, this is the best time to get in if you can figure something out that works, because, honestly, I don't think it can get much worse than this.

Before I started to research this market, I didn't realize how bad it was for people trying to add liquidity to the markets.

We always joke that we're the liquidity providers of last resort. In the old days, there were so many people doing that. They were just providing liquidity, bid offer, get in and out. It was great. If something big in the world does happen, if there's news, and stuff starts to move, there's not going to be anybody standing in the way. You'll see moves in stocks that you've never seen before.

Do you have a plan for when something like that happens?

Because the markets have been such garbage and there's not a lot of money there and its summertime, I haven't been trading too much. We weren't really ready for the Knight situation, because if we were on our game and making a lot of money, that day I would have been trying to find buying power from anyone to short millions and millions of shares. One of my friends has huge buying power, but he only used like 20 percent of it. Even I didn't use all of my buying power, because I was a little scared. I haven't seen this type of situation before, so it's fine to say you have a plan, but it's a lot different when it actually happens. You don't know exactly what is going to happen. The flash crash was to the downside, and it affected the whole market. Knight was to the upside. No one thought the stocks would go up in a glitch. So, of course I have a plan. If we flash crash again, I'll buy everything. That's the only plan I can give you, but it depends on what the news is. If there's no news like on that day of the flash crash, then yeah. I'll buy everything.

Do you read a lot about regulations and rules like Reg NMS?

I don't care about that kind of garbage. We've adapted to all kinds of rule changes, bans on short selling, etc. My profit margins are small. On average, I don't make very much per share, so provided they don't add a trade tax or stamp tax, I'll be fine, because all of those other rules everyone will just adapt to it. It does suck that if a stock goes down 10 percent you can't short on a downtick anymore, so we even have strategies that are geared toward stocks that go down 10 percent. We've adapted to all the rules just like everyone else.

I noticed that these stocks that go down 10 percent and trigger the uptick rule tend to have some predictable moves after it. Is that something that you noticed as well?

It depends on what kind of news there is, but generally yeah. If it's a large company, I believe even BIDU today triggered the 10 percent, which makes me even more attracted to it for a long. It's one of my rules. If the company is good and the news is not that important, I'll always buy when it reaches the 10 percent.

Because the short sellers can't whack the stock anymore?

Yeah, exactly. You have one variable in your favor at 10 percent. You look at every trade, and it's all odds. That one variable makes the trade that much more attractive.

November 2013 Update

How would you rate this year in terms of profitability compared to last year?

Worse. A lot worse.

Would you say that's because of the VIX coming down more and the Fed keeping everything stable?

It's very hard to make money when the VIX is at lows and interest rates are 0 percent around the world. There's just nothing to do, unless you bought the stock market at the beginning of the year and held all year. Then you would be doing fine. Intraday trading is pretty bad right now.

Being long stocks, buying dips, etc. Is that something that really isn't your style and you struggle with?

I guess. Maybe mentally I think the market shouldn't be up here. I'm biased. I would never in a million years buy the market here and invest.

If the market turns, you think you can do well by being short biased all the way down?

I probably won't be short all the way down, but at least there will be a lot more volatility, a lot more swings in the stocks I like to trade. I don't like to go trade GOOG and PCLN. They're so expensive and very thin. Some of the lower priced stocks I like to trade. I hope they'll come back into play with some bigger swings intraday.

I recall you made good money on the Facebook IPO. Did you trade the Twitter IPO?

I did trade it, but it was very boring. It was basically a nonevent. It opened way higher than it was priced at. It didn't do a hell of a lot. It had a quick move up to $50 but I was never going to buy at that level. I wouldn't buy it now. Maybe I would do it if it went to $20. Without being able to short it that day, it was useless.

The underwriters were doing something similar to FB in the $45 level of TWTR. They were trying to support it. Did you try to pull that move again of buying support and selling a little bit higher?

No, I left it alone. I didn't even attempt to buy it. I did work though. They always try to defend a certain level. The opening price was a good place to do it.

What was your best day this year?

My best days this year have been trading gold. The few times gold had violent moves down, I was pretty heavily short. Those paid me very well. I'm kind of looking for gold to have one more move down.

Were these big trades in gold just day trades, shorting breakdowns?

Actually, they've been mostly in the futures market with sell stops. Most of my trade ideas in gold start to happen while I'm in bed. I just put a sell stop in at a level where I believe there are a lot of stop orders. I just try to front run those orders and get in. I wake up before the pit opens in New York. A lot of times the move already happened before the pit opens in New York. When gold is down about $20 before the pit opens, usually it just continues the whole day. So I just stay in the trade for the rest of the day. Holding time is something like one day, a day and a half, that sort of thing.

Do you think a lot of those moves in gold happen overnight because it's such a global commodity with international liquidity and you just never know when somebody will decide to puke his position in the Asian session or something?

Gold definitely slows down after New York closes, but it's one of those things that when it's moving, it really pays to trade it almost any kind of day. Right now it's not. So in between New York and Asia it's useless. There's no reason to trade it.

What would you say was your worst trade of the year?

It was at the beginning of the year. I was trying to catch a bounce in the Japanese Yen. I got in very early, bad price, averaged down. It ended up costing me quite a bit of money.

I actually hate the Yen, but I just thought the move was way overextended. To this day, the Yen still hasn't recovered.

These type trades, bottom plays, would you say that this is quite a risky way to trade and you have to have a lot of experience to avoid big losses doing this type of stuff?

Catching a bottom is very difficult. It's dangerous. It's something that I do quite often. I wouldn't advise other people that are relatively new to trading to do it. I always have a reason why for buying at certain levels. I always have the levels I'm interested at. It's a risky strategy for sure.

I noticed that in a lot of these sell-offs after the block trades, it becomes very obvious that the stock is going to bounce. Before the block trades, there's a lot of stress in the trade, and it's hard to profit. But after, there's a lower stress opportunity. Is that something you noticed?

Yes. These block trades continue to happen. I still use those quite a bit. I don't know why and how it works, but it seems to work.

Maybe it's because there's a big seller, and when he gets taken, the market stops being distorted to the downside and it returns to normality in the form of a bounce?

More than likely that's what it is. The only problem these days is that you don't actually see the seller. You don't know who it is. Maybe the HFTs know or somebody knows. It's not like before where you could visibly see sellers on the screen on the offer. You're looking at nobody most of the time these days. I do believe that the algos that are in the buy side keep fading until they're ready to take that order. I'm pretty sure that's what's going on, but you don't know until after the fact. That's why you wait for that volume. Wait for the big dip, for the mini-flash crash, and then take the opposite side of the trade.

It's nice, because when that happens, you might be underwater in the trade briefly, but if you're in small you can actually scale into a pretty decent position. Once it starts going in your favor, you can actually buy or short more if it's an up move. I always like to average into a winning trade.

Would you say that in these bottom plays the time element is important? I noticed that if you try to play ten minutes in, it's usually a bad idea. Fifteen minutes too. After twenty-five or thirty minutes or more, it starts to work more effectively.

Basing that off what, the open?

The time from where the sell-off started.

Yeah, because a lot of times what these guys do, especially in the futures it's a very classic move these days, is that it makes a low. Churn it for half an hour, retest the low, break it by a couple of ticks, and then rally off that low. It's never as easy as spike down, low of the day, and rally from there. They never make it that simple. I agree that the bottom ticks take a while to form now.

Would you say that your countertrending style is harder to apply in this current market?

I would say it is, but I would also say that any strategy is difficult in this market. I don't know of anyone making money hand over fist. I don't even know automated guys making a lot these days.

Did you trade TSLA a lot this year?

Yes, actually, I traded quite a bit this year. Obviously I did quite well in the short side recently. I never lost any money on the way up. I was short in the $170s, and that ended up working pretty well.

Every time that stock makes a big move in one direction, it seems that it goes in the opposite direction, so I would imagine that you would do well there.

That's one I've done all right on. I'm kind of sad, because that's one where I bought this morning at like $121, sold at $123, and watched it go for $6 more.

In the premarket it was at $116. It seemed that it was a good entry there for a lot of people.

If I'd gotten up earlier in the morning, I probably would have grabbed some at $118 or something. It was already at $120 by the time I got up. I guess there were some headlines this morning in the premarket that moved it up off the low. Nothing would have been better than if that thing had flushed down to $110 at the open. I would have bought for sure, options and stock.

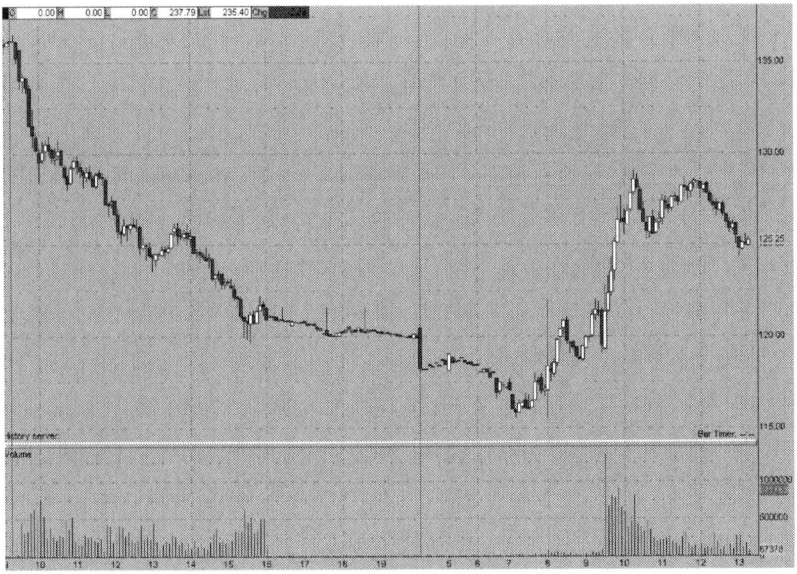

TSLA 5min chart. Source: MBTrading Desktop Pro

Do you think any big move in TSLA is usually a good fade?

This one in particular was, because it went down from $170 to $120 in a hurry. That's a pretty significant move. It was giving up about two-thirds of the up move from the breakout of $90 or $100 or whatever. It had to be interesting for some people to watch for the long side.

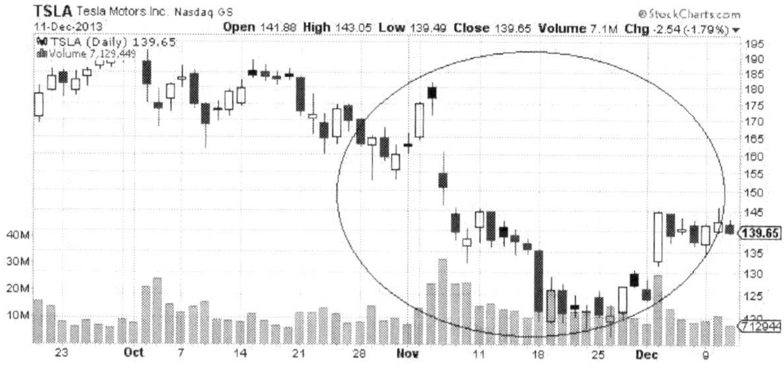

Chart courtesy of StockCharts.com

With regards to Fed days, do you try to be alert on those days for some big potential trades?

I always liked Fed days, but lately they've really sucked because rates are at 0 percent, and they're going to stay there for a long time, and the QE is not being changed and everybody knows that. Fed days have been horrible for the last three years except for the last two meetings. Those have been really good. The only reason they were good was because the market anticipated that they might start to taper, and Bernanke came out and said they weren't going to. That caught the market off guard a little bit. Rates aren't going up for the foreseeable future. If they start to taper though, then I'll start to short a lot.

The market now seems that it's run by the Fed. When they start to taper, then my guess is that the top will be in.

Do you think that when this train starts moving to the downside, it will be a little like gold in that it drops but it's still a good short?

Usually no. Usually there's a time to get in the long side as well. When the market is going to make a significant reversal, you have to get in before others. The market always goes down ten times faster than it ever goes up. You have to be very careful if you're shorting the market after it started to roll over. The bounces are violent. There's nothing worse than having bad timing in the short side. The long side is a little bit more forgiving.

Do you trade a lot of the small caps? The GOGOs of the world are doubling and tripling lately.

Those stocks I actually like. I've looked at GOGO but haven't traded it. Recently I traded ICLD. I play close attention to a lot of these stocks with low floats that double and triple, because a lot of these companies are in need of cash, and they raise cash into these moves. Again, obviously I like to be on the short side. I do get in the long side of these plays, but if I feel like they're going to do an offering, I don't play as long.

How do you manage your risk in these low float momentum stocks?

I won't hold overnight in those stocks ever, either side. That alone is pretty much the risk, because usually both announcements of offerings and news are done outside regular trading hours. Intraday, I just keep it tight. I've got a stop 10, 20, 30 cents away from my entry. Buying the dips and selling when it breaks to new highs works well in those.

Are you trading even less in the mid-day now because of this lack of volatility?

Everybody I know is trading less.

Do you wait for the breaking news to trade in those times?

I'm always waiting for news, but even the news has been slow. There's not much going on. Fannie Mae and Freddie Mac have been moving lately, and I played those some, but it's difficult to trade these pink sheet stocks.

Do you think that volatility expansion that you mentioned in the first interview is going to happen next year? The Fed is supposed to taper soon.

The problem with that is that now you have Janet Yellen saying that they might never taper. Honestly, I don't know. I think they'll have no choice, because they can't keep buying $1 trillion a year in open-market buying forever. They keep buying and trying to create inflation and get the economy going, but I don't think it will work even if they doubled the number. When it does happen, it's going to be even more interesting than 2008 I think.

How do you come up with the stocks you're going to trade in a specific day? Do you have a scan, friends that are throwing tickers around?

Both of those. I have a news feed. We have Briefing, Benzinga. I also use the volume list for NYSE and NASDAQ. Once I get about half a dozen stocks in play for the day, I probably have thirty to forty charts on my screen. Some of them I change every couple of days, some of them I trade all the time. Usually it's off one of those two feeds or the volume scanner.

And you're always in touch with your friends on Skype?

Yes, most of the time. At least a couple of guys.

It's like a private chat that you guys have?

Yes.

If someone launched a Bitcoin ETF, would you be excited to trade that?

Oh, fuck no. I'm not into Bitcoins. No thanks. They remind me of tulip mania, the dot com bubble, etc. Don't get me wrong, I think they can go to $5,000, but I'd rather own gold and silver.

But wouldn't they be a great day-trading vehicle both in the long and short side?

Oh, they would be a great day-trading vehicle. They go up and down 30 percent in an evening, so yes, that's true. The problem is the market is very illiquid, hard to get in and out. Spreads are wide. If you have an account with one of these Bitcoin brokers, the commission is ridiculous. You can never do what I do. Sure you can make swing trades on it, for example, but I don't think it would have a lot of participation if they created something like that.

Do you trade around short seller reports like Muddy Waters, Citron Research, TheStreetSweeper, that kind of stuff?

Sometimes. The thing with these guys is that the stocks they have recommended, like Z, QIHU, if you took those trades you'd be dead. Even HerbalLife (HLF) from Ackman, you would be totally dead.

I think Z doubled.

Z has doubled. QIHU probably more than tripled. HLF I think it tripled as well.

This has to be the worst short selling of all time, right?

It's difficult. Right now it seems that everyone is happily long. When everybody is long and they say the market is the best and you should sell all other assets, I like to do the opposite. I don't like the fact that everyone loves stocks. Like I said, I wouldn't be buying stocks here.

You don't invest the profits that you take out of your trading accounts in stocks in any way?

No, I don't have a lot of stocks right now. I own a few things, like NBG, which is like a lottery ticket. I own coffee futures. I have the Japanese market in the long side, but that's about it.

You mentioned that even the algos might not be making that much money. Do you think that the profitability of HFTs have peaked and now they're going to start to struggle?

As volume decreases, everyone struggles. HFT, humans, etc. Once volume picks up, it will be interesting to see how the algos react, because it won't stay like this forever. I don't know if we'll have a flash crash or what will happen once stuff starts to move, but I would expect the algos to make quite a bit of money once volume returns. This market could even get violent to the upside. Usually at the end of a bull market, if you want to call it a bull market instead of a Fed program, it gets violent to the upside too. I'm ready for anything. I just want something to happen.

How would you play a blow off top?

If it starts to show that it wants to put that sort of top, I'll be long every day, because that's when they really put the boots to the shorts. We are not there yet. Every time we go to new highs, we just kind of grind up. Other than a couple of days where it just outright ripped, mostly around the stupid government shutdown, which was scenario where it was a no-brainer long, it's a slow move up.

It seems that the only scenario where this market goes up a lot is when it comes from a sell-off.

Yes, as soon as people start committing to the short side, that seems to be about the time things just turn around violently and it goes back up.

It's like one giant TSLA.

Yeah, until it doesn't work anymore. Then all of a sudden everybody wants out at the same time. The charts are yet to indicate that we're going to roll over yet, and when it does happen, I think there will be plenty of time to get in. I can definitely see a 10 percent correction, and that's already 180 ES points or something. Back in the day, 10 percent wasn't that much, but we have almost doubled from those days.

Maybe trading it like TSLA is a good idea because the stock tanked from the top, but then it rallied it back and made a lower high in the daily. At that point it was a great short. Perhaps waiting for that lower high on ES is a good idea.

One thing that I really like on a weekly or daily chart is some type of new high bar and then a week that closes below the low of that high week. It's the high of the year, all-time, whatever, then you have a week that closes below the low of that high bar. Then things start to get interesting. That did happen around the government shutdown, but you never ever short that, because the government won't be shut down forever, and they won't default on their debt either.

Weekly Reversal Bar. Chart courtesy of StockCharts.com.

I noticed that some traders are good at buying breakouts and some are good at shorting them, but I never met anyone who'll do both very well. Is that your experience with your friends as well? Did you ever meet someone who can do everything well?

Some people are good at taking AAPL and trading it every single day. Other people, like me, want to trade a chart they like. I don't care what market it is. Futures, stocks, currencies, etc. You have to have your own style. I don't even care if you trade a stock like SIRI and try to make one penny a share all day long. It trades fifty million shares a day. Lots of people do it.

Would you say that this year it was really important that you cut down your mid-day trades, your marginal trades? And, if you hadn't done that, you would have lost some good money?

Yeah, I would say so. I've been struggling with the close lately. For some reason I've been wrong consistently, and I got caught short a few times.

I've been caught short there too a few times.

Even when it's a perfect setup and the market is totally weak, it's still never as good as a good short. I haven't run the stats, but I don't know how many times we have closed at the lows of the day this year. Maybe it's happened only ten times this year. That's how ridiculous this is.

Maybe it's not working because it's a perfect setup and everybody is shorting it.

No, nobody is really short. Not that many people are short. That's the main thing. Everybody is happily long. It's not like they're squeezing people to death. If everybody was short, we'd be getting some really violent up days, and we are not. I hope that's how the market does top. I hope it goes to 2000 next year, really quickly.

Do you do a lot of trading in the premarket and after-hours?

After-hours lately has been garbage. There's nothing going on. Sometimes when there are earnings out, it's OK. Premarket is OK when there's economic data out, but I don't really like trading those time periods.

Lessons from Chapter 10

1. Risk control despite strong views. Wayne has strong views on the markets, trading and HFTs, yet he still talks about how important it is to take losses, not letting losers get out of hand. He also mentions that he was careful during the flash crash and the Knight situations. It's better to be safe than sorry.

2. Big moves tend to end with big candles, big volume, and block trades. During panics or periods of euphoria, markets can easily overshoot. The HFTs will punish people when they're selling or trying to buy by offering worse prices. This can result in an end move that's composed by a big candle and a big volume bar.

The volume can be the result of the block trades Wayne talked about regarding his BIDU trade. It's a bit of a mystery who's behind these orders, but, for example: when a stock has a major down move and you see a big volume bar with big block trades, you have to ask yourself, "Does the guy who bought this entire sell order in one shot know something that others don't?" It can easily be the case that he has access to special information. He knows of other news that will come out later in the day (Wall Street research can frequently leak before it is made public), or that he simply knows it's a good value down there. In my experience, these big volume bars and big block trades also indicate that whoever was selling in a panic finally got taken, and now, without that selling pressure, the path of least resistance shifts and there's a better chance of a bounce.

The time element is important as well. It's not often that you see something tank a lot, bounce back, and that's it. Usually the momentum takes a while to reverse. In my experience, buying bounces off ten-minute sell-offs is quite dangerous in stocks, unless it's a quick scalp. After twenty to thirty minutes or more of selling, there's a better chance you actually have the bottom.

Bounce plays are difficult. They're definitely not for people without experience.

3. Adapt to changing market conditions. Wayne talked about the fact that when big orders got done it used to mean that the stock would continue in the direction of the trend, but these days they signal some type of momentum shift. He observed the market long enough and recorded enough observations in his mind that he noticed changing patterns and was able to adapt.

4. Surround yourself with great traders. During the Knight Capital glitch, he and his friends instantly knew there was something wrong with the stocks the program was buying. As a result, they were able to have their best day of the year. If you weren't experienced enough, you would just think those stocks were acting a bit weird or maybe that there was some kind of news, but he has a ton of experience which, combined with the knowledge of his Skype friends, made him confident the moves were unjustified, enabling him to score a big profit.

5. Be careful in mid-day. Wayne makes most of his money off the open and into the close. He waits for special situations during the mid-day period. Due to even fewer volatility and meaningful events in 2013, Wayne decreased his mid-day trading even more. He says it was an important adjustment in order to remain profitable.

6. This is the hardest time ever to start trading. This is an important lesson, because it can be both a good thing and a bad thing. The good thing is that it provides the opportunity for a trader to hone his skills and learn how to trade in the hardest markets he's likely to face. As Wayne put it, "Anyone who can get into trading at this time and make money will do very well in their career." The bad thing is that you can't get lazy. You'll have to work hard, study, and improve your trading every day. Profit margins in the trading business or the investing business are all down. If you don't make the technical adjustments for the HFT era, have the discipline to cut losses and follow good risk management rules, you will wipe out your profit margins.

7. You have to leave room even for great trades. Wayne talked about how great the setup was for his BIDU trade, yet he also mentioned that the trade would have

been good even if it went $1 or $1.50 against him. He also talked about this in the Knight trading situation, when he and his friends just kept on scaling in the trade. They were all down a lot at some point, but it all reversed when Knight shut their program down. The lesson here is that you have to leave room for trades. The level of HFT noise is quite high these days.

8. Scalping still works, but the game has changed. If you scalp in illiquid names you will get killed. The HFTs know you're there and they're going to take away your fills. You're supposed to scalp in issues with a lot of volume and liquidity, like ETFs or big cap stocks with thick layers.

9. You have to be careful about which ECNs you use in individual stocks. Some ECNs like EDGA or BX get hit first because they provide a rebate or low fees for liquidity takers. This provides the opportunity for someone sitting on a limit order to be **effectively ahead of others in the same level** due to the financial incentive. It's a way to subpenny the next guy, even though you're not an HFT. You can get filled when you would otherwise not by using the right ECNs instead of being too greedy for rebates.

10. Trading IPOs can be quite lucrative. It gives a trader the opportunity to interact with retail flow, capitalize in glitches, trade predictable patterns, or take advantage of artificial support levels that are the result of investment banks trying to support the IPO price.

11. The TSLA trade. The TSLA reversal off the premarket sell-off provided a good example of an overextended stock. TSLA is already a stock that tends to move back and forth a lot. That, combined with the drop from $180 to $115 in a short period of time, high short interest, and pre-market action made it a solid setup for a bounce play off that overextended drop. The fact that it accelerated to the downside pre-market signaled some kind of capitulation panic that presented the opportunity to enter a good risk/reward trade.

12. Trade less. If your style is not really matching well with the market environment, you have to trade less. It's easier said than done, but if anyone is serious about their trading career, this adjustment could be the difference between a profitable month and a losing one. Wayne's style is suited more to environments where things aren't just a stable uptrend "buy the dip" ride. He makes a killing during bigger volatility days or days where trends fail. Because he realizes the current market doesn't play to his strengths, he uses his discipline to trade less and waits for the right spots to remain profitable.

13. The Weekly Reversal Bar. If you want to get a sense of the big picture, look for a reversal of momentum with the Weekly Reversal Bar pattern. First there's a

weekly bar that makes a new high for the year or all-time high. Then the next weekly bar closes below the low of that bar. This weakening of the price action indicates a potential start of profit taking.

Chapter 11

Anonymous—The Former Winner

This trader was really struggling when I interviewed him. He had made some good money in recent years but then gave it all back in some instances that he recalls in the interview. Why did I decide to include his interview in this book? Simply because I believe there's a lot of be learned from failure. Most traders fail, and I believe being able to understand why that happens is a key factor in becoming and staying successful as a trader.

Most trading interview books only feature "successful" traders. I put successful in quotes because later on you find out that some of the traders ended up blowing up and you never get an analysis of what happened. What are some of the mistakes they made, lessons they learned, behaviors to avoid, etc.? This chapter is a reminder of why you have to stay humble, and why the markets are so dangerous. If you don't pay attention to the basic fundamentals, the market will take everything you have, and it won't even say "I'm sorry."

This interview was conducted in November of 2012

When did you decide to join this business?

I started probably four or five months before 9/11.

Was it hard in the beginning?

Yeah, starting out is difficult for probably any trader. It's hard to expect to make any money for the first six to nine months. If you can come out even, that's probably pretty good. I learned how to read the markets a little. I was trying to scalp for 10 to 20 cents, with 100 to 200 shares.

You started in a bear market. Were you comfortable short selling?

I don't think it mattered, because trading back then was so much different from now. I didn't take any risk. I would do a lot of spread trading. I would buy Exxon and sell Chevron against it. Buy one Pharma stock and sell one against it. Also, you couldn't short on a downtick. You could see that there was someone coming in trying to short the stock. I traded mostly NYSE stocks. You could see the specialist's book and find out that someone was trying to sell the stock, and you could get in front of him a little. Problem was that sometimes the specialist would hold the order and you wouldn't get filled. Now you have the HFTs. It looks like they provide liquidity because the spreads are narrower, but if there's a scare in the market they'll just take away that liquidity and there won't be any.

Back then you were just scalping, providing liquidity, and playing the market maker?

I used to trade Viacom A with the Viacom B. I would manually put orders all day long, 10 cents above and below the best bids and offers, and then go to the B stock if I got hit in the A stock. It was very little risk, but it was a lot of work putting orders in and out.

Back then in the NYSE, you could get price improvement. If an institution came in and bought 50,000 shares, the stock might print $1 up, and you could get filled $1 up. Now, wherever your order is, you get filled there. That makes it difficult for the day trader now.

Why do you think this happened?

Probably because the HFTs led to the end of the specialists, plus competition from the Island, ARCA, Instinet, etc. I used to trade a lot of NYSE stocks just for the price improvement.

How long did these easy-money days of market making last? When did they go away?

Probably around 2006 I started to take a lot more risk. I started to trade almost like a hedge fund. I would hold positions for three days, a week, etc.

So you went from having no overnight trades to having to do them frequently?

Yes, I started to have unhedged overnight trades.

You used to carry Viacom A hedged with the B, things like that?

Yeah.

You mentioned in the pre-interview that you had a good 2008 up to October.

Yeah, there was a ton of volatility there. When the recession was really hitting, politicians were doing all kinds of things. They voted against TARP, and then a week later they voted for it.

How did you give back your profits?

I gave back all of it in October. Right when the politicians got involved with TARP, the financials started to get crushed. I got caught long. I didn't think the markets would go down as much as they did.

How did you make the money in the first half?

I was playing countertrend, but I was really pressing my winners. When most people would take profits of 30 to 50 cents, I would try to ride for $1 to $2 of gains.

Letting the winners run as much as possible?

Yes. I got hurt at the end of 2008 and in the flash crash of 2010 as well. I tend to be overleveraged when there's value. A sports bettor likes to bet more if he thinks he's a 60 percent favorite to win. I would try to treat stocks like that. Problem is that if you get too leveraged you can't afford to let it go against you very much.

So you think you made a position size mistake?

For sure. Position size mistakes, leverage mistakes. I also got involved with options and 3x ETFs. Starting in 2007/2008 I was working thirteen hours a day. Although I was putting in that many hours, I wasn't doing the due diligence that a trader needs to do in terms of understanding risk/rewards of specific trades, keeping notebooks with charts, tracking where I was making money or losing money, times of the day where I was doing well/poorly. I just kind of got away from the fundamentals of being a good trader. I had no game plan like I should have, like having exit points or saying if I lost 3 percent or 5 percent, I should be out.

A lot of traders make most of their money at the open and the close. Was that true for you as well?

Most of the volatility is around the open and in the last hour of the day. I have stretches where I'm making all my money in the first hour and losing money in the last hour. Sometimes I'll over-trade in the middle of the day and get stopped in a lot of trades because the market just goes back and forth, and I waste a lot of commissions.

Yeah, I've done that a lot too. Do you have a theory on why the open is better?

Well, there are a lot of people sending orders around. A lot of times, stocks will just open up at extremes.

So you can fade the extremes?

Yeah, you can just trade against it. You can also see stocks in a range, and if it breaks out of that range in the first fifteen minutes you can go with that range.

How would you describe your style?

I would say I'm countertrend.

Have you stopped using limit orders?

When I'm getting out of a long or buying to cover, I'll use them, but to get into a position I will just use a market order.

I'm trying to do more technical trading nowadays, looking at charts, moving averages, support and resistance levels, etc.

Do you have any memorable trades from 2008?

I remember on October 4, it was a Friday, the market opened way up, but then it reversed and went to lows. I'd planned to see the Red Sox with my family, and I knew I was supposed to get out of my long position. It was an outside reversal day, and that was a bad sign for the following Monday. On Monday and Tuesday, I lost everything I'd made in that year.

A similar trade happened when the S&P downgraded the US credit rating in 2011. In that week there was a big open, and then the market reversed and went lower. Five days later the market was lower by 1,400 points or so.

I remember that.

I got hurt badly in the week of the S&P downgrade.

What do you think was your mistake in the trade?

It was a big outside reversal. The markets opened way up and then went straight down. All week I was thinking the market was overextended and I didn't get out of stuff.

You were overleveraged there?

I was way overleveraged.

You said that in 2009 and 2010 you did quite well, making a million dollars combined. How did you do it?

I played everything.

You mentioned sports betting and poker. You have a background in that?

I play Texas Hold'em, and I have a friend that gambled professionally as a poker player.

Do you try to look at the market from a similar perspective?

Yeah, you try to find the value in what you do, and if you do the trade a thousand times, the profits come. The more often you can do trades that you presume to be profitable, the better the chances are that you're going to be profitable according to the law of averages.

When you're going to do a trade, why do you sometimes prefer to express that view with options rather than the underlying?

You know what your risk is with the option. You can get a little more leverage, but mostly you know how much you can lose.

What hurt me in that downgrade situation is that I had some put spreads. I sold some and bought other strikes lower. At one point I sold my puts but kept the short.

Was it the same as 2008?

No, in 2008 I didn't sell options. I just bought calls and puts.

What happened in the flash crash situation?

We were probably down about 300 points and I bought the market. Greece was having riots. It's different now. When I started, all news that moved the market was what happened in the United States. Now everything out there affects the market.

It sucks, because I can't go negative in my account. Once it gets there I have to close the position. I was forced to take some major losses.

Have you always been a prop trader?

Yes, always.

Do you think there's an advantage to being a prop trader because you're around a bunch of other people you can learn from and see what works and doesn't?

I think there's an advantage there. I really haven't in the last four years, and that probably got me to take a lot more risk than I should have. There are some offices, though, where people don't want to share any ideas, or you might have a manager that will try to steal your system. When I traded Viacom A and B, I was away for six months and traded from home. When I came back, all of a sudden I saw a lot of people trading Viacom.

Do you do a lot of news trading? Try to quickly get in a trend after a piece of news hits?

I will try to. I have some news services that I pay for. Sometimes it's good, sometimes it's not. I may get the news quicker than other traders, but I'm not getting it quicker than other people.

I remember I was trading TEA a couple weeks back. There were rumors of someone potentially buying the company. I bought the stock, I sold some, and then I bought back in. The stock went below from where I bought it, so I decided to sell. Within about two minutes they halted the stock, and the news was that they were being bought out.

Normally you'll find that late in the week. Especially on Thursday, there will be all kinds of rumors. About 90 to 98 percent of them are false. Those are people trying to make money in the weekly options.

In these weekly options, there's what I call options vigilantes. They try to hold the stock at certain whole dollar levels on Fridays so they can collect the premium on both sides. It's like AAPL all of a sudden only moves in a $1 range on a Friday afternoon. All the premium in the calls and puts goes out. I see that a lot on Fridays. The markets make their move after the open and all of a sudden it spends four hours going nowhere.

I interviewed a trader who plays against takeover rumors. He shorts them and makes money that way. Do you play both sides or just buy them?

You can play both sides, but the risk is like in the TEA situation. They can halt the stock and you have no chance of getting out. You have to figure out mathematically where the value is. In that trade, if you shorted, you would lose $3 a share. You have to figure out if in the winning times you make enough to make up for that loss. If the trader makes money, then he probably does.

It's really rare, though, to see a buyout in the middle of the day. I can't remember the last time it happened.

Sometimes if the deal is in process and the rumors get out there, they'll rush the deal, but yeah, usually they'll happen in the mornings after a weekend. They work on it in the weekend.

The other day, NFLX had rumors, and then the news came out that Icahn had a 10 percent stake, and the stock rose a lot.

I believe the rumor was that MSFT was going to buy NFLX, but it was actually Icahn buying a stake.

Yeah, there were MSFT rumors on it.

Do you backtest at all?

No, not normally. I usually just call a friend that has all the applications for it. I recently looked at what AMZN and AAPL did on and around black Fridays and made some money that way.

Did you learn your technical trading by trial and error or from books?

You can read books and then do trial and error on it.

Of the technical that you use, which is the most useful?

I like the 50 and 200 moving averages. Also the outside day reversal that I mentioned earlier, where a stock opens higher at or going above the previous day's highs and then turns back and goes below the previous day's low. AAPL had an outside reversal day to the upside last week, and it just kept going for a few days.

What kind of equipment setup do you have?

I use five monitors, a Dell desktop, and an HP laptop. I'm actually shopping for a gaming computer now that can handle more monitors. I'm probably going to get one of those Alienware gaming computers with the i7 processor, gaming graphics cards, etc.

Do you use the trading software of your firm?

Yes. I use Lightspeed.

Do you find that it makes a difference using some software compared to others?

Yes, sure. Some platforms are more customizable, do different types of orders, etc.

Which news services do you have?

I use TradeTheNews and Fly on the Wall.

I've used TradeTheNews and found it much better than Fly. Why even have fly?

Well, TradeTheNews costs me $300 or so a month and Fly $30. On Fly, in the morning they have a list of upgrades/downgrades and things like that. Usually I want to know earnings dates so I can have less risk.

What is a good trade that you put on recently?

I caught the AAPL move up recently for something like $15 a share.

Do you think, because it has so much hype and news, AAPL becomes more inefficient than something like IBM for example?

Yes, it's definitely one of the most hyped stocks out there. In my experience this stock will go a lot higher than you think, and it will also go a lot lower. I tell people that if they're trying to buy it when it's down to wait, and then when they want to buy it, wait again, but the next time they really want to buy it then do it. AAPL is tricky, because they have a ton of cash and the PE is low.

Do you look at the L2, TS, and stuff like that? Is there an edge there?

I look at it, but in stocks like AAPL, there's so much volume that I don't even bother looking at it. I believe the L2 was much more useful years ago than it is now. I have it, but I don't look at it as much. It's better in stocks that aren't as volatile. You can see that there are a lot of stocks at a whole dollar mark. It's hard now, because people hide all their orders. The thing with these computers is that they can probably see where the orders are hidden, and the stop orders, etc.

What kind of advice do you give to people that are starting now?

Try to understand the risks and rewards when you go into a trade. Don't do trades because you're bored in the middle of the day. Keep records of where you're making your money and where you're losing your money. Hold yourself accountable to stops and taking losses. If you're trading with $10,000, stop yourself at $500 of losses in a position, and be done with trading that day.

So discipline? That is the number one advice?

Yes, don't take off things you're making money on, and don't let your losses run. It should be the other way around. Don't add to losses either, unless you're scaling in with a specific stop level. I've been trading for nine years, and my struggle is when I become a little cocky or arrogant. Then I have a bad day or two and want to make it all back. You have to treat every day as a new day.

Did you discover edges in the market by trial and error?

Yes, trial and error, writing down what works, what doesn't work. Certain things that might work for a year suddenly won't work the following year. You have to recognize certain patterns. If you're a new trader, try to play the trend rather than fight it.

Even in a year like this year, where markets aren't trending much and vol is low?

For a new trader it's probably better that the vol is low. He won't freak out, and the risk is a little bit less. Sometimes the market doesn't move anywhere for four months and it will be awesome for me. I would trade where I thought something was oversold or overbought, so I would go against the trend. A low vol market is very good for that. Sometimes when the market was really volatile I would find that I wasn't doing well, whereas people with algorithms would be doing very well.

I took a $10,000 account, trading 100 to 200 shares, to almost $1,000,000 in a year. A lot of that was luck.

Why was it luck?

I didn't have a good system but I had instincts for the market. Sometimes I'm very stubborn. I'll play a reversal but not put a stop in, and I'll take a much bigger loss than I should. In that account I would play 100 to 200 shares, then take it up to $15,000. Then I had a little bit more leverage. Sometimes I was able to parlay those gains into pretty good gains, then all of a sudden I would have over $100,000. Then it became a lot easier to make money. For many years I did very bad right in the summer. I would still not take summers off, because I was immature and stubborn.

Do you think your style is profitable and you just have to bet the right amounts and stick with your stops?

Yes.

Lessons from Chapter 11

1. The importance of appropriate bet sizing. Even though this trader has a background in sports betting and poker, he didn't incorporate one of the key elements of betting games—appropriate position sizing. In gambling, there's a formula: the Kelly Criterion. The Kelly gives you the perfect mathematical amount that you can bet for maximum long-term growth of your trading stake. It's a key sacrilege to go above your Kelly; the results of doing so are quite disastrous, as you can see in this chart:

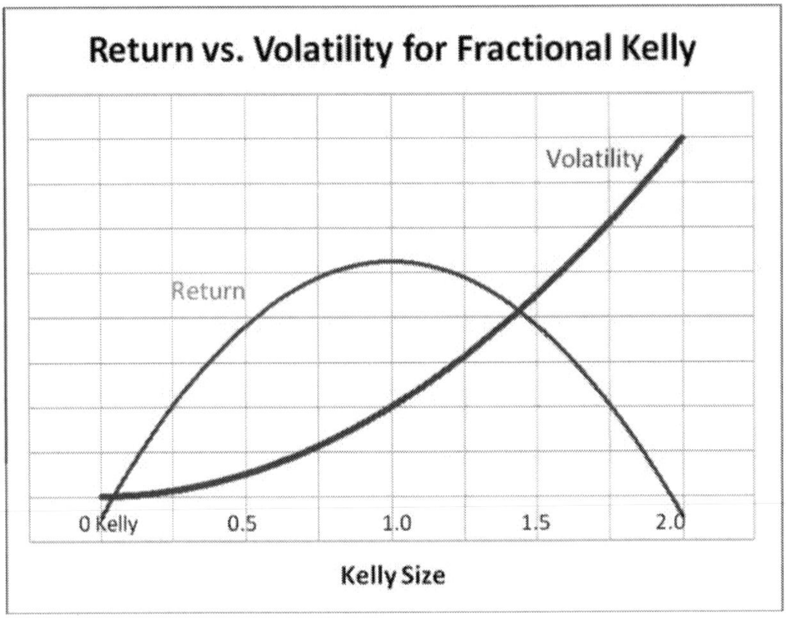

Source: drbobsports.com

What is striking about the Kelly is that if you bet less than the optimum amount (1.0), you'll cut your returns, **but you'll cut your volatility by an even greater amount**. To quote the article from drbobsports.com, which is the source of the chart::

"These graphs illustrate the long-term power of using Kelly sizing to increase one's bankroll over time, and beg the question, "If Kelly betting will lead to such incredible returns, then betting double or triple Kelly must lead to even higher returns!" Referred to as "overbetting," this misguided notion is one of the reasons that so many +EV sports bettors go broke just like their square compatriots. **It turns out that someone betting 1.5 Kelly has the same expected growth as someone betting 0.5 Kelly, but with tremendously wilder upswings and downswings, and much more risk.** Betting 2 Kelly actually has the same expected return as not betting at all: exactly zero, and betting more than 2 Kelly has a negative long term expected growth **even if you're making positive expected value bets**, and your bankroll will eventually fall to zero!

In conclusion, Kelly sizing is in fact, as has been stated several times, the point at which return is exactly optimal.

In addition to the dangers of overbetting, the Kelly Criterion also has large swings compared to flat betting. For example, a given positive expectation wager that compounds at 10 percent per time unit will eventually double, and of course grow to infinity. However, since the swings with Kelly betting are so large, **the initial bankroll actually has a 1/3 chance of being cut to half its initial value at some point before doubling.** To an academic, this is immaterial, since they can keep their eyes on the long run expected growth. **However, to investors who are often investing money for a shorter period of time and expecting immediate and consistent returns, this relatively high short term risk and volatility is unacceptable.**

However, because variance is exponentially related to return, we find that cutting the bet size in half causes only a nominal reduction in expected growth, but square roots the variance. In other words, if we were to bet one half Kelly unit on our 10 percent per time unit (with full Kelly) proposition, we would grow our funds at a slightly slower rate of 7.5 percent per time unit while our risk/variance/volatility would be the square root of what it was previously. **To use the previous example, we would now fall to 50 percent of our starting bankroll only 1/9 (rather than 1/3) of the time before doubling it—a much more tolerable level of risk for the average investor.**" (Emphasis mine)[39]

Does that mean that the Kelly is an appropriate number to use in trading? No, because unlike a lot of gambling games, you don't know the exact odds and the world is full of fat tails (even without overnight risk). In addition, the standard Kelly formula might not be appropriate for a trade that has multiple different scenarios for gains and losses (unless you tweak the formula).

What it does mean is that even if you're confident in your position, if you overbet you could easily have long-term negative returns even if the trade itself has positive expectation. If you overbet some but not by much, you'll still make money but with higher volatility than a small risk would create and with no additional profits! (But with plenty of stress and smashed keyboards.) It's nice to estimate probabilities and see what your Kelly is in a particular big bet you want to make simply just so you know where your risk should *not* be.

Example: If your Kelly is 10 percent of your account, you know that losing 10 percent is too much due to errors in estimation, black swans, halts, flash crashes, etc. You probably should bet half the Kelly or probably even less.

Betting a much smaller fraction of Kelly is the relaxation zone, because you're getting the most bang for the buck in terms of dollar-return/volatility ratio. Getting closer to the Kelly, you're starting to get more profits but your room for errors in

---

[39] http://www.drbobsports.com/essays.cfm?p=5

estimating your true probabilities is smaller. And your equity will fluctuate more, **so you'd better be mentally tough enough to handle the losses.**

Betting too little can also be a problem, because you leave money on the table; **however, this might be the only way to trade for people that are prone to tilting and revenge trading.** This trader is the perfect example of someone who needs to stick to the relaxation zone. Take a look at the chart again. The start of the volatility curve is where I would say the relaxation zone is. It's probably where most traders should stay in.

This former winner routinely made mistakes in terms of overleveraging, sometimes risking the entire account. This guarantees a long-term negative outcome even though he might be trading a positive expectancy discretionary system the entire time.

Jack Schwager in his excellent book *The Little Book of Market Wizards* describes a rule of thumb that can be used for traders when deciding how big a bet they should make in a trade:

> "Money Management doesn't have to be complex. Although there are entire books devoted just to the subject of money management, I believe a rule so simple that it can be described in a single sentence can get you 90 percent of the way there.
>
> Larry Hite, the cofounder of Mint Investment, one of the largest and most successful commodity trading advisors (CTAs) of the 1980s, was very clear about what he felt was the most important component of the firm's strategy: "The very first rule we live by at Mint is: Never risk more than 1 percent of the total equity on any trade." There you have it: effective money management in just one sentence.... This type of rule works because it prevents any single bad trade from doing much damage. You may still lose money trading, but you won't be knocked out of the game because of one or few bad trades that are allowed to accumulate losses without limit—a painful outcome experienced by many traders, even those with effective trade entry methodologies.
>
> There is nothing magical about the 1 percent limit; you could use 0.5 percent, or 2 percent, or whatever number is most appropriate for your strategy. The key point is that there is a strict loss limit on every trade. Effective money management is not a matter of complexity, but rather a matter of discipline. Even simple risk control rules will probably work fine, as long as you have the discipline to follow them."

If you do want to understand the technicalities of how the 1% rule was born, consider this: if you have a trade that can return 2 units for every unit risked (a 2 to 1 reward to risk ratio) and has a 50% chance of success (and most people would agree that is a good trade), the Kelly criterion formula would suggest you risk 25% of your capital. But because of fat tails (also called black/gray swans), estimation errors by the part of the trader, multiple bets at the same time (in gambling frequently only one bet happens at a time, whereas in trading you can face multiple losses from multiple trades), correlation among bets, multiple win loss outcomes, etc., betting only a fraction of Kelly is what is prudent. If you were to bet ¼ of Kelly, that would be 6.25%. But most people would not be able tolerate the drawdowns of such bet. A 50% chance loss will get you 4 losers in a row over 6% of the time. This would wipe out almost 25% of your capital. This is more than most people can tolerate, especially given that it will happen quite frequently while day trading, and an even bigger 50% drawdown would happen several times a year. As a result, you have to cut that 6% even further. A 1% to 2% rule of thumb makes sense considering these factors, with the higher percentages being reserved for high quality trades and lower percentages for lower quality trades. A beginner should probably go even below those percentages while he or she is learning.

2. Lack of exit points. The trader himself acknowledges he didn't have an exit point for a lot of trades he made. Because there's no maximum loss for a lot of his trades, he would frequently face gigantic losses, which guarantees massive volatility and possibly long-term negative account returns. As several traders mentioned in this book, the ability to take losses is the most important skill for a trader. Having an exit point is crucial so you know when to exercise that ability. This ability can be developed, and I describe my personal take on the subject in Chapter 15 in the section titled "The Boost Your Discipline Mini-Course."

3. Minimize outside distractions. The trader mentioned having a big long position without a stop in the market in October of 2008 and going to a Red Sox game.

The market had put an outside reversal day, which to this trader meant it was going lower. The fact that the big trade was a loser up to that point, combined with the distraction of having to leave the trading desk, meant that the trader had to take the loss. If you combine that with the technical input of the outside reversal, then it was a no-brainer to close the trade. He ended up holding that and gave back all the profits he'd made that year.

4. Divergence from the plan and trade style. The trader mentioned using options as a way to manage risk, because you know the most you can lose. He was in some put spreads in August of 2011. He then decided the market was oversold and sold his puts (but kept holding the short put part of the spread, a naked short). This left him without a hedge, vulnerable to a huge loss, and completely diverging from the whole idea of using options in the first place (limited losses). He diverged

from his plan then lost one million dollars over the following days after the S&P downgraded the US debt.

5. Keep detailed records. The trader himself acknowledges that he failed to keep track of his trading, what was working, what was not, the times of the day he made the most money, storing charts, risk/reward of specific trades, reviewing mistakes, etc. If you're struggling, keeping detailed records can make all the difference in your career. I use the free software Evernote for all my record keeping and would recommend other traders to do the same.

Chapter 12

Anonymous – The Secrecy of the Bot Destroyer

I was pretty excited about the possibility of interviewing the following trader. I was told he was quite aggressive and pretty effective at not just making money off market participants in general but also specifically from HFTs – that he was some kind of bot exploiter.

He was pretty skeptical about doing a phone interview. He told me in an e-mail, "I have some concerns about divulging information, and that is why I need the questions to be e-mailed. This will assure I give you the best answers I can while protecting my interest. I obviously won't be handing out free lunches to your readers. I will do an interview, but I want to be very cautious about the information I give. Send me some questions, let me look them over, and we can do a phone call." I then e-mailed a series of generic questions I use to get an interview rolling. Lots of times the interviews just take a direction of their own, and I don't stick with set questions, but for a general start they're useful. Turns out he didn't even give me substantive answers to the questions I sent. He answered them quickly without providing much information. I followed up with him, trying to schedule the phone interview but he never accepted it.

Why am I including the interview in the book? First, because there's some information in his answers – not a lot, but it confirmed some of other answers given by other good traders. The second reason will become clear in the lesson summary in the chapter's end.

This interview was conducted in August of 2012

What made you want to become a trader?

Lifestyle.

How long did it take for you to become profitable?

Six months.

What made a difference in turning that around?

Learning how things worked. When I began trading, I started with $5,000 and didn't know what ask was.

Biggest difference of back then to right now? Which strategies stopped working?

It's more difficult for individual traders to make money. Back then if you got into a losing trade, the market would bail you out with short term reversal. Back then the motto was "if you ain't fading you ain't trading." I've seen a lot of million-dollar-a-year earners who got used to this and didn't change and lost most of what they had earned over the years.

How has Reg NMS changed your strategies?

Well, it certainly hasn't made the market less fragmented. It has given HFTs and other professionals more advantages and angles over most. I try to adapt to the environment. If there are structure changes, you must change your strategies to adapt.

Since you have been trading for a long time, how has the market changed for you since the rise of HFT and algos?

Scalping is harder. Getting into and out of positions is more challenging. The biggest argument for HFTs is that they tighten spreads, but that's not exactly true. There's no depth to the liquidity. If you send an order for more than a 100 shares at a time, even if your size is allegedly concealed, you move the market more than you would have putting on the same size in the past. Spreads have actually widened for anyone who does over a 100 shares.

How did you do during 2008?

I did great.

How did you do during the flash crash?

Not as good as I should have.

How do you see the market evolving for short-term traders over the next ten years? Are you concerned it will get more efficient and that edges will close out?

Edges always change. Keep learning and hunting and you'll find something new. Sometimes you know there are edges and you can't take advantage of them. Dig deeper. Find a way to take advantage of them. I was short a stock last week, and I got a buy-in, so I had to cover. I tried several brokers to find shares. I found them and got short again. This company will be out of cash and gone in six months.

Best days?

$200,000.

Worst days?

$32,000.

How often do your strategies stop working? What kind of a cycle do you face?

Constantly.

Are market orders a sucker play?

Not always. If I'm really busy with more important things but I want the stock, I'll send a market order. I only do this on thick volume stocks though. I personally wouldn't do it with anything under a couple million a day average volume.

Did you extend your time horizon?

I would say I've added extended time horizon plays to my playbook, but more importantly I've been more strategic about getting in and out of positions. The way to think about this is that HFTs are like parasites and you're the host. They do not want to buy a stock unless you want to buy it. They don't want to sell it unless you want to sell it. So just know that when you send an order, it will have three or more times the impact on the market than it used to have. So buying 100 shares is like buying 300 shares. Your impact is intensified when getting in and getting out of positions, and for many traders that slippage was their entire earn.

How do you know when to pull the plug in a strategy that you're running?

You check the data, check that the story is intact, revaluate, and trade accordingly.

Do you think limit orders have weakened and marketable limit orders have become more important because of subpennying and penny jumping?

I take liquidity 90 percent of the time now. In the past, I provided liquidity 90 percent of the time.

Given the disadvantages of limit orders due to subpennying, in which situations do you use limit orders and in which do you not?

Subpennying is the scam of the century. You're essentially being forced to provide free insurance to those who can step ahead of your limit order by a subpenny. They know if the market moves they can dump the shares on you and lose almost nothing. Because of this, I only put in resting limit orders if I'm building a big position over a period of time where I anticipate getting fills at multiple price points.

Is there any edge in watching subpenny trades for predicting short-term direction?

Not for me. I see no point in that. You can't enter a subpenny order, so what are you going to do? Jump in there and pay their spread and trade with guys who have a tremendous edge on you entering and exiting the trade? I'm out.

What other advantages do HFTs and algos have over the traders besides subpennying?

Speed, commissions, exchange favoritism. If you ever want to see something interesting, follow the Clearly Erroneous Execution trades daily. You'll see some outrageous rulings. I've seen a $60 stock trade down to $58 on a mini-flash crash and NASDAQ, in their own words, has said, "Pursuant to Rule 11890(b), NASDAQ, on its own motion, has determined to cancel all trades in security." And the very same day, just an hour or so later, a $5 stock trades up to $20, and NASDAQ says this: "NASDAQ has reviewed the transactions under rule 11890 (b) on its own motion filing involving the security XXXXX executed between 13:31:00 and 13:32:00 (EST) today and has determined that all trades will stand. This decision cannot be appealed." If you inquire about this they'll tell you there are no firm rules, only guidelines, and it's at their discretion. Makes me think it's that who's on the advantageous side of those executions will determine the outcome of the ruling.

What kind of equipment do you use for trading? Do you have the latest hardware specs and top-notch, expensive software, or do you try to cut costs?

I have top notch hardware. I do not use a lot of paid software subscriptions aside from data. I have my own written instead.

Can bots be beaten on news trading?

If they misinterpret it they can.

What are some characteristics of winning traders you've seen over the years?

Aggression, resolve, being calculated, and having some gamble in you.

How confident are you in your ability to keep making profits over the next five to ten years?

I've no doubts. I'm a crusher.

What do you do with the money that you've earned but that is not needed for trading? Do you keep it in T-Bills or the bank, or do you invest in stocks, real estate, and businesses?

Guns, gold and land.

How important are your instincts? Do you trade off them frequently?

Yes, we call that on-the-gut trading. Most people can't do this profitably.

Did you trade the Facebook IPO?

I bought the open on IPO day and blew it out quickly. I've been trading it regularly and recovered the IPO day loss.

Do new catalysts and volume increase inefficiencies? Why?

Interpretation.

Are the consequences of computerized trading more reversals and overall noise in the price action?

I would say the reversal thing is true currently, but that might change. Overall noise is definitely true.

Do you read more rules and regulations and changes to rules and regulations?

I read a lot. I read more than I do anything else.

Do you avoid mid-day?

No, but I don't scalp it like I used to.

What advice do you have for an average trader dealing with the tough competition of HFTs and algos?

Join them, get a job, or study their weaknesses and take them down.

Lessons from Chapter 12

1. Surround yourself with great traders. Obviously this trader wasn't willing to share a lot about his strategies for a book, but I spoke with some traders that know

him personally, and they told me about a bit more about the strategies that he uses. The truth is that people are willing to share much more in a friendship situation or in a small group of people than they are in a more public forum. Why would you give away your secrets to the entire world? If a friend of yours asks about it, then you might be willing to share, especially if it's a trusted friend.

The late motivational speaker Jim Rohn had a saying that is so profound and extremely true. He used to say, "You're the average of the five people you spend the most time with." When you surround yourself with successful people, you can't help but start to absorb their mindsets, tactics, beliefs, etc. I know that for me personally, the idea of making several thousand dollars in a day through day trading was completely out of my concept of reality. But through the process of surrounding myself with great traders, I saw that this was not just common but extremely simple if you apply the principles of good trading—so simple that I started to have those days myself. This was one of the major reasons I decided to write this book. I wanted to learn from the best traders I could find. I wanted to not just understand their technical trading but also their mindsets, beliefs, etc.

There is even scientific evidence that behaviors are contagious. In one very interesting study done by Harvard and the University of California[40] it was found that when a friend of a study participant became obese, the participant was 57% more likely to become obese himself; when the friend was described as a "close friend" the chance went up to 171%. Humans are social creatures and we take cues from others as to know which behaviors are appropriate. This is why surrounding yourself with better traders and avoiding losing one's company is a key to short-term trading success. The good news is that the study authors say that this contagion effect should hold for weight loss as much as it does for weight gain.

How can you surround yourself with great traders? Reading this book is a great start, because most of the traders were less shy about their own take in trading than the Bot Destroyer, but there are several more options:

- Join a prop firm, not just so you can get more leverage (multiples times the retail leverage limits), avoidance of the PDT rule, and perhaps a better commission plan, but also because you get the chance to hang out with other traders. You can make friends with guys that might be killing the markets for years for large figures. You can learn from the managers there who probably know a lot about risk management since they have seen dozens of people blow up. Don't be shy about asking for advice. Worst case scenario is that they refuse to answer and you move on to the next person.

---

[40] http://tinyurl.com/lvkvaut

- Join a chat room. There a lots of day trading chat rooms out there, mostly paid. I never tried the free ones, because I know they tend to attract newbies and people who don't know what they're doing. I'm a member of a paid one, and it has helped me tremendously. By watching good traders alert their trades, you can understand more about what makes them act, good setups, risk/reward dynamics, the loss-cutting process, position sizing, etc. You won't necessarily be able to join the same trade. Usually that's not a good idea, as the slippage will hurt the profitability of the setup. (I say this happens usually, but that's not the always the case. Some of my best trades were trades off other people's alerts. The thing is, I knew they were great setups, so the move was going to be large.) By watching good traders in action, you can learn much faster than by just trading on your own. Don't be shy about asking traders questions through private messages. They'll be more willing to answer you than in public messages. Keep in mind that when selecting a chat room there will be a level of luck and randomness involved. Some of them will be good; lots will be bad. You'll just have to go through a level of trial and error until you find something that fits your style and the good trading principles that are outlined in this book. Don't subscribe for one-year plans until you've checked it out through a trial or a one-month package.

- Get a mentor. If you already know a great trader, try to think of ways you can get him to mentor you, even if it means working for him for free.

- Keep in touch with great traders through Skype. This idea was mentioned by a few traders in this book. They create their own private chat room on Skype. Needless to say, they'll be way more willing to share techniques, setups, and strategies there than anywhere else. Consider creating your own room and inviting good traders there.

2. Risk management. The Bot Destroyer's best day was more than six times the size of his worst day. This shows that he has his losses under control.

3. Take liquidity. Even though he's the Bot Destroyer, he still acknowledges all the advantages of the HFTs through subpenny prints, penny jumps, etc. He takes liquidity 90 percent of the time. I wrote about how to improve your executions when taking liquidity in Chapter 14 in the section called "Improve your order execution by using IEX as a smart order router."

4. Backtesting and programming. Even though it's not mentioned in the interview, I'm told by people who knows him that he backtests all kinds of stuff. He even said that edges always change. Backtesting is probably a key factor that he uses to adapt to changing conditions. He also mentioned writing his own trading software. Yes, it takes a lot of work, but in this HFT world, where edges are being

fought tooth and nail, being lazy about learning to code is not a good idea, especially if you're struggling.

Chapter 13

atticus – The Options Expert

The following interview will be hard to understand for a lot of readers. There are a lot of options terms and strategies that you might be unfamiliar with. I ask you to persevere and try to learn more about it, because this style of trading might fit your personality or you could learn things that will be useful for you.

This trader is very detailed and scientific about his methodologies. He has a deep understanding of options and option microstructure. I first came across him many years ago in the forums at Elitetrader.com (atticus is his nickname). He has run quite a few journals where he outlined daily what his plays were and which option strategies were best for each situation. He has made millions of dollars extracting profits from the markets, so even if you don't understand specifically what he means in a particular situation, try to understand why he was profitable or why his overall approach to the markets worked.

I included several footnotes explaining some of his option structures. If you're already familiar with options, you should be able to understand the strategies. If you're not, I would encourage you to read basic free tutorials on the web before tackling this chapter. If you still have difficulties understanding, I would recommend that you go straight to the lesson summary at the end of the chapter. I explain there in simpler language the lessons that I learned from this trader.

This interview was conducted in March of 2013

Why did you decide to become a trader?

My dad was a mathematician. He retired early from a teaching job to trade on the floor of the CBOE in Chicago. He had me fairly late. When I was born, my parents were already in their late thirties. I grew up with the *Wall Street Journal, Investors Daily, Barrons,* etc. around the house. I was also on math track. I graduated high school early, around fifteen. At sixteen I was looking for a job that I could actually do. I wasn't planning on starting an undergraduate program but taking a year off.

In the summer I worked as a clerk for my dad at the CBOE. I would run orders from the order desk to him. The pit in the CBOE was different from the CME. It wasn't a deep pit, just a couple of steps. I would reconcile sheets at the end of the day. I would look at the closing prices and see what I considered arbitrage opportunities at the time, but my dad would tell me immediately, "Those are stale quotes." Equity markets don't reconcile at end of the day to a fair value figure. They don't do reverse conversions and conversions and rolls to determine the prices.

I would look at discount arbitrages and deep in the money verticals and so forth. That really sparked my interest, because it looked like it was free money. I quickly learned that it wasn't. This was in 1983. The put market wasn't even ten years old yet. Calls started in 1973 in the CBOE, but you couldn't synthesize a put. It was hard to even get market data back then unless you were at the exchange, but then I decided to start an undergrad program.

While I was studying, I traded using a handheld device called a Quotetrack. It was an FM receiver back then. I was seventeen or eighteen, and my dad loaned me $60,000 to open my own account and trade for myself.

Do you think the fact that your dad was a mathematician helped you get on the right path?

I think so. It helped me understand that options are basically a probabilistic function. You're looking at the likelihood of price meeting X. You're looking at a logarithm distribution, and you can plot that in the chart. Delta, which is the first derivative of the price, is pretty close to the probability of expiration. In most markets, with libor where it's right now, you can pretty much use delta as the probability. That was basically how we looked at it, but that's where the math ends. I did algebra and calculus I and II, but I didn't follow in my dad's footsteps.

What happened to the first account that your father helped you fund?

I took it from $60,000 to about $25,000. At that point I just stopped trading. I told my dad that I only had about a third left. He told me to rethink what I was doing and stop for a while, not to trade on tilt and blow the rest out. It took about nine months to do that. In the next summer I decided to come back to trading from home. I bought a new Compaq DeskPro, I think it was a 286 at the time. I had a wireless FM desktop box for feeding the machine with data. I had Lotus1-2-3 as well. I decided to just trade at the end of the day, last thirty minutes before close, looking at the closing trend and trying to do directional bets in volatility.

Back then we had a Reg T margin that was much different than now. The parameters were much more conservative. You really couldn't do a lot of naked writing. I met a guy at the floor while working for my dad that I learned a few things from. He was one of the largest single name stock traders in the CBOE. I took his advice and sold straddles[41] on Friday at the close. Then I would convert to a butterfly on Monday morning. It was an unwritten rule they didn't even like to discuss outside the trading circles, but the CBOE guys, and to a lesser extent the Merc guys, were very specific when they would mark down their sheets for the weekend decay. Because it's not a continuous market, you don't wake up Monday morning and have the same prices that closed on Friday in terms of vol. They would typically mark down around noon central time or 3pm EST. My strategy would just front run that a little bit, taking the least risk possible, going closest to neutral as I could in single name stocks. I would sell ATM straddles in a basket of stocks in the indices, like GE, CAT, etc. On the following Monday I would take the weekend decay or vol mark down.

I would sell vol of something like 16 to 17 percent, then I would pick up about thirty basis points on Monday, buying it back the wings.[42] Or I'd sell the straddle. I would choose the closest wings that would give me a credit larger than the strike width, basically get a free butterfly.[43] If I couldn't get the credit, I'd just buy back the straddle. The rest of the week I would just do data mining. By the end of the summer I had about $50,000 from doing that, so I doubled the account with fairly low vol.

By the time 1987 hit, I was nearly break even in the original account. In '87 I shorted a ton of vol, and then the crash happened. I was on vacation, but we didn't have stuff like Wi-Fi. I was able to get out of my positions but ended up losing about 40 percent.

My dad actually ended up losing something like five million dollars, which was the bulk of our family's net worth at that time.

Did that event make you think the strategy was flawed?

I was only in the market two days a week. The rest of the time I was usually completely hedged, but because I was doing well I took some directional risk that I shouldn't have taken.

---

41 Selling an ATM straddle involves selling a call and a put at the same expiration and strike price. It's essentially a bet that the implied volatility is overpriced.
42 Buying the "wings" means that the trader has bought an OTM call and a put. This effectively hedges an ATM short straddle position against all kinds of risks.
43 A "fly" or butterfly is essentially a strategy where the trader is short 2 options in the "middle" and long 1 option in each "wing." Ex: short 2 100 calls, long 1 120 call and long 1 80 call. You are short volatility in the middle but hedged against tails events.

The VIX hit something like 300 back then, right?

It did hit some astronomical levels, but you have to understand that those bar charts contain maybe one trade of a guy capitulating at the low, and it wasn't representative of any real volume.

After '87 I decided to go to med school, and I knew I wasn't going to be able to trade actively, so I just traded two-to-three-month positions long-term vol bets. I would basically buy three-month butterflies and calendars to negate my Vega exposure.[44] A long butterfly is short volatility and a calendar is long volatility. I did a ratio of around one to five, so for each fly I would get about five calendars to negate my Vega, but the problem of that was that I was ramping my gamma, because both are short gamma. I was neutral in vol, but I had massive gamma figures.[45] It was a complex strategy, and my broker only asked about it when I called to put the orders in. I decided to go simpler and sold puts in stocks on which I liked the vol figure and bought puts in the index. At that point the skew or volatility smile in the index, even though we had the crash, wasn't that weighted toward the down and out strikes. In other words, if the index was at 500, the 450 puts weren't trading at a much higher vol than the 550 calls, maybe two hundred basis points more.

So I was trading this short dispersion strategy and making maybe 1 to 2 percent a month with very few drawdowns. I really appreciated the value of being hedged, even though a short dispersion has correlation risk.

Did you always trade from home?

Well, my dad had a JBO account with a trading firm. Essentially he had a market maker haircut instead of Reg T on options positions. He made an arrangement with one of the managers to let me trade the account, and we did really well there. What my strategies needed were looser margin requirements. Something that would cost me about $30,000 to do in a Reg T account would require $4,000 to $5,000 in the JBO

---

44 Buying a calendar involves selling an option in one month while also being long the same strike price option in another month that is after the month of the sale. The trader is trying to profit from differences in implied volatilities at different expirations. A calendar is long volatility because the long portion of the trade has a higher sensitivity to changes in volatility in the underlying than the short portion (in other words, it has a higher Vega).

45 This happened mostly because the calendars are highly exposed to near-term price changes in the underlying. Since the volatility "hedge" (that is, the long options part of the calendar) are for expirations many months from now, near term price changes can all of a sudden affect the price of the options portfolio a great deal (i.e. short gamma).

account. I turned his $250,000 account into $750,000 in the first year. We split fifty/fifty. After tax I had about $200,000.

In the trading firm, did you learn stuff from the other traders?

Not at all. I thought I would. There was a bunch of ex-floor traders, market makers and directional guys, but most of them were from the south side of Chicago. They had no aspiration to go to college. They wanted to be policemen, farmers, etc. They had very limited finance backgrounds, which was fine. My background was limited too, but a lot of them did things I just didn't believe in, such as doing point and figure charting, which is a massive smoothing of the data and I wasn't into breakout systems. I also met a guy that was in med school that I thought I was going to learn from, but I found out he was a complete degenerate. He had no bet sizing methodology. He would literally go all in when he really liked something.

Were you backtesting stuff or just feeling out when you thought something was mispriced?

There weren't a lot of backtesting tools back then. I have what is called eidetic memory. I can remember numbers very easily. I can recite pi out to maybe two hundred digits. I would have a really good memory in the stocks that I followed. I can recall the vol figure that I computed for an ATM straddle and the skew. I could recall the closing prices in stocks that I followed for maybe ninety days back. At some point I switch to the financial futures options and commodities. I was primarily trading options in T-Bonds, corn, beans, crude oil.

What do you think is the biggest difference between those options markets from those days compared to right now?

Electronic trading and the Internet changed everything, because when I started trading, single name and indices stock options spreads were really wide. For example: AAPL, the four forty-five ATM straddle for April expiration is about 40 to 50 cents wide, and the straddle is priced at $16 to $17. As a percentage of the value of the straddle, the cost is really small. Back in the '80s and all the way to maybe '98/'99, the ATM straddles would be maybe $1.50 wide. In one sense, when I had the JBO with the risk haircuts, even though I had margin treatment, I was still buying at the ask or hitting the bid, even though I was supposed to be a market maker. You would have to run your sheets, run what the fair value was. You would have a midpoint in every position, then you would derive what you were willing to pay in terms of edge loss due to the spread. Back in the '80s and '90s, vol was much higher. Most of the names I was trading had volatility above 100. These days vol is very low. You can get in and out with almost no edge loss due to tighter spreads, but unfortunately the vol is very low.

These stocks that had 100 vol, how you would assess they were mispriced? Do you look at fundamental data, news, or something else?

You look at realized vol. At this point we would have DDE links to Excel, and you could pump the data into a spreadsheet. I would just look at thirty-day realized vol figure in the stocks I traded. For example, JDSU was in the $80 to $90 a share range when the markets were already in the downswing from the bubble. You would look at historical vol of maybe 50 to 60, but you would have an implied vol of 120 in the options. That gave me the confidence. I would go 30 to 40 percent of my account in JDSU selling vol. It wasn't guaranteed, but the risk was so asymmetric. The reward would so outweigh the risk. All you had to do was hold it for three days and you'd be up $6 per contract. I remember prior to JDSU releasing its quarterly earnings report, the stock was at $79 a share. I sold the front month straddle at $22.05. There was about three or four weeks to expiration.

After earnings, the stock went up $6 or $7. All of a sudden the straddle was at $14. I bought the wings to convert into a fly.[46] At that point the trade was virtually locked up. I made something like $60,000 in that trade, holding for three days. The money wasn't enormous but the edge was. The one thing that kills me the most when I look back at my trading is that I wasn't larger in that period.

I also remember in the '99 to 2001 period there was something called RAIS in the CBOE. It was an execution system that if you traded twenty lots or less as a retail client, you would get FIFO treatment. The market maker wouldn't get filled before you. Let's say if we were both at $3.10 bid and $3.30 offer, I would get priority over the market maker. Back then there were no exchange links. You would have about five options exchanges. You would have options in COMS COM or tricom at the PLHX at $3.10 bid and $2.90 offer at the PSE. There was a huge arb there, and I got into that. I would buy in one exchange and sell it in another up to twenty lots. I would have a quick gain in a transaction that would take me about fifteen seconds.

I remember the first week that happened, I was totally unprepared for it. I had a programmer, but I was afraid to tell him about it because he could tell the whole world. I was just executing manually. On the first day of this arb I made about $180,000, with about $100,000 in capital in an Interactive Brokers account that I set up just for this purpose. Second day was about $280,000 or so. At that point I had to bring people in to execute the orders, about four or five people, and the edge immediately dried up. Exactly one week after this system started it stopped. The

---

46 In this case it was technically not a traditional butterfly (but rather an Iron Butterfly) because it involved being short both calls and puts in the middle but it's a similar structure. Converting a straddle into a fly cuts down the risk of exposure to fat tails or volatility increases.

markets were still there, but we would not get executed. Basically the OCC and the exchanges froze all the REIS transactions, so that was the end of that arb. About a month later I got a letter from the OCC saying that they were going to try to go after my profits in court. Then I got a letter from Timber Hill saying that they were going to represent me legally. The OCC never got a dime, so I'm very loyal to IB for that.

Did you regret telling other people?

Yeah, totally. I knew that if I'd been more discreet I could have milked it for at least a few months. The problem was that I was getting carpal tunnel syndrome from all the mouse clicking. I was literally executing five hundred transactions, if not more, about a thousand round trips a day. It's very hard to do it manually. I knew that these guys were very sharp, and they would be telling every family member about it, and the people they told would also start talking, and the edge would disappear and it did. I didn't know it at the time, but the guy who started the Archipelago ECN was much bigger than we were in doing this. He was making millions on it.

Was that the last time you saw easy edges like that?

Yes, there are some opportunities to do some reverse conversions in hard to borrow stocks so I could get shares in stocks that were reasonably hard to short.[47] These reversals would pay 70 to 80 percent a year, but they can pull the stock on you at any time. If the shareholders ask for the certificates, they can pull your borrow.

As the HFTs started to show up in the markets, did you have to lengthen the timeframe of your trades?

No, it's always a function of the volatility. The lower the vol, the more we have to go out. HFTs work both ways. For guys that are pure stock traders that try to make markets and collect rebates, the HFTs are brutal, because it's so mean reverting. If they put in a bid in a stock at $4.87, the HFTs will see that there's some natural demand, and they'll subpenny the deal. That doesn't happen to me at all. The HFTs actually help me because I trade a lot of stock, so I can hedge an options position. For example, if I'm short puts and I'm short the stock, HFTs help me get a better fill. The NBBO are narrower as a result of HFT interest. Since I'm not a directional trader

---

47 A reverse conversion can be achieved by selling a put, buying a call at the same strike and expiration while also being short the stock. Hard to borrow stocks usually have inflated premiums for a number of reasons, especially in the put side. This strategy tries to capitalize on that by having a credit after the option transactions which then is an almost guaranteed profit given that the position is hedged by being short the stock. But, of course, as atticus says, it's not easy to profit from because you can get your borrow pulled at any time, leaving you exposed to a decline in the stock.

in the primary market, the trade is now cheaper. HFTs for me are great, but I can understand that for guys at stock prop firms it's tough, because you get no swings. As soon as you put an order in and they're subpennying you or stepping in front of your trades you're constantly having to take liquidity and this hurts them. For me, since I always have been a price taker, the narrower spreads actually help me.

So the vast majority of your orders in options are taking the liquidity available?

Totally, all the time. I never buy an option at edge or sell an option at edge. If my methodology is dependent on getting in at the midpoint or below the midpoint of the spread then it's not robust enough. I can't depend on microstructure. If I'm a four leg spread and the spread is $30.00 x $31.00, my average fill is probably about $30.80. So I'm 30 cents off the midpoint. $30.50 is fair value. I'm paying 30 cents in edge loss, or about 1 percent on average.

When you sell options and tails and things like that, are you constantly scared of a black swan? How do you prevent a black swan from taking you out of the game?

I buy what are called "garbage puts." I don't buy a lot of upside protection, because we have the natural autocorrelation on vol in the upside. When prices goes up, vol goes down in inverse proportion. In the downside you need protection. I buy a lot of single name stock puts that are very deep OTM. Not so much for the vol sensitivity but for the delta gamma. If we do have a blow up, something that I paid a very low price for could easily go up ten to twenty times.

I'm also not always in the market. I'm not a passive trader that constantly sells vol like a lot of guys do. I feel strongly that if the vol is too low, there's not a duration that I can go out to that will fully compensate me for that vol, plus I'm exposing myself to that much duration and market risk. For example, I trade fairly large in the crude oil markets, but I tried to sell vol recently and just could not do it, because it's heavily correlated with stock index vol. So, I'm not always in the market, and certainly my income and exposures go down in low vol markets. These days I find myself buying a lot of close-to-the-money calendars in indexes, single name stocks, and commodities, because it allows me to sell a little bit of gamma and gain a little theta while also being long volatility.

You had that learning experience in '87. How did you do in October of 2008?

I would have to take a look at my spreadsheets. I know it wasn't great. I can tell you how much I lost in 9/11. It was about 19 percent, because Friday before the attacks I got a long signal in one of my Neural Networks systems. I was about 100 percent long in the Friday before 9/11. When the markets reopened I remember it was pretty orderly. It was down 5 to 6 percent, but I thought, "Wow, maybe I should stay in it." The loss was big though, so I took it.

I heard from some guys that if they get too big in an option, the market maker can tell and they try to shake the guy out by perhaps manipulating the prices. Do you think that's true?

Oh, it is. It's less of an issue now. There's the sell side that's making the markets. The Citadels, Susquehanna, Wolverine, etc. You also have the buy side, which is primarily hedge funds that are price takers for the most part, that trade huge size. They're not necessarily concerned about manipulation. They just want to get in or out. I remember a firm that I heard about that was trading 30,000 contracts a day in a fairly illiquid series. It turns out that if they lost their entire investment it would have been something like 1 percent of their AUM. I remember in the early 2000s, I was working for a fund of funds. I'd traded a fairly large number of flys for Best Buy. I routed an order to the AMEX, got a terrible fill, then I called a friend of mine who worked in a different number of single stock posts. I said, "Hey, bud, I got a really terrible fill from a broker." He said, "Oh yeah, I saw that trade. I didn't participate, but they were talking about it and laughing about how they raped the guy that sent that order." It was my fault for giving the broker any leeway in the trade.

You mentioned bet sizing. Do you have a mathematical algorithm for position sizing?

I do. I determine an edge in a position in terms of a five- to seven-day look in a thirty-day option, or maybe a two- to three-week in a quarterly option. I determine what my vol edge is, forecasting what is the likely realized vol over that duration. I determine what my edge is in terms of premium and percentage terms, then I apply essentially a Kelly criterion to that. I have it programmed in my iPhone, Android phone, and in my spreadsheets.

Do you go 100 percent of the Kelly?

No. I limit myself to 25 percent of my account in short vol trades, spread out in 5 percent blocks. So I might have a single name position that is 5 percent, an index position that is 5 percent, and so on. If I like something a lot I might go up to 25 percent of my account in any single trade, but I usually try to manage in 5 percent blocks.

Because the Kelly assumes that there are no fat tails, do you think it can be dangerous sometimes?

I have a nuclear risk figure, so if everything blows up, I know how much I'm going to lose. It's hard to do that in the dispersion trades that I do, but I look at things like

VAR[48]. If my two standard deviation, two sigma VAR is 20 percent of my portfolio[49], I'll have to reduce it. I monitor that in real time. I might reduce it by a quarter.

The primary risk that I look at, along with every trader that I follow, is our theta figure, because it's dollar figure.[50] It gives you basically a proportional gamma figure that we derive. If my dollar thetas are positive and are 5 percent of my book in total, that is way too much. I will have to cut it down. Let's say I'm short puts in stocks with long puts in indexes and my theta figure is 5 percent of my book. If it was 2 percent a week ago, that means the stocks that I'm trading are not well correlated, and I'm taking too much risk in the dispersion, and I have to reduce.

I've gotten to the point where the longer I've been trading, the simpler I've made the analytics. The biggest traders I know simply look at their theta figures, so I figured if it's good enough for them, it's good enough for me.

People who use Kelly in casino games usually do one bet at a time, but in trading there are multiple bets, sometimes correlated bets. Do you take that into account?

Sure. Everything is correlated. If I have a 3 percent bet in a single name, a 5 percent bet in an index, a 4 percent bet in a European single name, I don't see much difference between those. The DAX right now is pretty much leading our markets and so is Japan's. If I have a fairly large long delta[51] position in the United States, I would try to counter that with a short delta position elsewhere. The problem with that is that you also have to look at your modality of delta. If you have a short delta in the United States and a long delta in Europe, is the short delta in the United States unimodal? If it continues to go down does my delta position get smaller?[52] Does it become less sensitive or does it increase? If I have convexity to the downside, or positive convexity, that means I will gain more deltas as it goes down. Then I feel like I have a robust hedge. If I'm initially short deltas in the United States, and that delta flips bimodal, it flips sign, I won't consider it a robust hedge. I do try to keep my hedges unimodal. If I'm bearish in one market, I make sure that stays bearish. I

---

48 Value at risk. It's a statistical measure of risk over a certain period of time.
49 A two sigma VAR, in theory, would tell what is likely to happen roughly 95% of the time.
50 The Theta of an option or of an options portfolio tells you how much you are expected to lose per day due time decay. Ex: If you are long $500 in calls with a Theta of 25, in theory you're expected to lose $25 per day due to time decay.
51 Being long delta means he is exposed positively to a rise in the underlying price.
52 This would happen, for instance, if the short delta exposure was expressed by being short ATM calls. As the price of the underlying declines so will the value of the call. Your dollar exposure in the trade will also go down, leaving your hedge smaller and smaller.

don't worry as much about upside modality. If I'm bullish in another market and it flips to bearish after it rallies maybe 5 percent on the index, I will look for the mean reversion to maybe get me out. I make sure my hedges are true hedges. If I'm short delta, I make sure I remain short delta in the hedge.

What do you think enabled you to be able to consistently find edges for all these years you have been trading?

That's where the experience comes in. There's no impact other than experiences. Like I said, it's much easier now to move size. I can get in and out a thousand lots without moving the market more than a quarter point, but the vol is so low that it's just harder to find stuff.

Basically my edge is in terms of discretion, being out when I should be out and in when I should. Right now we are 11/12 vol on the VIX. The VIX figure is actually a strange number. The figure that they apply to the tails is indicative of the volume in the tails, but it's not the primary mover, because most people are trading ATM. It's not like I sit there and sell tails all day long and sell futures, because it just wouldn't be prudent if you consider the gamma of that. So I look at the ATM figure. If you're trading with 10.5 ATM figure, it's very difficult to sell vol in that level or even buy. Realized vol in the S&P500 is under 10. If I sell or buy 10.5 and I hedge discreetly in the underlying, I'm not going to make any money. There's no edge. I do look at what the dynamic hedging model would produce based on current realized vs. implied vol. If there isn't enough edge that I can hedge discreetly, I don't get involved long or short vol.

It's difficult. It forces you into single name vol, like earnings reports ramp up in vol trading duration (term skew). For instance, if May has an earnings report, you can buy May vol and sell April vol. As the date gets closer and people buy more and more May vol, you can profit. I trade a lot of calendars but only when I see an edge. When I do them, I'm not concerned what the broad market is going to do.

With regards to single name stock, when there's panic, does the implied vol get consistently too high most of the time?

Sure. Prior to the Dragi comments about bailouts you had days where the VIX would go from thirteen to eighteen, or something like that, without a big sell-off in the markets. You would have this asymmetric profile, and you always will, because essentially the VIX is bounded to ten or nine. It's like trading Eurodollars at 99.50. Can it go above 100? I don't think we will ever see that. The VIX is similar. There's a lower bound at around nine. If we drop 50 points in the S&P500, we would see twenty-two on the VIX. Would I be selling twenty-two on the VIX? I probably would but not in the index, but in single name stocks simply because I think there's less risk and better compensation. If the VIX is at twenty-two, names like Apple or Google might be at forty, so I'm being better paid there. I would not see twenty-two vol as necessarily a mean reversion selling point, because if it goes to twenty-two, it can easily go to forty.

I do look at technical stuff, outside reversals. If I was looking at the weekly chart, if I saw a high print of 1570 in the S&P500 and a low closing print of 1520, there's no way in hell I would be long any deltas or any market. Maybe gold, but even then you can get creamed as well as it can be a source of funds for injured equity accounts.

The equity markets are perceived to be small compared to FX or debt. They are, but the notional risk in equities drives everything. All of the psychology is really based off the equity market. The cab driver, the guy at the local bakery, everybody is looking at equity prices. I look at the equity markets as the sole barometer of where we are headed. Right now it looks great.

Because vol is so low, is it a good time to buy it? Maybe long-term vol?

There are very few instruments where you can get paid to hold. You can buy calendars in the VIX or some other vol instrument. The problem with that is you're short variance. Let's say you're technically long deltas in the VIX. Now you have modality again. If you're long deltas to say sixteen VIX and we are at twelve, then we have a day where the ES is down thirty to forty. We are going to have eighteen VIX. All of a sudden you're no longer long vol. There's no vol exposure. You're short so many deltas that there's nothing you can do about it. There's no hedge to it. It's essentially a write-off unless you can get back to neutrality on deltas.

There are very few things right now that you can do that you get paid to hold, so I'm not looking for that necessarily, but if we had an outside reversal day in the chart, or Bernanke swearing off of QE, I would probably be long vol regardless of what the print was, but we are so concerned with what could happen that any blip in the market is backstopped. That's the danger of buying vol here, especially in the VIX where you have an artificial curve based on absolute levels of volatility. Lots of times you see manipulation on the curve on settlement day.

I look at ATM vol. I look at twenty delta risk reversal, which would be the twenty delta put over the twenty delta call, and I also try to determine what the skew is. Right now I don't think it pays to be long vol into the summer months. Cyclicality says we're going to be slow here. If I had to be long vol I would love to be long vol in China, Singapore as a proxy for China, the Nikkei, and definitely in the DAX through some kind of synthetic calendar, long back spread/short delta.

The fact that you're not paid to hold to be long vol, couldn't that be a good thing? Almost no one is doing it, and maybe it's mispriced because everybody is short that trade.

Yes, it's definitely not crowded. I think people have become complacent due to all the backstops. If you look at Europe, with the confiscation of bank accounts in Cyprus and all of that, it's spooky. It's so difficult to buy vol when somebody just has to say, "Yeah, we don't have to worry about it. We're just going to print more money." When the dollar starts to fall against the euro, that's when it will be time to buy vol, because with all that's going on in Europe, there's no fix. The time to buy it will be when EURUSD goes above 1.30, 1.31. When we see inflation taking effect and that impacts the currency markets, I might start to position trade in vol.

When you trade single name equities, do you read the tape or look at stuff like L2 at all?

I don't look at that stuff at all. I look at closing trends, sector weights, and heat maps. I want to see where the large caps are moving. I look at the breath, relative value. I don't look at ticks or nominal statistics like that. If I see AAPL/GOOG, and I see networking stocks doing well and closing on the highs of the day, that might get me to short vol and get long delta. Basically the two trades that I believe exist are short delta/long vol and long delta/short vol. If you want to be short the market in any significant way, you don't want to be short vol. And if you want to be long the market you don't want to be long volatility. That's basically all you can do, and that is all that I do.

Do you use your instincts a lot to try to get a sense of what the stocks are going to do?

I certainly have as much analytics as I can in terms of setting up a trade, particularly in terms of bet sizing. I might commit up to 30 to 40 percent of capital if it looks like smooth sailing, but with EU as it's right now, I won't commit that much. Most of the instincts are discretion in terms of bet sizing depending on how the world looks. It's also a function of the fact that there's not as much opportunity. I'm virtually flat this week. I was short some vol in crude oil, and that worked out OK, but I'm very quick to take profits when I can.

In some of these plays that you do, do you use your experience that you accumulated over your career to sense when things are mispriced?

I think I mentioned on Elitetrader at one point, for each ticker that I follow I try to determine how the vol skew looks like in a percentage term.[53] I will also have an over/under on premium, so I know how the vol figure looks like in dollar terms. I will also price the complex spreads out in width, starting with a very narrow butterfly, say ten points wide, then fifteen, twenty, twenty-five. Beyond that point, the wings are so cheap, cheaper than half a point in terms of combined premium, so I stop tracking them. This gives me a relative value in terms of flys. I normalize them for dates as well. It gives me a variance figure, a vol of vol figure. I use a dollar figure on skew in the S&P500 and other indices like NASDAQ and the DAX that give me a relative allocation level. If the skew looks fat, if there's a large tail convexity, that gives me more confidence to sell vol even if ATM vol is relatively low. This indicates that maybe the tails are fat, there might be something fundamental coming up somewhere, but it won't be something that will impact the market for weeks to come. Maybe it will be just something transitory and it will be reverted back.

Any memorable trades from this year or last year?

I had a LEAPS position in AAPL maybe a year and a half ago. I sold vol prior to an earnings report and I was also short delta. I don't do this in indices, but occasionally I will do it in single names if I have a strong view. I felt that AAPL in notional terms couldn't support their valuation with the Android taking up so much market share. It was a fundamental shift. I saw so many people walking around with Androids. When the Galaxy Note came out, which is the Samsung's phone-plus-tablet device, I saw all my friends buying. I was in Midtown Manhattan and I saw like six of them in half an hour. I bought some LEAPS flies that were bearish. They essentially went up four fold after the earnings and the follow-through.

What kind of equipment do you use for trading?

I have the latest 12 core Mac Pro and two 30-inch Apple monitors. I also have some Macs that are dual boots for stuff like Excel. I have a Bloomberg as well. I run it on a Mac with Bloomberg Anywhere.

Does the Bloomberg subscription pay for itself?

I don't pay for it. I have some folks who supply that for me. I can do without it for sure. I use a small fraction of their analytics. Basically everybody in New York is collocated with their Bloombergs with extremely fast connections, whereas I'm far

53 The vol skew tells you what the difference is in implied volatilities between OTM, ATM and ITM options.

away with a 100Mbs connection. The latency is so high I can't get any meaningful edge.

Are you doing a lot of backtesting these days?

The more experience I have, the more trading I do, the less I backtest. I never put a lot of weight on backtesting. I used to do a lot of microstructure backtesting, seeing how orders would impact my overall results. With the spreads narrow now, I just don't do it anymore.

What do you do with the capital that you don't use for trading?

For the most part I move into cash. I will buy stocks but mostly to trade premium around it, like XOM to write calls on it. I might sell puts if I see a little skew there over the ATMs. As I accumulate premium over a few months, I'll convert them into additional shares. Once I get to the size that I want, I'll start to write calls against it.

What is the best book for somebody that wants to become a better options trader?

Anybody with a limited finance or statistics background should start with John Hull's *Options, Futures, and Derivatives*. With regard to equity options, I'd go with Sheldon Natenberg's stuff. If you want to know how to price synthetics, which are pretty basic math but most people don't know it, there's Allen Jan Baird's book on *Option Market Making*. That stuff can be very useful. For instance, if I'm bullish XYZ at $100, I think the stock will be trading at $102, but I think realized vol will drop, given that implied vol is autocorrelated component, instead of trading the synthetic iron fly, I may buy the put fly, because I want my body strike to be OTM at the next expiration, or at least touched.[54] This is simply because it provides a microstructure advantage. Deep ITM flys that have a deep ITM short component typically trade wider because there's more risk to the counterparty to trade out of.[55] I look at microstructure a lot when I trade. A lot of decision making is at that level, which is going to be the cheapest or most efficient way to express the trade.

Any last words of wisdom?

It's tough, because people learn about options and feel that they have to take positions, but there's so little juice out there right now. I would say for people who have a stock background, if they can make money there, continue there, and don't

---

54 The iron fly would be short a put and a call in the "middle," whereas a long put fly would be short two puts in the middle. This difference can provide the trader an advantage in certain situations due to microstructure even though they express a similar bias.

55 This provides the trader an additional vol "juice" to capture by selling the option.

go to options. People used to have 4 to 5 cents of edge, now they have a fraction of a cent in edge. Sometimes they feel like they need to go into options because of that. I know guys that trade very large with major prop firms or NASDAQ market makers that left the game for options because they could not beat the sell side. I know guys who have made millions over the last few years simply selling puts on bank stocks because they used to make markets in bank stocks. Unless you have a lot of capital and you can sit on your hands, it's just not a market to get into here. The vol is so low. It does not pay to be long vol. It does not pay to be short vol. You're naturally forced to go out of the curve in terms of time. Unfortunately, the longer you go, the bigger the Vegas will be and the more volatility risk you'll have. You can't trade short-term, because there's no juice. You can't trade long-term, because you have juice but the vol figure is so low. I would not recommend anybody to go into vol trading at this point.

Lessons from Chapter 13

1. Protect yourself against black swans/fat tails through garbage puts. A lot of people think selling volatility is a money loser in the long-term, because occasionally you get hit by a fat tail or black swan and lose a large amount. This definitely can be true if your risk management and position sizing is poor; however, if you protect yourself against such events using way OTM options, you can reduce those risks.

It's important to understand that picking nickels in front of a steamroller is not always a bad idea.[56] This can be counterintuitive for people that were trained to look for good risk/reward trades. They see a one to ten gain to loss payoff ratio and naturally are turned off and think people who engage in that kind of trading will lose everything. This is probably correct for 95 percent or more of participants who engage in that sort of trading. This is not the case with the Options Expert. It's pretty easy to prove that a one to ten win loss ratio can be extremely profitable if your win percentage is high enough. The real issue is making sure that ten-unit loss is really ten units and not five hundred during a once-in-a-lifetime sort of event.

Perhaps an example can illustrate this situation. Let's say stock ABC is trading at $50. It then proceeds to drop $20 in a week during a series of bad news. You notice that IV is at 200 percent. You believe that is completely mispriced and this was created by an irrational panic by investors. You decide to sell vol by selling the ATM

56 I understand this statement is controversial but stay with me.

straddle. But what if the stock goes to $0? If you do this type of trade enough times, at some point you're going to get hit by some kind of massive bad news, perhaps accounting fraud or maybe the SEC suspends trading in the stock (after which the stock doesn't trade for weeks, gets delisted and usually opens down 90 percent in the gray sheets market). In order to protect yourself against such an event, you can buy way OTM puts for, say, $15 strikes. You'll still get hurt by the fat tail. After all, your short put position will lose way more than your short call premium, but the garbage puts locks in the max loss you can possibly have. This enables you to have a loss that is consistent with a Kelly criterion style risk metric and thus prevents long-term negative account returns (as well as instant account blow ups).

Selling vol in this manner is similar to running an insurance company. You're taking the opposite side of a bad trade (the bad trade being buying vol), but **you must have a large enough bankroll** compared to your maximum loss, otherwise your equity volatility will be large and you'll possibly have long-term negative returns. This style of trading is not for everyone. It requires rock solid risk management and discipline. Otherwise one day you can make a mistake and end up facing such a big loss it can set you back dramatically. If you do trade this style, always be willing to sacrifice some profit in order to reduce the risk of a large negative event through the use of garbage options.

2. Have a sound position-sizing and risk management methodology. As you can see, The Options Expert has a very specific position-sizing method. He is the most detailed about it of all the interviews I conducted. He limits his exposure to 25 percent of his account in short vol trades, spread out in 5 percent buckets.

He derives how much he should bet from the Kelly Criterion formula. Keep in mind that in options it's frequently the case (but not always) that you know exactly how much you're going to lose, so you can get closer to the Kelly percentage in a lot of trades. This is not the case in stock or futures trading, where you can be hit by halts, overnight gaps, etc. For those types of situations you have to be lower than a conservatively estimated Kelly just to be safe.

He uses a "nuclear risk" figure of 15% for a two sigma VAR event (if he notices that it is 20% in his real-time monitoring, he will reduce it to 15%). A two sigma event will happen more frequently than what a normal distribution probability model would tell you, but it's important to keep in mind the following things:

A. He is taking risks based on "account size," not net worth. He has money in long-term investments, cash, etc. His true economic exposure is smaller than that.

B. Even if he faces a significant loss (say 30-40% of his account in a several sigma event) occasionally (like an insurance company), he can still grow his account quite well. As of matter of fact, the Kelly criterion frequently suggests risking a significant % of your bankroll if you have a great system. The key is to have these losses under control.

3. Dispersion trades. If you like a stock and its vol figure (meaning, you think vol it's too high), you can short its puts and then buy puts in the index. This enables you to win by being right about the stock rising and/or profiting as the implied volatility decreases. You also won't be exposed to broad market situations like the VIX going to 40, or something else along those lines. There's correlation risk of course, but at least you diminish your overall market risk. If this position is of meaningful size, you are probably better off also buying some "garbage" puts in the single name stock in order to further reduce your risk. If it's not (if the stock goes down 80% and it doesn`t threaten your account in a significant way), you can probably do without it.

4. The importance of sitting on your hands. The Options Expert had no problem saying that he wasn't trading much recently, given the lack of opportunities. He says one of the keys of his success is the discipline of being in the market when he should and not forcing trades.

5. Use theta as a risk figure for your options portfolio. The theta gives you a dollar figure that you can use to manage your exposure. It's used by a lot of big time options traders.

6. Books. He recommends a few books for traders looking to become better options traders. If you're looking to expand your knowledge in that area, they're a good start.

7. Microstructure. Some options strategies might be superior to others, even though they express a similar bias. This is due to microstructure differences in the backstage of the trades. If you want to improve as an options trader, learning microstructure could provide you with additional knowledge that you might find useful.

Chapter 14

The Trader Toolbox - Tricks, techniques and methods to fight against HFT

A lot of interest in the area of high frequency trading (HFT) and market structure reform has risen since events like the Flash Crash, and the book *Flash Boys*. In this chapter, I'm going to outline some tools that can help traders deal with modern markets.

First, let me say that learning deeply about the mechanics of modern markets won't turn a losing trader into a winning one (most of the time). The key elements of sound trading will always include having a good methodology (with positive expectation), the discipline to follow it and sticking with sound position sizing limits. These elements are timeless and have to be present regardless if we are dealing with a market run by specialists/market makers or by HFT computers. In my view, knowing more about HFT driven markets can help in two areas: first in your order execution and second in designing your methodology. Let's go through them one by one.

Order Execution

What market making HFTs frequently do is monopolize the spread and force market participants to take liquidity. They achieve that by "penny jumping" by one cent anyone who sends a passive limit order. They also buy the rights to interact first with retail order flow from brokerage houses, preventing you and me from having passive limit orders filled because we have less order flow to interact against. What they also do is cancel orders when traders try to take that liquidity, widen out their spreads a little bit and make more when the participant hits that spread. Anything that can prevent those things from happening can help reduce your "trading costs" and add a bit to your bottom line. There are many tools available (that traders don't seem to be aware of) that can help them to prevent cancelations when taking liquidity, increase their price improvement exposure, not be forced to hit the spread, etc. Using these tools won't be the Holy Grail—you won't all of a sudden turn profitable—but it will add a small percentage to your profits at the end of the year. Perhaps something in the range of 1% to 10%. These extra profits can add up.

For example, let's say a business decides to learn more about tax strategies with the help of a good accountant. The business won't necessarily triple its profits or double the sales of its next product. It might, however, legally decrease its tax bill by 5% and have additional capital at the end of the year that otherwise would not be there. Those small percentages compounded over the years add up to a fortune. This is very similar to techniques that prevents you from being "gamed" by HFTs. It adds up a bit to the bottom line at the end of the year and it accumulates exponentially over time due to compounding.

Designing your methodology

You can develop your strategy a little bit better knowing how modern markets work because right away you know what is unlikely to work for a human trader. For instance: most of the traders interviewed mentioned that they do not try to compete with HFTs and advise others to do the same. The reason is because these firms invest a lot in getting special advantages through expensive equipment, privileges and order types. If you are not willing do to the same, making a profit at the end is pretty much impossible. When designing your methodology, you can be pretty sure that a system that tries to scalp the market around for a few cents with very short-term time horizons (a few seconds to maybe a minute) is very unlikely to succeed except in unusual circumstances.

Also, because HFTs monopolize the spread, you have to give extra care to the order routing part of the strategy. Even if you use passive limit orders in an attempt to not pay the spread, the HFT firms will increase your costs indirectly through adverse selection. You will get filled in all of your losses (because the market is going against the passive limit orders), but sometimes you will miss fills in some winning trades (because the HFTs will sit in front of your order until the market is ready to go in the direction you predicted). Unfortunately, you will only find out about this when trading with real money as a backtest is unlikely to factor that in. If you are aware of adverse selection, you can avoid this problem and design a more realistic system.

In this chapter, I'm going to outline some tools that can help the order execution side.

Tool 1: Improve your order execution by using IEX as a smart order router

Since this book was first published (March 2014), an interesting exchange has gained the public's attention after the large success of the book *Flash Boys* by Michael Lewis. The IEX or The Investors Exchange was created by Brad Katsuyama and his colleagues from the Royal Bank of Canada after they realized that the US stock market was severely lacking an exchange that would actually respect and be fair to the investors and traders who were bringing their business there. The main idea is that they will not allow special advantages to HFTs that are routing their orders to their exchange. The way they achieve that is through several methods:

-Limited amount of order types. Unlike the main exchanges who, for a fee, allow almost any kind of order type (even if unfair) to be created.
-No maker/taker rebates.
-No collocated HFTs. They simply refuse to allow HFTs to be collocated in their exchange.
-A 350 microseconds latency for any order action taken by a participant (enter, cancel, revise an order), which ensures the IEX Matching Engine has sufficient time to receive and process changes to the NBBO (national best bid and offer) before a fast participant can receive and act upon the change on IEX.

This last point is a very important one. Recall that, in Chapter 8, Eric from Nanex talks about how HFTs can cancel orders from other places faster than order routers from exchanges can spread out the balance on an unfilled or partially filled order. This lets the HFTs widen out their spreads and make a little more on the transaction than otherwise would be the case.

How can a trader use IEX to its advantage and improve its order execution?

You see, the way IEX works, you can route an order, say buy 10,000 shares of PG, to IEX (which currently is an ATS, a dark pool, but soon it might become a displayed exchange) and if there are orders to sell PG there you will get executed for whatever amount is resting there for up to 10,000 shares. If there isn't the full amount that you want, they will re-route the balance of your order to the 11 registered displayed stock exchanges (3 from NYSE, 3 from NASDAQ, 4 from BATS and the Chicago Stock Exchange). The thing is, Katsuyama and his colleges are the folks who created Thor, the system that is used to combat HFT's games by getting orders to hit all the exchanges/ECNs at the same exact time to prevent them from cancelling or changing their orders after they discover your interest.

Because IEX is run by folks who know a lot about these HFT games and who were creative about how to work around it, you can expect that they will be intelligent about how IEX routes out your orders. This creates an interesting tool to traders: using IEX as a smart router. They have a proprietary method in which they re-route orders to other pools of liquidity (they are currently trying to patent it). What they do disclose is the following:

-After leaving IEX, the order does not go through dark pools or internalizers first (which is the case with quite a number of retail brokerages smart routers). Frequently orders that hit dark pools tip off HFTs, which allows them to cancel their orders in other places. Because routing to a dark pool is a shot in the dark, you don't know if there are any shares there at all—your upside can be limited and the downside of alerting HFTs is significant.

-They have direct data feeds to the exchanges that they are trying to hit. This means that their order router is looking at the present rather than looking at the past, which is the case with the SIP.

-They will hit those 11 exchanges in a specific sequence and routing logic (which is proprietary), but it is designed as to not allow the HFTs there to cancel or modify orders in other places when they see the buy or sell interest.

-Their own 350 microsecond delay prevents HFTs at IEX from reacting to buy or sell interest faster than their smart order router can spread out the client's order to the other displayed exchanges.

IEX's new order routing approach doesn't use (or need) Thor for several reasons:

First because their technology is much better than it was at RBC. RBC, being a broker dealer, didn't have much incentive to get the fastest connections to the exchanges or the best hardware. They weren't in the "arms race" to zero latency, whereas IEX's hardware and connections are as good or almost as good as the top HFT firms these days.

Secondly, because their router is centrally located among data centers in New Jersey, they don't need to spread out orders in a Thor-like fashion because they are quite close to the other data centers (and the exchanges housed within).

At RBC, they were routing off lower Manhattan. Signals had to travel up the Hudson River, and across into New Jersey (NJ), before reaching each of the data centers sequentially: first Weekawken (BATS), then Secaucus (Direct Edge), then Cartaret (NASDAQ) and finally Mahwah (NYSE). The time it took to reach each data center was relatively consistent, and predictable. This enabled the HFTs to play their games.

By having their router close to the other data centers in NJ, there is no need for Thor anymore. Any difference in reaching different destinations will be so tiny that it won't matter.

With this unique architecture, you can expect significant improvements over other simple routers. The results from their own statistics show that is indeed the case: they have a 97% fill rate (data from April 2016). What this means is that if you send an order for 10,000 PG and it is sent out to the displayed exchanges (because it couldn't get filled at IEX), if there are 10,000 shares at those displayed exchanges (at the NBBO), you are likely to get 97% of it filled. This resolves the problems that a lot of traders have of having the market disappear on you when you are trying to work out a big order. The cost of using their smart router is also not significant—just $0.0001 per share (about $1 for a 10,000 share order).

Currently (as of April of 2016), there are three retail brokerage houses that allow order routing to IEX. They are Interactive Brokers, Tradestation Securities and Lightspeed. Having an account for bigger orders at those brokerages can decrease your costs dramatically (as a long as they don't charge extra fees for that route). It's also important to ask your brokerage (in case it's not one of the three) to enable IEX routing. The more clients demand it, the more they will feel forced to do it. As a result, traders and investors won't have to rely on the inefficient and frequently biased smart routers the some brokers offer.

As is the case with a lot of advice in this book, try it out and see if your results improve.

Tool 2: Have good entries, avoid chasing.

This isn't a direct tool like the others in this chapter. It's more like a guideline that can keep you out of trouble. In this new HFT era, there is a lot of "noise" in the price action. You will notice that both stocks and futures tend to have a lot of back and forth regardless of what the trend is. This poses a challenge to traders because this movement tends to make you doubt your position constantly. For instance, one of most costly mistakes traders can make is to "chase" a stock down or up without a significant catalyst (breaking news or key breakout/breakdown). The problem with doing that is frequently the instrument you are trading will go the other way and you will spend a much higher percentage of the time in the trade with the pain of being down in the trade. That pain can drain your mental capital and induce you to make mistakes. You might get nervous about your position and exit just when it's about to go in your direction. Or you might get frustrated by the back and forth and just give up on the trade. When you do give up and the stock does what you expected, you might chase it again and start the process all over. This might put you in a position where you are "chopped around" constantly. This tends to happen also because when you chase, a lot of the time, other people did the same. The play becomes crowded and HFTs/smart players will push the other way to create a shakeout of the weak hands.

You might notice that in trades where you are up a lot, you don't tend to get chopped around. The fact that your entry is from a much lower/higher level (depending on whether you are long or short) gives you a profit cushion that makes it psychologically much easier to ignore the noise and stick with the position. These positions are much easier to manage. A lot of the time, they almost manage themselves.

When you do have a poor entry point in the trade, one of the things that you can do is what I call going into "bad average entry mode." Let's say ABC stock is in a channel of between 20.04 and 20.20. As it trends lower to test the 20.04 level, you decide to "chase" it down short at 20.07 in anticipation of the breakdown of the channel. This is a bad average price entry because it's on the low end of the channel. But one of the things that you can do to improve that entry is to take a small profit (with passive limit orders) at say, 20.04/20.02, 20. This will effectively give you a bit of a profit cushion and potentially prevent you from making mistakes when the lower end of the channel holds and the stock shoots back up to 20.20. If you took no profits in the lower end, you might get nervous and end up chasing the stock up and covering at the top end of the channel . This is exactly the opposite of what one should do when an instrument is stuck in a channel.

By taking a bit of the profit quick, it's as if you shorted at 20.13 or so. **A better average that will make you more resilient to the HFT back and forth.**

Now if you short 20.07 and it immediately comes back up to 20.20, then you will have a problem. If the stock keeps you in pain for long enough (let's say, an hour), you might just give up on the trade even though your thesis might still be intact.

The best way to trade that example, of course, is to short on the higher end of the channel, say at 20.17. Not only will the profit cushion make it easier to hold the trade, but you will also make more per trade because of better priced entry. The overall profitability of the trade will be higher (you are actually benefiting from the HFT noise) and the trade also will spend a smaller percentage of the time in the red. You also lose less when wrong. The overall "gain to pain" ratio of having good entries makes that style easier to trade than chasing entries. If you do decide to chase, at least do it with small size.

This idea doesn't apply only to sideways channels. It also applies to uptrends and downtrends. In trends, you usually want to be getting in when there is a short-term reversal of that trend. In an uptrend, you want to be buying dips and downtrends, shorting rallies. The principle is the same: the gain to pain ratio will be superior and psychologically is a less demanding style.

When is it okay to chase and not care as much about entry? Usually, when there is a catalyst—whether it is significant breaking news or a significant technical event (breakout, breakdown, loss of a key point). In that case, it's unlikely the stock will go back and forth around your entry. Its either going to go in your favor quite quickly or its going to go against you quickly, so it's okay (sometimes necessary) to chase.

Tool 3: Hidden Orders

Ever since the publication of the book *Dark Pools* in 2012, it became public that ECNs and exchanges were accommodating HFTs firms by offering them special order types that most market participants don't get. These order types enable HFTs to decrease the amount of "adverse selection" they are exposed to and to be at the top of the queue, which are key components of profitable market making.

Most HFTs firms have dozens (if not hundreds) of special order types at their disposal by exchanges and ECNs. Retail traders who want to be able to fight back and cut down their trading costs should learn and implement useful order types that are available to them.

There is an interesting tool that is not very well known by traders that can help you decrease the amount of HFT "gaming" your orders suffer. Hidden "native" orders are orders that sit on an ECN or exchange and that, in theory, are not seen by anyone. I say in theory because the exchanges/ECNs have broken the rules before in order to accommodate HFTs. It's possible that some of them have leaked information about hidden orders at some point.

These orders are different from iceberg/reserve orders. Iceberg orders show up on the Level 2 window and on the direct feed data that HFTs receive. They usually appear as 100 shares and give HFTs an opportunity to "penny jump" the order by going in front of it by 1 cent. This exposes the order to adverse selection, meaning they will get out of the way when they see a shift in the short-term supply and demand and stay ahead of you by 1 or a few cents when they don't. You tend to miss out on fills that you want and get fills that you don't want.

Lots of traders report the experience of having a stock move down or up right to the point that their limit order does not get filled by one cent (or get partially filled). Sometimes this happens due to randomness, but a lot of the time this happens because HFTs use passive non-HFT orders as insurance. If they are bidding for a stock, they know that if they get ahead of you by 1 cent, they can get their fills and try to sell on the ask. If all goes well, they make the spread; if it doesn't and the stock looks to drop, they dump their shares into your orders. You get your fill but now you are also underwater in the trade (or you left money on the table for a buy to cover order while exposing yourself to a squeeze).

A useful way to diminish this passive order gaming is to use "native" hidden orders. With these orders, the HFTs tend to only find out where your orders are after they have been executed (whether in full or partial). Let me give you an example: let's say you are short 1,000 shares of stock ABC, it's trading at $35, and it then proceeds to drop as you expected. You decide to take profits in the $34.60-$34.65 area because you think there will be some support at $34.50. You put a hidden buy order for 500 shares of ABC, native to ARCA at $34.64, 200 shares at $34.63 native to NSDQ and 300 native to NYSE at $34.63. When I say native to the ECN/exchange, I mean that it will only interact with the order flow of that ECN/exchange. For instance, if someone sells 500 shares of ABC at $34.64 at NYSE, you will not get filled because your hidden order was sitting at ARCA. Hidden orders can even be traded through, meaning, you can see prints below the price of your buy order. This disadvantage can be countered by using what I call a hidden order "net." You use several ECNs/exchanges that have the most volume, instead of just one. That way you have multiple order flows to interact with.

By having your orders distributed that way, when the stock drops and stops in the $34.60s area, you will avoid being used as insurance for HFTs looking to make markets. If the stock really drops quickly, say from $35 to $34.50, it won't make much of a difference whether you are using hidden or lit (displayed) orders. It's on the marginal situations where your orders are on the bottom or close to the bottom that hidden orders can decrease your trading costs by exposing you to less adverse selection.

With the lit orders, having the HFTs penny jump you and prevent you from getting filled at or close to the bottom can cost you significant profits as the stock reverses higher and you are forced to hit the ask in the $34.70s area. With the hidden orders, the HFTs can still game you in a similar fashion, but they can do it only after they find out that there are hidden orders at a certain level. In a fast moving stock with good volume, by the time they find out it's too late. Your order is likely to at least been partially filled.

In addition, HFTs don't like hidden orders because even though they can find out that they are at a certain level, they don't know when they get cancelled or entirely filled and the free insurance is gone. They do like to use a trick against these orders, odd lot trades. Sometimes, in order to find out if there are hidden orders in an exchange/ECN, they will send out orders for a tiny amount of shares (usually less than 50). When they discover the hidden liquidity, they can penny jump it or just keep sending odd lot orders to annoy and/or increase the trading costs of the trader behind it.

Routing a Hidden Order Net

Which routes to use to best increase the chance your hidden order net will capture most of the volume in a particular stock? You have to be aware of where, currently in the US, most of the volume is going through. As of January of 2016, volume is distributed as follows:

Notional Value Summary | Volume Summary | ☑ Auctions ☑ Odd lots ☐ Combine

Today | 5 Day Avg. | MTD Avg.

Jan 18, 2016	Tape A NYSE	Tape B Regional	Tape C Nasdaq	Total	% of Mkt	Today % of Mkt
Matched Volume						
NASDAQ (Q)	583,398,034	211,404,521	570,817,257	1,365,619,811	15.23%	0.00%
NYSE (N)	1,108,097,091	0	0	1,108,097,091	12.35%	0.00%
NYSE Arca (P)	335,165,445	428,490,133	242,793,876	1,006,449,454	11.22%	0.00%
EDGX (K)	279,845,708	183,579,297	231,771,424	695,196,430	7.75%	0.00%
BATS BZX (Z)	286,943,765	166,033,733	155,874,505	[illegible]	6.79%	0.00%
BATS BYX (Y)	188,127,318	104,752,913	90,184,011	383,064,243	4.27%	0.00%
EDGA (J)	114,620,674	71,063,346	56,758,408	242,442,428	2.70%	0.00%
NASDAQ BX (B)	106,534,891	53,103,625	56,570,719	216,209,234	2.41%	0.00%
NASDAQ PSX (X)	35,106,843	24,801,949	27,319,653	87,228,446	0.97%	0.00%
CHX (M)	12,949,759	21,833,832	8,802,317	43,585,908	0.49%	0.00%
NYSE MKT (A)	0	9,694,481	3,597,225	13,291,706	0.15%	0.00%
NSX (C)	50,705	3,102	17,955	71,761	0.00%	0.00%
FINRA & TRF Volume						
NASDAQ (DQ)	1,420,605,937	649,517,752	773,125,177	2,843,248,866	31.70%	0.00%
NYSE (DN)	192,179,225	66,446,981	97,112,437	355,738,642	3.97%	0.00%
Total Consolidated Volume						
Total	4,663,625,395	1,990,725,665	2,314,744,963	8,969,096,023	100.00%	0.00%

Source: BATS Exchange.

By the table, you can see that in a NASDAQ stock (Tape C), NASDAQ and ARCA do most of the volume (over 35%). For a NYSE stock (Tape A), NYSE and ARCA do most of the volume (about 36%). For AMEX stocks (Tape B), ARCA and NASDAQ do most of the volume (about 32%).

When routing your net in a NASDAQ stock, the better routes are NASDAQ (sometimes still called Island by some brokers) and ARCA as a secondary route. When trading a NYSE stock, the better routes are NYSE and NASDAQ. For AMEX, ARCA is the main one and NASDAQ is a secondary route.

The Weaknesses of Hidden Orders

Hidden orders are not the Holy Grail. They just happen to be useful in certain conditions. In what situations are hidden orders not a great tool?

As a rule of thumb, if you have a large order or if the stock has low activity, the benefits of hidden orders are limited.

For large orders, having your net sit on the bid and ask for a long time till it's completely filled might allow the HFTs to find out what you are doing with odd lot trades or just be looking at "phantom" trade executions. When they do find out, the amount of adverse selection you are exposed to increases because now they can penny jump you. The other weakness of these orders (not being exposed to all the order flow but only from the exchange/ECN you are native to) is still there. If you combine that with more adverse selection, that might have little or no added value over displayed orders.

In low activity stocks, the problem is similar. It's going to take longer for your order to be executed. There is more time for you to get hit with odd lot trades (which increases your costs if your broker has a minimum commission charge) and for HFTs to discover what you are doing.

When to use Hidden Orders

The ideal scenario for hidden orders are stocks with a good amount of activity going off in the bid and ask, and a significant spread. This is usually the case in momentum stocks that are higher priced or some small caps.

The spread has to be large because otherwise it is just not worth it to try to save it. If you are trading something with a spread of 2 cents or less, you might be better off just taking liquidity. If the spread is 10-20 cents or more, then it's worth it. In fact, it can get quite expensive to hit that big of a spread over and over again.

Where hidden orders are really useful is when your stock is moving fast in a direction and you have a tough time with HFTs stopping right in front or order. In this case, having a net of smaller sized hidden orders nicely distributed in different exchanges and ECNs can pretty much guarantee that you will get fills with less adverse selection than otherwise would be the case.

Another situation where they can make you money is when you see a trade setup in a large spread stock that you believe is profitable **only if you get in without paying the spread**. If you get filled with the hidden order, that's great—you get to participate in the trade. If you don't (because the move happened before your fill), it's not a big deal anyway because hitting the spread would turn the trade into a loser. You have a free shot at being in those trades. Over the course of a year, being in these trades can add up to a lot of money.

Pre-market and after-hours

Pre-market and after-hours trading is also a period where hidden orders can be a good tool at your disposal. First, because the spreads are usually huge, paying it without a piece of fresh news is extremely costly. What a trader can do is to put hidden orders in front of displayed orders in those sessions and participate in some of the "market making" that happens outside of regular trading hours. There won't be a lot of activity or volume, but the gain is so large that it can be worth it.

The way I play is to try to close my swing/overnight positions by having orders sitting at these extreme levels and checking the next day to see if I got a fill. Most of the time you won't, but it's cheap to try it and occasionally you will get filled. Even odd lots trades are not a big deal there. If a stock closed at $40 and you get hit for 20 shares selling at $40.98, you are still profitable even after commissions.

Keep in mind that sometimes it's better to have your order displayed instead of hidden. You want to show to someone nervous about their position where the liquidity is so they can hit it.

Also remember that other people will be using hidden orders too, if your lit order has been sitting in the market for a while. It's quite possible that there will be hidden orders in front of it at the same exchange/ECN.

Tool 4: Dark Pools

Dark pools recently have been the subject of many headlines recently, mostly due to alleged illegal activities from the banks that operate them. For instance, Barclays is said have given High Frequency Traders (HFTs) unfair advantages[57] over traders and investors in order to boost its trading activity and revenues.

In this section, I'm going to explain what dark pools are, how they can be used by traders to reduce trading costs and when they should be avoided in order to achieve the same purpose.

First, what is a dark pool? The technical term for them is ATS (alternative trading system). They are essentially mini exchanges that match buy and sell orders without displaying them to the market. If you route a buy order (say, buy 50,000 shares of MSFT) to a dark pool, in theory nobody knows your order is there. You have the possibility of getting filled for your entire order without "spooking" the market by displaying a large bid in the Level 2 window. A lot of smart routers tend to go through dark pools first before they hit the displayed exchanges/ECNs; as a result, your order would be exposed to that order flow before other participants. Another benefit of dark pools is that because the order is not displayed, sometimes you get the benefit of not having to hit the bid or ask in order to get your order executed. If you send a displayed order and have it appear in the Level 2, frequently, high frequency traders will jump ahead of you by one cent. This sort of "penny jumping" is done automatically by computers. While it has to be adjusted manually by us humans, this is annoying, time consuming and inefficient. By having that order in a dark pool, you can be in front of the HFT bids and asks, in theory, without them knowing about it, and you can get the order flow of that dark pool to save you the spread.

Another benefit of dark pools is that when you send liquidity taking orders that go through them first, you tend to get access to additional liquidity not shown in the Level 2 that is inside the NBBO (National Best Bid and Offer). This tends to reduce your trading costs because it reduces the spread that you have to pay. Example: You try to buy 1,000 shares of PG at 80.02 in a market quoted at 80.01 x 80.02, your smart router hits a dark pool before the displayed market and gives back a fill for your entire order at 80.015. You just saved half a cent, which comes out at $5. Over the course of a year, these savings add up.

---

[57] http://tinyurl.com/zgazjdn

Does that mean that dark pools are the Holy Grail for traders and investors to reduce their trading costs?

No. In addition to the unfair advantages that high frequency traders might be getting in dark pools, there are other issues even through legal means. For instance, Eric Hunsander from Nanex did an expose on how modern markets are rigged.[58]

In it he demonstrated that a large order (in this case a buy order for 20,000 shares of Ford) alerted HFTs about his buying intentions because it hit dark pools first before the displayed markets. The HFTs then proceeded to cancel their orders from the displayed exchanges. The trader behind the order ended up only getting 12,133 shares (and 600 were from the dark pool). In this case, having the order go through the dark pool first was an extremely bad deal.

The question now is: if you are looking to decrease trading costs, when should a trader use dark pools and when he should avoid them?

It all depends on your order size. As a rule of thumb, if you are executing a small liquidity taking order (you are hitting the bid or ask), you want to go through as many dark pools as possible. The additional liquidity will give you fills inside the NBBO and reduce the spread that you pay. Some brokers allow you to expand the number of dark pools that your order will go through. Being aware of this option can help you expose your order to dark pools when you think that is valuable. Ask your broker if they offer such an option.

If you are sending a small liquidity providing order, you want to use a dark pool that has a lot of activity in that stock. This will enable you to not have to sit with a bid or offer for very long, get taken and save the spread. Not a lot of retail brokerages allow routing to dark pools. Ask your broker if they have such options.

On the other hand, if you are executing a liquidity taking large order, you want to go through as few dark pools as possible. As explained by Nanex and evidenced by a lot of frustrated traders, when HFTs notice dark pool activity a lot of the time, they tend to cancel their orders in the displayed market. HFTs know that dark pools are used by institutional traders looking for liquidity. Since institutions usually have a lot of stock to buy and sell, HFTs can make more by widening their spreads. In the case of large liquidity adding orders, it's also problematic to use a dark pool. Barclays and Credit Suisse are both being accused of wrongdoing when dealing with institutional orders. And these are just two banks—there are dozens of dark pools out there. Every time you send your larger orders to dark pools, you run the risk of being taken advantage of by executives looking to increase their market share. The benefit of you having your block trade executed is significant, but so is the cost of having your intentions exposed to HFTs. Choosing the right dark pool becomes crucial.

---

[58] http://www.nanex.net/aqck2/4661.html

To summarize, I created the following table of how traders and investors can use dark pools to decrease trading costs. The definitions of small, medium and large orders have to do with how much of a market impact you expect to have. For instance: if you want to buy 400 shares of ABC and there are 5,000 shares bid and 6,000 offered, you have a small order as this is not expected to have much of a market impact. If you are trying to buy 20,000 shares, it's a large order. A medium sized order would be somewhere in between. There is a fourth category for huge orders (say 50,000, 100,000 or even 1 million shares) – these are institutional orders that require more advanced techniques to conceal your intentions and require multiple executions over many hours/days. Those techniques are beyond the scope of this section.

Keep in mind that some larger spread stocks without a lot of liquidity (typical of small caps), sometimes even something as little as 200-300 shares, is expected to have market impact.

Small Orders	Medium Orders	Large Orders
When taking liquidity: You want to go through as many dark pools/market makers as possible. Some brokerages allow you to expand the number of dark pools and market makers your order goes through. Turning this option on is an attractive choice. See the Brokers section bellow.	**When taking liquidity:** This is where trader discretion and experience comes in. You have to be able to judge whether your order will have a market impact or not. The more impact you expect to have, the less you should rely on dark pools.	**When taking liquidity:** You want to go through as few dark pools as possible. Preferably only IEX. IEX has a 350 microsecond delay to its HFTs and participants. This prevents them from outracing the IEX router and cancelling their orders from displayed exchanges. By not going through dark pools first, you can avoid a cascade of cancellations that happen when dark pool activity is detected by HFTs.
When adding liquidity: You want to use a dark pool/market maker that has a lot of activity in that stock. This will help you quickly get filled and save the spread. Not a lot of retail brokerages allow routing to dark pools, but some do.	**When adding liquidity:** This is where trader discretion and experience comes in. You have to be able to judge whether your order will have a market impact or not. The more impact you expect to have, the less you should rely on dark pools.	**When adding liquidity:** You want to be as careful as possible. A lot of dark pools are alleged to have engaged in wrong doing. Some might be leaking out information about orders. You should only use a dark pool that you really trust.

Two other variables you have to take into account are how quickly you want to get in or out of a stock, and how fast the stock is moving.

You want to get your orders executed fast	**You are not in a rush to execute your orders**
Because you want to get in or out as fast as possible, you should go through as few dark places as possible. Having your intentions exposed while routing your orders becomes a bigger issue given that you are going to be hitting the bid or the ask more aggressively. Getting executed becomes more important than a small price improvement a dark pool could bring.	Because you are not in a rush, you should hit as many dark places as possible for the price improvement. Having time to work your order means that you can break a larger order into smaller blocks. The same principles for smaller orders would apply in this case, even if the orders were large.
It's a fasting moving stock	**It's a slow moving stock**
You want to go through as few dark pools as possible. In a fast moving stock, the downside of having your intentions exposed will be large. The subsequent HFT move will be more costly, likely several times any price improvement a dark pool could bring.	You want to go through as many dark pools as possible routing your order. The downside here is not as large. If HFTs detect your intentions, it might not even impact the price very much (especially if you can wait a few minutes until you route another order). Unless your order is quite big, you can afford to seek price improvement in these types of stocks.

Brokers: Retail brokers like CenterPoint Securities give access to a lot of dark liquidity through their special routes like CPCIT(Citadel), CPKCG (Knight), CSFBDESK (Credit Suisse), and others. That extra liquidity can help when traders are looking for price improvement or for fills when dealing with the Short Sell Restriction.

Interactive Brokers has an option called "Seek Price Improvement" that is turned off by default. If your order is small, turning the option on can decrease your trading costs and expose you to additional intra NBBO liquidity.

Dark pool orders definitely have a place in a trader's toolbox. Don't be scared by the headlines you read on the financial websites. If you understand them and know how to use them, you can use your judgment of when they are likely to decrease or increase your trading costs. Being aware of how much market impact you are likely to have and how your broker routes your orders can further help you in decreasing those costs.

Tool 5: Inverted Exchanges and ECNs

Most traders and investors are used to the standard exchanges where you post a limit order and get a rebate when you get filled and whoever was in the other side of the trade has to pay a fee to hit that limit order. Not a lot of people are aware that some exchanges actually have that classic fee schedule inverted. That is, you have to pay to add liquidity and get paid to take liquidity. One might ask, "Why would I want to pay to add liquidity?" There is actually a lot of uses to those routes. In this section, I'm going to explain some of them and why they can be invaluable in decreasing the amount of adverse selection your orders suffer from.

Most HFTs or smart routers these days follow a cost conscious approach when they are routing liquidity-taking orders. That is, when they are looking to buy on the offer or sell on the bid, they will be looking to hit the routes that will cost them the least first, then will hit up the other pools that are more expensive. What this means is that the routes that are cheap to hit (take liquidity) are getting taken first, which means they are exposed to less adverse selection than the routes that are more expensive to hit.

With the routes that get taken first, you will experience less often the frustrating situation where the market goes right to your price, stops there and reverses with no fill or a partial fill to your order. With the most expensive routes, usually you will only get your order filled when the market is blowing right through your price. This usually means you are wrong (in the ultra-short-term sense).

Which are the routes that are expensive and which ones require a lower cost to hit? Below there is a quick table. Keep in mind that the exact amounts of rebates and fees paid by you will depend on your broker, how much volume they do with the exchanges and how much of the rebates they will pass onto you, among other factors. This is just a general estimate that might not be entirely accurate for your situation. Consult your broker for confirmation of these figures. These values can change at any time.

Stocks above $1

Format: Venue - Rebate/Fee to add liquidity – Rebate/Fee to take liquidity

High Rebate Venues		
EDGX	+0.002	-0.0029
BATS/ BZX	+0.002	-0.003
ARCA	+0.0025	-0.003
NASD AQ	+0.002	-0.003
CHX	+0.002	-0.003
NYSE	+0.0016	-0.003
PSX	+0.0025	-0.0029

Balanced Venues		
EDGA	+0.0005	-0.0002

Low or no Rebate Venues		
BATSY -BYX	-0.0018	+0.0015
BX	-0.002	+0.003

Stocks below $1

High Rebate Venues		
EDGX	+0.00003	-0.30%*
BATS/ BZX	0	-0.30%
ARCA	0	-0.30%
NASDAQ	0	-0.30%
CHX	+0.00009	-0.30%
NYSE	0	0
PSX	0	-0.20%

Balanced Venues		
EDGEA	0	0

Low or no Rebate Venues		
BATSY- BYX	0	-0.10%
BX/BZX	0	-0.10%

These figures are not applicable to hidden orders and assume no special relationship.

As warned, these figures might not be entirely accurate for your situation. Also, for some HFT firms who do a lot of volume with any given exchange, the figures will look completely different as the increased volume leads them to better deals in terms of more rebates and lower fees.

The key is to understand the overall category of the routes that you are using. Take ARCA for instance: while the exact rebate/fee figures can fluctuate depending on the broker/firm relationship with ARCA, overall, it seems safe to categorize ARCA as a high rebate/high fee to take venue. Same thing with BX—looking at its fees, you can categorize it as an inverted exchange. You have to pay to post orders there and orders that hit you are the ones that collect the rebate (although the amounts will vary).

How is this useful? There are some instances where using an inverted or balanced route can be quite beneficial. Below are some instances where you might want to consider using them.

-When the Short Sell Restriction (SSR) is on and you really want to short a stock fast. Stocks under the SSR can only be shorted on an uptick. What this means is that you cannot hit the bid and get short the stock. This rule forces shorts to post their orders on the offer. Sometimes stocks under the SSR stack up massive offers because everybody is trying to short it when it becomes obvious that the stock is about to drop. Here is a screenshot of the Level 2 of a typical SSR short stack up:

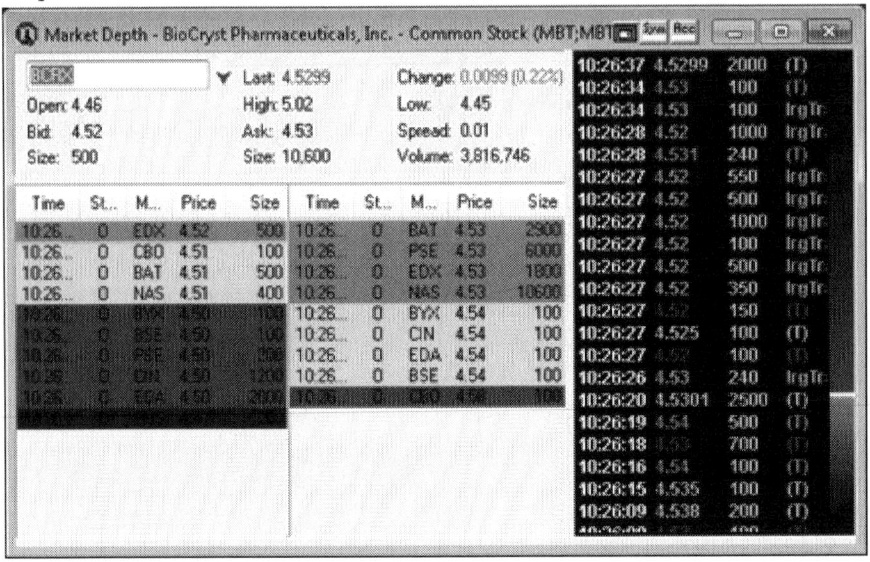

Source: MBT Desktop Pro

When this happens, shorts that are desperate to get in the stock tend to only get filled when they push the price down enough that buyers are ready to take out the entire offer. One way to mitigate this issue is to use balanced or inverted exchanges to post your orders. This way, the occasional buy orders that hit the offer will, most of the time, hit your order first.

In the example above, if you were to post a 3,000 share short order on EDGA or BX, anyone looking to buy some of that stock is likely to go through you first because you are offering an economic incentive for them to do so, whether in the form of a small BX rebate or a tiny fee from EDGA. They can save the 0.003 of hitting EDGX, NASDAQ, BATS or ARCA (PSE). Most of the smart routers from brokers or HFTs tend to incorporate some form of venue cost analysis in through algorithm.

-When you are trying to save the spread in stocks with a lot of competition at any given price level. Stocks that have small spreads with lots of exchanges at any given price can be a candidate to use balanced and inverted exchanges. Frequently, if you use high rebate venues such as BATS or EDGX, your order tends to only get filled when the supply and demand has shifted and the entire quote is rolling through you. You get the rebate but you also become underwater in the trade. You will also miss out on some winners as you never get filled. Of course, you can adjust your order up to make sure you get a fill and don't miss the trade, but the bottom line is that you only tend to get filled when the quote is rolling. You get that 0.002 rebate, but you face the additional cost of being down on the trade.

How much is that cost? Let's say you are trying to buy it at $10.00, the offer is at $10.01. You post your order on EDGX at $10.00. You get filled but the quote rolls and now it's at $9.99 bid and $10.00 offered. You got a 0.002 rebate but now you are "down" 0.005 as the fair value of the stock is $9.995 (the mid-point) and your average entry price is $10.00. On net, you "lost" 0.003.

If you use a balanced route like EDGA instead, you can face a quite nice scenario. If you get filled at $10.00 without the quote rolling or significantly weakening, you will be "up" 0.005 (you got filled at below the current mid-point fair value of $10.005). You also get paid a tiny rebate of 0.0005 for a total "gain" of 0.0055.

The thing that a lot of traders miss about chasing rebates is that the benefits are easy to see. You look at the broker statements and can see all the rebates you collected that helped you offset the commission costs, enabling you to trade virtually for "free." The downsides are hidden; they come in the form of adverse selection, and also in the form of missed fills and partial fills that can have enormous costs. Let me give an example to illustrate this issue.

Let's say trader John is bearish in the stock ABC, a highly liquid stock with a small spread, usually 1 cent. He shorts 3,000 shares at $11 with a liquidity taking order. He is in a rush to get in as he thinks the collapse is imminent. He does not think it is prudent to post limit orders (whether in high rebate or no rebate venues) as he thinks the move down is about to happen. Fortunately, he is correct and the stock proceeds to collapse to $10.30s. Happy with his profit and expecting some sort of bounce at some point, John decides to start to scale out of his trade starting at $10.35 all the way down to $10.22. He posts 600 share orders using BATS every 3 cents down. So he has the following buy orders setup. Buy 600 routing BATS at 10.35, 10.32, 10.29, 10.26, 10.22. John is happy to see that he is getting filled in his orders all the way to 10.22. At that price, some trades go through, but it then proceeds to reverse. John got no fill at that price and then he watches as the price quickly starts to bounce. He rushes in to send a liquidity taking order for his last 600 shares and gets filled at 10.30.

While John is happy to have made money in the trade, he could have made a little bit more had he not been so greedy for rebates. His last order was filled at 8 cents premium to where he wanted simply because he tried to get an additional 0.002 rebate. The risk reward of such a proposition was 4000 to 1, meaning he risked 4000 units in order to get an additional 1 unit. No trader would consciously accept such proposition. Had John used a balanced or inverted venue, he could get at least some partial fills or perhaps a full fill at the low price, which would more than make up any fee or lack of rebates.

As John learned, the benefits of rebates are easy to see. It's the downsides that are hidden. With that exercise in mind, we can come up with a simple rule for order execution in a HFT era that can be useful to remember:

The smaller your edge and the more adverse moves against your position you expect, the more aggressive you should be in terms of price and routes. The larger your edge and less adverse moves against your position you expect, the less aggressive you can be in terms of price and routes.

At 10.20s, John had a small edge on the trade; most of the move had happened. That's why he was scaling out of his trade. He was already expecting a bounce, what I call "adverse volatility." What he should have done instead was to have used a more aggressive route such as EDGA or BX and perhaps have chosen a little bit higher price. That's all hindsight of course—there is no way for John know that the price would bottom at exactly 10.22. What he can know is that **rebate chasing when he has a small edge and expects adverse volatility in the trade is a mistake.**

There is also the psychological damage of seeing the price reverse on you and having profits evaporate. Some traders are prone to tilt and make even more mistakes as a result. There is also the factor that John might not have been watching the stock when it reversed and might have ended up covering at an even worse price. If he used that principle to guide him instead, he would have been more aggressive when he saw that his edge had dwindled and he started to expect adverse moves against his position a certain percentage of the time. He would be less aggressive in other circumstances.

When is it ok to chase rebates? Going back to that principle: when you have a large edge and expect less adverse moves against your position. Anyone familiar to think in terms of profit expectation might be thinking "why even exit the trade?" This is true. Mathematically it doesn't look sound to do. The thing is, sometimes traders have psychological reasons for scaling out early and "locking" at least some profits. They simply "must" take some profits off the table as even just the thought of having those profits disappear might make the trader suffer. The actual event of losing the profits could set off an emotional meltdown in the trader and lead to a cascade of mistakes. Those mistakes also have a dollar cost, which changes the mathematical expectation calculation. All of a sudden what is irrational becomes rational again.

In this situation, it's ok to post orders in high rebate venues and scale out gradually. There is, however, a probably even superior alternative which is to wait for the price to start to turn against you by some amount and then use a liquidity taking order to "lock" part of your gains. Let's say you are up $4,000 in the trade, and you feel that you must lock some of that for mental reasons. Because your edge is large and you don't expect a lot of adverse volatility, you are probably better off waiting for some kind of adverse move to start to take some gains rather than to post high rebate orders at random. This way you let your gain ride for a while and still get to lock profits without risking missed or partial fills.

Going back to John's scenario, instead of using aggressive routes, could he have used liquidity taking orders when the price started to reverse? It's an interesting debate which strategy is superior. If you think about it, liquidity taking orders are the most aggressive types of orders. They are, on the surface, the most expensive. In reality, they can actually be the most profitable as the better priced exits can offset pretty much any liquidity taking fees or lack of rebates. Given that they are the most aggressive, it's entirely consistent with the rule to use them. Which method is superior depends on so many factors that are specific to the stock that it's hard to say exactly which one is better. For instance, if it's a "noisy" stock that jumps up and down, a lot passive limit orders can actually benefit from the noise if the trader puts the orders in the extreme side of the mean reverting noise. You can actually profit from it. If it's a smoother stock, then a liquidity taking order is superior because when it turns you can actually trust there is something new going on and the adverse move against your position has started.

Chapter 15
Additional Advice, Resources and Tips

1. Trading Psychology

In this book I tried to emphasize the more technical aspects of trading and not as much on psychology. This is not to say that trading psychology is not important. Lots of traders mentioned the ability to take losses as the most important trait a day or swing trader needs. I simply didn't want to write another trading psychology book with lots of simple advice when market microstructure and strategies have become more important than ever. As far as psychology goes and how to improve in that area, I can provide the following tips some people might find helpful.

1.1. Read *The Six Pillars of Self-Esteem* by Dr. Nathaniel Branden.

I highly recommend this book to pretty much anyone in any career, even if they don't think they need to improve their self-esteem. The author goes through what he believes are the six keys to enhancing self-esteem that he observed in decades of study and work that he did as a psychotherapist.

Have you ever wondered why some athletes, like Tiger Woods, Novak Djokovic, or Sebastian Vettel, seem like natural winners who would often perform even better in high-pressure situations and somehow get an advantage over others even though their opponents were performing just as well? Sure, they're talented, but in any field there are countless examples of talented players who never reach their full potential. (In tennis, off the top of my head I can name David Nalbandian and Marat Safin.) Also, in most fields in the top ten to twenty, pretty much everybody is talented. Self-esteem provides one clue as to why some people perform better than others when they have similar skillsets. A lot of high performance athletes talk about the important of mental toughness and psychology in their performances. Djokovic himself said that whether or not he goes for big shots at key moments plays a large role in his big matches against Federer and Nadal in Grand Slams. He said that as he matured as a player and person, that process got easier.[59]

For a person with high self-esteem, success feels natural. It doesn't produce anxiety to be close to it (or if it does, its level is lower than a person with low self-esteem). Your mind is more relaxed. You're better equipped to perform in the way

---

[59] http://tinyurl.com/lsdsdbq

you trained, because you feel deserving of the success you're about to achieve. A person with high self-esteem is unlikely to engage in self-sabotaging behaviors that can drastically impact the long-term outcome of a career.

I suspect that mental stability (helped by a good level of self-esteem) is probably one of the major factors why Tiger Woods was so good at playoffs (he's at 11-1[60]). Think about it. He essentially had to play these playoffs against a guy who just played really well, had the run of his life in a major, yet he would win over and over again. Was it golf skill that made the difference? It's unlikely to be a major factor, because they both had played the tournament and scored the same exact amount! (Which is why the game went to playoffs.) And even if skill was a factor, it certainly can't be so large as to enable him to win so often (again, his opponent had the same score as Tiger did on that golf course over the weekend, so he clearly adapted well to the course, and along with Tiger he was the single best golfer out of the entire field).

To me, it's clear that it's his psychology that gives him the edge. Because he feels deserving of winning and success, he doesn't get nearly as anxious as his opponents. As a result, his higher level of relaxation enables him to do what he has already trained himself to do countless times. Meanwhile, his opponents who lack the same level of entitlement feel stressed and are more likely to engage in poor decision making, negative thinking, sloppy execution, and self-sabotage. In a quick format like in the playoffs, these differences can turn a small or nonexistent skill advantage into a gigantic overall edge.

Woods is also 14-1 when going into the final round of a major with at least a share of the lead. When he's playing well, he stays that way. Meanwhile, a player with poor self-esteem might just get into a negative mindset, telling himself, "I'm leading. I hope I don't screw it up," and he might perform poorly as a result.

Interestingly enough, his downfall in recent years could at least be partially explained by psychology. Ever since he went through a media scandal and his reputation was shattered, his performance has declined significantly. It didn't help that he suffered injuries and had to change his swing, but the decline in his performance has lasted so long and the amounts horrific performances (even before his more serious injuries) have been so numerous that it suggests he has also lost his old confidence. Steve Siebold, an expert on mental toughness training, suggests his problem could even be depression: "As a former professional athlete myself, and after working with top amateur and professional athletes in many different sports on the mental aspects of performance for more than 30 years, I'm convinced

---

60 In a binary format like golf playoffs where one mistake can cost you the win this sample size is significant. It's far more likely he was a significant favorite in these playoffs than him being a 50 to 55 percent favorite who got on a lucky streak.

there's a lot more going on with Tiger Woods. In fact, there's nothing physical about it. It's a mental health problem and everything I see points to depression."

"For the longest time Tiger Woods was immortalized as a God in the golfing world. So imagine what it feels like when every day another story appears in the press bashing the heck out of him. One minute he's a living legend and now everyone's beating up on the guy. That kind of love/hate relationship is enough to drive people over the edge when it's a private matter, so is it really surprising that Woods is spiraling out of control with all the questions, speculation and public chatter constantly following him around?"[61]

In trading, you can see some people who, due to a lack of self-esteem, would frequently feel undeserving of profits after a certain number (say, more than $15,000 a month). These traders would all of a sudden lose their courage and not take risks they know they should, because they don't like the discomfort of being up so much. They'd rather stay "where they belong," with smaller profits, than grow as a trader and reach new levels of profitability.

Other manifestations of poor self-esteem in trading would be taking reckless risks, desiring to be right at all costs, refusing to acknowledge your strengths and weaknesses, refusing to take a loss, gambling, poor planning, among others.

The first time I read Nathaniel's book was when I was seventeen and I was struggling severely with extreme shyness, anxiety, and depression. I'd already tried all kinds of different methods to overcome it (NLP, lucid dreaming, self-hypnosis, and others), but they all failed because they didn't go to the heart of the matter. They didn't change the day-to-day behaviors that were affecting my self-esteem. In my case, it was a lack of self-assertiveness (one of the pillars of self-esteem) when dealing with other people, along with not living consciously enough (engaging in self-deception). For others it might be lack of accountability (the second pillar). They might keep blaming people for their mistakes or just refusing to acknowledge their imperfections. These kinds of destructive behaviors accumulate in the unconscious mind and add up to an overall assessment of your self-worth that comes out through an experience (that is even more than just a feeling) of you being pleased with yourself or not.

That book literally saved my life. After I read it, I immediately implemented several changes in my life and noticed that my self-esteem greatly improved. I'm forever grateful to the person who recommended that book to me, which is why I'm now recommending it myself.

I understand that the word *self-esteem* has lots of different meanings to different people. The truth is that the author of the book does not endorse the mainstream definition of the term, meaning "feeling good about yourself." Lots of things can make you feel good about yourself, like a drug, a love affair, a quick reckless profit,

---

[61] http://tinyurl.com/pjpfbqc

etc., but they're not necessarily good for your self-esteem as he defines it. He also doesn't believe you can have too much self-esteem as some psychologists think. "It's no more possible to have too much self-esteem than it is to have too much physical or mental health," he says.

A lot of the misconceptions about self-esteem exist due to poorly executed "empirical" studies that don`t use good methods or an intelligent definition of the word self-esteem.[62]

Note that in trading, it's frequently said that you ought to keep your ego in check, otherwise you'll end up fighting the market. Nathaniel has a different definition of the word *ego*. He talks about the ego as a good thing. The ego we hear about in the trading world he refers to as "pseudo self-esteem." This is all just semantics, however. There's no conflict between his principles and good trading psychology. I'm just mentioning this so people don't get confused.

I probably won't do the book justice if I try to summarize it. If you're serious about becoming the best trader you can be, check out that book and do the exercises in it. He also has an Audible audiobook "The Psychology of High Self-Esteem," which is terrific.

1.2. Understand, manage, and increase the activity of your pre-frontal cortex.

The key to understanding why the pre-frontal cortex (PFC) is so important to traders is knowing which human activities and behaviors are controlled by it. This area of the brain, amongst others, is responsible for:

-Orchestration of thoughts and actions in accordance with internal goals.

-The ability to differentiate among conflicting thoughts, determine good and bad, better and best, same and different, future consequences of current activities, working toward a defined goal, prediction of outcomes, expectation based on actions, and social "control" (the ability to suppress urges that, if not suppressed, could lead to socially unacceptable outcomes).[63]

-Forecasting the consequences of a current behavior on a long-term goal. Controlling immediate reactions to a stimulus.[64]

It is essentially the discipline muscle. I use the word "muscle," as do many neuroscientists, because, like a muscle, it strengthens when it is used regularly and

---

[62] Some studies ask people about how high their self-esteem is, which hardly qualifies as good evidence of such given how often people deceive themselves and how differently people can interpret that term. These are just a few of the problems with a lot of the studies that are out there.

63 This information is derived from studies with people who had damage to their pre-frontal cortexes.

[64] Neuroscientist Jordan Grafman Ph.D.

it weakens when it is not. Research has indicated that activities that use the PFC increase its size and efficiency.

Sometimes it's very hard to do the "right thing" when it comes to a particular trade or decision because we essentially have two brains.

According to Nobel prize-winning psychologist Daniel Kahneman, we have the System 1 brain (impulsive, fast, automatic, emotional) and the System 2 (slow, logical, conscious, calculating) brain. System 2 is mostly controlled by the PFC. What happens a lot of the time to losing or struggling traders is that because they never really fully developed their System 2 brain, they spend a lot of their trading using the System 1 brain. This leads to all sorts of career-ending mistakes, such as not taking losses, adding to bad trades, oversizing to make the money back, overtrading, and gambling.

If you want to be effective as a trader, you will have to develop and improve your System 2 brain. Learn what helps it, harms it, and what activities outside trading can develop it further. I developed a quick, practical mini-course that you can use today to understand and develop your PFC and make your System 2 brain more effective. If you stick with the course, even if it's a little hard at first, you will notice that difficult things will get much easier as you develop your PFC muscle. Discipline will become second nature.

The Boost Your Discipline Mini-Course

The key to having discipline is developing your *willpower*, which is self-control, the ability to do or say the hard thing when your emotions want you to do or say something else. The good news is that anyone without brain damage can do it (really, we have an entire area of the brain dedicated to this—saying "I can't do it" won't cut it). The bad news is that it's going to be a little annoying at first because, like a muscle, if it's a little out of shape, it can take effort, but once you get going, it gets easier, just like physical exercise. Even if you don't think you need more willpower, I encourage you to practice activities that boost it. Just as you can't be too physically healthy, you can't be too mentally healthy, either. The sky is the limit when it comes to being in good mental shape.

I would highly recommend you pick up the book or audiobook *The Willpower Instinct* by Stanford psychologist Kelly McGonigal, Ph.D. Her work is tremendously practical and easy to understand (something you don't see very often coming out of academia). Her book is filled with techniques and experiments, all proven empirically in rigorous tests and in her in-person course, The Science of Willpower, to boost the area of the brain responsible for willpower, the pre-frontal cortex (PFC). Here are some of her key techniques and understandings about willpower that you might find helpful:

1. **Sleep has a large impact on willpower.**
2. **Meditation can boost your willpower.**
3. **Being self-critical, harsh on yourself, or feeling guilty increases the likelihood of future willpower failures.**
4. **An attitude of self-acceptance decreases the likelihood of future willpower failures.**
5. **Blood sugar crashes can hurt your willpower.**
6. **Willpower can be restored by being in nature, listening to music, spending time with people you like, and exercise.**

Let's go through one by one.

1. **Sleep has a large impact on willpower.**

According to McGonigal, eight hours of sleep does wonders to recharge the brain and its willpower capacity. In one of the studies, she mentions that it was tested whether adding a five-minute, breath-focus meditation would help people suffering from substance addiction.

The meditation actually boosted test participants sleep by one hour. That increase predicted whether the subject would relapse and give in to addiction in the future. The PFC consumes a lot of energy. When we operate under sleep deprivation, according to research, the body and the brain have their sugar metabolism impaired. The PFC and many other areas of the body won't be able to operate effectively under those conditions. The condition won't improve even if you create a blood sugar spike by eating high carbohydrate foods. It does improve when you have a good night of sleep. (For scientific references and sources related to McGonigal's work, check out her book.)

In my own trading, I notice that if I have a bad night of sleep, I get impulsive. I overtrade and losses get more irritating by a factor of several times. When you are sleep deprived, it's crucial that you do one of these two things: either take the day off or trade defensively. If you were already thinking about taking a day off to take care of things outside trading, days following a bad night of sleep are perfect for that. Go ahead, deal with your issues, and enjoy yourself. You will be back, fully charged, the next day.

If you do decide to trade though, **decrease your position size and only trade the best trade setups**. It sounds easy, but the fact that your PFC will be on shutdown mode can make following this rule challenging. However, it can literally save you thousands of dollars (my worst trading days by far are days where I slept poorly the night before). On these defensive trading days, try to sleep during the mid-day session. This accomplishes two things: first, it keeps you out of trouble by not trading during the least profitable time of the day when your PFC is under-functional, and second, it re-charges your willpower for the close, when you are likely to have more profitable opportunities.

2. **Meditation can boost your willpower.**

Meditation is becoming more popular these days, and for good reason. Research indicates it provides all kinds of benefits, ranging from lower stress, less anxiety, and better focus, to more creativity and better memory.[65] One of the greatest hedge fund managers of all time, Ray Dalio, says, "Meditation, more than anything in my life, was the biggest ingredient of whatever success I've had."[66] I notice that when I'm not meditating regularly, my trading suffers noticeably. All of a sudden, my brain will lose its discipline and start to seek stimulation. When I have a losing trade in a stock, my tendency is to try to overtrade my way out of it. After a few hours, I notice that instead of putting in ten trades in a day, I did twenty, thirty, or something along those lines.

The mid-day session becomes particularly problematic because it is already quite boring. Without meditation, it is even more boring. It becomes easy to justify some trades and start to overtrade your way into giving back your morning profits.

---

65 What Happens to the Brain When You Meditate (And How it Benefits You)- http://tinyurl.com/kszjg3x

66 Other practitioners include Tiger Woods, Kobe Bryant, David Blaine, and three-time Olympic gold medalists Misty May and Kerri Walsh.

But this habit goes beyond just trading. I'm in a much better mood when I'm meditating regularly than when I'm not. It is harder for me to get irritated, and my tolerance for pain increases (which helps with losing days and drawdowns).

According to research, meditation is a great way to develop your PFC. Yes, it will be difficult at first. That's the whole idea. If you are the type of person who has a hard time doing nothing for twenty minutes a day, then you are exactly the type of person who would benefit from integrating meditation to your life. If your mind just won't stop thinking about all kinds of things, you start to feel silly doing something so boring, and you keep thinking about checking Facebook or Twitter, your brain is addicted to seeking stimulation (The System 1 brain). Stimulation seeking can be quite harmful to a trading account; it's a hard habit to break, but it is possible if you start slowly and don't try to do too much too quickly. I would recommend starting with even just a few minutes of meditation a day, then as you get more focus and willpower you can increase to 5, 10 and eventually 20-40 minutes. How do you practice meditation? Here is a simple technique that I use daily that can help:

Breath Focus Meditation Technique

Sit down, away from your computer or cellphone (or any other type of stimulation), in a comfortable place. Set an alarm for the length of time you plan to do it. I recommend you start with one to three minutes, so you don't get discouraged. Just stay there and focus on your breath. Just listen to it—the sounds, the in and out. You might find it helpful to say, "Breath in, breath out," if you have trouble concentrating. Listen to your breath, and try not to move or scratch yourself. You might feel an urge to do so; that is your System 1 brain trying to get its way. By using your PFC and not giving in, you are getting it back in shape, teaching your brain that you won't give in to desire instantly. Just accept that the urge is there. Don't fight it. Just experience it, fully feel it, stay with it, and it will dissolve by itself.

As you focus on the sounds and sensations of your breath, you will begin to have all kinds of thoughts and ideas. That is fine and expected. Please don't think that meditation is "not thinking." This is not the case, and even if it were, we are trying to develop the PFC, not reach some kind of nirvana. I don't subscribe to the "spiritual" aspects of meditation, and it is not necessary to do so to collect its benefits. If you have thoughts and lose focus of your breath, try to catch yourself doing it and bring your awareness back to your breath, over and over again. Once the alarm goes off, you can go back to your daily routine.

This simple technique can make a significant difference in your trading. First, because it might improve your sleep (though the evidence for that is not yet broad and conclusive, personally it works for me), you will wake up more refreshed and with more willpower. Second, because even though it takes willpower to do it, according to McGonigal, these sorts of willpower using activities "end up giving back far more willpower than they take." You will build a willpower reserve and make your PFC bigger and more effective. Meditation is like a gym for a trader.

I would recommend the reader to research about meditation, read articles and books about it, and try out different techniques to see what works best for you.

3. **Being self-critical, harsh on yourself, or feeling guilty increases the likelihood of future willpower failures.**

This is a huge one because most western societies really drill into people's mindsets that they have to be a success, make a lot of money, and achieve things; otherwise, they are losers. This can be a problem, especially for males, who seem to identify themselves more with financial success than females. The result is that it can make people hard on themselves when they face setbacks, make mistakes, and don't align their behaviors with their goals.

In one interesting study, it was tested whether feelings of guilt and self-criticism in dieters affected their ability to stick with a diet. The researchers gave a doughnut and lots of water (to increase the feeling of being full) to two groups of dieters, then told one group that it was okay to feel guilty, that everybody indulged once in a while, and asked them not to be hard on themselves. To the other group, nothing of this kind was said. Then the researchers put out three bowls of candy (carefully chosen to appeal to all kinds of preferences). They told the dieters that it was a "taste test" and they could eat as much as they wanted, and asked them to report on the quality of the candy. The dieters who were told that it was okay to indulge and to not to be hard on themselves ate only 40% as much candy as the dieters who didn't receive that message.

According to McGonigal, "There is abundant research that shame and guilt are the biggest triggers for further relapse." That is true in gamblers, also. "The worse they feel about losing money, the more likely they are to gamble again," she says.

As a trader, it's important to understand that when you make mistakes, such as not following your rules, overtrading, or taking bad setups, the first instinct when you lose money is to curse yourself, yell, and break things. You might feel an urge to criticize yourself, to call yourself a terrible trader or an idiot. All this does is create stress, and when the body is stressed it will prioritize the systems that deal with short-term emergencies, and this will make you more impulsive (the System 1 brain will begin to dominate), which makes it harder to face a willpower challenge (such as following your rules or taking the day off).

Self-criticism will also make you feel bad. You'll feel an irresistible urge to try to make the money back because it will change your mood and make you feel good again. **Your dopamine receptors become more sensitive under stress**. This makes chasing good feelings more tempting, and it can be quite a challenge to overcome this urge. This is a deadly combination because you will be revenge trading and operating as your impulsive self.

There is evidence that smokers who look at horrifying images on the back of cigarette packages are likely to smoke more and feel good about smoking than smokers who didn't. **Stress is the enemy of willpower and discipline.**

There is also the "what the hell" effect. If you break your rules, act undisciplined, and feel shameful and guilty about it, you might just say, "Ah, what the hell. I'm trading so badly today, I might as well just keep going and try to turn this around," which only increases the chance of further mistakes. How to deal with these urges to criticize yourself? How to deal with unwanted emotions and difficult trading days? That's where the next willpower finding comes into play.

4. **An attitude of self-acceptance decreases the likelihood of future willpower failures.**

One study mentioned by McGonigal separated smokers into two groups. One taught the technique of "surfing the urge" to deal with strong desires and temptations. The other was a control group that didn't learn it. Then, for an hour, they stretched out the process of picking up a pack of cigarettes, opening it, picking out a cigarette, picking up a lighter, etc. During that hour, they were not allowed to smoke. They had to deal with an unfulfilled urge throughout the whole procedure. After this procedure, they were allowed to do whatever they wanted. They went back to their lives and tracked how many cigarettes they smoked. The group that was taught to "surf the urge" ended up cutting back the amount of cigarettes they smoked by 37%, an impressive result given that the test group was not asked to cut back on cigarettes or even to keep using the technique that they were taught!

What is the "surfing the urge" technique? They were told that urges always pass, whether or not you give in to them. When they felt a strong craving, they were supposed to imagine that desire as a wave in the ocean. It would build up, but eventually crash and disappear. They had to imagine themselves riding that wave, not fighting it, resisting it, or trying to "get rid of it," but just to experience it and notice how it felt. If you apply this method to your own desires, urges, and cravings, you will notice that they will be less powerful. They tend to dissolve when you fully experience them.

I personally use a similar procedure that is described in the book *The Six-Pillars of Self-Esteem* (in the self-acceptance chapter). Here's a brief summary of how it works:

Self-Acceptance Procedure

If during your trading session you experience urges to average down, overtrade, criticize yourself, punish yourself, or break things, etc., first, fully feel your emotions and notice how they affect you. Awareness can be very helpful. Stay with the emotions. Don't just acknowledge them and move on to other things. Take your time. Second, don't try to get rid of these emotions. Fully acknowledge that they are occurring and accept them. Accepting doesn't mean liking or being proud of them; it just means that you recognize them as expressions of yourself at this point in time. You might not particularly like them, but you recognize that it's happening and allow yourself to experience them. Third, relax your muscles. Frequently when people deal with unwanted emotions, they contract their body in an effort to suppress their feelings. Fourth, take a deep and slow breath while remaining aware of the emotions and not resisting them.

This simple procedure is likely to make it easier to go through the experience without letting the emotion take over your behavior. You will find that it sometimes helps a lot, sometimes just a little, but you will be relatively better off than you were before you did it.

5. **Blood sugar crashes can hurt your willpower.**

The PFC uses a lot of energy to function. It is one of the most sugar-hungry parts of the brain. According to neuroscientists, when the body's blood sugar is unstable and starts to drop, the body interprets this as a signal that you could be facing starvation or scarcity soon. As a result, it goes into conservation mode, and the PFC partially shuts down. Being in a more impulsive state is more beneficial during a short-term energy crisis. This hurts your willpower and discipline.

It's important to preserve a stable blood sugar level throughout your trading session if you want to be at your best at all times. One of the ways that you can achieve that is to eat foods with a low "glycemic index" (GI) and avoid foods with a high GI. The GI is a measure of how quickly the blood sugar rises after ingesting a particular food. There are many free articles and books in this subject, as well as free food tables available on the internet that show what kinds of foods destabilize your blood sugar and which ones keep it stable.

The standard American diet (S.A.D.) is not very helpful for traders because it is filled with high GI foods, especially for breakfast. At lunch, it doesn't improve much. The results of that are sugar and insulin spikes, which helps willpower in the short-term, but then the blood sugar crashes lead to a lack of activity in the area of the brain that traders need the most, the PFC. Lunch is particularly important because, right after that, you face the mid-day session, where profitable opportunities are less abundant. Spending hours in that time period with an underworking PFC is not a great recipe for profits. In fact, some traders may notice that they "lose" their discipline in the afternoon and end up giving back their morning profits. Their blood sugar instability can explain why. A S.A.D. diet also leads to diabetes and diabetes-like conditions in the long-term, which will hurt your brain's ability to use sugar. Needless to say, this hurts your willpower.

If you want to improve your health and willpower, consider improving your diet gradually by adding low GI foods and reducing high GI foods.

6. **Willpower can be restored through being in nature, listening to music, spending time with people you like, and exercise.**

When you use a lot of willpower regularly, sometimes you can feel "drained." The PFC consumes a lot of energy and, like a muscle, it can get fatigued. We can develop it so it gets larger and with bigger reserves, but there is still a limit on how much effort it can exert.

It's important to integrate life activities outside trading that can "recharge" your PFC. This is so when you are trading your willpower is at its maximum, or close to it. According to McGonigal, activities that can restore your willpower are things like being in nature, listening to music, spending time with people that you like, watching a movie or series (for less than two hours), physical exercise (exercise is especially useful because it also builds your willpower reserve; just like meditation, it takes willpower, but it gives back far more than it took), among others.

This willpower finding also should help some traders take vacations and days off without feeling guilty about it. If you want to trade optimally, having periods where you are not trading (and using your willpower reserves) can do wonders because they will recharge you and your willpower reserves. When you come back, you will trade better than you would otherwise. Don't feel too guilty about the money you didn't make while you were on vacation because you might end up getting it anyway, due to superior decision-making when you come back.

Note: I only wrote about some of the main ideas and methods that I have learned from these two authors, but there is a lot more in their published works than I could possibly cover in this chapter. If you are serious about improving yourself as a trader, I would encourage you to explore their work and understand their concepts more deeply.

2. Recommended Broker

Interactive Brokers - www.interactivebrokers.com

Interactive Brokers, popularly called IB, is good broker to have for any day trader. Their commissions and fees are lower than most retail brokerage houses out there. These savings add up to thousands of dollars at the end of a year. They have good trading software and order types, and through their platform, Trader Workstation, you can customize anything that you can imagine. They also support several types of advanced orders **and, more importantly, the so-called "native" hidden orders** (which was mentioned in this book as a way to getting around HFT tricks and advantages). If you are an IB client and don't know about native hidden orders, definitely ask them about it. It can improve your order execution and cut your costs. Their abundance of routes for listed stocks also helps when you are trying to take liquidity because you can directly route your order to an ECN or exchange. They also have great borrows for shorts and additional layers of security to make sure your account won't be hacked and your money stolen.

IB has a minimum of $10,000 for new clients ($3,000 if you are age 26 or younger), and their accounts are SIPC insured.

3. Hardware and computer technical help

You definitely need a good machine to trade with, but keep in mind that day trading is a low CPU intensive activity. If you check out your Windows Task Manager, you'll notice that even with all your trading software opened, Internet browser, news feed, etc., your CPU usage will rarely stay above 50 percent for much longer than a few seconds. What this means is that you don't need to invest in the latest generation processor (a second or third generation Intel core i3 or core i5 or an equivalent AMD chip is likely to be fine for most traders). You're better off investing in things like RAM memory and a SSD (solid state drive).

For RAM, get at least 6GB DDR3, ideally 8GB. The thing is, a lot of computer programmers and software companies get lazy with memory usage, so programs these days tend to eat up a lot of RAM, even if they don't necessarily need to use it that much if they were coded properly. Make sure you get enough, because if you don't your operating system will start to write data to your hard drive (or SSD) when it runs out of RAM. The speed of that operation is magnitudes lower than of RAM memory.

Along with enough RAM, definitely get a SSD (and install Windows on it). A SSD is essentially a high-speed hard drive. Even if your desktop or laptop didn't come with one, you can just buy it online and install it yourself (there are plenty of videos teaching that on YouTube). A SSD, depending on the model and brand, will be about five to ten times faster than a regular hard drive. In practice this will translate to:

- All the programs you use will open much faster and some will run faster as well.
- Windows will run faster.
- Faster boot and shutdown speeds.
- Faster installation process for new software and security updates of existing software.
- Copying, editing, and moving files will take less time (for backups this is extremely useful).

A lot of computers these days are shipped with the top processors, but without an SSD, which is suboptimal to say the least, for most people, the hard drive speed is the biggest bottleneck in terms of day-to-day performance—not the processor. My SSD is probably one of the best investments I've made. It enables me to get much more work done in less time. It also helps when you have to reboot your machine and reopen all the programs during regular trading hours. That alone can save you thousands of dollars over the years.

4. How to Best Accumulate Market Knowledge become a Student of Price Action and Market Situations

Lots of traders that I interviewed mentioned that a key element of their success was the accumulated experience of having watched the markets for a long time. They ended up building a database of charts, situations, setups, and observations in their heads, which can provide them the confidence to take trades today because they have seen it all before.

One software that I've been using to speed up the process of this mental database building is the popular free program Evernote. What's nice about it is that I can quickly take a screenshot of a Level 2 window or a chart, paste it to Evernote, write a small note about it, and then have it stored in the Cloud. The fact that you have to type out the lesson or observation should help increase the chance that your brain will retain that information and be able to use it in the future. You can also go to your notes database at any time and review the main lessons and charts that you have accumulated. This will further help your brain retain that information. Below there's an example of how I use this program:

To take a screenshot of just one specific window (like a chart window or Level 2) just hit Ctrl+PrintScreen. (The PrintScreen button without Ctrl will take a screenshot all of your workspace.) Then you just hit Ctrl+V in an Evernote note and you can write what you learned about the situation. When you close the Evernote window, everything is saved and sent to the Cloud automatically.

I always try to write on Evernote when I have a big loss, or make a big mistake. It isn't a loss if you learn something from it—**you're paying for an education that might make or save you ten times that amount in the future**. I'm a big fan of trading small (100 shares or even less) and writing what you learned in Evernote. I've accumulated lots of lessons and insights about how markets work and how to day trade stocks as a result of that.

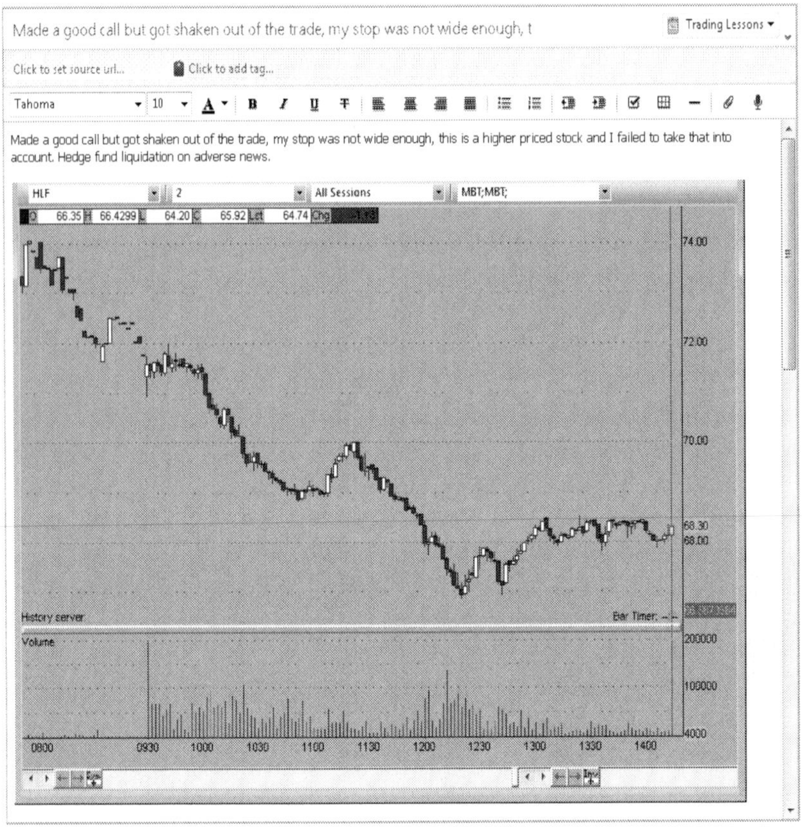

Source: Evernote and MBTrading Desktop Pro

Chapter 16

The Core Principles of Good Short-Term Trading

After conducting a lot of these interviews and analyzing my own trading results, I've come up with a list that I believe are some of the core fundamentals of short-term trading. When I've had a losing day or I'm going through a difficult period, 80 to 90 percent of the time it's because I've violated these principles. Following them can literally save you thousands of dollars.

Think of these as simple heuristics (rules of thumb). They might not be applicable every single time, but most of the time they work if you stick with them.

The core principles are:

1. Do the majority of your trading during the most profitable periods of the day. Have the vast majority of your risk exposure in those periods as well.
2. Trade less or don't trade on days where you're struggling physically, emotionally or psychologically.
3. Surround yourself with great traders.
4. Have the discipline to take losses.
5. Have the patience to trade the best setups and avoid marginal setups.
6. Accumulate as much market experience as possible.
7. Avoid adverse selection.
8. Do your premarket preparation work.
9. Have wide enough stops to avoid the noise.
10. Never show your hand.
11. Size your positions correctly, don't overbet, and never risk your account.
12. No matter how confident you are in a specific setup, there's always at least a 10 percent chance that you're completely and utterly wrong.
13. Seek to be exposed to big gain/small loss situations and avoid exposure to small gain/big loss trades.
14. Be very careful when trying to catch a bounce or short a top.

1. Do the majority of your trading during the most profitable periods of the day. Have the vast majority of your risk exposure in those periods as well.

These periods are the open (up to roughly one hour and a half after the opening bell) and the close (the final hour of the day). Trading during the mid-day period is very tempting sometimes, because you'll see chart formations that probably worked for you many times. You'll start to think there's no reason not to take it since you have made lots of profits off it over the years. The thing is, in an HFT world there are simply fewer moves during that period. A decent move in any direction will frequently retrace back to the other direction as the market making algos take profits or provide support in an attempt to take profits (the stock gets stuck in "market making channel"). What gets a move following through is volume, and that is frequently absent in the mid-day session.

Lots of reliable signals, such as red to green/green to red moves, breakouts/breakdowns, and other technical patterns fail more often during mid-day than in the open and the close.

Does that mean you shouldn't trade mid-day and that patterns don't work? No, it means that you need a better overall setup to trade. You don't want to take a marginal setup, because it will fail more frequently and that can upset you for later in the day (it can cost you mental capital for the close). Instead of, say, shorting a green to red play that you believe is OK (but not great), you pass up the play and wait to see how it trades in the close. You do take plays that you believe are great setups when it starts to move (or when there's breaking news), but I can't tell you how many losses I've had simply because I wanted to trade the same patterns and setups I did at open during the mid-day—but the truth is that they don't work as often.

The reliability of patterns and setups depend on the time period in which they happen. That's what a lot of technical gurus and people selling courses won't tell you.

This applies to your risk exposures as well. Your larger sized positions should be in the open/close and you should cut down your size significantly in the mid-day session (unless that great setup or news play shows up).

2. Trade less or don't trade on days where you're struggling physically, emotionally or psychologically.

This is another one that when I violate I will frequently face losses that I don't normally face. It happens especially when I trade on poor sleep. This hurts my decision making tremendously. I will feel more emotional about trading and get really afraid of missing out on a great play, and this leads to hanging onto losers due to fear of getting out right at the reversal point.

I will also feel more impulsive to put trades in. This makes my broker rich and hurts my account. If you feel that on a particular day you're struggling for any reason, immediately cut down your size dramatically. Don't trade mid-day at all, and live to fight for another day. A wise trader once said: "**You have to know when to wave the white flag.**"

Sometimes I do what I call "defensive trading" days. I simply trade the open and close (the most profitable periods) and for the rest of the day I either just monitor the markets, hardly putting any trades in, or I leave the trading desk to enjoy the day outside.

3. Surround yourself with great traders.

Most of the traders that I interviewed stay in touch with other good traders. They learn from them by watching what they're doing, right and wrong. They can ask for advice in a private setting where it's more likely they will get a useful answer. It's very difficult to get good by being isolated and just trading by yourself. People are social creatures, and they tend to absorb beliefs, mindsets, techniques, strategies, tricks, from the people they spend most of their time with.

There are many ways you can surround yourself with great traders. Some of them include joining a trading chat room, joining a prop firm, starting a Skype group and getting good traders in it, or getting a mentor. Also, try to decrease contact with losing traders that you might be in touch with.

4. Have the discipline to take losses.

Lots of traders interviewed mentioned this one as the number one factor in their success and in the failure of others. In the previous chapter, I outlined in the section "The Boost Your Discipline Mini-Guide" how can anyone can develop discipline through willpower boosting activities and mindsets. Being able to take a loss is like being able to swing at a baseball for a hitter. Without it, you can't really have a trading career.

5. Have the patience to trade the best setups and avoid marginal setups.

The thing about marginal setups and why they should be avoided is the fact that they're marginal probably due to the probability of success being lower than you're used to. As a result, they'll inevitably lead you to losses. If these losses destabilize you mentally, it will cost you money in trades later on that day. Perhaps you'll mismanage a great setup and as a result profit $1,000 less in a great trade just because you tried to make $200 in a marginal trade earlier. This math won't work out over the long-term.

Taking marginal trades will also require focus while you're in the position. This might hurt you in other positions or prevent you from seeing a potential trade that could be setting up.

Trading is different than other activities because so much depends on your mental game instead of just technical execution. *It's important to take care of your mental capital just as much as you take care of your trading capital.*

An idea related to this is putting more money in the better setups and put less money in the less good ones. This is obvious, but it is violated so frequently it deserves mention. The more you like a specific setup or trade idea, the bigger you should bet; the less you like it, the less you should bet. Traders frequently violate this when they average down. They're not adding to the position because they all of a sudden like the setup more (though they'll claim that), they do it because they don't want to take a loss in the trade. It is also violated when the trader starts to trade bigger on lower quality trade ideas in the afternoon to make back losses from earlier in the day. The first hour is the best hour. That's the hour to make the larger bets. The mid-day period should have less size as the profit expectation and probability of the trade being a winner are lower.

A violation if this rule tends to happen when traders "chase" a trade because they just can't stand the idea of missing out on it. As mentioned in Chapter 14, trades that have been "chased" tend to be specially challenging due to the fact that they expose the trader to a higher amount of financial pain relative to the gain. Having good entries at attractive prices tend to make trading a lot easier, especially in HFT dominated markets.

Traders also violate this when they refuse to bet big on the rare instances where their edge is very large. As a famous trading quote goes, "It takes courage to be a pig"—and not being a pig can cost big profits.

A good tip related to this principle is to **never take an overnight trade that doesn't have a very significant edge**. The reason is that if you do have a loss on that trade, you'll start the day with a mental capital hit. You might have to trade the most important hour of the day (the open) being upset, on tilt or in a revenge trading mindset. You might also overtrade mid-day or mismanage trades through the day. As a result, the small or marginal edge from the overnight trade will be completely wiped out when you factor in the consequences for the next day if you do take a loss (especially a big loss). If you do take it, at least go with small size.

6. Accumulate as much market experience as possible.

Lots of the traders interviewed can do amazing trades and bank huge profits not because they're superhuman but simply because they have seen that situation come up so many times that it would be unnatural not to take the trade. Their confidence in the setup is effortless. They can "sense" it will work. All they have to do is to size their position in and be ready to take a loss if that particular time is one of the unusual instances where the setup doesn't work.

This principle goes hand in hand with being patient regarding your trading career. In this area, don't expect to do as well as many other traders do right away. You have your whole life to get good. Focus on accumulating market knowledge and following these principles of good trading and (assuming you're disciplined) the profits will come. Use a program like Evernote to record observations and save charts. Lessons learned can be beneficial in this regard.

7. Avoid adverse selection.

Using limit orders and collecting a rebate can be very seductive, because it gives you an illusion of savings. You don't pay the spread, and you pay less in commission due to rebates, but you suffer from adverse selection (you tend to get filled when you're wrong in the short-term and not filled when you're right). Adverse selection is a hidden cost. You have to balance not paying the spread plus the rebate with the cost of suffering adverse selection.

If the security you're trading is not very liquid, this cost can turn a profitable strategy into a losing one. Many times I fell for this trap and tried to save a few cents by using a limit order when buying a stock. This is especially a problem in larger spread stocks. I would miss lots of winning trades and wish I'd paid the spread instead. As Dennis Dick says, avoid trading larger spreads and illiquid stocks, but if you can't, wait for the spread to narrow down and don't be afraid of paying it.[67]

8. Do your premarket preparation work.

If the first hour is the most important hour of the day, then being prepared for it by doing your premarket work is critical. You should know which stocks you are planning to trade or watch, setup price alerts at key levels, see what is in play, assess how you're feeling (see if principle 2 will have to be applied), find problems in your trading setup (Internet connection issues, mandatory broker software updates, etc.), check your borrows, among other things.

9. Have wide enough stops to avoid "the noise"

As Jeff Goldman explains and Eric Husander proves, there's a lot more noise intraday these days as a result of HFT activity. I can't tell you how many times I've made a great call in a stock but was shaken out of the trade by having too tight a stop. It's one of the top mistakes made by traders in the era of HFTs. It is critical that you leave enough room to avoid being played in these games. It's not just that you'll be hit by small losses constantly, but you'll also suffer a mental capital drawdown (you just lose confidence in what you're doing and start trading badly), which might prevent you from reentering the trade, thus you miss it and hurt your mental capital further.

10. Never show your hand.

When the HFTs or other participants see that someone wants to get size in or out, they'll make that person pay. These HFT firms make millions of dollars squeezing every cent out of big orders. It is important that you learn to use hidden orders (native, not broker hidden orders), iceberg orders, and never get too big in a security. The bigger the position size mistake you make (relative to the liquidity available), the more you will be **exponentially harmed**. This is due to the efficiency in which HFT firms detect big orders (the bigger the position you are trying to liquidate, the more time they have to find you) and the nature of auction markets (in an auction market system, such as the stock market, the price is set by the highest price someone is willing to pay and the lowest price someone is willing to offer).

---

67 In my experience, this principle applies more to NYSE, NASDAQ and AMEX securities but not as much to OTC stocks.

When your hand is exposed, these HFT firms will try to milk your order for the most you are willing to pay (if you are short) and the least you are willing to offer (if you are long). This is why is so dangerous to get involved in crowded plays in a HFT world. HFTs and other smart participants will try to 'squeeze' the crowd out of a play and shake out the weak hands.

This principle also goes along with not being a rebate sucker (principle 7).

11. Size your positions correctly, don't overbet, never risk your entire account.

In Chapter 11 I explained why overbetting is completely unnecessary—it not only increases the volatility of your returns, but it also decreases the returns, so it costs you money to overbet. There are also all kinds of risks when you take large leveraged positions intraday that some people forget about, such as trading halts, merger and acquisitions news, bankruptcy filing news, etc. Betting too much also hurts your returns because losses will decrease your mental capital and lead to inferior trading decisions later in that day.

12. No matter how confident you are in a specific setup, there's always at least a 10 percent chance that you're completely and utterly wrong.

Several times in my trading career, I've been completely convinced of a certain outcome. I'd done my analysis, seen the numbers, and simply didn't see how I could not be correct. The market then, of course, proceeded to show me that I was completely and utterly wrong. The result was a loss in my trade. It's a very useful rule to have to believe that there's always a 10 percent chance that you're completely wrong. Is 10 percent a magic number? No, but it helps you satisfy the human tendency of wanting to be right (after all, there's a 90 percent chance that you're correct), but at the same time keeps your risk management alert system in check, because you know there's a chance you'll have to face a big loss. This prevents you from overbetting, ignoring price action, refusing to take a loss, not reassessing a trade based on the news, etc.

The truth is that when you have a position in the markets, you're always exposed to black swans, fat tails and unlikely events. By assuming that a certain percentage of the time you'll be hit by something unexpected, you ensure that you won't blow your account up one day by being too confident.

13. Seek to be exposed to big gain/small loss situations and avoid exposure to small gain/big loss ones.

Nassim Taleb in his magnificent book, *Antifragile*, talks about how there are two types of exposures that people typically are exposed to. One where people make or lose small amounts and then make it big when an expected event occurs, and one where they make small amounts for a long time and then face a huge loss when an expected event occurs. Perhaps a graphical display of this idea can help you understand:

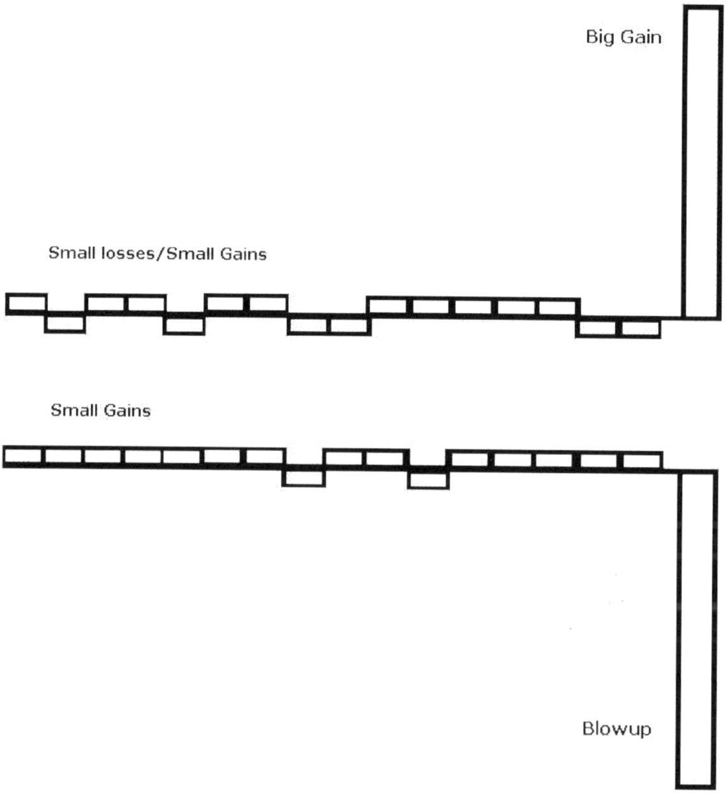

The second exposure model is dangerous because you never know how big that loss is. Recall from Chapter 11, Lesson 1, that if you go a lot above your Kelly position size, you are expected to have long-term negative returns, even if you are trading a system with overall positive expectation. This model is the most seductive because, psychologically, it is the easiest to trade. You keep making small amounts every day, you get more reinforcement that you are a good trader, but then one day the "system" doesn't work and you give back all you made and then some, perhaps even going into debt with the broker. What are ways you can be exposed to the first model and avoid the second? Here is a quick list:

- Trade the best day trade setups. They are the ones with the best risk/reward ratio due inefficiencies in intraday asset pricing. They usually happen at key support/resistance levels, when news is fresh, when momentum starts shifting, etc. The more you accumulate market experience, the more you will notice these inefficiencies.
- Buy OTM (Out of the Money) options in situations where there is potential for a big move. You can be exposed to extremely asymmetrical payoffs by doing so.

- Be careful with overnight trades (in particular, big positions with leverage). The additional risks will prevent you from controlling the loss size and expose you to bigger, unexpected losses. You will populate your trade results distribution with additional big losses that would not be there otherwise.
- Be very careful with short selling. Short selling, by its very structure, is a small gain/big loss trade. The most you can make is 100%, but the most you can lose is unlimited. This does not mean that you should not short; it means that when you do, controlling your risk is the number one factor that you should pay attention to, especially if you are carrying a trade overnight. A big (say 25-50% of your net worth) overnight short is one of the riskiest positions you can possibly have because in a fat tail/short squeeze scenario, you could literally lose everything and then some. Volkswagen stock, for instance, closed at around €210 the day before its big squeeze. It opened at €350 the next day and rallied all the way to €1000 over the course of the squeeze (btw, the stock looked very weak before all of this). Anyone carrying a big overnight short was forced to take a large loss as the gap up prevented any risk control. The US stock Medbox (MDBX) made an even more amazing squeeze in 2012, going from $40s all the way up to $210 in one day (and most of it was in a gap up).

These types of black swans are unpredictable (and it's hard to dodge them through good analysis because you only have to be wrong once to lose everything), so cutting down the size of overnight shorts is a necessity because you never know when you will be caught on the wrong side of one. Of course, it doesn't pay to insure yourself against an event that will happen once, say, every 10,000 years, but for one that could happen once or twice in your lifetime, it definitely pays. As a rule of thumb, assume that one day you will short a stock overnight and it will open up 300% against you (similarly to the two previous stocks mentioned), and then size your position accordingly (a loss of anything more than 30% of your net worth, in the mega-squeeze scenario, is probably too large). Of course, always get out when a stock is making huge moves against you, no matter how painful.

2015 update: In 2015 another amazing squeeze occurred. The biotech stock KBIO went from a close of roughly $2 to an afterhours high of $19, a gigantic run in a just a few hours (the next day, it peaked at $24-$25 in the pre-market session). Unfortunately for me, I was short the stock overnight at $2. I was following a deeply flawed simplistic liquidation analysis that was running around on Twitter. In this case, however, this rule saved me. Because I was ready for a 300% move (even though it might seem a little paranoid) against me and I assume there is always at least a 10% chance I'm wrong, I never sized the position aggressively (as I rarely do in an overnight short). In this case, the gap up was even more extreme than my rule would indicate (a short could have covered anywhere from 200% to 900% depending on how quickly he saw the event). I ended up being flat on the stock at $17.50. While it was the worst loss I ever took, it was still just a few percentage points of my net worth and 1/10 of my year to date trading profits. Had I not followed the 300% rule, I could have faced a devastating loss. I will probably be assuming a 500% move from now on in order to size overnight shorts, for further protection.

- Don't average down or up. This is what blow ups are made of because you are increasing your risk exposure in a low quality trade (you are going against the momentum, which is very dangerous in an HFT world because the algos exacerbate these trends) while your mental capital is being depleted. You will end up having a lot of capital at risk while making poor decisions and the computers will be pounding the trend against you. All it takes is one trade where you keep adding into for you to lose everything in a gigantic loss. Remember the Kelly chart.
- Stick with your stops. If you frequently let your losses ride, some of your small losses will turn into bigger ones. You will populate your trade results distribution with additional big losses that wouldn't be there if you stuck with your stops.
- Avoid shorting OTM options unless you are experienced and have rock solid discipline when it comes to bet sizing. Selling OTM options can yield small gains for a long time, and then lead to a huge loss when an expected event occurs. People are seduced by these gains, and they will frequently look at historical data to find comfort in running this strategy. The issue is that there are always new things that "never happened before," so historical data can lead you to a trap. The reader might recall that the Options Expert from Chapter 13 engages in some option selling in his speculative activities. The difference is that he will also buy way OTM "garbage" options to lock in a maximum loss in the trade. He also understands bet sizing better than the average trader.

14. Be very careful when trying to catch a bounce or short a top.

Bottom picking is a quite risky and difficult strategy to execute. It requires a lot of experience and risk control to be done successfully. Some of my largest losses, as is the case with a lot of traders, have come from trying to catch a bounce too early. Frequently, things go much lower because of the momentum and panic. In October of 2008, no one would have imagined that the S&P500 could go down so much in a single week. As a result, many people blew up.

As a rule of thumb, always assume that the chance that you are correct and the bottom will start is similar to the chance that the selling will take the asset significantly lower than you think. This doesn't mean you shouldn't take the trade; it means that if you do take it, get out as soon as it looks like you are wrong (asset makes new lows or breaks below a key level).

Another way that some traders play it is by scaling in. When things look oversold, they start to buy a small position and add when they look even more oversold. If the bounce happens, great, they will ride for a while and sell. If it doesn't happen, they have an "uncle point," a point where they will be out, no matter what.

Why should they be getting out at that point? Because the chance of a bounce is similar to the chance that it will go significantly lower than they think, and it might very well stay there. This is a point that some traders might not realize. Sure, it might bounce, but it still might not make the trader even in the trade because it went significantly lower than what he thought.

Realizing that you are just as likely to be right as you are to be wrong will force you to think in terms of reward to risk ratios and protecting your account instead of trusting that the bounce will come.

This idea might not be completely accurate statistically, but as a risk management heuristic, it works.[68]

---

68 This principle can also be applied to picking tops and/or shorting parabolic up moves. Assume that the chance it will go quite a bit higher is similar to the chance that you will get the top.

Epilogue

I hope that throughout this book you were able to improve your trading results by learning from the experience and wisdom of other traders. Trading has gotten more difficult in recent years due to the rise of HFTs, but good traders will always adapt and improve. In this book there is a lot of knowledge, advice, and tips on how to adapt to these changing conditions and be successful. I encourage the reader to re-read the chapters from time to time.

Writing this book was a hard task for me, mainly due to lack of time, but somehow I was able to pull it off. When I started the interviews back in August of 2012, I'd just decided to start to day trade actively. I had no idea what was going to happen, but I knew I had no choice because I had bills to pay and really didn't want to get a "real" job. The uncertainty of what kind of result I would get, combined with the need to pay lousy bills, made me work really hard to learn from the best guys I could find. The result of this journey is this book.

Society frequently looks down on this profession and links it to gambling (sometimes rightly so), but the truth is that being trader, having the freedom of working when you want, taking vacations at any time you want, and having your results depend entirely on you is one of the best feelings a person can have. You feel like you have destiny in your hands and are free to enjoy your life.

If you're willing to work hard and be disciplined, trading is and always will be one of the best jobs on earth.

About the Author

Fernando Oliveira is a full-time trader who was born and resides in São Paulo, Brazil. He made a living off poker and online casinos from 2004 to 2012. In 2012 he transitioned to day trading US stocks and futures. He holds a Technical High School diploma in IT and is a college graduate in Financial Management.

He can be reached at beathft@gmail.com

On Twitter @neweratrades

His website is www.beathft.com

Printed in Great Britain
by Amazon

40685828R00206